FLY
GIRLS

FLY GIRLS

How Five Daring Women Defied All
Odds and Made Aviation History

KEITH O'BRIEN

An Eamon Dolan Book
Houghton Mifflin Harcourt
BOSTON   NEW YORK
2018

For information about permission to reproduce selections from this book, write
to trade.permissions@hmhco.com or to Permissions, Houghton Mifflin Harcourt
Publishing Company, 3 Park Avenue, 19th Floor, New York, New York 10016.

hmhco.com

Library of Congress Cataloging-in-Publication Data is available.

ISBN 978-1-328-87664-5

Book design by Emily Snyder

Printed in the United States of America

DOC 10 9 8 7 6 5 4 3 2 1

For Mom, Dad,
and that great solo flier
Grandma

If you will tell me why, or how, people fall in love, I will tell you why, or how, I happened to take up aviation.

— LOUISE THADEN, *Pittsburgh Post-Gazette*, 1930

Contents

Part Three

Introduction

IN 1926, THERE were countless ways to die in an airplane. Propeller blades snapped and broke, and planes went down. Wings failed, folding backward or tearing away completely. Control sticks got stuck, sending airships hurtling toward crowds or hangars. And all too often, engines just stopped in midflight, forcing pilots to scan the ground below for a farmer's field or a cow pasture—anyplace where they might land in a hurry. "In such a crisis, there is no time to think," said one early pilot. "You either automatically do the right thing or you die."

In clear skies, pilots often made the wrong choice. In bad weather, they had even fewer options. Storms, squalls, rain, snow, and fog made flying almost impossible. In open-cockpit planes, raindrops felt to pilots like little bullets hurled at their faces at a hundred miles an hour. Goggles fogged up, paper maps blew away in the wind, and aviators became disoriented. A pilot, in moments like these, was instructed to find railroad tracks on the ground—"the only discriminable object in an absolute gray of land and sky"—and follow them. By doing so, a lost flier could find the nearest town. But flying at a hundred and twenty miles an hour just fifty feet off the tracks was treacherous too. In one such case, a pilot plowed his plane into a mountainside when the railroad entered a tunnel. Worse still, pilots could do everything right—navigate through the fog, dodge the mountains, survive emergency landings—and still lose, for reasons out of their control. In the

1920s, plane builders typically used wood to construct their machines, then stretched linen over the wings, like pillowcases, and pulled the thin fabric tight around the spruce spars. These lightweight materials, covered in a protective lacquer, helped make flying possible. But the wood could rot and the fabric could tear, dooming even the best fliers. As one aviation manual pointed out, "Many pilots have been killed in wood fuselage ships."

Crashes in 1926 killed or injured 240 people—a small but significant number, given that the vast majority of Americans never flew and that the government couldn't be sure that it was counting every accident. Federal agents gathered their figures not from official calculations but, often, from newspaper reports. Plane manufacturers had no required regulations—and instructors, no required training. Flying, one pilot noted, "is no place for slovenly methods or ideas." And yet, more than two decades after the Wright brothers first flew at Kitty Hawk, North Carolina, the slovenly climbed into cockpits every day, frightening the public and, at times, even themselves. "Would you ride in a lot of planes you know or with some of the pilots you know?" one man asked his fellow pilots at the time. "You know you would not." It was too dangerous. Even the so-called aviation experts were often unable to explain what caused planes to crash. Investigator: "Plane went into ground, nose first, causing complete wreck, so that it is hard to really tell what happened." Investigator: "The reason for failure is hard to ascertain." Investigator: "Completely destroyed by fire."

By the mid-1920s, the fledgling aircraft industry, eager to prove planes were safe, latched on to one idea capable of creating positive news coverage, marketable heroes, and excitement all at once: plane racing. Small affairs at first, the events quickly grew until pilots were competing against one another for headlines, fame, and the equivalent today of millions of dollars in what became known as the National Air Races. Soon, air-minded Americans weren't just reading about their favorite pilots darting across the ocean; they were watching them whip their planes around fifty-foot-tall pylons at these races or hearing them scream across the country in one race in particular: the greatest test of speed, strength, and skill financed by important men with large egos, the Bendix Trophy race. "It has become," one pilot said of the Bendix, "one of our national institutions, like the World Series."

These races were often fatal for pilots. Too risky for discerning men and, according to many men and the media, no place at all for women. In the late 1920s, newspapers and magazines routinely published articles questioning whether a woman should be allowed to fly anywhere, much less in these races. That such questions could be posed—and taken seriously—might strike us today as outlandish. But they were all too typical of the age. American women had earned the right to vote only a few years earlier and laws still forbade them to serve on juries, drive taxicabs, or work night shifts. It is not surprising, then, that the few women who dared to enter the elite, male-dominated aviation fraternity endured a storm of criticism and insults. They weren't aviators, as far as the men were concerned. They were petticoat pilots, ladybirds, flying flappers, and sweethearts of the air. They were just "girl fliers"—the most common term for female pilots at the time.

But in 1926, a new generation of female pilots was emerging, and they refused to be pigeonholed, mocked, or excluded. Instead, they united to fight the men in a singular moment in American history, when air races in open-cockpit planes attracted bigger crowds than Opening Day at Yankee Stadium and an entire Sunday of NFL games— combined. These were no "sweethearts," no "ladybirds." If the women aviators had to have a name, they were fly girls—a term used in the 1920s to describe female pilots and, more broadly, young women who refused to live by the old rules, appearing bold and almost dangerous as a result. As one newspaper put it in the mid-1920s, "The people are exhorted to swat the fly, but it is safer to keep your hands off the fly girl."

It's a story that plays out over one tumultuous decade when gender roles were shifting, cultural norms were evolving, and the Great Depression had people questioning almost everything in America. At the beginning, in 1927, even independent women interested in aviation would think of themselves as mere cargo to be ferried from point to point. At the end, just a few years later, women would compete head to head against men in that great transcontinental race for the Bendix Trophy. A woman, many believed, could never beat a man in such a competition. But in 1936, one woman did, in a stunning upset that finally proved women not only belonged in the air—they could rule.

Among them were wives and mothers, divorcées and heiresses, teachers and bankers, daredevils and starlets. And five women in particular: Ruth Elder, a charming wife from Alabama who paid the price for going first; Amelia Earhart, a lost soul living with her mother on the outskirts of Boston and desperate for a way out; Ruth Nichols, a daughter of Wall Street wealth in New York, hungry to make a name of her own; Louise McPhetridge Thaden, a small-town dreamer from rural Arkansas who wanted it all—a job, a family, fame—but in the end would have to make a difficult choice; and Florence Klingensmith, a young pilot from the northern plains whose great gamble in the sky would alter history on the ground.

In the decades to follow, only one of these five women would be remembered. But for a few years, before each of the women went missing in her own way, these female pilots captivated a nation, racing across the ocean or across the country, hoping to beat one another and longing to beat the men. At times, a hundred thousand people swarmed dusty airfields to watch them compete, darting through the sky in their colorful planes of robin's-egg blue and pale orchid, scarlet red and gleaming white, purple and cream and cobalt and silver, and racing—an impossible tale playing out in a deadly sky in an unforgiving time.

It began on the Kansas prairie, with a hard wind blowing.

PART ONE

1

The Miracle of Wichita

T HE COAL PEDDLERS west of town, on the banks of the Arkansas River, took note of the new saleswoman from the moment she appeared outside the plate-glass window. It was hard not to notice Louise McPhetridge.

She was young, tall, and slender, with distinct features that made her memorable if not beautiful. She had a tangle of brown hair, high cheekbones, deep blue eyes, thin lips programmed to smirk, and surprising height for a woman. At five foot eight and a quarter inches — she took pride in that quarter inch — McPhetridge was usually the tallest woman in the room and sometimes taller than the cowboys, drifters, cattlemen, and businessmen she passed on the sidewalks of Wichita, Kansas.

But it wasn't just how she looked that made her remarkable to the men selling coal near the river; it was the way she talked. McPhetridge was educated. She'd had a couple years of college and spoke with perfect grammar. Perhaps more notable, she had a warm Southern accent, a hint that she wasn't from around Wichita. She was born in Arkansas, 250 miles east, raised in tiny Bentonville, and different from most women in at least one other way: Louise was boyish. That's how her mother put it. Her daughter, she told others, "was a follower of boyish pursuits" — and that wasn't meant as a compliment. It was, for the McPhetridges, cruel irony.

Louise's parents, Roy and Edna, had wanted a boy from the beginning. They prayed on it, making clear their desires before the Lord, and they believed their faith would be rewarded. "Somehow," her mother said, "we were sure our prayers would be answered." The McPhetridges had even chosen a boy's name for the baby. And then they got Louise.

Edna could doll her daughter up in white dresses as much as she wanted; Louise would inevitably find a way to slip into pants or overalls and scramble outside to get dirty. She rounded up stray dogs. She tinkered with the engine of her father's car, and sometimes she joined him on his trips selling Mentholatum products across the plains and rural South, work that had finally landed the McPhetridges here in Wichita in the summer of 1925 and placed Louise outside the coal company near the river.

It was a hard time to be a woman looking for work, with men doing almost all the hiring and setting all the standards. Even for menial jobs, like selling toiletries or cleaning houses, employers in Wichita advertised that they wanted "attractive girls" with pleasing personalities and good complexions. "Write, stating age, height, weight and where last employed." The man who owned the coal company had different standards, however. Jack Turner had come from England around the turn of the century with nothing but a change of clothes and seven dollars in his pocket. He quickly lost the money. But Turner, bookish and bespectacled in round glasses, made it back over time by investing in horses and real estate and the city he came to love. "Wichita," he said, "is destined to become a metropolis of the plains."

By 1925, people went to him for just about everything: hay, alfalfa, bricks, stove wood, and advice. While others were still debating the worth of female employees, Turner argued as early as 1922 that workers should be paid what they were worth, no matter their gender. He predicted a future where men and women would be paid equally, based on skill—where they would demand such a thing, in fact. And with his worldly experience, Turner weighed in on everything from war to politics. But he was known, most of all, for coal. "Everything in Coal," his advertisements declared. In winter, when the stiff prairie winds howled across the barren landscape, the people of Wichita came to Turner for coal. In summer, they did too. It was never too early to begin stockpiling that vital fuel, he argued. "Coal Is Scarce," Turner told customers in his ads. "Fill Your Coal Bin Now."

He hired Louise McPhetridge not long after she arrived in town, and she was thankful for the work. For a while, McPhetridge, just nineteen, was able to stay focused on her job, selling the coal, selling fuel. But by the following summer, her mind was wandering, following Turner out the door, down the street, and into a brick building nearby, just half a block away. The sign outside was impossible to miss. TRAVEL AIR AIRPLANE MFG. CO., it said. AERIAL TRANSPORTATION TO ALL POINTS. It was a humble place, squat and small, but the name, Travel Air, was almost magical, and the executive toiling away on the factory floor inside was the most unusual sort.

He was a pilot.

WALTER BEECH WAS just thirty-five that summer, but already he was losing his hair. His long, oval face was weathered from too much time spent in an open cockpit, baking in the prairie sun, and his years of hard living in a boarding house on South Water Street were beginning to show. He smoked. He drank. He flew. On weekends, he attended fights and wrestling matches at the Forum downtown. In the smoky crowd, shoulder to shoulder with mechanics and leather workers, there was the aviator Walter Beech, a long way from his native Tennessee but in Kansas for good. "I want to stay in Wichita," he told people, "if Wichita wants me to stay."

The reason was strictly professional. In town, there were two airplane factories, and Beech was the exact kind of employee they were looking to hire. He had learned all about engines while flying for the US Army in Texas. If Beech pronounced a plane safe, anyone would fly it. Better still, he'd fly it himself, working with zeal; "untiring zeal," one colleague said. And thanks to these skills—a unique combination of flying experience, stunting talent, and personal drive—Beech had managed to move up to vice president and general manager at Travel Air. He worked not only for Turner but for a man named Clyde Cessna, and Beech's job was mostly just to fly. He was supposed to sell Travel Air ships by winning races, especially the 1926 Ford Reliability Tour, a twenty-six-hundred-mile contest featuring twenty-five pilots flying to fourteen cities across the Midwest, with all of Wichita watching. "Now—right now—is Wichita's chance," one newspaper declared on the eve of the race. "Neglected, it will not come again—forever."

Beech, flying with a young navigator known as Brice "Goldy" Goldsborough, felt a similar urgency. The company had invested $12,000 in the Travel Air plane he was flying, a massive amount, equivalent to roughly $160,000 today. If he failed in the reliability race—if he lost or, worse, crashed—he would have to answer to Cessna and Turner, and he knew there were plenty of ways to fail. "A loose nut," he said, "or a similar seemingly inconsequential thing has lost many a race." And so he awoke early the day the contest began and went to the airfield in Detroit. Observers would have seen a quiet shadow near the starting line checking every bolt, instrument, and, of course, the engine: a $5,700 contraption, nearly half the price of the expensive plane.

"Don't save this motor," the engine man advised Beech before he took off on the first leg of the journey, urging him to open it up. "Let's win the race."

Beech pushed the throttle as far as it would go. He was first into Kalamazoo, first into Chicago. With Goldsborough's help, he flew without hesitation into the fog around St. Paul, coming so close to the ground and the lakes below that journalists reported that fish leaped out of the water at Beech's plane. While some pilots got lost or waited out the weather in Milwaukee, Beech won again, defeating the field by more than twenty minutes. He prevailed as well in Des Moines and Lincoln and, finally, the midway point in the race, Wichita, winning that leg by almost seven minutes despite a leaking carburetor.

"It's certainly good to be back home again," Beech said to the crowd of five thousand people after stepping out of the cockpit. "The old town looks good to me, and wonderfully restful after the strain of hard, fast flying."

A beauty queen, Miss Wichita, presented him with a gold-plated key to the city. And six days later, back in Detroit, in front of a much bigger crowd of thirty thousand people, race officials gave Beech the Edsel B. Ford trophy and a check for $2,500. He and the other pilots had covered a total of sixty-one thousand miles, flying on despite eight accidents, twelve forced landings, and one fatality, when a taxiing plane hit a man on the ground, shredding his body with its propeller. Six planes didn't finish, and two had to be shipped home in boxcars, unable to fly anywhere anymore. But if the point of the Ford tour was reliability, Travel Air, with Beech at the controls, had proven something. The phone back in Kansas began ringing with plane orders—

and praise for one man. "Walter Beach," full-page ads declared, misspelling the name of the new hero, "Wichita's Own."

At the Hotel Broadview downtown, the city's elite honored Beech that September with speeches and toasts. Jack Turner presented him with a fur-lined flying suit, and the publisher of the *Wichita Eagle* compared him to Christopher Columbus. But Beech deflected the attention to his navigator Goldsborough, to their moneyed backers, and to all the hard-working men of the boarding houses on South Water Street.

"Let us consider," Beech said, "that not every hometown boy is a fool. Let us consider listening to their arguments of what they can do. Pick out a miracle that is possible for them to accomplish."

MCPHETRIDGE KNEW SHE was shirking her work, shorting Turner with her lack of coal sales. But she couldn't help it. Day after day, she drifted to the Travel Air hangar in the tall grass east of town, sticking out amid the grease-stained mechanics, fuel men, and pilots but feeling at home among them. As a girl back in Bentonville, she had longed to accomplish miracles of her own.

McPhetridge once jumped from the second story of a barn just to see what it felt like. She drove her father's car long before she was old enough to have a driver's license, and she sometimes did things just because others said they couldn't be done. In Bentonville, townspeople liked to turn out for funeral processions, watching the deceased clatter by in a casket pulled by a horse-drawn cart. Once, to impress the other children, Louise accepted a dare to run along behind the procession, climb aboard the moving cart, and hang upside down by her knees near the casket as it rolled down the road. It was a trick that the kids in town thought impossible until Louise finally did it, earning the wrath of her parents and the admiration of her peers.

Now, lingering at the airfield in Wichita, McPhetridge was flirting with trouble yet again. It was only a matter of time before her boss Jack Turner found her there when she should have been selling coal. McPhetridge expected to get fired when it finally happened. Instead, she got a phone call from Walter Beech himself.

He and Turner had a proposition for her, a different job. They wanted her to work for Travel Air's new West Coast distributor, D. C. Warren. With a young woman at Warren's side—especially a tall, blue-eyed woman like McPhetridge—reporters were sure to pay attention to Travel Air.

"Warren has agreed to take you out to San Francisco," Beech told McPhetridge at their meeting. "Your salary won't be high, but he will teach you this aviation business and see that you learn how to fly."

McPhetridge was stunned. Her parents were too. They had long known that their daughter was unusual, a challenge. Her mother had even accepted the fact that Louise would never be a traditional woman, but was destined to work. "In competition with men," her mother predicted.

But this was too much, even for them.

"Oh, Louise," her mother said, disapproving. Her father wasn't pleased either. He considered calling Beech to officially state his opposition to his daughter's taking this job and perhaps to her flying anywhere, with any man, ever. But Louise talked him out of making the call.

"It is," she told her parents, "the one thing I want to do."

Not long after, in early April 1927, she said goodbye to her family, to her job selling coal, and to everything else flat and unfulfilling in Wichita and climbed into a Travel Air plane headed west. It was cold in Wichita that morning, almost freezing. Yet the sky over the prairie was blue, giving McPhetridge a clear view of the ground from the passenger seat of the little plane bound for the coast. By nightfall, she had reached San Francisco.

2

Devotedly, Ruth

ACROSS THE CONTINENT from McPhetridge in California, another young woman pondered a move of her own. She lived in a house so big it required no street number. The Nichols family gave their address as simply Grace Church Street, Rye, New York. It was about twenty miles north of midtown Manhattan, in quiet Westchester County, nestled near the ocean on the Connecticut border, and visitors summoned to the house couldn't miss it—all three stories of it—with its sprawling property and servants' quarters.

But inside, the house was dark and scary for children. Dead animals mounted on the wall stared down on the formal proceedings. A massive grandfather clock ticked away, tolling morosely on the hour. In the dining room, proper manners were to be observed while the family ate off fine china. And any child who broke the rules might be forced to answer to the owners of the house, Erickson and Edith Nichols, and possibly banished to dine with the family's servants. In 1925, there were three of them.

The oldest child, a daughter, had at least one thing going for her: she wouldn't be there for long. Ruth Nichols was expected to marry well. She was to cut short her education—no college for Nichols—to make sure that happened. And like any girl raised in New York and steeped in old money in the 1920s, Nichols understood the deal. From a young age, she knew that one day she would make her debut, and all the papers would cover it in their society pages. Then her parents would find her a husband and plan a wedding, and all the papers would cover that too. It didn't matter if she wanted to resist. Her parents had a plan for Ruth, and she felt compelled to follow it to please her parents—especially Father.

Ruth simply couldn't disappoint "Daddykins," as she called him. Or "Motherkins," a practicing Quaker devoted to God, her husband, and Ruth. "My precious Ruthie," she called her, "the blessedest girl." "Thee mustn't worry, dear. Just trust our Heavenly Father." And yet, Nichols was worried, increasingly burdened with anxiety and guilt and an important question: "Did I have a right to live my own life?" Shortly after her eighteenth birthday, in early 1919, she got a taste of what that might feel like.

A flier named Eddie Stinson from Detroit was in Atlantic City giving rides, and Ruth's father wanted her to have one. He paid ten dollars for the privilege and put his daughter on board Stinson's open-cockpit JN-4, a primitive, single-prop biplane of Great War vintage that pilots called a Jenny. Every fiber in Nichols's body told her not to fly. She had never even ridden a roller coaster, much less a Jenny capable of flying about seventy-five miles an hour. But Nichols refused to reveal her panic to Father. Instead, she stood next to Stinson and smiled. There was Nichols, five foot five and blue-eyed, all dimples and plump cheeks, wearing goggles, a helmet pressed down over her brown hair, and a leather coat two sizes too big.

The plane took off and soon Stinson began to laugh. He wasn't going to just fly; he performed a loop, flipping the Jenny upside down to impress his passenger. Nichols—eyes shut, stomach churning—was not amused. But she survived the flight, and by the end of it, inexplicably, her fear was gone. "I felt," she said later, "as if my soul were completely freed from my earthly body."

Just a few months later, emboldened by her moment in the sky, Nichols left home against her father's wishes, forsaking marriage in favor of a different path: an education at Wellesley College, an elite school for women near Boston. "College life," she told her mother, writing home that fall, "is simply great!" There were masquerades to attend and student government meetings too. There were lazy days spent swimming at a nearby lake and joyful nights singing school songs in the moonlight. Nichols competed in wheelbarrow races and late-night games of charades that devolved into noisy squabbles. She learned lessons that had nothing to do with her assignments and she also took part in the time-honored college tradition of sleeping late on weekend mornings. "So late, in fact," she told her mother once, "that our dining room was closed." Unable to get breakfast with the other students, Nichols was forced to make a meal out of what she had on hand in her room—ice cream and cookies. A decadent treat, true college living, and Nichols told her parents about all of it in letters she sent home, signing them with love.

"Devotedly, Ruth."

HER PARENTS WEREN'T giving up just yet. After Nichols's sophomore year at Wellesley, her mother and father pressured her to walk away from school. The offer: a winter in Miami. The goal: "to become a lady." And this time, Nichols listened—for a while. That winter, she agreed to go to all the dances, theater parties, and Junior League activities that her mother scheduled for her. But she also wanted to use the time to learn how to fly, so she approached a well-known instructor in South Florida named Harry Rogers.

"How much are flying lessons, Captain Rogers?" she asked him one day near his seaplane on the water.

"They come high," he replied. "Sixty dollars an hour."

It was the sort of money that made learning to fly impossible for most people. But not for the daughter of Erickson Nichols. Ruth was almost twenty-one now and had a bank account flush with her father's money. She agreed on the spot to pay Rogers five hundred dollars for his services—a snap decision that surely got the attention of the young pilot, a machinist's son, with his flight school on the water.

Wellesley College, it was not. In the lessons, Rogers cursed at her, yelled. Their discussions were more like shouting matches, only it wasn't a match; Rogers was winning. "For Pete's sake," he'd tell Nichols when she was flying, "don't ask me why! Do it because I tell you!" Other times, he just insulted her, calling her "dumb," "the dumbest," a "nincompoop" flying at "numbskull speed."

Nichols weathered his abusive lessons with Junior League grace, kissing her instructor on the neck after she soloed for the first time.

"I'm a flier now, Harry!" she said.

"A flier, my eye," Rogers replied. "You've only just begun. But maybe," he added, "just maybe, you'll make it yet."

She returned to college in the fall of 1922, graduated in 1924, and then decided to sail around the world aboard a luxury liner that was attempting to become the largest ship ever to circle the earth. Nichols was thrilled with the pioneering spirit of the trip, with her fine stateroom, and with the fact that the numbers were in her favor. There were many single men on board and only about half a dozen young women. "Allowing," Nichols said, "more men per person."

But soon she was at odds with herself, waffling between two poles: her parents' world in Rye and the world she wanted to create; the life of a society girl and the life of a pilot; the marriage that was expected of her and the adventures she wanted to pursue on her own. Increasingly she was sure of only one thing: the next time she went around the world, she was going by plane.

There was just one woman she'd have to beat.

3

Real and Natural, Every Inch

AMELIA EARHART ENTERED the office on Boylston Street in Boston seeking guidance. She didn't like asking for help. Public confessions of weakness — or failures of any kind — weren't her thing. But by August 1926, there was no escaping the reality anymore: Earhart was adrift.

A lifelong nomad — attending six high schools and living in five states before the age of eighteen — Earhart had finally managed to get herself lost. She was staying with her mother and younger sister, not in Boston but five miles north, in Medford, a middle-class city of clerks, electricians, and office workers on the banks of the Mystic River. Her father was a continent away in California, possibly drinking too much again. The drinking had helped ruin her parents' marriage, this time most likely for good. Her own relationship with a bookish engineer wasn't exactly a raging love affair. And Earhart, once filled with ambitious dreams — she was going to be a doctor, an engineer, a poet — had little to show for her life. She was twenty-nine years old and unmarried with a résumé as thin as her past was scattered.

Earhart had worked for a while as a nurse's aide in a military hospital; had tinkered with photography, then dropped it; had toiled as a telephone-company staffer, then moved; had driven a truck for a spell, delivering sand and gravel; and had briefly attended classes at Columbia University in New York — twice — dropping out each time for personal reasons. Life seemed to be pulling her away, pulling her to Medford.

The house there was on Brooks Street, not far from the river at the top of a hill. And though it wasn't the life she wanted, it certainly could have been worse. Earhart got a job as a tutor, and she was good at the work. She had always loved words, writing poetry under the nom de plume Emil Harte, and she at least had the means to escape Medford every now and then. Earhart had a car, a yellow open-top roadster, that she was known to drive fast on the streets around Boston, so fast that friends named the car the Yellow Peril.

Still, for Earhart, it was a difficult time. She kept a scrapbook filled with clippings about female achievers making news; she cut out the stories and pasted them on the pages as motivation, perhaps, or proof that anything was possible. Headline: "Woman Wants to Be a Skipper." Headline: "First Woman Named Court Commissioner." Headline: "Modern Woman Again Breaks Tradition." Yet here she was in 1926, roughly as successful as her poet alter ego Emil Harte—a nobody. She couldn't attend college, "owing," she told a friend, "to financial difficulties." And the tutoring work ended too soon, like all the other jobs she'd had before it. If there was a time to ask for help, it was probably now—a fact that even the independent Earhart surely understood. On August 18, 1926, she turned up on Boylston Street in Boston's Back Bay to register at the Women's Educational and Industrial Union, an employment bureau run by women, for women.

She was case no. 49166—just another applicant seeking work at the WEIU and willing to stretch the truth to get it. Earhart lied about her age, saying she was only twenty-seven. She embellished her education, adding three semesters to her time at Columbia and making it appear as if she had attended just one high school—Hyde Park High in Chicago—for four years. She fudged her background too. She wasn't a relatively inexperienced tutor with limited work around Boston. Instead, she boasted, "I have had five years of tutoring experience, as well as class work."

Earhart was reframing the story to her liking, sanding off the jagged edges of her imperfect world. But even she was realistic about her job prospects. Gone were the dreams of medicine and engineering. Instead, Earhart told the WEIU, she would be happy to find work as a hostess, an English teacher, or "anything connected with an aeronautical concern."

The screener at the WEIU was impressed with the woman sitting there. Earhart was five foot eight with dark blond hair, gray eyes, and a voice that was both thin and strong, wobbly and direct, and, either way, dignified. She was well read and articulate, and the WEIU screener noted both characteristics, scribbling comments about Earhart in thick black ink in the margins of her registration card:

"An extremely interesting girl—very unusual vocab—is a philosopher—wants to write—does write."

But one detail about Earhart stuck out most of all.

"Holds a sky pilot's license?"

It was a question, not a statement. On an application filled with lies, this detail about flying was by far the most unbelievable.

And it was true.

THE FIRST TIME Earhart tried to fly, the military wouldn't let her. It was during the war, and she was a nurse's aide at a hospital in Toronto, not a soldier. The second time she tried to fly, she had just moved to Los Angeles with her parents, and a pilot agreed to take her up for a fee—a short ride made possible by her father. The third time, in early January 1921, would be different. Earhart approached a female instructor at an airfield in Los Angeles with a question.

"I want to fly," she said. "Will you teach me?"

The instructor, Neta Snook, liked Earhart immediately—her directness, her scholarly demeanor, how she carried herself, sitting up straight in the cockpit, how she walked around the field with a book tucked under her arm, and how she wore her hair. Quietly, at home, Earhart had been cutting off her hair one inch at a time so that her mother wouldn't notice the gradual change to a bobbed haircut.

The two were almost the same age. Both originally hailed from the Midwest—Earhart from Kansas, Snook from Illinois—and each felt alone in California. Earhart was still shaking off the failure of having left Columbia the first time and getting used to life in the family's new house on Fourth Street in the city. Her father, for the moment, wasn't drinking—a miracle that Earhart credited to the Christian Science church he was attending. But she couldn't be sure how long that would last. And money was tight enough for the Earharts that they were taking in boarders to help cover expenses. Earhart didn't even have the money to pay Snook at first. Snook agreed to teach Earhart on credit, accepting Liberty bonds for her services. But Earhart realized right away that lessons wouldn't be enough. She needed a plane of her own. "I want to fly," she declared, "whenever I can."

To do it, Earhart was willing to make what was, for her, the ultimate sacrifice: she took a boring office job, opening, sorting, and filing letters in a mailroom. "Unskilled labor," Earhart said. Then she turned to her family for help, asking her sister, Muriel, if she owned anything that Amelia could sell or if she could part with any money. Her mother, possibly sensing her daughter's earnest desperation, finally stepped in to assist. Pooling together Amelia's savings, her mailroom wages, some money from her sister, and a small inheritance Amelia's mother had recently received, they amassed enough cash to buy Amelia a Kinner Airster—a two-seat, open-cockpit biplane, made right there in Los Angeles—for about two thousand dollars. The Airster was smaller, lighter, and faster than Snook's hulking airship, a real step up. But Snook didn't see it that way. "All in all," Earhart's instructor noted, "it was not a plane for a beginner."

Twice, she and Earhart crashed it. Once, the cause was a lack of gasoline, human error. Another time, they crashed on takeoff when a troubled cylinder slowed their ascent. This left Earhart with two choices: nose the plane down to gain speed and slam into a line of eucalyptus trees at the edge of the airfield, or pull up, lose airspeed, and plummet to the ground. Earhart chose the latter—"I would have done the same," Snook said later—and down went the plane, smashing the propeller and landing gear but not injuring the two women. Earhart had thought to cut off the ignition switch before impact, reducing the chance of an explosion. She'd also apparently thought to bring makeup, which she began applying as soon as it was clear that they had survived the crash. "We have to look nice," Earhart told Snook as she sat in the cockpit of the busted Airster, "when the reporters come."

The reporters *were* coming. The West Coast aviation press soon took note of Amelia Earhart, who was not just flitting around on weekends but participating in air rodeos and briefly setting a female altitude record, flying over fourteen thousand feet. Just as notable, as far as her sister was concerned, Earhart was, apparently, falling in love—with Sam Chapman, one of the boarders in the Earharts' home. He was tall, redheaded, and, above all, it seemed, understanding. Chapman was content to stay quiet while Earhart spoke to reporters and made at least one bold prediction. The next time she went east, she said, it would be by plane, in her Airster. "A Lady's Plane as well as a Man's," said full-page Kinner ads in Los Angeles, capitalizing on Earhart's growing name recognition. "Read what Miss Earhart has to say after flying a KINNER AIRSTER."

They weren't reading about it for long. Almost as quickly as Earhart made headlines in California, she disappeared. By 1924, she was drifting again. Her parents' marriage was over and Earhart was headed back east, but not in her plane. She was going by car, in her open-top roadster, the Yellow Peril. Her plane had been sold, and what little fame Earhart had managed to garner flying it around Los Angeles was gone too. All she had left from her time in California was Chapman, her boyfriend, who was from Massachusetts and also moving back east. They were engaged now — that's how Chapman described their relationship to others, anyway. Engaged and sure to marry. "In the near future," he vowed. Because they were happy. "Happy indeed," Chapman declared, telling others that the pair enjoyed quiet strolls and long talks. He was thirty years old by then and quite possibly the most patient man in New England. While Earhart stewed in Medford, Chapman lived at home with his mother in seaside Marblehead, twenty miles away, biding his time and working at Edison Electric. The Edison building in Boston was on Boylston Street, just blocks from the WEIU employment bureau; so close, in fact, that Earhart would have nearly passed Chapman's employer on her visit there — a reminder, surely, that there was an easier path for her if she wanted it.

She could marry Chapman; he was waiting, offering stability and security. Life in Marblehead, with its sea breezes, had to be better than her purgatory in Medford. Chapman also seemed to understand that Earhart was different from other women. "Real and natural," he thought, "every inch." But Chapman's letter of recommendation to the WEIU was decidedly less passionate about the woman he called his fiancée, reflecting something about the man or about the couple. "Miss Amelia M. Earhart," he wrote, "is all right."

There would be no marriage anytime soon. Earhart was going to work, hoping for aviation but getting something else instead. The union placed her at Denison House, a settlement home in Boston's Chinatown that focused on helping immigrants acclimate to life in America. Given her lack of education and experience, Earhart had the best possible job a woman like her could reasonably hope to get. She was a social worker.

Outside Denison House, the tangled streets of Chinatown bustled with life and noise. The neighborhood was filled with Chinese-goods stores and Syrian restaurants, Oriental-rug dealers hawking carpets and crowded streetcars rumbling by on elevated tracks, churning up the dust of the city—a city that had no hold over Earhart. All she needed was a chance, and she'd be gone. "When I leave Boston," she admitted to a friend, "I think I'll never go back."

4

The Fortune of the Air

G ENTLEMEN," THE DARE began in a public letter dated May 22, 1919. "As a stimulus to the courageous aviators, I desire to offer, through the auspices and regulations of the Aero Club of America, a prize of $25,000 to the first aviator of any allied country crossing the Atlantic, in one flight, from Paris to New York or New York to Paris, all other details in your care." It was signed "Yours very sincerely, Raymond Orteig."

He was forty-nine, a Frenchman by birth and a gourmet with a love of fine wine and big hotels. Orteig owned two of them in New York City, mingling with ease among a high-class clientele who enjoyed his company and his French accent. But he was also at home among aviators, the young fliers who sometimes stayed at his properties, especially during the war. And more than any other single factor, perhaps, his dare—the Orteig Prize—sparked air fever and the aerial competitions that would come to consume Americans during the next decade.

Orteig himself appeared to have little in common with the dashing airmen that typically made the newspaper. He was short and stocky, bald on top and gray everywhere else, peering out on the world with eyes that were at once dark and joyful. But the refined Frenchman never forgot his humble beginnings. He was a shepherd's son, raised in a small town in the Pyrenees, near the Spanish border. More important, perhaps, he was an immigrant. At the age of twelve, he came by ship to the United States because it was his best hope of a good life. Go to America, his grandmother had told him, bidding the child farewell. "And see what you can do."

Orteig arrived in New York with just a few francs in his pocket and fell in with other French immigrants, getting a job at a restaurant and working his way up from busboy to waiter to general manager to, finally, owner. By 1902, just twenty years after coming to America, Orteig owned both the Hotel Lafayette on Ninth Street and the Brevoort Hotel on Fifth Avenue, serving guests at marble-topped tables in his cafés, on his terraces, and in his bars, where, for a long time, women were not permitted. The hotels felt, to Americans, anyway, like Paris — in part because of all the wine Orteig served, even after Prohibition laws took effect in 1920. It was a party, and one that could not last. In 1926, lawmen cracked down on Orteig, sending undercover agents into his hotels to buy alcohol and then padlocking the doors of the Brevoort's main dining room, hurting business.

But Orteig assured the Aero Club of America that he was still good for the twenty-five grand that he had pledged for a successful transatlantic crossing. He offered a bank guarantee to prove it. And in late 1926, just as the shuttered dining room at Orteig's hotel was reopening, pilots — long wary of ocean flying — finally felt confident enough in their little airships to attempt the thirty-six-hundred mile journey for the Orteig Prize. By accident, almost, the Frenchman's money was about to start a race that would forever shrink the world, ending lives and launching careers, inspiring countless men to fly and encouraging a few women too. "This flight," said former war pilot Harold Hartney, "will be one of the greatest feats ever performed by an airplane — if it succeeds."

SUCCESS, EVERYONE KNEW, was unlikely at best. To fly across the ocean, a pilot needed a plane large enough to carry the necessary amount of fuel — up to seven tons — but still light enough to actually get airborne. If he miscalculated, the plane would barrel off the runway on takeoff, plowing into power lines, fences, or trees, and the people inside would die. "Dashed to pieces," the New York Times put it, "and burned alive." If he'd calculated correctly, the pilot had a new problem: navigating. Over land, he could use maps and landmarks to help reach his destination. Over water, he had to rely solely on a compass, adjusting for winds that might be blowing him off course. Or more difficult: he had to operate a sextant, which required sending a crew member out onto a wing or a special catwalk built onto the plane to get a clear reading. The pilot himself couldn't leave the controls or even daydream for fear of losing airspeed, altitude, or both. Then, inevitably, darkness would set in—an all-consuming darkness, over a wide expanse of water—and the pilot would begin to get sleepy, listening to the steady lullaby of the engine and nothing else. No other sound.

"Every once in a while, I caught myself nodding," admitted Ernie Smith, a pilot who was part of the ocean-hopping craze of the late 1920s and flew with a navigator from San Francisco to Hawaii. He found the task both stressful and dull. At times, he doubted that the instruments were working. Other times he focused too much on the instruments and nearly drifted off to sleep, sending his plane into a dive. Around dawn, somewhere over the Pacific Ocean, the aircraft's engine began to sputter, having sprung a gas leak, the sort of problem bound to arise on a long, arduous flight. The men, still seven hundred miles from land, prepared to ditch into the ocean and probably die there. They released a crate of pigeons—their version of a flare. "No use drowning them," Smith said. Then they prepared to pile into a rubber lifeboat, wondering if it would even float. It was only manual labor that saved them. By using a hand pump in the cockpit, Smith managed to squeeze just enough gas into the engine and will them closer to land. They crashed on an island thirty miles short of Honolulu, shaken but alive and proof of just how hard it was to fly across an ocean, especially the Atlantic. The pilots on this route chasing the Orteig Prize had to fly roughly twelve hundred miles farther than Smith did—more time for things to go wrong. And still, they went. René Fonck was first.

HE WAS A FRENCHMAN, like Orteig, with a record of shooting down 126 German planes during the Great War. For him, Fonck said, the trip wasn't about money but something bigger: bringing France and the United States together. To that end, the debonair thirty-two-year-old ace would leave not from Paris but from New York's premier airport: Roosevelt Field, twenty-five miles east of downtown Manhattan, on Long Island. Its clay runway was a hundred and fifty feet wide and more than a mile long, and Fonck would likely need every inch of the

5,580-foot strip to get his plane—a giant tri-motored S-35 Sikorsky—into the air.

On September 21, 1926, the great flier appeared at dawn at Roosevelt Field, looking dapper in a blue uniform and acknowledging the crowd of a thousand people lined up on both sides of the runway. Just before 6:30 a.m., he climbed aboard the large silver plane with his three crew members. He tested the Sikorsky's engines, opening them up and letting them roar until the airship trembled and the crowd cheered. Finally, he accepted a last-minute gift of croissants, courtesy of Orteig. He jokingly tested their weight before placing them aboard the overloaded plane, and then, with a salute, he bade America adieu.

The Sikorsky—heavy with gas and weighing fourteen tons—lurched down the runway like an elephant with wings. It hit forty miles an hour, then sixty-five—then a problem. One of the wheels on the landing gear failed under the strain, breaking and slamming into the plane's left rudder. Unable to stop, unable to take off, and now unable to steer, Fonck did everything he could to keep the wounded ship from barreling into the crowd. But there was no way to stop it from crashing. It skittered off the end of the runway, cartwheeled on its right wing into a small gully, and burst into a fireball, belching fifty-foot flames into the morning sky. Two crew members died in the inferno; two others escaped, including Fonck, who was small enough to push through a narrow hole in the busted plane, dodging the whirring propellers and the fire. It burned for more than an hour, consuming the Sikorsky, the bodies of the men, and the grass for fifty feet around the wreckage while Fonck watched, dazed and delirious, blood oozing from his forehead.

What happened, he said, could not have been helped—an assessment that aviation experts later confirmed. Fonck's crash was "probably unavoidable," they explained, "a typical sacrifice in the development of aviation." The plane was too heavy and the wheel had failed.

"It is," Fonck said, "the fortune of the air."

He still wanted to try to cross the Atlantic, and others did too. But they did no better than the Frenchman. In April 1927, seven months after Fonck's failure, two American transatlantic planes crashed in final test flights, injuring or killing the airmen on board. Then, in early May, it was France's turn to fail, and it did—in a new and devastating way. French pilot Charles Nungesser had been superstitious about his transatlantic flight from the start. He didn't want to give interviews about it. "Too much news," he said, "will affect my luck." He didn't want to say anything, really. "That's my idea of being careful." He just wanted to work on his airship, check every inch of his thirty-two-foot biplane capable of landing on both land and water and known as *L'Oiseau Blanc* —the *White Bird*.

Nungesser had the fuselage adorned with his personal symbols: a skull and crossbones and a coffin flanked with candles, all in black. Because Nungesser wasn't just any pilot; he was the Hussar of Death— that was the nickname he'd earned for his work killing Germans in the war. Shrapnel couldn't hurt the Hussar. Bullets couldn't either. Nungesser had been wounded and so had his navigator, François Coli. Coli wore a patch over one eye, but as a seaman's son, he could still navigate better than most men. There was no question that they would bring Orteig's prize back to France, where it belonged. "Warmest congratulations and expression of my admiration for your magnificent crossing of the Atlantic," the French minister of war wrote to Nungesser and Coli—*before* they had even arrived in New York. "Your exploit marks an unforgettable date in the history of French aviation."

On the morning of the departure, in Paris, with the crowd shouting *"Bon voyage"* in the predawn darkness and reporters pressing the airmen for last-minute information, Nungesser was calm and cool, acknowledging none of the hysteria. He just shrugged.

"We'll see you soon," he told the crowd.

He and Coli—working on just two hours of sleep—climbed into the cockpit and began shouting directives at the mechanics on the ground. Then the plane was moving, speeding down the runway, and struggling to get aloft, like the other transatlantic planes before it. Twice, the *White Bird* briefly took leave of the runway, jumping ten feet into the air. And twice it came back down again, heavy with fuel. By this time, the plane had traveled nearly three thousand feet, and it was closing in on trees and a stream. The crowd began to panic, shouting at Nungesser and pleading for him to make it.

Finally, he did. With just fifty feet of runway left, the *White Bird* limped into the gray light over Paris, three hundred feet in the air, then seven hundred, then twelve hundred, safe. After thirty minutes, Nungesser and Coli disengaged their landing gear and dropped it to the ground. They didn't need wheels anymore. In New York, they would land in the harbor, at the feet of the Statue of Liberty, their country's gift to America. A welcoming party, led by the mayor, was already waiting for them there with a detailed schedule for the heroic fliers. A tugboat would ferry them to Pier 57 on the Hudson River. There, they would board an ocean liner to dine and sleep off their fatigue in private staterooms. After that, they would make the rounds: banquets, theater engagements, teas, and a Friday-night celebration in the grand ballroom of the Hotel Astor. The ballroom was already booked. The invites had gone out, and more than a thousand people planned to attend. All the organizers needed to make it happen was Nungesser and Coli. The men were expected by late afternoon on Monday, some thirty hours after leaving Paris. And on the Battery, in New York City, people gathered, pressing against the wall by the water and scanning the horizon for a speck of white — the *White Bird*.

No plane.

Fog moved in, and rain. Still, the people stayed. By four o'clock that afternoon, ten thousand New Yorkers had gathered to witness the moment, and 250 police reserves worked overtime to control them. Some sky watchers bounced around on speedboats; others packed into pleasure steamers. A tugboat was chartered specifically for French officials and a second tugboat was waiting with Nungesser's younger brother Robert on board and three doctors from Bellevue Hospital, just in case. There were fresh beds made up in the cabin to provide rest to the weary fliers and hot coffee brewing to warm them.

No plane.

By nightfall, the fog had lifted, the rain had stopped, and most of the people had left, giving up on the French fliers and moving on. But the welcoming party remained. Officials lit up the harbor with searchlights and beacons, straining to see a small light in the low clouds over the bay. If they arrived in the dark, Nungesser and Coli were to flash the plane's light in a prearranged signal: long, then short, Morse code for *N*.

Still no plane.

Nungesser's brother comforted himself with the notion that Charles must have landed early — in Newfoundland, perhaps — to escape bad weather. And back in Paris, his mother sought solace in prayer, climbing the great hill of Montmartre and holing up inside the Church of the Sacré-Coeur. "My prayers will save him," she said. Both were wrong. Nungesser and Coli had vanished somewhere over the ocean. Exactly where or how or why, no one could ever say. Searchers never found the men or their famous plane. But reporters quickly found a new would-be transatlantic conqueror to shower with praise and glory. He had landed at Roosevelt Field in New York the very same week, a twenty-five-year-old airmail pilot from Minnesota: Charles Lindbergh.

RAYMOND ORTEIG WAS beginning to worry about the role his prize played in luring good men to their deaths. With each tragedy, he was forced to answer questions or release statements professing sadness: "I greatly deplore the unfortunate accident . . ." In the case of his missing countrymen Nungesser and Coli, Orteig had to do even more than that. The hotel owner, already on the hook for the $25,000, put up an additional $5,000 for anyone offering tips leading to their rescue or the discovery of their missing plane. There was little reason to believe Lindbergh's effort would end any differently. Orteig had always imagined that the man who won his prize would have a crew, or at least a copilot, to help him. Yet here was Lindbergh, flying alone and traveling light.

"Are you only taking five sandwiches?" one reporter asked him.

"Yes," Lindbergh said. "That's enough. If I get to Paris, I won't need any more. And if I don't get to Paris, I won't need any more, either."

"No coffee?" another reporter asked.

Lindbergh—six foot three and thin enough to have earned the nickname Slim—just laughed. He didn't drink alcohol. Didn't smoke cigarettes. Didn't chew tobacco. Coffee?

"No," he replied. "I won't need any."

His plane, like Nungesser's, had just one engine. Also alarming: it was smaller than the doomed *White Bird*, four feet shorter from nose to tail and two feet shorter across the wings. At least one prominent aviation engineer declared that the *Spirit of St. Louis*—built for Lindbergh with money donated by wealthy Missouri investors—was too small to succeed. Even Lindbergh joked that his plane was like a "death chamber." "It's a tight fit in this cockpit," he said. Still, shortly after midnight on May 20, 1927, he made up his mind: he was going. Lindbergh left his room at the Garden City Hotel on Long Island, headed to the airfield in the dark, conducted his preflight preparations until dawn, and then folded his lanky frame into the plane's small cockpit.

"Ready, Slim?" a mechanic asked.

"Ready," Lindbergh replied.

It was misty and foggy at Roosevelt Field, raining off and on—questionable conditions, at best, for flying. Even taxiing down the runway was a problem. The wheels of Lindbergh's tiny plane sank into the soft clay, slowing his progress. And the airship, carrying the heaviest load it had ever shouldered, labored to get into the sky, horrifying the five hundred people who'd gathered to watch. Lindbergh was running out of runway. He had to take off now or crash, like Fonck, into the fast-approaching gully at the end of the muddy strip. Running out of time and space, he slammed down the elevators on the tail, trying to pull the plane's nose up. It lifted slightly, and the tail followed.

Lindbergh was aloft, though still not out of trouble. He was so low, maybe just fifty feet off the ground, that witnesses at the end of the runway could see his face through the cockpit glass—and they thought Lindbergh looked old, suddenly aged by worry. Pilots who were watching wondered if he might ditch. The plane was headed straight into a thicket of trees. But Lindbergh found a narrow break in the highest branches, guided his plane through the opening, cleared the treetops by just a few feet, and then disappeared, swallowed by the morning mist.

The takeoff was neither the safest nor the best. Across the ocean, Lloyd's of London refused to place any odds on Lindbergh's success after his inauspicious start. The famous insurance broker declared that the risk of failure was too great. The American public, weary of air disasters, was just as concerned. Desperate for news about Lindbergh, people jammed the switchboard at the *New York Times* with ten thousand phone calls that day, the highest volume the newspaper had ever recorded, while others observed moments of silence, praying for the American aviator. At a boxing match that night at Yankee Stadium, the fight emcee asked the typically raucous crowd to stand and honor Lindbergh, and forty thousand fight fans did just that, removing their hats and turning their faces to the night sky. At that moment, Lindbergh was hundreds of miles out to sea, needing all the prayers he could get.

But the American press had already written this story. Lindbergh's takeoff wasn't dubious; it was "daring" and "magnificent." And young Lindbergh wasn't reckless for having tried it. He was a "lion," reporters wrote, who had temerity and a keen, thoughtful mind, with his eyes fastened on the goal, his jaw set, and his instincts true. "Defeat and death stared him in the face," the *New York Times* wrote the morning after Lindbergh's takeoff, "and he gazed at it unafraid."

When he touched down at Le Bourget airfield thirty-three hours later, nothing could hold back the crowds surging forward to embrace Lindbergh. A hundred thousand Parisians knocked down iron barriers around the runway and pushed past soldiers armed with bayonets just to be near him. Back home, crowds gathered from Times Square in New York to Lindbergh's hometown of Little Falls, Minnesota, tossing their hats into the air. Factory whistles shrieked and church bells rang; offices were closed and school was canceled. Lindbergh was paraded through four cities on two continents: Paris, Cherbourg, Washington, and New York. But realizing that this wasn't enough—that people wanted more—a wealthy aviation enthusiast paid Lindbergh a small fortune, $50,000, to keep touring. In the summer and fall of 1927, he visited another ninety-two American cities in his famous plane for more parades, speeches, radio broadcasts, and galas.

The flier grew tired of all the attention—the "hokum," Lindbergh called it once—criticizing the slow speeds of the parades, complaining about the gasoline fumes that made him nauseated, and sending out his new manager to run interference with the reporters who were chronicling his every gesture and analyzing his every word. "Awaiting," one radioman said, "Lindbergh . . . Lindbergh is coming down the gangplank . . . Walking slowly . . . His hat in his hand, quiet and dignified . . . A darn nice boy."

He had won Orteig's prize and everything that came with it—the book deals, the movie offers, the lucrative sponsorships, and the adulation. But Raymond Orteig, the man behind it all, felt like a winner too.

"I feel a lot lighter," the Frenchman said.

"Lighter by $25,000?" a friend joked.

Orteig shook him off. It wasn't about the money. "Lighter in the heart," he explained.

With Lindbergh's success, Orteig felt as if a burden had been lifted. No one else would have to die trying to fly across the ocean to win his money. But Orteig and others hadn't counted on the female pilots.

They would do it for free.

5

The Fairest of the Brave and the Bravest of the Fair

L ouise mcphetridge, Ruth Nichols, and Amelia Earhart heard about Lindbergh's flight the way everyone else did: on the radio, in the newspaper, or from friends eager to share the exciting news. McPhetridge had just arrived in Oakland and was settling into her new job selling Walter Beech's Travel Air planes. Earhart had only recently started doing social work at Denison House in Boston. By her own admission, she was barely flying anymore. And Ruth Nichols couldn't catch a break. She and her foul-mouthed flying instructor Harry Rogers still saw each other from time to time. But Rogers wasn't calling Nichols—not even to shout at her—leaving her to face an unwelcome reality: she was no aviator. In the spring of 1927, Nichols, twenty-six, was working in the women's department of a bank on Forty-Second Street, still living in her parents' house in Rye, and watching as a different Ruth—Ruth Elder, younger and prettier, flirtatious and Southern—made plans to come to New York to capitalize on American air fever and upstage all the other women with a story sure to interest air-mad reporters.

Elder was thinking like a man and talking like Lindbergh. She was going to be the first woman to fly the Atlantic, or she was going to die trying. Either way, Elder was about to prove two points: a woman with a good plane and a bold plan was impossible to ignore—and easy to disparage.

RUTH ELDER BREEZED into Long Island that September, four months after Lindbergh's flight, landing at Roosevelt Field with the subtlety of a gale. Her colorful sweaters were tight, and her brown hair was bobbed in the latest style. The Alabama native almost never appeared without a rainbow-hued scarf wrapped around her head, pinning back her wild curls. Her airship was equally eye-catching; the single-engine Stinson Detroiter monoplane was a brilliant shade of orange. The color choice had less to do with flair than practicality. In a wide expanse of gray-blue ocean, the floating wreckage of an orange plane was easier to spot than the remains of, say, a silver one. But Elder—and her male copilot, a Floridian named George Haldeman—had no intention of putting her plane in the water. It was too beautiful, too perfect, all the way down to the name painted on the fuselage in large, sweeping cursive script: *American Girl.*

"Gas bought, runway ready, plane dandy, pilots OK," Elder told reporters in their first meeting at Roosevelt Field, already commanding their attention with her looks, style, and distinctive high-pitched voice. "Give us a weather break and we'll take off then."

"What's your hurry?" one reporter asked.

"Say," she replied, "I've been dreaming and planning this ever since I first learned to fly two years ago. Then Lindbergh did it—and I was more determined. I want to be the first girl to turn the trick. I'll do it—I and Captain Haldeman."

"Do you only want to fly to Paris because you are a girl?" another reporter asked.

"Well, they've got pretty evening gowns there, I hear," Elder joked. Then, more seriously, she added, "I've never been to Europe. Might as well go this way. Get some clothes. Doll up a little. Come back by boat, taking it easy. No flying back for me."

The reporters wanted to know everything about her. Was she married? Engaged? Or were she and Haldeman together, maybe? No, Elder replied. No and no—especially to the last question. "Say, listen," an insulted Haldeman interjected, "I'm married." Was Elder afraid and would she back out in the end? Be honest. Or would her family ultimately talk her out of it? No, she replied again, and no. "They've been perfect peaches," she told them.

Elder had been in New York for a half an hour. Hadn't even left the airfield to check in to her room at the nearby Garden City Hotel. And already the New York press was picking her apart. Reporters described her nose: "Perfectly powdered." They called her vain, criticizing her purse or her knickers, and they pushed the twenty-four-year-old woman again and again to admit that she wasn't truly serious about her transatlantic plans.

"What is this you're doing?" another bewildered newspaperman asked her. "Advertising a movie? Or just getting yourself well enough known to be offered a vaudeville contract?"

"Oh, no," Elder said. "I'm really going to fly to Paris." Didn't they understand? "I'm here to fly," she said. "Quickly."

Looking out at the reporters and, beyond them, the long clay runway where Fonck had failed and Lindbergh had prevailed, Elder must have felt as if she'd flown the *American Girl* not to Long Island but to an altogether different world. She was from Anniston, Alabama, one of seven children raised by Sarah and J. O. Elder downtown on Noble Street. The house there was the latest in a string of modest homes rented by the Elders with money J.O. made as either a farm laborer or a molder in a pipefitting shop—all of which wasn't good enough for Ruth, J.O.'s third-oldest child and thrill-seeking daughter. She left home shortly after her eighteenth birthday and moved sixty miles west to Birmingham—"the city," Elder called it.

She rented a room in a boarding house there and her parents figured she'd be back in Anniston soon. Instead, Elder began leading a life that she kept secret and now desperately hoped to hide from the New York reporters. She got a job selling lingerie in a department store—and she got a husband. But the marriage didn't take. She was divorced and then, in May 1925, married again—this time to Lyle Womack, an electric-sign salesman. Together, the pair moved to Lakeland, Florida, where, for a time, anyway, they lived an ordinary life east of Tampa. Elder got a job in a dentist's office and Womack helped introduce his young wife to flying—and, also, to some Florida businessmen who were fond of both golf and schemes.

In Elder, the men chasing Lindberghian fame saw an opportunity. The Floridians wanted to put Elder over the ocean with George Haldeman, a well-known local pilot, doing most of the flying and Elder doing most of the smiling. They pitched their idea to some wealthy snowbirds from West Virginia on a golf course in Lakeland, and these men saw value in the plan. As financial backers, they would make money by shooting footage of Elder and selling it to Hollywood. There was just one caveat: she would have to say she had never been married. The men were marketing a product, and it couldn't be labeled "Mrs. Lyle Womack."

The West Virginians, intrigued, agreed to put up $35,000 to buy a plane and make it happen, believing Elder was the right woman for the job. She was, men liked to point out, the most beautiful pilot they had ever seen. "So pretty," one said, "that it doesn't seem right." She was, to put it another way, "the fairest of the brave and the bravest of the fair." She would make it to Paris — or she wouldn't. She would live to tell the tale — or she would die. Either way, the reporters would get their story. Either way, the West Virginians were insured. And either way, Elder figured, it was better than playing out her years working at a dentist's office in Florida and making dinner for her husband. The trick was getting Haldeman to teach her to fly — and then getting him to go with her across the ocean. He hated instructing women. Inevitably, they always ended up crying about something, Haldeman complained. But Elder wore him down, not with her beauty but with dogged determination.

"I've lived for a while without amounting to a plugged nickel," she told one reporter after arriving in New York. "I want to do something that will make people notice me, that may give me an opportunity to get somewhere in the world."

"Is it worth risking your life?" the reporter asked.

"Yes, it is," she replied.

There was really only one way for Elder to screw up the deal — by losing to another woman who had dreams, money, and a plane of her own. That woman was staring out at the ocean too, three hundred miles to the north.

THE JACK RABBIT was typically the main attraction at Old Orchard Beach in Maine. The roller coaster drew big crowds of tourists in the summer. And if visitors didn't have the stomach for the Jack Rabbit, they were sure to enjoy the spinning cars of the Whip next door, the views from the Big Eli — the town Ferris wheel — or any number of other attractions in the Palace Arcade, hemmed in by Grand Avenue, West Surf Street, and the sea.

Old Orchard Beach, on the jagged coast of Maine, fifteen miles south of Portland, was a resort community, designed for the enjoyment of Bostonians and New Yorkers in the summer. The 1927 season had been especially busy. Visitors there held masked balls and dances, dined on lobster, and found ways to make Prohibition-mandated non-alcoholic gin properly alcoholic once again. Miss America herself made an appearance there that August.

But the most enthralling story that summer was the increasingly plausible notion that Old Orchard Beach would be a future hub for American airplanes heading to Europe. Its location was ideal. A pilot seeking the shortest possible route to Europe didn't fly straight out to sea but rather followed the curvature of the earth. On the Great Circle route, as it was known, a Europe-bound plane would fly up the coast of Maine, over Nova Scotia, past Newfoundland, and then out over the open ocean. That meant that any plane leaving from Maine instead of New York saved not only time but weight in gas. And it was comparatively easy to leave from Old Orchard Beach because of the nature of the sand there: it was flat, firm, free of rocks, and—at low tide—stretched for miles. A plane was limited to just a mile's worth of runway at Roosevelt Field but could have almost three times that distance at Old Orchard Beach. Most important, perhaps, the resort community already had the infrastructure in place to handle air traffic. For years, a pilot named Harry Jones had been giving flying lessons at the beach. He had a hangar not far from the carnival rides at the Palace Arcade, and, soon, he had a new client: Frances Grayson.

"Please keep my plans fully confidential," Grayson told Jones. "You know how uncertain everything is in aviation." But as soon as possible, she hoped to come to Old Orchard Beach, take off from there, and beat Ruth Elder across the Atlantic Ocean. "We are not flying into the 'movies,'" Grayson said, brushing off suggestions that she just wanted fame. Rather, she felt, they were flying into history. And like Elder, she was willing to die doing it. "I would rather give my life to something big and worthwhile," she said, "than to live longer and do less."

Reporters considered Grayson the opposite of Ruth Elder in almost every way. Where Elder was beautiful, Grayson was plain—"the Flying Matron," newspapers called her—with a toothy smile and a doughy face. And where Elder was part of a new breed of American woman, Grayson was considered old. She was thirty-five, matronly in-deed as far as the men were concerned. But what did they know about Frances Grayson?

Not long ago, back home in Muncie, Indiana, Grayson, the oldest daughter of Minnie and Andrew Jackson Wilson, had been as beguil-ing as Elder. Her mother had died young of a botched hysterectomy. Her father owned a grocery store on West Ninth Street, and every-one there just called her Willie. But she was more than just a grocer's daughter with a boy's name. She was an actress, a musician, and a lo-cal stage star. The society pages of Muncie's two newspapers dutifully chronicled her recitals and her appearances in town at picnic parties, benefits, and luncheons. Frances's marriage to postmaster John Brady Grayson in September 1914 was also big news. She walked down the aisle in her father's home wearing an ivory satin dress and meeting her groom in front of the family fireplace, which was framed in white and yellow roses.

The marriage took Grayson to a rural outpost in her husband's na-tive Virginia. But she didn't stay at home like a good Southern house-wife, a decision that may have taken a toll on her relationship with her husband. Instead, Frances Grayson appeared at suffrage events, lobbying for a woman's right to vote; she returned to the stage as an actress and toured the Northeast; and, ultimately, she divorced her husband, feeling like a failure, feeling small—like a mere atom. "But some day," Grayson said, "I hope to make that atom count for some-thing." She moved to New York and left the arts for real estate, where she excelled. By 1927, she had sold $2 million in property, opened an of-fice on West Thirty-Fourth Street, and managed to convince a wealthy Danish woman to give her $38,000 to finance a bold plan: a transat-lantic flight for her, a woman. Grayson hoped to fly with a crew from Old Orchard Beach all the way to Copenhagen in a new plane built in Queens by Igor Sikorsky.

"Don't worry," she told her family. "I am not going to fail."

Sikorsky had built Fonck's doomed airship the previous year, but its fiery end at Roosevelt Field didn't worry Grayson. Her plane, known as the S-36 Flying Boat, was brand-new and totally different. It had both pontoons and retractable wheels. In the air, it soared on massive wings, seventy-two feet from tip to tip. And on water, it floated like a seaworthy vessel, bobbing on its fuselage. Aviation experts hailed the

Flying Boat for its "almost unlimited possibilities." Grayson believed it was so sturdy that it could ride the waves at sea for weeks if necessary, and she thought it the most beautiful machine she had ever seen. At Sikorsky's factory in Queens, she stood in the shadows, day after day, watching the men build it and waiting for her chance—a mere atom no more.

"I am," Grayson said with growing confidence, "a child of destiny."

RUTH ELDER HAD no idea who she was anymore. By day two in New York, reporters were breaking the news that she had lied. Elder was currently married and had been before. By day three, the reporters' endless questions about these lies had reduced Elder to tears— and bargaining. She wept, trying to persuade them to keep the details about her marriages out of the papers. When that didn't work, she wept again as she tried to explain herself.

"American women believe that a married girl's place is in the home and not in the cockpit of an airplane. I don't want to turn them against me—to outrage their belief of the girl's place in life. That is why I evaded direct answer to the first questions concerning my marriage."

She insisted that everything else they knew about her was true. "I'm no bluffer or faker," Elder said. She would still be the first woman to fly across the Atlantic. But already, she was facing challenges on that front too. The first was in the form of Sikorsky's S-36 Flying Boat, delivered to Frances Grayson no more than a mile away. The second was a host of new rules suddenly being imposed by Roosevelt Field.

Joseph Lannin, who'd bought the field after selling the Boston Red Sox a decade earlier, declared that, effective immediately, transatlantic planes using his runway had to have more than one motor, had to be fitted with pontoons, and had to have a radio. Elder's *American Girl* met none of Lannin's new standards. Worse still, the people closest to her—her husband, her family, and even her financial backers in West Virginia—were beginning to bail.

The problem, as they saw it, was mathematical. Since Lindbergh's success in May, only one other plane had made it across the Atlantic. Every other ship had failed. One pilot flying a seaplane had ditched near a schooner to save himself. Five weeks later, an American explorer who had succeeded in flying to the North Pole in 1926 got to France with a crew of three. But unable to land in a driving rainstorm once they arrived, they'd turned back for the Normandy coast and crashed in the water. Everyone aboard the plane survived, which was more than most ocean fliers could say that summer. In August alone, sixteen people died in planes that were preparing to cross or actually crossing the sea. The death toll included skilled fliers, navy men, and two female passengers, a princess from England and a schoolteacher from Detroit.

The worst single event was a race from Oakland to Hawaii sponsored by the pineapple industrialist James Dole. Two planes in the Dole Air Race disappeared over the Pacific — five people dead. Then a third plane vanished trying to find the other two — two more people dead. Then three weeks later, just before Elder and Grayson arrived on Long Island, another plane was lost. This airship was owned by one of America's most prominent men: William Randolph Hearst, publisher of the *New York Daily Mirror.* Hearst hired two experienced pilots to fly the plane to Rome and reserved a third spot for the *Daily Mirror's* bespectacled managing editor Philip Payne, who would recount the amazing flight to the world. And Hearst's men knew exactly which runway they wanted to use to get into the sky: Old Orchard Beach. "If a loaded plane cannot rise here, I doubt if it ever could," said Hearst's pilot J. D. Hill, a man who had eight thousand hours of experience in the air.

On the first clear afternoon after Labor Day, the plane roared down the beach at Old Orchard with an escort of police motorcycles beside it. It needed more than two minutes and a mile and a half of sand to get into the air, but takeoff was otherwise uneventful. The plane was soon streaking like a dart up the coast and then well out to sea. By midnight, it was some 350 miles east of Newfoundland. "All OK," the plane radioed to a passing ship in the dark. "Making good time."

Then, at 3:17 a.m., for reasons unknown, the crew sent out an SOS. And by the time searchers found the plane, a week later, it was just pieces, wreckage — a chunk of wing, a few gas tanks, and a mangled wheel — indicating, experts said, that the plane had hit the water nose-first at an estimated ninety miles an hour.

That settled it, aviation experts said: no more ocean flying. Too many good men, heroic men — "fine young men," Secretary of Commerce Herbert Hoover called them — had been lost, and too many funerals had been held. At the latest one, for the *Daily Mirror*'s Philip Payne in New York, ten thousand mourners attended. If the men couldn't do it, the women—Elder and Grayson—shouldn't even try. In early September, as news broke of the women's plans, officials in both Canada and the United States began pressuring lawmakers to ban, or at least regulate, ocean flights. Eddie Stinson—the man who'd built Elder's plane, the *American Girl*—agreed that such legislation was necessary, effectively raising questions about his own airship. "It is asking too much of an airplane motor to run continuously for 30 to 50 hours under adverse weather conditions," Stinson announced. "The success of Colonel Lindbergh should not be accepted as a standard for the capabilities of modern airplane motors." Perhaps most significant, Lindbergh himself was now inclined to oppose ocean flights—at least those flights, he said, made for "publicity" purposes. The man who had nearly crashed on takeoff at Roosevelt Field in an effort to win Orteig's twenty-five-thousand-dollar prize refused to comment directly on Elder's, Grayson's, or any other flier's attempt to cross the ocean. But during a stop in Atlanta on his goodwill tour, the world's most famous aviator seemed to question the women's transatlantic plans. "It is rather useless to take off on flights involving great hazards unless there is some definite and worthy purpose in view," Lindbergh said. "I see no object in flying across hazardous ocean wastes unless there is a real purpose in mind."

By early October, the federal government threw up yet another obstacle. The US Weather Bureau stopped supplying pilots with ocean weather reports, information that had been a staple for pilots for months. The reason—officially, anyway—was budgetary. Still, Ruth Elder refused to give up. She endured the reporters' questions, ignored her critics, and submitted to every test that officials in New York forced on her. She took their physical, and passed. She took their licensing exam, flying the *American Girl* solo in front of crowds of gawkers on Long Island, and passed. Finally, after a month of delays, she and Haldeman got clearance to take off and awoke on the morning of October 11 to blue skies over Roosevelt Field. Elder was finished crying and tired of waiting. If she was going to beat Frances Grayson, the time to go was now.

"They shall not stop me," Elder said.

═══

THE MORNING OF Elder and Haldeman's departure, a team of mechanics pushed the *American Girl* out of its hangar and across the grassy landscape to the long runway that made European flights possible—Fonck's runway, Lindbergh's runway, now Elder's.

There, a crew loaded the plane with everything Elder might need: 520 gallons of gas, two rubber suits supposedly capable of keeping Elder and Haldeman afloat for up to seventy-two hours, a fourteen-pound emergency radio kit to send SOS signals, and a large knife to use to cut through the fuselage and escape the sinking plane in the event of a water landing. Finally, just behind the pilots' seats, they tucked away some simple rations for the trip: twelve sandwiches, six bars of chocolate, four dill pickles, two quarts of coffee, and one quart of beef tea, all packed up together in a basket.

With the basket on her arm, Elder looked like she was off on a picnic, wearing tan knickers, a green-and-red-plaid sweater with golf stockings to match, and her trademark rainbow-colored ribbon around her head—the "Ruth ribbon," girls in New York were calling it. But even as she stood there smiling for the storm of photographers, her mind was elsewhere. Elder was thinking about Grayson, who had jumped north to Old Orchard Beach in her Flying Boat the day before and, as far as Elder knew, might head out at any moment, beating her across the sea.

"Is she going?" Elder kept asking.

Hours dripped away. Still, they were on the ground. Too windy to take off.

"We'll wait," Haldeman said.

Elder could hardly believe her poor luck. But by afternoon, her mood began to change. She slapped mechanics on the back when her personal weather report came in, assuring the fliers of clear skies for three-fourths of their journey—if they left now. She heaved a sigh of relief when she learned that Grayson didn't appear to be leaving Maine that day. Then, to help pass the time, she admired the smooth contours of her little orange plane, running her hand down its nose. "We'll make it," she said, as if trying to reassure herself. Just before five o'clock that evening, with the sun dipping low over the runway, Haldeman and Elder made the call: despite the gusty skies, they were going. They turned around to fly into the wind, as all planes do. Haldeman pulled a fur-lined suit over his clothes and climbed into the cockpit with all the joy of a man heading to his own funeral, while Elder, equally bundled up against the cold, waved to the crowd that had gathered to see her. Her signature hair ribbon was hidden beneath her aviator's helmet. But her smile was still there as she said farewell.

"Goodbye, everybody."

A policeman planted a kiss on Elder's cheek. Haldeman steered the *American Girl* to the far end of the runway, and then let the engines idle for a few minutes, churning up clouds of red dust. Finally, he hit the throttle and the plane began to roar, racing down the runway.

Like everything else involving Elder in recent weeks, the takeoff was a first-rate New York circus. Five hundred people and scores of automobiles were positioned where the plane had been sitting all day. But since Haldeman had turned it around at the last minute to fly into the wind, the *American Girl* was now barreling toward the spectators, whom airfield officials hadn't bothered to move to safety. A companion airplane with a photographer on board rumbled along next to the *American Girl,* hoping to get exclusive shots of Elder's takeoff. Other pilots, hoping for views of their own, were already in the air. And to add to the chaos, the *American Girl* had the usual problem: it was too heavy and running out of runway.

Seeing the orange machine speeding toward the crowd, police sounded the alarm, blowing whistles to scatter the masses. Spectators, now horrified, began to run. By one account, the *American Girl* had six hundred feet of runway remaining when its wheels finally left the ground. By another, it had only a hundred feet. Some people at the end of the runway ducked, fearing that the plane would strike them as it flew overhead. Then they looked up into the sky and cheered. Elder was up and away, flying into the darkness.

Based on storm forecasts, Haldeman had decided not to take the shortest route, following the Great Circle, but to fly straight east from Montauk Point, at the tip of Long Island, cross over Nantucket, and follow the steamship line toward Europe — a long haul in a little plane. As a result, by eight p.m., land fell away behind the *American Girl.*

In the cockpit, Elder and Haldeman were thrilled, taking turns at the controls and singing to pass the time on the first night. "I'm on my way to gay Par-ee," Elder said, making up lyrics to go with a popular tune they both knew. But by morning — when they were fifteen hours into the flight and still less than halfway there — they began to have problems. The plane had been bucking a steady headwind since it left New York, and as a result, it was consuming more gas than had been expected. Haldeman ran the numbers and figured they had just enough fuel to get to Paris. But that was before the second night, when, for more than six hours, the *American Girl* pitched and rolled in a large and violent squall. Had they been over land, they would have come down and waited it out. But since that wasn't possible, they flew on in total darkness. "Black trouble," Elder called it.

They could feel the plane failing, hear the engine struggling. Ice was forming on the wings, crusting up in the twenty-seven-degree temperatures outside, making the plane even harder to fly, and forcing it down—down toward the sea. The compass bounced around; they were surely off course now. Worst of all, perhaps, the *American Girl* was bleeding oil, an apparent leak from who knew where. With every hour, the oil pressure was falling.

Somehow, despite everything, they outlasted the storm. "It's all over!" Haldeman shouted to Elder when he finally saw the moon again. But they couldn't outfly the oil problem. By the second morning of the flight—a stunning thirty-two hours after takeoff and at least eight hours away from landfall in Europe—they had to consider ditching. They brought their wounded bird down low over a Dutch oil tanker, the SS *Barendrecht*, that appeared like a miracle on the surface of the ocean. It was the first ship they had seen in more than twelve hours and their best shot now at survival.

How far are we from land? Elder asked in a message she tossed to the deck of the ship inside a cardboard box. *And which way?*

The plane circled while the sailors painted their reply on the deck.

True S 40 degrees west, Terceira, Azores 360 miles.

Elder and Haldeman hadn't even made it to the Azores.

"We are going to land!" Haldeman shouted to the men on the deck of the *Barendrecht* as he made one final pass. "Pick us up!"

Haldeman zoomed away, looped back, and prepared to ditch while Elder grabbed the large knife they had packed. Her job: carving a large hole in the fuselage of the plane so they could get out and avoid drowning. As she plunged the knife into the plane's skin, Elder felt as if she herself had been slashed open. But she had no choice. They were done flying. It was time to swim.

The Dutch crew tossed each flier a line, safely reeled them in, and then, a short time later, watched as the *American Girl* burst into flames, slipped beneath the waves, and sank.

IN MAINE, on the day of Elder's departure, Grayson had no intention of going anywhere. She and her crew awoke that morning in the empty Brunswick Hotel to find a hard frost—the season's first—on the ground outside, a temperature of thirty-eight degrees, and a stiff wind blowing up the beach. Winter was coming. The day would be for tests and ceremonies only. The Flying Boat needed a proper name—the *Dawn,* Grayson decided to call it—and she wanted to make a show of its christening. She invited the governor's wife, Dorothy Foss Brewster, to do the honors and Maine's First Lady agreed, despite her own reservations about Grayson.

"Prayers of women everywhere," Brewster told Grayson before a shivering crowd on the beach, "will go up for your success, if you shall decide if it is now wise for you to start. The hazard of the enterprise, however—and the question as to its fruits—lead me to express what I believe to be the earnest entreaty that you may decide to wait."

For weeks, like Elder, Grayson had been defending her plans against a torrent of criticism. What she was attempting to do, Grayson argued, was certainly as worthwhile as what Lindbergh had done. It didn't matter that she wasn't flying the plane herself. The *Dawn* was a seaplane going from America to Denmark—a trip that had never before been attempted—with a woman on board. "This is a pioneer flight," she kept saying. It was a costly one too. In addition to the money from Denmark, Grayson was draining her own savings to make it happen. Friends worried that she was going broke. Now, at the christening of her own plane, she was fighting off criticism again. The fact that it came from another woman surely made it harder to bear. As Grayson replied to the governor's wife, before the Mainers and the reporters, she chose her words carefully.

"It is decidedly an honor to have the First Lady of the state christen our wonderful ship," she said. But Brewster and everyone else needed to know that Grayson was going to Europe no matter what. "In urging me not to go," Grayson told the governor's wife, "I feel you have assumed as great a responsibility as if you had advised me to go. The *Dawn* will awake American women to greater efforts and bind closer the women of two continents."

Sufficiently fired up and surprised by the news that Elder had left New York just after five o'clock that evening, Grayson briefly considered going that night too, right away. But it was already well after dark, and the *Dawn* needed to be fueled up, a process that took hours. She had no choice but to summon the skills that she had honed as an actress and pretend it didn't matter to her what Ruth Elder did. "Well," Grayson said, "I wish her Godspeed and all the success in the world. There's glory enough for both."

She was proceeding with her plans. Twice during the thirty-two hours that Elder was in the sky over the Atlantic, Grayson made arrangements to take off. And twice she canceled them due to weather. The first cancellation was mostly precautionary. The second time, she and her crew nearly lost the *Dawn* in a raging tide that blew in and swamped the plane on the beach. Still, Grayson felt good about her prospects. Despite the surge of salt water, the hull hadn't sprung a single leak. Even better was the news she got later that day while warming herself by the fireplace in the lobby of the Brunswick: Ruth Elder had failed. She was alive and unharmed, but she had lost, bailing out near the Azores. "Congratulations," Grayson immediately cabled Elder from the hotel. "My prayers followed you."

Now it was her turn. Grayson had the plane and the crew to do it. Wilmer "Bill" Stultz, a farm boy from Williamsburg, Pennsylvania, was a decorated twenty-seven-year-old pilot with training in both the army and the navy. Grayson worried about what she called his temperament; Stultz was known to drink. But no one questioned his flying abilities. Meanwhile, Brice "Goldy" Goldsborough, Stultz's navigator, was considered one of America's best. A wagon maker's son from Iowa, Goldy had guided Walter Beech to victory in the 1926 Ford Reliability Tour. More important, he had been specializing in compass navigation for eight years, building the instruments with his large hands. If anyone could chart Grayson to Denmark, it was Goldy. But early on, he hardly got a chance to do his job.

Three times in the nine days after Elder failed, Grayson and her crew managed to take off from the beach. And three times, they turned around and came back, hobbled by the weight of the airship, mechanical problems, and, increasingly, fighting among Grayson, Stultz, and Goldy. It was, by any measure, a miserable time to be at the beach in Maine. Since Grayson's arrival, the state had seen record rainfalls, as much as four inches on some days. When it wasn't raining, it was storming. One gale and then another. "Gray fog, gray clouds, all is gray," Grayson wrote one day while staring out the window. "And the lashing of the waves, the rain, the wind, remind me that it is almost November."

In Old Orchard Beach, she had become an attraction, like the rides at the Palace Arcade. Some weekends, despite the worsening weather, thirty thousand people poured into the beach town to catch a glimpse of Grayson. And the strain of it all—the weather, the failures, the crowds, and the questions—was beginning to take a toll. Recently, Grayson and her crew had argued over flight plans in the lobby of the Brunswick. Now, after Stultz turned around and aborted the third attempt due to a sputtering engine, Grayson insinuated he was planning a mutiny.

"One day a pilot is willing to take you," she said, "the next day he is not." Stultz was out, and that was just fine with him. Snow was already falling at Moosehead Lake up north, making air travel dangerous at best. A Sikorsky engineer had calculated that if even one-sixteenth of an inch of ice formed on the wings of the *Dawn*, it would add two hundred pounds to the plane and make it difficult to fly. "The danger is obvious," the engineer said. Grayson would have to wait until spring. "Figure it out for yourself," Stultz said, pondering the ice. "What would this mean to the *Dawn* over the Atlantic?"

Grayson decamped to New York. But she wasn't giving up just yet, and by December she had a new plan. She'd leave from Roosevelt Field on Long Island two days before Christmas with a new pilot and a mostly new flight crew. Only one man was returning to fly with Grayson: her reliable navigator Goldy. In October, the thirty-six-year-old man had every confidence in their plans and their plane, barely waving to his worried wife, Gertrude, from the cockpit of the *Dawn* before the multiple takeoffs in Maine. But after his final preparatory meetings with Grayson in New York in late December, Goldy was shaken. At home in Brooklyn two nights before his departure, he paced the floor for hours, clutched Gertrude in his arms, and cried out—irrationally, it seemed to his wife—saying he could not live without her. The next night, he returned home at midnight, agitated, and announced they were leaving the next day. Again, he clung to Gertrude, who begged him not to go with Grayson. There was still time for him to back out.

"Do you think the damn woman is worth risking your life for?" Gertrude asked.

At Roosevelt Field the next day, December 23, Goldy was so lost in his own thoughts that he nearly walked into a spinning propeller. Again and again before boarding the *Dawn,* the navigator came back to kiss his wife goodbye. Gertrude had never seen him behave in such a way, and as the plane took off that evening, she had a feeling she had never experienced before. "I feel that I shall never see Brice again," she told a friend as she watched the *Dawn* disappear into the sky over Long Island.

It was 5:07 p.m. and already freezing in New York, with snow and colder temperatures promised as the plane moved north. And up the coast, aviation enthusiasts were waiting. They stood at established checkpoints to scan the night skies for the *Dawn*.

Nothing.

Morning came in Newfoundland—the *Dawn*'s scheduled refueling stop—and still there was no plane. It was Christmas Eve, and across America, families gathered around radios to sing carols together in a coordinated national program. Twenty million voices singing as one, from living room to living room, reading off song lists published in their local newspapers and marking the end of a miraculous year.

And still, nothing. Grayson's famous plane, flying at a low altitude up one of the most populous coasts in the world and over some of the globe's busiest shipping lanes, was missing. "Direct all vessels patrolling off New England coast to keep sharp lookout for Miss Grayson's plane," the US Coast Guard instructed sailors in a message. Ships, planes, navy destroyers, and even blimps came streaking into the region to take part in a search that, by the time it was over, covered a stretch of ocean almost three times the size of New Jersey. But they never found even a propeller blade from the *Dawn*, leaving people to speculate wildly: the plane had gone down near Newfoundland. It had made an emergency landing much farther inland. It was somewhere in the hinterlands of New Brunswick or Quebec. It was still out there, floating on the ocean. Back in Muncie, Indiana, Grayson's father canceled his Christmas plans. "That's all off now," he said, holing up in his grocery store, where he had a telephone to stay in touch with the newspapers. He was sure his daughter was alive—somewhere— awaiting rescue in her reliable seaplane. "Built to float for two weeks," her father said. Others were just as definitive that they must be safe on land. At least two people in Newfoundland, including a clergyman, were convinced they had heard the thundering engines of the *Dawn* in the sky. In one account, Grayson's plane arrived there sixteen hours late. In another telling, it was twenty-five hours late. "I submit the following as absolutely correct," one eyewitness said. Finally, at least three radiomen across a stretch of a thousand miles reported hearing the plane's last radio message — an impossibility.

Off Cape Cod: "Plane down."

In Bremen, Maine: "Can't exist long."

In Newfoundland: "Where are we? Can you locate us?"

If any of them was true, it was most likely the one heard off Cape Cod. A wireless operator aboard a steamer collected the message via Morse code at 7:30 p.m. And it was consistent with other reports placing the *Dawn* over Cape Cod at that time, including an account from a British schooner that was eighteen miles offshore that night. Outside the schooner, it was dark and windy, a moderate gale. The seas were high and visibility poor in winter skies spitting sleet and snow. But the men aboard the schooner all agreed on what they heard. It was the unmistakable sound of an airplane engine, so close it was frightening. And then a loud splash. And then nothing but the sound of the sea.

"Please tell me the truth," Gertrude Goldsborough begged the reporters who came to her home in Brooklyn. "Is there any hope?"

There was not. Grayson and her crew had vanished, and officials quickly blamed Grayson for the outcome. They had told her it was too cold to fly. They had told her to stay as close to land as possible on the night of December 23 to avoid stormy weather. Clearly, she hadn't listened. "We did everything we could to dissuade Mrs. Grayson from attempting an ocean flight in winter," the US Weather Bureau's top meteorologist declared on Christmas Eve with the massive search just under way. "But she was very determined and overrode our objections."

Soon, the newspaper columnists were piling on. Grayson's flight had been a daredevil stunt, they said, a suicide mission.

INITIALLY, ANYWAY, Ruth Elder got better treatment. From the moment she reached dry land on the European continent — safe, still beautiful, and now famous — people wanted to celebrate her transatlantic failure.

"There she is," Parisians shouted when they first saw her in late October.

"That's Ruth."

"Vive l'American Girl."

She was fifteen days late to her destination, ferried there by the SS *Barendrecht*, a second ship, and then a different plane. But the crowd at Le Bourget airfield in Paris didn't seem to mind, surging around her, pressing close to kiss her, and frightening the young woman at first with their enthusiasm. *"Bon,"* Elder said, speaking what little French she knew amid the crush of her admirers. *"Très bon."* French officials feted her with a dinner that night. Others took her shopping for dresses, making Elder feel, she said, like "Cinderella." "Why, I'd never had two dresses at a time in my life," she marveled. They even arranged for her to meet the mother of the missing Charles Nungesser. She kissed Elder with affection on both cheeks and made a personal plea. "Find my son for me," she said. "I know my boy is alive."

Elder seriously considered the idea. In her transatlantic flight, she had fallen short, and Haldeman had done most of the flying, yet she'd still traveled 2,623 miles, the longest flight ever by a woman. If she could secure a plane and more financial backing, she said, maybe she'd go in search of Nungesser. In the meantime, there were parties to attend, speeches to give, and contracts to review. Hollywood producers and vaudeville shows were reportedly offering Elder a total of $400,000 for her story, for her time, for her face, for her name. Fireboats and photographers met her when she returned to New York by ocean liner two weeks later. President Calvin Coolidge greeted her in Washington a few days after that, and people back in Anniston, Alabama, invited her home for "Ruth Elder Day."

On December 20, as Grayson was preparing to take off from New York, thousands of people lined the streets of Anniston to catch a glimpse of Elder riding in an open car surrounded by mounted police, fire trucks, and marching bands. They queued up to shake her hand in a receiving line afterward, and they paid to attend a dinner in her honor that night, a meal topped off with a dessert of cakes with white icing and frosted red letters. The letters on the cakes spelled out *R-u-t-h.* "Oh, I don't know how to say it," Elder cried, looking out on the faces of her hometown. "But the people have just been wonderful."

Only they hadn't—not always. In Paris, the French called her by the pejorative nickname "the Happy Midinette" or "the American Midinette." Translation of *midinette*: "silly young girl." In Anniston, people pushed her into gimmicks, auctioning off kisses from her at ten dollars apiece to raise money for charity. And in New York, Elder's snubbed husband, Lyle Womack, disparaged his flying wife every chance he got. He felt belittled by reporters, who referred to him as "Mr. Ruth Elder," and by Elder, who had briefly denied his existence. Her proper name, Womack declared, was Mrs. Womack, "not Ruth Elder." He said he expected her to abandon flying in order to return to doing what she did best: keeping house. "Ace-high housekeeper," Womack said in one of the few compliments he paid his wife. "I'm very much in love with her," he added, "but I won't bask in her glory."

They argued from the moment Elder stepped off the ocean liner back in New York and Womack tried to kiss her.

"Don't be a fool," she told him.

Within months, she was divorced—her second failed marriage—with Womack charging Elder with cruelty, fodder for still more headlines. Madame Nungesser checked out on Elder too. She dismissed the idea of sending the female flier in search of her son after getting a good look at the American Midinette. "You are too little to do such things," Nungesser told Elder. "It is men's work." In the end, even the *Anniston Star* couldn't resist taking a shot at its most famous citizen. "The nation will hope that Ruth Elder and other girls will stay on the ground hereafter," the *Star* wrote. "It is folly in anybody but a lion tamer to enter the lion's cage."

Perhaps most hurtful, prominent American women criticized Elder too. A leading female sociologist dubbed Elder's flight "a mistaken thing for a young girl to do." Eleanor Roosevelt, whose husband, Franklin, was soon to run for governor of New York, called Elder's attempt "very foolish." And Winifred Sackville Stoner, founder of the League for Fostering Genius, found nothing genius about Elder. "She showed courage," Stoner said. "But what good did she do?" The nation, she suggested, would be better off if Elder pursued something more worthwhile. "This afternoon, I am having as my guests at tea a number of high school girls who have won prizes for fast typing," Stoner said. "Any one of them in being a fast, accurate typist does far more for the community than does a dozen . . . Ruth Elders."

Elder was as famous as she had always hoped to be, and she was also completely lost, burdened by criticism and almost absurd expectations that none of the men had faced either before or after they'd attempted to fly across the ocean. As Elder parted from her parents in Anniston that December, she nearly broke down in tears. She couldn't spend Christmas at home. A train was waiting to take her north. She was booked for a weeklong vaudeville appearance in Cleveland. She had to go.

"Well, goodbye," she told her parents from the steps of the train. "And tell everyone in Anniston goodbye, and ten thousand thanks."

The train pulled out of the station at 7:30 p.m. And outside the windows, the Alabama landscape rolled by in the dark. It was almost Christmas Eve and Ruth Elder was all alone — no husband at her side and little support around her beyond those looking to cash in on her fame. Only one American female aviator, in fact, had publicly stood up for Elder, defending the embattled flier against her many critics.

It was another Ruth — Ruth Nichols.

6

Flying Salesgirls

T HE HOUSE IN RYE had never felt gloomier to Ruth Nichols than it did on New Year's Eve 1927. She was closing in on her twenty-seventh birthday and was forced to admit she was neither the woman she'd hoped to become nor the girl her parents wished her to be. Nichols wasn't married, wasn't engaged. She was keenly aware that other society girls in New York thought her old — "old hat," Nichols believed — and also aware that, for all her big talk of flying, she wasn't doing much of it. As the clock ticked toward midnight, Nichols, alone in the big house, didn't seem to have any direction; only doubts — and a lingering question.

"How could I escape?" she wondered.

The headlines about Ruth Elder and Frances Grayson in recent weeks could not have helped Ruth Nichols's state of mind. Unlike Grayson, Nichols was a real pilot. And unlike Elder, she didn't require hasty licensing exams by New York officials. Nichols had been flying for years and had even made a handy list of her many achievements in the air in case anyone wanted to review them: 1922, first flying lessons with Harry Rogers in Florida; 1923, first solo flight in a seaplane; 1924, first American woman to get a seaplane pilot's license. Then, in the summer of 1927, just before Elder landed on Long Island, another breakthrough: Nichols became just the second woman ever to receive a transport pilot's license. She could — theoretically, anyway — fly any licensed aircraft, which was more than Elder or almost any other

American woman could say. But when given a chance to criticize Elder, Nichols declined to take it. "I would not call Miss Elder foolhardy," Nichols told reporters.

With herself, however, she was always less generous, and she was especially critical of herself that New Year's Eve. By the end of the night, Nichols was studying her face in a mirror, intent on finding all its flaws. Her mouth appeared droopy, her blue eyes frightened, and her expression not young anymore. It looked sad.

Just then, the telephone rang. It was her old instructor Harry Rogers on the line, calling Nichols not with curses or insults but with an opportunity. Within the week, he and a wealthy aviator, feeling air fever, were hoping to make the first-ever nonstop flight from New York to Miami in a seaplane currently bobbing in the waters off Rockaway Beach in Queens. And the savvy Rogers had noted, by reading the New York papers of late, how to attract bold headlines to a flight: bring a woman.

"Want to come along?" Rogers asked Nichols.

"When do we start?" she replied.

Nichols had experience making the New York–to–Miami run. She had flown it months earlier, with her aunt, in two days. Rogers, with his home in Brooklyn and his seaplane business in Florida, had experience on the route too. Eight years earlier, he'd piloted the first airship to go from South Florida to New York in a single day, landing once to refuel and setting a record for a flight up the East Coast: sixteen hours and thirty-five minutes.

A daily service between the two cities remained elusive eight years later. But a nonstop flight with Rogers and Nichols at the controls, timed to arrive in Miami during a convention of newspaper editors, could help change that. With navy destroyers and blimps hardly finished combing the seas for the wreckage of the *Dawn*, Nichols headed to Rockaway Beach the next morning, New Year's Day 1928. She met Rogers there, spent the night in a boarding house, and got her first look at the airship that would make the trip: a single-engine Fairchild seaplane with silver pontoons, yellow wings, a red fuselage, and seats for four passengers inside a heated cabin. Sherman Fairchild, the manufacturer, had big plans for his new machine, and Nichols was part of them. She might as well have been given the title of marketing director, because if she and Rogers made it to Miami, reporters' interest in Nichols would help spread the word: Fairchild planes were safe.

On the morning of January 4, Nichols, sporting white knickers, a lavender sweater, and a brown chamois coat, climbed into the cockpit of the plane. She carried a weekend bag filled with a wardrobe change for a party that night on Biscayne Bay, and she didn't want any attention. Nichols hoped to keep her takeoff with Rogers a secret, then make a surprise landing on the blue water near the Royal Palm Hotel in Miami. But of course, the reporters found out — Fairchild likely saw to it — and they chronicled her historic flight south.

At 7:55 a.m., Rogers hit the throttle, and the pontoons of the plane skimmed off the icy waves in Queens and rose over Rockaway Beach, tail-heavy with extra fuel tanks installed where the passenger seats should have been, but aloft. An hour later, they passed over Atlantic City, rising to twelve hundred feet, the sun warming the air and the plane humming along at ninety miles an hour. And by 11:00 a.m., they were flying due south off the coast of Virginia, with no land in sight and Nichols at the controls. The water below glistened in the winter sunlight, and the skies were blue. Nichols could see for miles. Despondent just a few days earlier, she was giddy now, flying the Fairchild plane for four hours, a third of the trip to Miami, and riding a steady tailwind south.

They hit a squall near Savannah but rode it out and then struggled to fly in the dark after the sun set over Daytona Beach. But they soon spotted the bonfires lit to guide them, burning near Rogers's air terminal. At 8:05 p.m., almost exactly twelve hours after they had left New York, Nichols and her companions touched down on the water in Miami — a perfect landing before a waiting crowd of photographers, their flashbulbs firing in the dark, and handlers, who ushered the flight crew into the dining room of the Royal Palm, where the newspaper editors were waiting.

They greeted Nichols with cheers — a rousing ovation — and also intimate questions about her life. "Please," she begged reporters, "let's not put in any more personal things." She wanted the story to be about flying. "I have always been interested in aviation," she said, "especially as a safe and interesting way to travel." With her flight in the Fairchild, she believed she had proven it was possible for men and women alike. "The trip was so comfortable," she said, "and the cabin was quiet enough so that a businessman could have dictated to his stenographer."

A pleased Sherman Fairchild hired the well-spoken Nichols within the month at a salary of sixty dollars a week. Her new, if unofficial, title was "flying salesgirl." Nichols was no longer looking at her face in the mirror in her parents' house in Rye; she was seeing it in the pages of newspapers across the country. She cabled home to let Mother and Father know she was all right and to make one request—that no one meet her at the train when she returned to New York. "Absolutely request no demonstrations," she said, "and no family, nor relatives, of any sort." She hoped to arrive in the city as she always had, unnoticed. Nichols even threatened to change trains if she learned reporters were waiting for her.

But in some ways, she also embraced the attention, realizing it was her best shot at what she wanted most: escape. Nichols might have asked reporters not to write about her personal life, but she also prepared a detailed press release with information about her personal life. She wanted the world to know she wasn't just a socialite. She was a sportswoman who could do it all: play hockey and perform onstage, mush dog sleds and hold piano recitals, ride camels and dance, ride motorcycles and golf. She claimed that she could even box. "Only a wee bit," Nichols said, "so please don't tell anyone. Am not pugnacious, nor like a rooster."

Ruth Nichols was bigger than that. She was becoming a brand.

WALTER BEECH, the Wichita aviator, had never lacked for ego. But after the craze over Ruth Elder and Frances Grayson in the fall of 1927, he must have felt like a visionary for placing the young Louise McPhetridge under the supervision of D. C. Warren in the West Coast office of Travel Air in Oakland. At sales stops across California, from Fresno to Sacramento, Warren did most of the flying at first, but the crowds turned out to see McPhetridge dressed in high boots, officer's trousers, a silk shirt, and a jacket, with colorful bandannas wrapped around her neck. At times, the Californians pushed up against her, ten deep in places, making McPhetridge feel like a sideshow curiosity as she entertained the crowd and uttered pithy sales slogans in her Southern accent. "Fly high," she told prospective buyers, "and avoid the rush."

But back in Oakland at the home airfield on the marshy shores of San Francisco Bay, McPhetridge was learning to be a pilot; this was no show. And sometimes, on their sales trips, Warren let her fly all by herself.

"Here," he said one afternoon in Bakersfield, handing McPhetridge a map after a day of selling planes. "You get us home."

For the next three hours, while Warren read the newspaper and dozed in the copilot's seat, McPhetridge flew, essentially alone, navigating with the map on her lap and the stick in her hand over 260 miles of plains, valleys, mountains, and, finally, fog near Travel Air's home in hangar no. 3 in Oakland. The men on the ground there appreciated her grit. When there was work to be done on an engine, McPhetridge got as greasy as any of the mechanics. Warren soon learned she was quite a saleswoman too. On one trip alone that summer, McPhetridge, who'd had little interest in peddling coal, sold twenty planes at $12,000 apiece—a big score that proved her worth to Walter Beech's company. By early January 1928, just eight months after she had arrived in California, McPhetridge was no longer a sweet-talking showpiece of a salesgirl but the manager of the Travel Air office in Oakland, reportedly the only female manager of an airplane distributorship in the nation.

The position was cause for still more curiosity about—and celebrity for—McPhetridge. Out of roughly twenty-nine million adult women in America in 1928, less than a dozen had pilot's licenses on file with the US Department of Commerce. According to official figures, McPhetridge had a much greater chance of dying of whooping cough, of the flu, of scarlet fever, of the measles, in a car crash, in a train crash, in a coal mine, in a sawmill, or even in a plane than of earning a license to fly a plane herself. Female construction workers easily outnumbered female aviators. Female electricians did too. Indeed, there were more women working as lumbermen, rafts men, policemen, newsboys, railroad foremen, and switchmen—fields so male-dominated that the job titles specified that gender. Still, McPhetridge said, "I don't see anything strange about a woman selling airplanes. Women sell automobiles, real estate and other things. Why can't they sell airplanes?"

In May that year, to help bolster her argument, McPhetridge got America's 1,943rd flying license. Orville Wright himself signed the paperwork. And the achievement drew the attention of one man working at the airfield in Oakland: plane builder Herbert von Thaden.

Thaden, who preferred to use the *von* as a middle name, was the son of German immigrants, Otto and Hattie, born in Chicago. Herb's father died in 1899 when Herb was just one, after which Hattie moved with her little boy to Cincinnati. There they lived among other immigrants in an apartment building on Vine Street in a predominantly German neighborhood not far from the Germania Hall, the Germania House, and the German Mutual Insurance company. Hattie got a job as a florist; her son, Herb, gravitated more toward machines and math. In 1916, at age eighteen, he began flying planes in rural Ohio. In 1917, he honed his skills in the US Army. And in 1921, he graduated from a prestigious college that catered to his interests: the Massachusetts Institute of Technology. He tinkered with hot-air balloons for a while but ultimately turned his attention back to his first love — airplanes — hoping to build a new kind of airship constructed entirely out of metal.

It was, in 1928, a novel — and some thought impossible — notion. Planes had almost always been built out of wood. Plane designers knew how to work with the material. It was easy to cut and shape and it was light. But Herbert Thaden — wide-chested and handsome, with a gladiator's jaw and thick hair sculpted into a stylish flat-top — thought differently than most people. Where others saw impossibility, he saw a math problem, something he loved. A metal airplane would not only protect pilots in crashes, Thaden said, but prove more durable in all types of weather and make mass production feasible. The future was clear, he believed. It was metal aircraft.

At the airport in Oakland, while McPhetridge was selling planes, Thaden set his mind to building one. He was twenty-nine. He had been flying planes for almost half his life and he knew what he wanted. He wanted engineers who were also pilots; no one else need apply. He wanted a stockpile of a light corrugated metal called duralumin. Once he acquired it, he and his engineers got to work building a plane that was thirty-five feet long and fifty-three feet across the wings, with a roomy cabin and a fuel capacity that enabled it to fly for six hours. It was one of the first metal airplanes ever built in the American West, and there was no doubt about who made it. The name was painted across the metal ribbing on the tail: *Thaden Metal Aircraft*. Thaden himself called it the Argonaut, and not long after the first model was finished, in February 1928, he invited one person for a ride — Louise McPhetridge.

They seemed to be an odd pairing, the freewheeling McPhetridge and the calculating Thaden; the daughter of Arkansans and the son of German immigrants; the small-town female pilot and the math-minded MIT grad. But Thaden didn't want to change McPhetridge or corral her. He didn't want her to stop flying either. He liked her just the way she was, a dreamer different than him, but also the same. Thaden understood why McPhetridge loved flying, and McPhetridge understood why Thaden was so obsessed with it too, always jotting down ideas on scraps of paper that gathered like snow around him wherever he was working. In aviation, little details mattered. Thaden was great at figuring those details, and McPhetridge was starting to realize that she needed to be too.

Just four months after McPhetridge arrived in California, the Dole Air Race competitors prepared to dash across the ocean from Oakland to Hawaii for the pineapple tycoon's money. They took off from McPhetridge's landing strip on the bay, churning up clouds of dust, and then some of them vanished, never to be seen again. That same month, a Stanford University student crashed less than a mile away. One of the wings on his plane had buckled and fallen off in midflight, sending his airship spinning to the ground. The Stanford kid's leg and skull were crushed, and he died en route to the Alameda Sanitarium. It was only a matter of time, perhaps, before McPhetridge would be headed there too.

In the summer of 1928, a plane she was flying stalled on takeoff. It wasn't one of her Travel Airs but an open-cockpit Waco biplane owned by a mustachioed flying instructor called William "Sandy" Sanders. Sanders was known primarily for three things: flying fast and often dangerously; being the first aerial sheriff in Alameda County, officially deputized with a ceremony; and getting arrested just a day after that ceremony for being drunk and punching another aviator in a fight witnessed by police. McPhetridge was flying his Waco that summer day in 1928 because Sanders was drunk again. He needed someone to ferry him from Alameda to Oakland, a short hop down the bay. McPhetridge volunteered for the job, and right away, on takeoff, there were problems with Sanders's Waco. The temperature gauge spiked. McPhetridge, at the controls, tried to open the shutters to cool the engine with fresh air. But the control lever was stuck. She hollered at the inebriated Sanders, who was sitting closest to the shutters, to open them by hand, but it was too late. The engine quit—and that's when McPhetridge made her mistake. Instead of landing straight ahead on whatever ground she could find, she tried to turn back for the airport. With the turn, the Waco couldn't recover. It lost airspeed, and down they went, McPhetridge and Sanders, the plane spinning out of control for four hundred feet and then crashing into the marsh.

McPhetridge blacked out. She had no memory of hitting the ground, only waking up in the sanitarium to the horrible sound of Sanders wailing in pain. Later, she got the news: he was dead. Investigators declared the crash wasn't her fault. Sanders's plane had stalled; it happened sometimes. Too often, actually. But McPhetridge, who'd suffered only minor injuries, knew better. In her mind, she could hear her instructor's advice: "Always land straight ahead." She hadn't listened. Overconfident and inexperienced, she had failed at a critical moment; a man had died as a result—and she blamed herself for it, never forgetting how one little mistake, one quick, panicky decision, or one misstep when checking over a plane on the ground could change everything.

The stories about Sanders's death didn't last long in the Oakland press, but the tragedy nearly overshadowed, for McPhetridge, the other big event that summer: she and Thaden got married, stealing away to Reno, Nevada, by train in late July 1928 to make their love official before McPhetridge returned to Wichita and Bentonville on a trip she had previously planned. They had hoped to keep the wedding a secret, at least until McPhetridge got home to Arkansas. But people saw them in Reno, and the news made the West Coast papers: Louise McPhetridge was now Louise McPhetridge von Thaden, although she soon dropped both the McPhetridge and, like Herb, the von.

"Gosh," Herb joked in a letter he sent to Louise in Bentonville, "it's tough to be notorious like we are."

Oakland suddenly felt lonesome without her. "Don't stay too long," he begged her.

Louise promised him she wouldn't, that she'd be back soon—and she always kept her promises.

7

The Right Sort of Girl

THE PUBLISHER WAS LOOKING for the "right sort of girl." He'd know her when he saw her. She needed to be a worthy representative of American womanhood, a girl who could "measure up to adequate standards." She needed to be proper, but perhaps not too proper; attractive for photographs, but perhaps not too attractive. Finally, she needed to come from a good family—to have "good breeding," the publisher called it—and be possessed of poise, intelligence, and, if possible, a pilot's license. This woman wouldn't be doing any actual flying, but it would look better if she could—and New York publisher George Palmer Putnam was big on appearances. He claimed that the transatlantic flight he was secretly arranging in the spring of 1928 was a "sporting-scientific adventure." But like others before it, this flight was about a narrative that Putnam, an experienced storyteller, could package and sell. He wanted to put the first woman over the ocean.

He was a storm of a man, blowing hot or cold depending on his personal atmospheric pressure, and he pushed across the paved landscape outside his family's publishing house in New York City impervious to obstacle. No matter Putnam's mood, he was hard to ignore. In a city that loved its blue bloods, Putnam's blood ran bluer than most. His family had been in America since Colonial times. His ancestors had fought the British in the Revolutionary War, serving with distinction as brigadier generals and major generals. His great-grandfather was born in Massachusetts in 1778 while George Washington's troops were on the march. And his grandfather, the first George Palmer Putnam, became one of the biggest booksellers in New York after cofounding a publishing house around 1837. Originally called Wiley and Putnam, it later became just Putnam. His roster of authors and friends included some of the biggest names in American letters — Nathaniel Hawthorne, James Fenimore Cooper, and Washington Irving, among others — and the business continued to thrive after his death in 1872. The bookseller's children, one of whom was George's father, took it over, renaming the house G. P. Putnam's Sons.

Putnam — GPP to friends — initially resisted the family business, if not the family money. As a young man, he went west, settled in Bend, Oregon, bought the town's newspaper in 1911, started writing scathing editorials to ease his blood pressure, and turned the sleepy pioneer weekly into the only daily within a hundred miles. But unsatisfied with just a newspaper, Putnam ran for mayor and won, becoming, to locals, "the boy mayor of Oregon." This was an adventure, and adventure was something Putnam craved, even after he returned to New York, following his father's death in 1915. He wrote a novel about a rich, selfish New Yorker who moves to Oregon, finds himself, and saves the day. He hiked Yellowstone National Park, spending so much time there that he claimed to know most park rangers personally. He sailed for six months, exploring the Atlantic and Pacific Oceans with a team of scientists. And a year later, in 1926, he led a four-month trip to the Arctic — the Putnam Greenland Expedition — skirting icebergs in a schooner. Putnam and his men greeted Eskimos, dined on auk's eggs, and, most important, collected specimens — "prizes." They killed terns and fulmars, narwhals and walrus, sleeper sharks, bearded seals, and a pair of polar bears. One bear was killed for pure sport; Putnam's crew shot it, skinned it, and lashed its hide to the rigging of the schooner. The other was dispatched out of necessity. The men wanted to take two polar bear cubs alive. To do it, they had to kill the mother, which they did, shooting a single arrow through her heart. Then, with the large bear's body floating in the water, they lassoed the two angry cubs, dragged them aboard, named them Captain Bob and Baffin Belle, and brought them back to New York to deliver to the Bronx Zoo. On the deck of the schooner, the two cubs clawed at their cages while an ecstatic Putnam looked on, thrilled with his polar bears and excited to be making news. As a friend once put it, trying to be nice, "George Palmer Putnam did not wear shadows well."

With the spotlight now on aviation, Putnam wanted in, of course. In 1927, he acquired Lindbergh's best-selling memoir for G. P. Putnam's Sons. Then, just months later, in early 1928, Putnam heard a rumor that briefly stopped his manic mind from racing.

"Pull your chair over," Putnam told a connected East Coast businessman, Hilton Howell Railey, in a meeting in New York in late April that year. Two airmen in Boston, Putnam informed Railey, were secretly preparing a seaplane for a historic flight taking a woman across the Atlantic. Railey lived in Brookline, just west of Boston; maybe he could check it out for Putnam.

Railey — a New Orleanian by birth and a scout for Putnam's schemes — didn't always appreciate Putnam's hard-charging attitude. But on this day, the publisher was calm — and Railey was game. He had started as a reporter for the *New Orleans American,* the *Philadelphia Evening Ledger,* and the *New York Evening Post,* riding along with ambulance drivers to get his scoops. In the rumor Putnam was selling, Railey smelled a story too.

"What if it's true?" he asked. "What then?"

"If it's true," Putnam said, "we'll crash the gate. It'd be amusing to manage a stunt like that, wouldn't it? Find out all you can."

It didn't take Railey long. By midnight, at the Copley Plaza Hotel in Boston, he had found his two airmen: a mechanic named Lou Gordon and a pilot whose name had filled the East Coast papers for weeks the previous fall. It was Frances Grayson's original captain, Wilmer "Bill" Stultz. Railey was no idiot. He plied Stultz with Scotch — the pilot's weakness — to get the answers he needed. Putnam was soon on the phone with a big-time lawyer, and he had his confirmation: a female operation was indeed in the works. There was just one hitch in the plan. The woman who had commissioned the flight — the wealthy Amy Guest — had backed out. Her family didn't want her flying across the ocean. They needed a new girl now, "the right sort of girl," and Railey wanted to find her.

AMELIA EARHART DIDN'T seem any closer than she had been to marrying poor Sam Chapman, who was still waiting for her at his mother's home in Marblehead. But the social-work position at Denison House in Boston's Chinatown suited her well. For one thing, it had freed her from Medford, where her mother and sister were living. By the spring of 1928, Earhart—almost thirty-one years old—had moved in with the other social workers on Tyler Street, buzzing around the tight corners of Chinatown in her fast yellow car and impressing her bosses as well as the foreign-born people she was serving.

Many of them were struggling under new anti-immigration policies. Exhausted by floods of refugees pouring into the country from troubled nations around the world, Congress and the White House had set quotas restricting who could come in and from where. It wasn't an accident that these quotas favored white Christian immigrants from Northern and Western Europe while making entry difficult—if not impossible—for Italians and Mexicans, Russians and Poles, Jews and Africans, Chinese and Japanese; "the undesirables," the press sometimes called them. The quota law, as it was informally known, broke up families, preventing wives and children who were from the undesired lands from joining husbands and fathers in America, and the law also helped turn immigrant smuggling into a big business. Desperate people paid five hundred dollars each at times for a long-shot chance of getting to America, a chance that often didn't pan out and lined the pockets of the smugglers while leaving the would-be immigrants right where they started. "We might speak of it as highway robbery," one US official declared at the time. "The stories of the hardships that are undergone by people who try to enter this country 'by the back door' are sometimes hard to believe."

In her position at Denison House, Earhart surely heard these stories and others, getting a snapshot of America that most never saw. She organized evening English classes for immigrant men and women. She often followed up on their lives personally, making visits to their apartments in Boston's South End and sharing home-cooked meals around their tables. She was by turns a teacher, a counselor, and even a nurse, driving sick children to the hospital in the yellow car that the kids loved so much. And always, she was writing, taking notes. "I shall try to keep my contact with the women who have come to class," Earhart wrote in one such note. "Mrs. S and her drunken husband, Mrs. F's struggle to get her husband here, Mrs. Z's to get her papers in the face of odds—all are problems that are hard to relinquish after a year's friendship."

Also hard to relinquish for Earhart was flying. Even as she embraced social work—and, indeed, considered writing a book about it—she found ways to get herself into the air. Using her Los Angeles connections, she joined a group of men building an airport in the nearby town of Quincy. Once, to help promote Denison House's annual carnival, she borrowed a plane, took off, and tossed advertisements from the cockpit. A few months later, in the fall of 1927, she flew again, but this time to prove a point.

A famous German woman, Thea Rasche, was performing stunts in Quincy for a crowd of two thousand people, Earhart among them, when her plane went down in a swamp. Rasche was uninjured. "It is nothing," she said, climbing out of the wreckage. Wanting to make it clear that Rasche's crash was not related to her gender or to the flying skills of women in general, Earhart immediately found a plane at the airfield, took off while the crowd was still fixated on the crash, and completed Rasche's program without incident. Reporters took note of the flier from Denison House while Earhart herself took note of other women who were flying. The same month that Rasche crashed, Earhart reached out to a woman she had been reading a lot about that year: Ruth Nichols. "Because your picture has been appearing lately in Boston papers, I make you the victim of an idea which has been simmering for some time," Earhart told Nichols. "What do you think of the advisability of forming an organization composed of women who fly?"

Nichols thought it was a fine idea. "I suggest herewith," Nichols told Earhart, "and do hereby nominate, second and vote for yourself as Chairman pro tem."

By April 1928, the organization that Earhart and Nichols had discussed remained an elusive plan. But in provincial Boston, anyway, there was no doubt about who was the best-known female aviator in town. It was the social worker with the gray eyes, the one answering questions about aviation on Tyler Street, the one writing stories about it in local society magazines, the one increasingly pushing women into the fray. "Flying is still a man's game," Earhart said that spring, "like automobiling was in the beginning." But she believed New England women might help change that—and soon. "I have hope," she said, "that this year will see many more women flying."

If Amy Guest's secret seaplane had been sitting in a hangar in New

York or Miami, Wichita or Oakland, or anyplace else, George Putnam likely would have found another man, not Railey, to gather the intelligence he wanted. That man surely would have suggested a different woman to ride with Stultz and Gordon across the Atlantic. Thaden might have received the invitation; Nichols might have too. And maybe Nichols should have. Nichols and Putnam were almost neighbors, living less than two miles away from each other in Rye. But in Boston in early 1928, if you were looking for a female aviator, there was only one call to make. "Call Denison House," a retired navy man told Railey, "and ask for Amelia Earhart."

The call came in during the afternoon rush at the settlement house as children scampered around. Earhart at first declined to take it; she was too busy, she said. But the man on the phone insisted it was important and Earhart relented.

"You don't know me," a man said on the other end of the line. "But my name is Railey—Captain H. H. Railey." And his reason for calling—intentionally vague at first—quickly came into focus throughout the course of the conversation and in a face-to-face meeting later that same day at Railey's office on Federal Street, just twelve blocks from Denison House. "I might as well lay the cards on the table," Railey told Earhart. "Would you fly the Atlantic?"

IT WAS, FOR HER, the first of many questions. The male backers wanted to know everything about her. Was she strong? Was she educated? Did she really know how to fly? And if so, how well? They wanted to know if she'd hold them liable in the event of a disaster. They wanted to know what she'd do afterward in the event of a success. And they wanted to know if Earhart would risk everything in exchange for no compensation while the men involved got paid and stood to get rich for their efforts—$20,000 for Stultz as captain and $5,000 for Gordon as mechanic.

The initial meeting in Boston was exciting; the second meeting, in New York about ten days later with Putnam, Guest's lawyer, and a third evaluator, was, for Earhart, "a crisis." Mindful that the men were examining everything about her—her grammar, her looks, her demeanor—Earhart struggled to find the proper balance. If she came off as too weak, she might be denied the trip. If she came off as too strong, too beautiful—or, in her words, "too fascinating"—she might lose on that count too, as the men wouldn't want to drown the second coming of Ruth Elder in the cold waters of the Atlantic. Faced with that conundrum, Earhart tried to strike a tone of mediocrity, neither forgettable nor memorable.

With Putnam, it seemed to work. He was in one of his moods that day, stewing in the halls of G. P. Putnam's Sons on West Forty-Fifth Street. Consumed with other matters, he kept Earhart waiting for an hour. When they finally sat down, Putnam claimed to take no notice of her looks one way or the other. His lasting impression was that she didn't like him — and the feeling was at least somewhat mutual. Back at Denison House in Boston, Earhart told her boss, Marion Perkins, that Putnam had left her feeling cold and had hurried her onto a north-bound train at the end of the day with hardly so much as a goodbye. "Didn't offer to pay my fare home, either," Earhart complained. Still, she felt good about her prospects and the answers she'd given to the men's questions, one of them most of all.

"Why do you want to fly the Atlantic?" one of the evaluators had asked her.

Earhart thought for a moment and smiled.

"Why does a man ride a horse?" she replied.

She got the job — with no pay and no chance to fly herself, but presumably she'd have control of the flight. By agreement, Earhart was the commander of Amy Guest's $60,000 tri-motored seaplane — the *Friendship*, it was called. Stultz and Gordon were to report to Earhart. But over the next three weeks, she barely saw the plane — orange with golden wings, seventy-one feet across — or the men at their hangar across the inner harbor in East Boston. There would be no arguing with the crew over weather maps, as Grayson had done, or staging impromptu press conferences, as Elder had. Putnam and the other organizers wanted to keep everything secret, which meant that Earhart had to stay away, posing for publicity photographs on the roof of the Copley Plaza Hotel in goggles and a helmet but not going any-where near the *Friendship*. Earhart didn't even tell her mother, father, or sister what she was doing. Only a couple of people knew: Chapman in Marblehead, and Perkins at Denison House. "I'll be back for sum-mer school," Earhart promised her boss in early May.

For much of the next three weeks in Boston, it rained. On the days when it didn't, it was often cold. East winds blew in fog that enveloped the city, *Friendship* and all, so thick at times that people thought the harbor was on fire. Downpours washed out Red Sox games at Fenway Park, sending baseball fans scurrying for the stadium's tunnels. Temperatures as low as twenty-four degrees left a hard frost on crops. Twice, when the weather seemed to break, Earhart and her crew awoke at 3:30 a.m., ate hurried breakfasts, took a tugboat to the orange plane floating in the water in East Boston's harbor, and tried to take off. And twice they failed—the plane was too heavy or the weather too foggy. Other women were mobilizing their own transatlantic plans now; sooner or later, one of them would get across. Just as troubling, rumors were beginning to spread about the secret operation in East Boston. Putnam couldn't keep it out of the papers forever. The *Friendship* needed to get off the water—and get away. On the morning of June 3, Earhart and her crew tried again, following the usual routine: Waking at 3:30. Packing coffee and cocoa. Whispering on the waters of the harbor in the dark and then breaking the silence by starting the three 220-horsepower engines of the *Friendship*.

Earhart squatted on the floor of the fuselage against the auxiliary gas tanks, quiet, wearing a fur-lined flying suit and high-laced boots. Faced with the likelihood of crashing and dying or disappearing and drowning—"It is," said one critic, "a 50-50 bet"—Earhart hadn't said goodbye to her loved ones. Instead, she wrote letters to be delivered if things went wrong.

For her sister, the schoolteacher in Medford: "Even though I have lost, the adventure has been worthwhile. Our family tends to be too secure. My life has really been very happy, and I didn't mind contemplating its end in the midst of it." For her father, far away in California: "Hooray for the last grand adventure! I wish I had won, but it was worthwhile, anyway. You know that. I have no faith that we'll meet anywhere again, but I wish we might." Finally, for her mother, a will of sorts: "My regret is that I leave just now. In a few years I feel I could have laid by something substantial, for so many new things were opening for me."

From the beginning that morning, the flight was troubled. It took five tries for the plane to get off the water; it was too heavy, at five tons. To make it, they had to shed not only gas and gear but backup pilot, Lou Gower. Without his 150 pounds on board, the *Friendship* finally hit fifty miles an hour, enough speed to get airborne, and rose above the harbor with the sun. Almost immediately, the cabin door failed, bursting open. Gordon and Earhart, caught off guard, nearly fell out the door and into the sea. They finally managed to secure the busted door with string—not ideal—but there was nothing they could do to overcome the problems they faced once they made their scheduled stop the next day on the Great Circle route north: Trepassey, Newfoundland, a colorless outpost on a gray ocean. They landed there to refuel and spend one night but ended up staying two weeks, grounded by the weight of the heavy *Friendship* and socked in by the weather. It was often foggy in Trepassey in spring and summer, a meteorological lesson that Earhart and her crew learned the hard way. "I do not know why they selected this port," one curious local said. But it was too late to change their minds. While the press pushed its way into Amelia's mother's home in Medford—"What in the world are you doing here?" a surprised Mrs. Earhart asked a reporter she found in an upstairs bedroom— Earhart waited in the fishing village at the edge of nowhere, marooned by poor planning.

"What is in store for us?" she wondered.

She fretted over newspaper reports that said she was flying to recoup a lost fortune. Not true. She worried that Stultz—a drinker like her father—might get his hands on some alcohol. She suffered through countless bland meals of canned rabbit and turnips, weathered storm after storm, and waded through a sea of personal doubt. Two other women were planning to cross the ocean now; one of them had made it as far as Newfoundland too. "Our competitors are gaining on us," Earhart complained. But she was stuck in Trepassey, stuck with Stultz, who was increasingly moody, drinking, and overruling the commander of the *Friendship*: Earhart.

"I know the liquor flows," Earhart wrote in her diary, always worried about alcohol, given her father's problems. "Is it possible we have been here so long? . . . We are just managing to keep from suicide . . . Oh, if only we can get away soon . . . This has been the worst day in my life."

It was like Frances Grayson's transatlantic quest all over again, only without the tease of success. Despite multiple takeoff attempts in Newfoundland, Earhart's plane couldn't even get off the water. "All of us," she wrote, "are caged animals."

The official forecast on their thirteenth morning in Trepassey—"this trap," Earhart said—was no better than any other. There were two storms out at sea, fierce enough that her female rival across the province refused to fly. But Earhart was tired of waiting.

"We're going today," she said and informed a Paramount cameraman and also Stultz, who appeared agitated and hung over or possibly still half drunk from the night before. "Not sober," the cameraman noted. Stultz argued with Earhart in sight of the reporters; Earhart prevailed, and just before eleven o'clock that morning, a small boat delivered the tense crew of three to the orange plane on the water. Stultz was gray with doom. He predicted that if they had to land on the rough seas, the Friendship would crack up and sink. But Earhart, wearing pants and a short leather coat, tried to find a positive spin, noting they had a twenty-mile-an-hour westerly wind blowing them toward Europe. "We have a dandy breeze behind us," she said, "and we are going in spite of everything."

In the cove near the little village, the plane rumbled across the water at full speed for roughly two miles, trying to hit that magic number: fifty miles an hour.

But it fell short. No lift.

They dumped gas and tried again, and then a third time. Still nothing.

The orange plane had been sitting on the coast of Newfoundland for so long now that locals didn't call it the Friendship anymore; it was the Trepassey Plane. And it looked as if today's efforts to leave would end like so many others had in the days before it—with Earhart and her two male companions walking back to their rooms for yet another canned-rabbit dinner. But on the next pass, the Friendship briefly caught air, tasting the sky before running out of water in the cove and coming back down again. Stultz turned the plane around, taxied to the far end of the harbor, and, at 12:18 p.m., hit the throttle one last time. This attempt took seemingly forever: three minutes of full-throttle push, the plane breaking away from the waves and then slumping back down, trying but failing. And yet still going, still gaining speed.

Fifty-five miles per hour. Sixty.

They eased off the water and into the air, flying for the first time in weeks. The Friendship lumbered west for five miles, circled back to the east, and flew over the harbor at an altitude of just eighty feet. Then the plane disappeared in the northeastern sky.

FROM THE FLOOR of the fuselage, behind the men, Earhart watched Newfoundland drift from view, recording the takeoff and everything that happened next in a log. She didn't have a seat, and the cushions that she had hoped to use had been tossed out with the gas to shed weight. In the stripped-down cabin, she was forced to make do with what she had, and she crouched on a pile of flying suits and did what she could to fend off the cold. At times, it was just forty-two degrees inside the plane. But it was still better, Earhart thought, than Trepassey. While the men flew, she chronicled what she was seeing—her only job— writing about icebergs of clouds, mountains of fog, and Stultz at the controls, taut and alert. "Many hours to go." She noted the air pockets that tossed them around, the darkness that enveloped the plane that night, and the left motor coughing too much. "Sounds like water," Earhart wrote. She passed the long hours by jotting down random thoughts about adventure, poetry, and life, keeping one discovery she made a secret: the bottle of alcohol she'd found in the cabin, smuggled aboard, presumably, by Stultz.

Mostly, though, she just sat there, wishing she knew how to operate the radio so she could at least help Stultz and Gordon. By dawn the next morning, the men needed all the assistance they could get. The left engine was still misfiring. They were bouncing from one thousand feet to five thousand feet, trying to dodge the clouds. They were running out of gas, and, worst of all, they were lost.

Back at Denison House, the immigrants were asking Marion Perkins questions.

"Where is Miss Earhart now?"

"Is she still flying?"

"Is she coming back soon?"

Perkins had no answer, no way to know. Even Earhart and her crew didn't know where they were.

Then, just before nine o'clock that morning, they caught a break in the clouds and spotted something below. "Two boats!" Earhart wrote. But the ships were going north and south, respectively, cutting across the plane's path, not east and west, parallel with it, the way ships generally crossed the Atlantic. "Why?" Earhart wondered.

Stultz and Gordon didn't know either. And with about an hour of gas left, they began to question everything. Were they that hopelessly lost? Completely turned around? Where was Ireland? Would they crash? Should they ditch near a boat? Earhart—given a job now—tried to get a note to one of the steamships below, dropping a message as Ruth Elder once had. But Earhart's message, tossed from the plane in a bag weighted down with two oranges, missed the deck by a wide margin, splashing into the sea.

"Well," Stultz said, "that's out."

It was, in Earhart's estimation, a "mess." Then, through the mist and the fog on the horizon, they saw it: land. It wasn't a shadow or a cloud, and it wasn't Ireland either. Somehow, the *Friendship* had missed that country entirely. They were flying over boat traffic in the Irish Sea, between Ireland and Great Britain, heading for the shores of Wales.

Stultz landed on the water about a half a mile off the coast and taxied to a buoy, where he and Gordon fixed a line to keep the plane from floating away. For a long time then, they just sat there, unnoticed. There were no cheering crowds, no celebrations, no photographers with flashbulbs firing. These would be, in some ways, the last quiet moments Amelia Earhart would ever have. By lunchtime, she was a global commodity to be bought and sold with the full power of the Putnam publicity machine at her back, ready to crank out a book about her exploits and arranging for homecoming parades across America.

In New York, reporters pressed to learn more about the woman and the breaking news about her personal life: Earhart was engaged to a man named Sam Chapman. "That's really a private matter, isn't it?" Earhart asked reporters. "Let's leave it that way." In Boston, 250,000 people lined the streets—roughly one-third of the city's population—to welcome her home, and two thousand social workers, mostly women, crammed into a room at the Copley Plaza afterward to greet her personally. They wanted to see her, touch her, write hymns about her. At one of the many celebrations that summer, five thousand girls in Chicago cheered Earhart—in song.

But the greatest celebration of them all, Earhart thought, was in Medford with her mother and sister and Sam Chapman. Twenty thousand people lined the streets there to welcome her home, and Earhart waved to them from the seat of a Pontiac, Chapman at her side. He rode along on the running boards of the car down the crowded streets of Medford, he and his girl — a couple, but not for long. She was leaving Chapman behind, for reasons neither would ever reveal but that seemed obvious to Earhart's sister. Chapman, despite all his patience, thought Earhart too strong, her sister believed, while Earhart, despite staying with him for so long, thought Chapman too weak. The *Friendship* flight had, among other things, helped make clear their differences. Chapman would never marry, dying single and young, and Earhart would never again live in Boston or Medford, leaving New England behind as she'd once promised she would if ever given the chance.

She was moving to New York to spend the summer with George Putnam and his wife at their estate in Rye and writing the book that Putnam wanted. It was the story of a heroine who conquered the ocean like Lindbergh and even looked like him. Many Americans thought so. She was a modest young woman, an "all-right girl." "The best-known girl in America," newspapers called her. "A slender girl . . . a pink-faced girl . . . Decidedly feminine to look at, but enjoys masculine sports . . . The girl is not a prude." She was, as Putnam liked to say, "a little lady."

"What's the matter?" Hilton Railey asked Earhart at one point that summer amid the crush of celebrations. "Aren't you excited?"

"Excited?" she replied. "No."

As Earhart saw it, she had achieved little with her *Friendship* flight. "I was just baggage," she told Railey. "Like a sack of potatoes." It was a harsh assessment, perhaps, yet one that many men shared, clicking their tongues in disapproval while America fell in love with the flying social worker. Among her loudest critics was an old friend of the missing Frances Grayson: pilot Harry Jones, at Old Orchard Beach in Maine. Jones had no problem with men flying over the ocean. "Men who do it," he said, "are high heroes. I mean men who actually contribute something to the crossing." But Earhart, he said, had contributed nothing. "She was a liability," Jones explained, "a distinct liability" — adding weight to the plane just by sitting there. "She might well have been replaced with two hours' gasoline supply."

Earhart was famous, yes. But famous for doing nothing — and she knew it.

PART TWO

8

City of Destiny

FROM HIS OFFICE inside the Ambassador Hotel in Los Angeles, Cliff Henderson wasn't planning just any airplane race. He wanted to build the future, staging a show where previously there had been only dust, creating a world where anything was possible and making—from the flesh of mere men—gods.

This was how he thought of his work, anyway. It was the only way he could think of anything, really—in grandiose superlatives. For Henderson—a handsome man, trim and compact at five foot eight and about a hundred and fifty pounds—everything needed to be bigger than it had ever been, better than expected, and flashy. Aviation officials agreed; if they were going to hold a national air race in Los Angeles in the late summer of 1928 that would truly cash in on Lindbergh, Earhart, and American air fever, Cliff Henderson was the promoter they needed.

The idea of an air race wasn't new. Almost as soon as planes were flying, pilots were squaring off in small-time speed dashes held in Dayton and Tulsa, Kalamazoo and Little Rock. There was fame to be won in just competing; Walter Beech had learned that firsthand in the Ford Reliability Tour. For years, aviation officials had even staged a national meet, the National Air Races. Yet, to date, they had been underwhelming, at best, primarily revealing not the splendor of flight but its primitive state and humbling dangers.

At the national races in Philadelphia in 1926, heavy rains turned the city's dirt runway into a muddy quagmire, almost a foot deep in places. In the muck, some planes couldn't take off. Others got stuck and needed to be towed away by tractors. Still others stalled out in the spray of mud and water. But mishaps were common in air races, no matter the weather. On one day in Philadelphia alone, three planes went down. On another, twenty planes competing in a long-distance derby just failed to show up. They'd gotten lost, apparently, in the fog of the Allegheny Mountains, and it was difficult to know if the pilots were safe. Just as troubling to race organizers, the crowds at times were lackluster. That same week in Philadelphia, "Polish Day," celebrating immigrants from Poland, drew more people than the races.

Spokane, Washington—the host of the 1927 races—managed to do better, offering $50,000 in prize money and attracting record crowds of thirty thousand fans on some days. Still, the 1927 races reeked of amateurism. Prison inmates cleared the airfield-to-be of hazards, "juggling," according to one account, "a ball and chain with one hand while they tossed rocks with the other." And the location, in eastern Washington, was likely too remote. The site attracted cowboys and, as one report noted, "heaps of Indians," but not enough people from big cities. Now, in 1928, Los Angeles hoped to change all that. Bidding against San Francisco, Atlanta, and Des Moines for the right to host the races, the city promised to almost double the crowds, vowed to triple the amount of prizes, and guaranteed clear skies. "Ideal climate," promotional materials noted. "There is sunshine 355 days a year in Los Angeles County."

In the end, the other cities couldn't compete. National race officials awarded the 1928 event to Los Angeles, home of Cliff Henderson, a salesman who could satisfy the big promises the LA folks were making.

HE WAS A QUAKER and an Iowan, the fourth of five children, all of whom had grown up poor. "With wooden spoons in our mouths," Henderson liked to declare, "not silver ones." The Hendersons took pride in hard work, living by the family motto that "a dollar earned was the best kind of dollar." His father ran a drugstore in the little town of Shenandoah, and his mother raised chickens, pigeons, and rabbits on the six acres they had there. It was Cliff's job to sell the animal meat and also the crops they grew—radishes in spring, sweet corn in fall—with the help of his closest friend and trusted partner, his older brother Phil.

Phil was quiet where Cliff was loud, and careful where Cliff was brash; he moved with the precision of a slide rule while Cliff tore through the streets of town like one of the tornadoes that blew through in summer. Together, they were a dangerous and effective pair, not afraid to get dirty to get what they wanted. Motivated to buy a Buster Brown wagon on display at the hardware store downtown for $2.75—a small fortune to the boys—Cliff and Phil raided their barn for cow manure, piled it into a cart, and sold it as fertilizer for a penny a load. Almost three hundred trips later, they had the wagon they wanted.

"Now we gotta get a Shetland pony!" Cliff said.

Phil—who was two years older—just shook his head. "Mom says they cost lotsa money."

"Two hundred dollars," their father informed them.

But Cliff was determined, and Phil helped craft a plan to make his brother's dreams come true. They would sell seeds, walnuts, and the pelts of an elusive prey—muskrat. In a good week, they caught five, skinned them, and sold the pelts for thirteen cents apiece. Pretty soon, they had what they needed—"lotsa money"—and the pony was theirs. The boys named her Black Beauty and learned to ride her, then used her in Cliff's latest project, the Henderson Brothers Circus, a backyard event drawing children from miles around. All the kids wanted to see the pony, the tricks she could reportedly do, and the boy emcee at the center of it all: Cliff Henderson.

Shenandoah couldn't hold him. Neither could the family's next stop, Akron, Colorado, a cattle-ranching settlement on the high prairie east of Denver where the Hendersons moved, seeking land and a better life. Cliff knew he could never be happy there, working for ranchers and killing coyotes for pay. So in the summer of 1912, at just sixteen, he left home for nearby Fort Morgan. He was working as an auto mechanic there and sleeping above the garage at night when he got the phone call that changed his life.

The man on the line was E. L. Ferguson. He was driving that summer from Philadelphia to San Francisco in a truck loaded down with three tons of soap, hoping to make the first transcontinental delivery by motor truck. He was stopping for one night in Fort Morgan and had called the auto shop, essentially, for directions. Ferguson hoped someone at the shop could tell him the best road to Denver and, beyond that, to Wyoming, a wild and often trackless stretch. Henderson, who'd answered the phone by chance, saw his opportunity. He offered to personally guide Ferguson and his crew of roughnecks to Denver. The men were thankful for his help, and once he had guided them that far, Henderson begged Ferguson to let him stay with the truck all the way to California. Ferguson, seeing the boy's worth, agreed to the plan. It was Henderson's parents who needed convincing.

"Can't you see it my way?" Cliff pleaded.

"No, I say," his father replied. "No."

But his mother must have known it would be impossible to stop him now. She agreed to let her son go west under a few conditions: that after the truck reached San Francisco, Cliff would go to Los Angeles, where they had relatives; that he would finish high school there and go to college; and that he would be, as his mother said, "a good boy." Cliff agreed.

"I'll live up to my word, Mother," he said.

Pushing west across the plains, with muddy ruts for roads or no roads at all, Ferguson's truck was lucky to go eighty miles a day. But Henderson felt like he was seeing the world, visiting the big cities of Cheyenne and Reno and accompanying his older traveling companions into brothels at almost every stop along the way. The men let Henderson watch and then tried to persuade the boy to claim a prostitute of his own. It became an almost nightly game between Henderson, the men, and the half-naked women, and Henderson was winning. Remembering his Quaker mother back home, he declined the women's advances, and he left the brothels and the truckers behind shortly after they arrived in San Francisco. He was going, by ship, to Los Angeles, as he'd promised.

But Henderson never forgot the celebration that greeted the truck at the end of its transcontinental journey in San Francisco. The mayor was waiting for them; a brass band was too. Crowds of people attended two luncheons at the city's finest hotels to honor them, and reporters pressed the heroic Ferguson for details of the hard road west.

"In that country, we were not touring," Ferguson said. "We were building roads."

It was like going to showman school. Henderson was taking notes.

IN LOS ANGELES, Henderson could easily have gotten lost, misled by charlatans or blinded by shiny objects in the California sunshine. No doubt his options were limited. Upon arriving, he moved into a room in the attic of a boarding house on Figueroa Street, paying his rent by peeling potatoes, washing dishes, and mowing the lawn for the widow who ran the house—a life hardly better than the one he'd left behind in Colorado. But Henderson had a plan to escape.

He enrolled at Manual Arts High School and got a job working afternoons at a drugstore. The job helped get him out of the business of washing dishes at the boarding house and allowed him to splurge on dinners of egg sandwiches and grape juice. But it didn't take him away from school, his primary focus. At Manual Arts, he ran track and played basketball and managed both squads, and he served as the school's student-body president and an assistant yell leader, standing before the crowd at pep rallies and chanting: *"Raggity! Haggity! Boom! Bah! . . . Manual Arts! Rah! Rah! Rah!"*

By graduation in 1916, Henderson was so popular and connected it was like he had lived in Los Angeles his entire life. He was in love with a dark-eyed woman named Helen Avery and proud to be enrolled at the University of Southern California. He began attending college there that fall, studying law and playing basketball for the Trojans despite his lack of height, and by the end of his freshman year, Henderson was named captain of the team—the first freshman captain at the school. He was, according to his fellow students, "the bright and shining light among the USC players." When the Great War broke out, he enlisted and served as an ambulance driver near the front in France and later in Germany. When he got the chance, he transferred to the air service and got his first taste of flying. Then, upon returning to California at the end of the war, he set up a new life for himself yet again. Instead of going back to college, he married Helen and opened a car dealership in Santa Monica. He was doing what he loved most, selling, and he reunited with the man who helped him do it best: his brother Phil.

Their Nash dealership on Main Street near the beach was soon out-selling every other dealer in the region. No one could keep pace with Henderson and his unusual sales promotions. FREE AIRPLANE RIDE WITH EACH USED CAR, his signs promised. Henderson—who had lit-tle flying experience but enough money to buy an old plane—flew the buyers personally, making a name for himself as "the Babe Ruth of Motor Row." Pretty soon, that name was all he had. By September 1927, Cliff Henderson Motors was at least twenty thousand dollars in debt, with car buyers defaulting on loans in droves and Henderson left holding the bag for their failures. Creditors came for him, and, despite all his success, he had almost no cash on hand to satisfy their demands. He was liquidating his dealership, selling his house to cover his losses, and rethinking everything, when he heard about an opportunity to promote something new: the 1928 National Air Races. "It will mean a big thing to Los Angeles to have these races here," one of the mon-eyed backers behind the 1928 bid said.

Henderson was desperate to get the job, using every connection he had to cast himself in the best possible light. He even wrangled a let-ter of recommendation from the lieutenant governor of California, a fellow war veteran, who described Henderson as a man of character and integrity. "I have no hesitancy, whatsoever," the lieutenant gov-ernor said, "in recommending him." In the end, the local backers—officially calling themselves the California Air Race Association—lis-tened. They hired Henderson as manager, promoted him to the board, and asked him to help solve their biggest problem first: LA, the home of the 1928 air races, didn't have a real airport. "Los Angeles is what is called the average American city," humorist and local resident Will Rogers joked that year. "That is, the politicians are arguing over where to put their municipal airfield."

IT WAS AN argument with big implications for all of Southern Califor-nia. Los Angeles—home to 1.4 million people at the time—was one of the fastest-growing cities in America, almost tripling its size over the previous eight years. It boasted some six thousand factories, mills, and plants, churning out tires, paper boxes, and steel pipes. Cars, already, were everywhere. And because so many people were visiting the re-gion, experts predicted that the city might one day have more than two million residents. "Los Angeles," one declared, "is a city of destiny."

Technically speaking, this city already had eleven runways, plus there were ten more in nearby towns. But like most airports in America in 1928, these fields were little more than ragged, reasonably flat patches of grass or dirt with no lights and no amenities. The Los Angeles City Council, the air race committee, and the committee's newest hire, Henderson, were hoping to change that, reviewing multiple sites to lease or purchase outright.

They knew what they wanted: a field free of hills, tall factory chimneys, and electrical wires, objects that might kill a pilot; level land that did not flood and, ideally, did not fog; and a square and large area that was close to the city but not so close that planes were buzzing over homes. By the spring of 1928, they had narrowed the list of potential sites down to three, and Henderson knew which one he wanted: Mines Field, named after the real estate agent trying to sell it. It was a thousand-acre-square bean and barley field in Inglewood, about thirty-five minutes from downtown Los Angeles. The prevailing winds were from the southwest and moderate. The soil was perfect—sandy loam. Its potential was limitless. That's how Henderson saw it, anyway, as he began to shop the idea around town that spring, telling people that they should hold the National Air Races at Mines Field, a place later known worldwide by just three letters: LAX.

"Imagine, if you can, the material benefits Inglewood will get," Henderson said, pushing the Mines Field idea in a meeting that May. "The exposition will be one of color and brilliance. The name of Inglewood will be known internationally. It will be indelibly printed on the air-minded world. You will have secured the greatest aeronautical meet on account of your ideal geographical position."

But if the officials wanted all these things to happen—if they wanted Los Angeles to be a truly great city, an air-minded town in an air-minded time—they needed to act now.

"Line up, gentlemen," Henderson told them. "The opportunity is not only knocking on your door—it is crashing down your door. It is by far the greatest opportunity that has ever come to a small city in California. *Grasp it!*"

LOCAL OFFICIALS AGREED to hold the races in Inglewood, and Henderson hustled to get the bean field ready in time. Up went seven miles of barbed-wire fencing around the perimeter and in went a grandstand with seating for twenty thousand people. Up went an exposition hall with 284 booths and in went three runways, all coated in oil to keep the airplanes from stirring up clouds of dirt. Finally, in a crowning touch, workers erected a statue of Charles Lindbergh that had been donated by an Italian sculptor. The field was ready—just in time—and the races were as big as Henderson had promised. That September, he awarded a record $200,000 in prizes. He drew a paid attendance of three hundred thousand fans, and at least another three hundred thousand watched for free on the streets of Inglewood. He overcame every obstacle, even the death of an army lieutenant who drove his plane into the ground during the first weekend of the races in front of thirty thousand frightened fans.

The showman's great show was missing only one thing, really: women. For the most part, in 1928, women just watched—from Cliff Henderson's grandstand or from the overflow chairs that he borrowed from the church down the street to accommodate the masses or from one of his stages. There were dancing girls to greet the crowds, and model girls to sell the latest aviation styles, and attractive girls on display on the arms of hero pilots or next to the silver trophies they hoped to win—"two score of the most beautiful girls," reporters promised. They just weren't in the air.

9

If This Is to Be a Derby

THE FLYING WOMEN kept their silence—and, at first, their distance.

That September, while Henderson orchestrated his show in Los Angeles—"Yours for America first in the air," he told people—Amelia Earhart, Louise Thaden, and Ruth Nichols stayed far from Henderson's spotlight and his stage, either by choice or by necessity.

Nichols made preparations to fly west, hoping to compete in the New York–to–LA derby that Henderson had organized as part of his races and then meet up in Los Angeles with Ruth Elder at the Famous Fliers ball to be held at the Biltmore Hotel. But Harry Rogers was going to be doing the flying in the derby, not Nichols. She would just be along for the ride. And in the end, Rogers's plane never got off the ground in New York, anyway. There was to be no derby, no headlines, and no ball at the Biltmore for Nichols.

Earhart fared better—at the start, at least. It had been quite a summer for her, with those parades across the country celebrating her transatlantic achievement, luncheons with her new friend Nichols in New York, and her significant lifestyle upgrade—she'd vacated Denison House in Boston's Chinatown to live with Putnam and his wife at the Putnam estate in Rye. Nothing if not efficient, Earhart cranked out the ocean-flying memoir that Putnam wanted—breezy, modest, and short—finishing it by the end of August. Then, on the last day of the month, one week before Henderson's races were to begin in Los Angeles, she flew west with Putnam in the new airship she had acquired: a two-passenger, open-cockpit Avro Avian biplane.

But it had been a while since Earhart had flown a plane herself, and it showed. At her first stop that night in Pittsburgh, Earhart plunged the plane's right wheel into a rut or a ditch—"A hidden ditch!" she exclaimed—ripping away the landing gear on the grassy runway, standing the Avian up on its nose, shattering the propeller, and cracking one wing. While Earhart checked in at the glamorous Schenley Hotel, known for accommodating Hollywood stars and US presidents, Putnam put a team of mechanics to work around the clock in Pittsburgh to fix Earhart's busted plane. He couldn't have his newest star author sitting around on the ground; her book was due out in just ten days. And within forty-two hours, she was back in the sky, flying west. She made it all the way to California before the end of the air races—her first cross-country trip by plane. Yet once in Los Angeles, Earhart did everything she could to avoid attention, refusing even to land at Mines Field, self-conscious that people would be watching. She chose instead to come down in Glendale, twenty-five miles away.

"I don't profess or pretend to be a flier," Earhart admitted after arriving at the races. "I am just an amateur."

UP THE CALIFORNIA COAST in Oakland at that very moment, Thaden felt like an amateur too. A terrible flier. A fool, actually.

Like Earhart and Ruth Elder, Thaden had received an official invite to the races. She had a red button to wear and a yellow card, invite no. 906, that would give her access to Mines Field. But for Thaden, the timing of the races could not have been worse. It had been less than three weeks since she'd crashed that borrowed airplane on takeoff in Alameda, going down in the marsh and killing Sanders. It had been only eleven days since Thaden was cleared of any wrongdoing in the crash. Pilots back in the Bay Area had only just finished eulogizing Sanders—"one of the most capable fliers on the Pacific Coast"— and attending his funeral, just a few miles from where the plane crashed. They escorted his body to the cemetery on a green hilltop in Oakland with views of the bay in the distance. Then they watched as a dozen men gave Sanders the final tribute he would have wanted: a flyby, planes soaring low in formation over his hole in the ground.

Thaden, still on crutches, forced her way out of the Alameda Sanitarium to be there for the funeral and dropped flowers on Sanders's grave. Making it to the races 350 miles south was an altogether different proposition. While her bosses, Walter Beech and D. C. Warren, flew to Los Angeles, and her husband, Herb, drove there to give speeches about his ideas on metal airplanes, Thaden stayed away, or at least stayed out of the newspapers.

But in whatever ways the crash was changing her, whatever guilt weighed upon her, Thaden showed no fear in returning to the sky that fall in Oakland. On the contrary, just as soon as she had recovered from her injuries, she began taking chances like never before, pushing herself. "I am not a good pilot," Thaden said, sounding almost defiant about it. But she was working to change that. "Some day," she added, "I hope to be."

In early October 1928, Thaden prepared to set the altitude record for a woman. At a time when pilots cruised under five thousand feet and often much lower, believing the air at high altitudes to be too thin, too dangerous, Thaden sought to go higher. Her goal: shatter the world female record of seventeen thousand feet, and keep going. It was a stunt that required, in addition to a sturdy Travel Air plane, six things: a certified barograph to measure barometric pressure; two certified altimeters sealed in the cockpit to confirm her altitude; a warm, fur-lined flying suit; a parachute, hopefully reliable; and an oxygen tank. The first five items were easy enough to acquire. It was the tank that caused problems. Thaden was forced to get one from a local machine shop and then improvise to make it work, using rubber tubes and an ether mask borrowed from a nearby hospital.

"You must be very careful," an intern at the hospital told her.

If she didn't get enough oxygen at high altitudes, Thaden could pass out. But if she got too much, she could also lose consciousness. When Thaden pressed for details to learn how she could strike the right balance, the intern essentially shrugged.

"Well," he said, "that's hard to tell."

In early December, after weeks of preparation, she went anyway, taking off from the airport in Oakland and climbing into the cool air above the bay in her open-cockpit Travel Air. She planned to gain eight hundred feet per minute for the first five minutes, level off around 18,000 feet after little more than an hour, and then climb again —50 feet per minute this time—forcing her plane into short dives, when necessary, in order to ramp up more speed to go higher. But once aloft, she was almost too uncomfortable to think about anything. The fur-lined suit she was wearing was too warm for the low altitudes and not warm enough for the higher flying. The parachute straps cut into her shoulders, and the chute itself pushed her up in the seat. Sitting higher than usual, she had to be careful to keep her head down or she'd catch bursts of ice-cold air in the face over the windshield. Meanwhile, her makeshift oxygen mask kept obstructing her vision. Still, with eyes darting between gauges and altimeters, she revved the throttle and kept climbing, half sweating, half frozen, and rising higher into the fog. At 18,500 feet, it was nine degrees outside. At 21,000 feet, it was zero. At 25,400 feet, it was six below. Thaden had the record; she was so high in the air that if the engine had died, she could have glided all the way to Sacramento or Stockton. It was time to come down.

In the days ahead, the National Aeronautic Association — the private aviation sanctioning body behind the growing sport of flying — checked the barograph and the altimeters on Thaden's plane. It determined the readings to be wrong and credited Thaden with reaching only 20,260 feet — a disappointment for her, but still a record for a woman, almost four miles above the earth. Thaden now wanted more. "All world's aviation records for women," she declared, "should be held by American women pilots."

Four months later, in March 1929, she claimed her second record, this one for endurance. She took off in Oakland carrying twelve hundred pounds of gas and flew nonstop in the air over the city for twenty-two hours and three minutes, almost five hours longer than any female pilot had ever stayed at the controls of a plane. "Well, I made it," she said upon landing. "But, gosh, I'm tired." In April, Thaden added still another record to her résumé: speed. Over a two-mile stretch in the sky above Oakland, she hit 175 miles per hour in her Travel Air and set a sustained record of 156 miles per hour — faster than any woman had ever flown. In each record-breaking flight, Thaden hadn't come anywhere close to threatening the men's records, established almost exclusively by military pilots flying military planes, often with full military crews. Men in recent months had flown almost twice as high as Thaden, 128 hours longer (with a crew of five officers), and in one case, with an Italian war ace at the controls, 160 miles an hour faster.

Still, an advertisement that spring in the *San Francisco Examiner* described Thaden with four words: "World's Leading Woman Flier."

Herb would have loved to see it for himself. He was proud of Louise. But his metal Argonaut airplane had sold in California, a big success. Then, in February of that year, his company sold—an even bigger development—moving Herb and the Thaden Metal Aircraft Company from hangar no. 3 in Oakland all the way across the country to Pittsburgh. Unable to personally inspect the Travel Air plane that Louise would be flying, he sent his wife telegrams offering last-minute advice and support. "I wish I were there," he said, "or you were here." But there was no point in her rushing to Pittsburgh when she still had what Herb considered important work to do in Oakland. "You stay, until everything is propitious," Herb told her. Until her work was finished.

By April, with the speed record in hand, Louise had finally had enough. She headed east to join Herb at his new office in an industrial strip on the banks of the Ohio River. Almost exactly two years after arriving on the West Coast, Thaden was finished selling planes at Travel Air, her time in Oakland done. She claimed to be finished chasing records too. "No more of the sensational flying," she promised. "I'm not going out for any more records."

She hoped to set up a flight school in Pittsburgh and teach women to fly. There was only one thing that could delay her—one particular contest. Thaden wanted to compete in Cliff Henderson's air races.

HENDERSON WAS STRUGGLING that spring, torn between Los Angeles, his home, and Cleveland, the host city for the 1929 races, vacillating between professional excitement and personal grief. In February, he flew by airmail plane to Ohio to interview for the job of managing the 1929 races—a job that he got. The great showman was coming back for more, and his wife, Helen, was thrilled for him. But the couple hardly had time to enjoy the news.

Just thirty-one years old, Helen was sick and getting worse every day for reasons doctors couldn't explain. They diagnosed her with inflammatory rheumatism, a catchall term used to describe all sorts of autoimmune problems at the time. All Henderson knew for sure was that he was watching his wife grow so weak that she couldn't walk; that he had to carry her around the house or to the car for the leisurely drives they liked to make out to Mines Field to see the airplanes; that she was slipping away. In late February, after getting the job in Cleveland, Henderson drove his wife to the field one last time. Shortly thereafter, Helen slipped into a coma from which she never awoke. She was dead by early March.

Henderson—only thirty-three and now a widower—was reeling without Helen. "My pal," he said, "my companion, my everything." Her death would have been hard enough to deal with in Los Angeles. In Cleveland that April, trying to plan the 1929 air races, it was almost unbearable for him. He passed weeks in a fog of depression made worse by his loneliness and the weather. Late-winter snowstorms blew in off Lake Erie. His new office at the Cleveland Hotel was empty and cold—just a storeroom. He was starting all over again in the Midwest and dealing with all sorts of problems—including, most notably, the problem of the women.

Elizabeth Lippincott McQueen, a fifty-year-old socialite from Beverly Hills, was the first to begin making noise. At Henderson's races in 1928, McQueen and six other women had hosted a breakfast for out-of-town pilots and announced they were forming a new group, for women only: the Women's International Association of Aeronautics, the WIAA. "Our objective," McQueen said before the breakfast, "is to interest women in aviation, particularly those women who have members of their families engaged in aviation activities, and to foster air-mindedness in every possible way."

It sounded harmless enough at the time. But McQueen—blessed with glamour and a tony address near Wilshire Boulevard—was a woman of many talents. She not only flew planes; she wrote, lectured, climbed mountains, rode horses, cared for her Maltese terriers, and posed for photographs with her sixteen-year-old parrot on her shoulder. She had personally trained the parrot to sing opera. She wasn't going to host a fancy breakfast and move on. By the spring of 1929, McQueen seemed to focus entirely on one goal: getting Henderson to approve an all-female transcontinental race, the first women's race ever staged. "Yours for America first in the air," Henderson had told people again and again in 1928. Now, McQueen was trying to hold him to that.

"You are no longer a local figure in this great cause," she told her fellow Angeleno Henderson in the spring of 1929. "But you have become a national one—and it is our sincere desire to uphold your hands in your good endeavors to make America first in the air." All of America, she meant—the women, too. "Will you kindly consider a women's contest race to the Cleveland air races?" she began asking men in power. "Would it not be the first woman's race? If so, I am sure it would attract unlimited attention throughout the entire United States."

Henderson was intrigued. The women pilots were too. One by one, they signed up for McQueen's race: Thaden and Earhart, Nichols and Elder, and others. McQueen was planning a true derby for them, from Clover Field in Santa Monica to the primitive dirt field that Henderson was helping to prepare in Cleveland, a long-distance event just like the men had tackled at the National Air Races in both 1927 and '28. "I see no objection to having a race start at Clover Field or any of the Los Angeles airports," Earhart told McQueen. Thaden was also excited, signing up as soon as she reached her new home in Pittsburgh. "I wish," she said, "to be officially entered." After all, this was no exhibition. McQueen had helped secure $10,000 in prizes for the winners of the derby.

But race organizers in Cleveland—all men—soon came down against McQueen's plan, saying they were "emphatically in opposition." They doubted the women had the stamina to fly all the way from California to Ohio, a distance of two thousand miles. "They feel it would be too much of a task on the ladies," Henderson's boss, race chairman Floyd Logan, informed McQueen, and he proposed instead a much shorter trip—from, say, Minnesota or Nebraska to Ohio. This was a journey the women could handle. "A two day trip into Cleveland," Logan said. The organizers also suggested one more rule change: each woman had to fly with a man.

Thaden was furious. In New York that May, she and Earhart met to discuss the proposed changes and how they—two of the most famous female aviators in the world—would not abide by them. As Thaden saw it, Henderson and the men were trying to turn the women's derby into a "pink tea affair"—a precious little race for precious little women flying their precious little planes.

"If this is to be a derby, let's have it one," Thaden said. "Otherwise, we will be the laughingstock of the aeronautical world. You know—'Women can't fly. Can't navigate. Have to do this and that, in order to do anything.'"

Earhart agreed. She might have been even angrier than Thaden about the men's proposals. By the spring of 1929, she was a published author as well as an editor at *Cosmopolitan* magazine in New York, and she was ready to throw the full weight of her name behind a bold plan. They'd boycott the women's derby. Not go at all. On June 11, only a few weeks after meeting in New York, Earhart and Thaden put this plan into action. Earhart publicly denounced the men's plans as ridiculous, sure to turn the women's derby into a joke. Already, Earhart said, she'd heard Hollywood starlets were registering to enter the race, because under the newly proposed rules, brave men could fly the women to Cleveland. If that's what race organizers wanted, that was fine. But they needed to know that Earhart, Thaden, and every other real female pilot was going to skip it.

"If we can't fly the race and navigate our own course through the Rockies, I, for one, won't enter," Earhart said. "None of us will enter, unless it is going to be a real sporting contest. How is a fellow going to earn his spurs," she added, "without at least trying to ride?"

It was national news and terrible press for Henderson, still grieving and toiling away in Cleveland. There was no choice but to strike a compromise—and race organizers, spooked by Earhart's statements, quickly crafted one. The women, they said, could fly alone, without men, all the way from Santa Monica, as they wanted. Furthermore, they declared, each entrant had to be a real pilot with a hundred hours of experience in the air and fifty hours of previous cross-country flying. No fame-seeking starlets allowed. In exchange, the women had to agree to make stops and overnight stays along the way so the grueling journey would be more manageable—fifteen stops in all. "Tentative derby route for ladies event includes Oklahoma City and Tulsa," Henderson informed McQueen, as well as such glamorous destinations as Yuma, Arizona; Abilene, Texas; and that great air capital on the plains: Wichita, Kansas. "Your cooperation in interesting these cities will be appreciated," Henderson told McQueen.

The women agreed. It was the best offer they were going to get. Now Thaden just needed to secure a plane for the derby, and an old friend had a lead on one. It was the man who had given Thaden her job selling coal, the man who had introduced her to Walter Beech at Travel Air, the man who, in Wichita, anyway, seemed to know everything.

"I will give you a little confidential information," Jack Turner told Thaden. "But probably you had better not say that I told you and be sure not to tell anybody else."

Beech was building a new plane in his growing factory in the tall grass east of town. "A very fast ship," Turner told her, "and only one." She should inquire about it. Write a letter or call Beech—and soon.

"Probably," Turner said, "the company would loan it to you."

10

There Is Only One Cleveland

T RAVEL AIR, BY the summer of 1929, was no longer just a little outfit on the Kansas prairie; it was one of the largest plane manufacturers in the country, supplying reliable airships to the world's most famous fliers. The aviator who'd won the Dole Air Race from Oakland to Hawaii—surviving while so many others died in the Pacific—had flown a Travel Air. Charles Lindbergh, in making publicity-grabbing airmail deliveries, flew one too, painted deep red and pushed out of the factory in Wichita in record time by Walter Beech himself. Across the country, distributors like Thaden's former boss D. C. Warren were lining up to sell the Wichita-made product. In 1929, Beech —now president of the company—had 116 such dealers nationwide, projected to sell $2 million worth of planes that year alone. Each one was built in the factory east of Wichita, the factory churning out two planes a day—the factory where Louise Thaden arrived that August, inquiring about Beech's new plane.

It was brutally hot when she got to town, reminding Thaden of all the reasons to dread Wichita in summer. It hadn't rained in weeks. The prairie was parched and dusty. The corn was shriveling in the fields, and the wind offered no break, just insulting blasts of hot air. In the last week of July and the first week of August, thermometers in Wichita hit a hundred degrees five times, sending weary Kansans, with no air conditioning to cool them, in search of relief wherever they could find it. At night, they wandered the sidewalks in their pajamas. And by day, with no end in sight, they filled the indoor swimming pool at the Elks club and the Orpheum Theatre on East First Street downtown. The theater that month was bringing something to Wichita for the very first time: a talking movie in full color.

But Thaden had no time for picture shows. She woke every morning in a sweat, agitated and worried—worried about the other women, her competition, acquiring planes that summer all across the country. Earhart, who had owned her Avian biplane for just a year, was already moving on to something better. That July, she sold the Avian in hopes of buying a Lockheed Vega, the plane preferred by men seeking speed. The bullet-shaped Vega, with its engine covered by an aerodynamic cowling, had dominated the air the year before, in 1928. A Vega set the record for a transcontinental flight, flying nonstop from New York to Los Angeles in eighteen hours and fifty-eight minutes. The same model had won at Henderson's air races too, beating eight other planes across the country through stormy skies. A Vega was surely the plane for Earhart—and she got an orange one. "Conspicuous in nearly every great competitive air event," Lockheed advertisements proclaimed, "you will find a world-famous, Los Angeles-built Lockheed 'Vega' Monoplane . . . the commercial plane with a fighting performance."

Ruth Nichols was also working that summer to line up a race plane of her own. She tried to acquire one from the well-regarded Command-Aire manufacturing outfit in Arkansas. No luck. She asked to borrow one from a banker in Chicago and also a wealthy publisher there. Again, no luck. She reached out to Walter Beech in Wichita, but all he could offer Nichols was a plane owned by one of his junior engineers. It was a Travel Air that Beech assured her would outrun anything, but it wasn't new, and Nichols would have to pay the insurance, an estimated six hundred dollars, and split her winnings with the engineer. "This is the best I can do," Beech told Nichols. Again, no luck.

By the summer of 1929, Nichols was heavily invested in setting up aviation country clubs across the nation. She hoped they would one day be like golf clubs, but for plane owners. And in her push to get the job done, she was bleeding money and receiving some upsetting notices in the mail. "It is with a deep feeling of personal loss that I inform you of the fact that your check which I cashed for Mr. Bedford in Chicago came bouncing back like a spanked gazelle," one business associate informed Nichols that summer. "Including the protest fees, I am bereaved of $116.02." The man wanted his money but was trying to be nice about it. "P.S.," he wrote in longhand beneath his typed letter. "Let's neither of us get mad."

Nichols, the daughter of wealth in Rye, quite possibly couldn't have afforded the plane insurance that Beech was requesting, a reality that would have shocked most people, and certainly Beech, given everything the papers wrote about Nichols as a socialite. Instead, just before the women's derby that August, Nichols borrowed a different plane at no cost: an open-cockpit machine known as the Ken-Royce made by Rearwin Airplanes in Kansas City and loaned to Nichols by R. A. Rearwin himself. He personally mailed in her air-race application, believing his biplane, twenty-five feet long and thirty-five feet across the wings with a 185-horsepower engine, was fast enough to win—and at least one other aviator agreed. "I have all my dough on you," Nichols's old instructor Harry Rogers told her. "We are all expecting nothing but first."

By August, Thaden was beginning to wonder if she'd even have a plane to join Earhart, Nichols, and the seventeen other women in the transcontinental race, each expecting to win and all but two of them assisted by mechanics who would fly ahead and handle any problems with the planes at every stop along the way. The famous Ruth Elder had acquired a Wichita-built Swallow. And while airmen still treated her like a joke—in one West Coast airport, they had posted a picture of Elder in the ocean under the caption "Where are we?"—Elder took her preparations seriously. When not acting in Hollywood movies, hosting luncheons at Los Angeles's most fashionable cafés, or greeting her guests wearing sporty, low-backed frocks, Elder was training, flying long-distance to Seattle and learning acrobatics in the sky. "I've just finished making two flying pictures in which I never got off the ground," Elder complained that summer, recounting her movie scenes in dummy planes. "My contract forbade me to fly." Now she hoped to silence her critics by practicing and studying. "Because one never can know all that is to be known about flying," she said, "for new things come up all the time."

Gladys O'Donnell, a mother of two children from nearby Long Beach, was another contender. She had a Waco plane. Four other women were flying Walter Beech Travel Airs, including three sure to compete for the silver cup and the ten thousand dollars in prize money. One of them was Blanche Noyes, an actress turned aviator whose husband was an airmail pilot from Cleveland. The other was Florence "Pancho" Barnes, the moon-faced, big-talking wife of a California minister. And the third was the aptly named Marvel Crosson, an attractive middle-class woman from San Diego who was breaking Thaden's records that spring and lying about her age. The newspapers reported in the summer of 1929 that Crosson was twenty-five, which itself was a marvel since she was born in 1900. But one detail about her was not debatable: Crosson, a former saleswoman like Thaden, wasn't going to be returning to her job at the department store at Fifth and C Streets in San Diego anytime soon. With her Travel Air ship, she was a true pilot now, one who had logged hours flying not only in San Diego but in Alaska. She was going to be hard to beat. "Marvel Crosson," one newspaper declared, "is a sure winner." Crosson certainly hoped so. "I have given up my life to prove that women are the best pilots in the world," she said.

Thaden—who had no mechanic to accompany her and, for a long time, no plane—seemed at least a little intimidated, sweating it out in Wichita and picking up her plane some two weeks after Crosson. Her Travel Air biplane, when finally delivered, was blue and yellow, with a streamlined cowling covering the engine just like Earhart's Lockheed—a real Walter Beech beauty, but also flawed from the start. Spewing carbon monoxide into the cockpit, the motor nearly killed Thaden on her test flight to Fort Worth. She landed there dizzy and confused. But Beech fixed the problem by running a pipe from the edge of the cowling into the cockpit. Thaden would have fresh air now, especially if she shoved her face into the hole of the pipe. It was the best she could hope for, given the time constraints. Crosson, Earhart, Elder, and others were already in Santa Monica, planes ready. Thaden had to go, and she landed in Los Angeles on August 13, five days before the race was to begin. She wasn't the last one to arrive, at least.

Nichols was still limping west, hobbled by her troubled Rearwin plane that had to make three forced landings on the journey to the starting line of the women's derby. In the last of the three—caused by a leaking oil line and an overheating engine—Nichols had to march for miles across the desert wastes of remote western Arizona, stepping over rattlesnakes and tarantulas in search of help. That she managed to find it amid a sea of sagebrush was a miracle. That she ultimately made it to Santa Monica in time to start the race was another one. Refusing to miss the derby, Nichols persuaded a few local mechanics to fix her plane and even convinced one of them to fly with her the rest of the way to California, just in case, despite his obvious misgivings about flying with a female pilot.

She arrived making apologies that were quickly picked up by the national press. "I'm very sorry that there's been so much publicity about this landing in the desert." Nichols was embarrassed about it because, as she pointed out, she'd never crashed, was always safe. And now, because of everything, she had missed the festivities that the other women had enjoyed that week. There'd been breakfasts to attend, dignitaries to meet, movie cameras to smile for, and photo ops to stage, all the women standing together next to the trophies they could win.

"Come on out here, Louise," Elder begged Thaden at one photo op while holding a trophy in her hand.

"Come on, Marvel."

Elder, a film star now, was comfortable in front of the cameras. Thaden, Crosson, and others shied away. But there was one gala at which every woman was expected to appear: the Aviation Ball at the ornate La Monica ballroom on the shores of the Pacific Ocean. "See Amelia Earhart, Transatlantic Flyer," advertisements said. "See Marvel Crosson, the highest flying woman pilot in the world. See Louise Thaden, who stayed in the air longer than any other living woman . . . See Them — Hear Them — Talk with Them — Just Before They Fearlessly Start the Long Flight to Cleveland."

On Saturday night, the eve of the races, Thaden and Earhart, Elder and Crosson, Noyes and O'Donnell, and all the rest — except Nichols — stepped into the La Monica. They eyed one another and then the place cards at their seats. The cards bore a simple message for the women.

"There is only one Cleveland. Find it."

ACROSS THE COUNTRY, Cliff Henderson was waiting. The widower had pushed through months of darkness that spring, distracted by work and buoyed by letters sent to Cleveland by his dead wife's mother.

"You'll not have time to answer—and never mind that," Helen's mother wrote to Henderson. He was busy, and she understood. She just wanted Henderson to know she was thinking of him—and rooting for him. "Live life to the full," she begged him. "There is no reason to be sure we will have any other day." As if taking this message to heart, Henderson threw himself into planning the 1929 races, helping to organize the women's competition and then working to make the Cleveland event bigger than the one in Los Angeles the year before. "It is," he declared, with his usual dash of bombast, "the most complete layout that has ever been attempted in connection with the air races in the history of the country."

He was planning an opening-day parade in Cleveland, hoping to clog its streets with fifty thousand people. He was staging not just another exposition in the city's brand-new auditorium but an elaborate musical on the new esplanade outside. The show, *Wings of 1929*, was itself worth the one-dollar admission price to the races, Henderson figured. Then there were the races themselves. Three great towers, called pylons, had been erected at the field, creating a racecourse in the sky. Some three hundred pilots would compete, flying around them. Excited locals had already purchased $100,000 worth of tickets to witness the spectacle. To make it even more alluring, Lindbergh was scheduled to appear, and Henderson personally traveled to Washington, DC, to woo another celebrity: President Herbert Hoover himself. In a ceremony on the lawn of the White House, Henderson handed the president an oversize invitation to the races.

"This looks formidable," the president said, eyeing the giant envelope. "Is there something inside of it?"

With that, Henderson tore it open, revealing an invite signed by the mayor, Henderson, other notable Clevelanders, and one hundred thousand local schoolchildren, filling ten feet of paper with earnest, hopeful signatures, begging White House officials to come to Cleveland. "A very lovely invitation," the president said, eventually agreeing to send some of his top officials to the races. "Now all we need is the cooperation of the weather man," Henderson said on the eve of the event. "And, if you'll excuse the bromide, we're all set for the greatest show on Earth."

It began with the women in Santa Monica. The morning after the gala, on the shores of the Pacific, Clover Field was crawling with spectators. They mobbed the starting line on the earthen runway, pressed in to give the women bouquets of flowers, and swarmed over a nearby hill with a view of the field. Some twenty thousand people in all looked to size up the female pilots before they flew to their first stop, San Bernardino. Famous aviators were there. Hollywood stars, like Will Rogers, were too, and, of course, the reporters came out. It was, for Henderson and the air races, a bonanza of publicity. Californians were doing more than paying one dollar per car to come to the field. They were also placing ads sponsoring the women—"We admire your courage . . . We wish all the lady fliers the best of luck . . . Hail the New Womanhood!"—and they were even wagering on them. "Pick the Winner of the Women's Air Derby," one advertisement said. "Win $10."

It was enough to rattle even Thaden, who was no stranger to crowds. Her hands were sweating as she climbed into the open cockpit of her blue and yellow Travel Air and waited for her turn to take off. She and Earhart and the other women had asked for this moment, this chance to prove themselves. Now that it was here, about to unfold on the field in Santa Monica, both Thaden and Earhart realized there was more than just winning at stake. No matter who won, all twenty of them needed to make it safely to Cleveland or they would all face criticism for failing.

"The men, you know, have been somewhat worried about such a long flight for us," Earhart said that week in Santa Monica, "and they seem to have visions of us smashing up all over the countryside. So the thing for us to do is to prove their fears have been foolish."

Thaden agreed. All summer, she had been saying the same thing, that the women couldn't just be good. They needed to be perfect. "One hundred percent perfect," Thaden stated and, she added, "unduly careful." "If the derby is run off without a mishap, it will be a big boost for aviation in general," she said. But the opposite was also true. "If there is a mishap, the derby will defeat itself."

On the airfield now, Thaden began saying her goodbyes.

"Good luck, old girl," she told Crosson. "See you in San Berdu."

She wished Earhart luck too. "See you later."

Then, waiting in the cockpit, Thaden waved to Noyes, sitting in the Travel Air at her right—once and then, a bit awkwardly, a second time. Noyes waved back, hit the throttle, rolled down the field, and pushed her plane into the sky—up and away. It was 2:18 p.m. and Thaden was up next, watching for the starter to drop his flag. "When the white flag falls," he told her, "you take off."

She checked everything one last time: her parachute, her safety belt, her controls, her maps, her stabilizer adjustment, and the tube Beech had run into the cockpit to solve the carbon monoxide problem. She hoped she would be able to breathe. She pulled her goggles down, wet her lips, and, when the flag fell, gunned it, pushing her Travel Air plane down the 2,890-foot dirt runway, following Noyes into the air, rising over the crowd, and banking east for San Bernardino.

This part of the trip was quick, just seventy miles, the first of fifteen stops over the next nine days. They were divided into two groups: light planes and—the main division—heavy ships. The times between each of the stops across the country would be added up, with the winner being the pilot with the fastest aggregate time across the 2,400-mile route. Like a golfer shooting three double bogeys on the front nine in a tournament, a woman making mistakes early on in the air would have to live with them and hope to overcome them. But it would be hard. Even a small problem along the way—a mechanical failure or getting lost for half an hour—could set a pilot back, forcing her to lose precious minutes that would be difficult to make up later.

Thaden had no such problems on day one, finishing in second place, twenty-nine seconds behind the colorful Barnes, and followed closely by O'Donnell, Crosson, Noyes, Nichols, and Elder. Earhart finished a distant eleventh, almost sixteen minutes off the lead. The problem for Earhart was mechanical. On takeoff in Santa Monica that afternoon, her starter switch had shorted out, prompting a fast return to the field and a quick fix before she went on. Another competitor didn't take off at all, late to arrive in Santa Monica. A third woman flew too far, landing in Redlands, several miles past San Bernardino. A fourth didn't fly far enough, landing at the wrong airstrip, fifty miles short of the town. All were effectively eliminated. And one woman did finish but pancaked her plane on landing, coming down hard from ten feet off the ground and cracking the undercarriage of her plane in front of five thousand people straining to see through the clouds of dust. Up until that moment, the race had been known by its official name: the National Women's Air Derby. But in newspapers across the country the next morning, reporters began sneaking a different term into their stories, a reference to a popular product that women used every day: the powder puff.

The pastel-colored puffs, used to apply makeup, were made of velour or wool and came in three compact sizes. Packed in neat little cellophane envelopes, they sold for ten cents or a quarter at drugstores. Every woman needed one—or five. As one advice columnist put it, "A clean puff is of the utmost importance to the woman who is at all fastidious." The term was everywhere in 1929. There were salons called the Powder Puff, the Powder Puff Shop, and the Powder Puff Beauty Parlor, and now there was this race, the "Powder Puff Derby," as newspapers began calling it. "The Cosmetic Caravan." Will Rogers—who had been there for the takeoff in Santa Monica—piled on too. In his nationally syndicated column read by millions of Americans, Rogers coined his own term for the race: "the she derby." "They are aviators," he said, "but they are still women. They were only out 60 miles when they all struck and wanted to have it their way."

The comments didn't sit well with the women. Rogers, however, wasn't joking about the strike. After arriving in San Bernardino, the derby contestants began protesting the late addition of yet another stop: Calexico, California, 150 miles south, on the Mexican border. They drafted a statement saying that, given the lateness of the notice and the poor conditions of the Calexico airstrip, they were refusing to fly there; they argued that they should skip it, stop in Yuma, and then fly on to Phoenix as previously planned. While race organizers in Cleveland threatened to disqualify any woman who didn't follow their directions, the women back at the airfield were dealing with yet another development.

"Beware of sabotage."

The cryptic message arrived via telegram that day, and shortly after dinner that night, the women believed they had proof of, if not sabotage, then at least tampering. One woman returned to her plane after dinner and found every switch in the cockpit turned on, every throttle moved. "Gas, ignition, primer, everything," she reported. Worried now, all the women returned to the airfield to inspect their planes, watching over them and working on them until after midnight. By the morning of day two—tired after just four hours of sleep—the women seemed to be losing on every front. The race organizers in Cleveland were forcing them to at least fly over Calexico for a visual check-in before turning east for Yuma and Phoenix. Worse still, the alleged saboteurs had gone to work overnight—or so it seemed to some of the women. Arriving at the airfield in San Bernardino before dawn, they found problems with their planes that they could not explain. One pilot had a clogged gas line. Another, Elder, was dealing with a problem so simple as to be alarming: the ground crew had filled her oil tank with gasoline, not oil. Even if it was just an honest mistake, it was cause for concern—and questions. Yet the women still took off, starting at 6:00 a.m., swooping low over Calexico as directed, and stopping later that morning in Yuma, an airfield that seemed more like a sandbox than a runway. The sand was so deep that the wheels on the women's planes dug in upon touchdown, bringing the machines to an abrupt halt that tipped their tails forward in the air and shoved their propellers toward the ground. Thaden nearly flipped her plane on its nose and then watched the others roll in, cheering them on in the suffocating heat.

"Stall it in—stall it in, atta girl . . . Now hold that tail down. HOLD IT DOWN! . . . Oh, Lord. I hope they all make it."

Earhart was the one who didn't. Upon landing in the deep sand, her orange Lockheed lurched forward and bent its propeller—a problem that could not easily be fixed in the desert 175 miles east of San Diego, the nearest large city.

"Anything I can do?" Thaden asked her, trying to offer support.

"Well," Earhart replied, "yes, there is."

She was having someone fly in another propeller from Los Angeles in a rush. Perhaps, she proposed, the other women could wait until it arrived. Maybe just three hours. "Why, sure we will," Thaden told her.

It was beyond hot in Yuma. "My brains are getting addled," Thaden said, cursing. But waiting there for Earhart seemed like the sporting thing to do, and the women were nothing if not good sports. In the air, when passing each other, they waggled their wings in greeting, even though doing so made them lose valuable seconds. Earhart was flying in a cabin, not an open cockpit, so she carried some of the women's luggage, even though the extra weight could clip her speed. And once, over a desert town that she had visited the year before on her long flight west, Earhart circled low and wasted five minutes to give people who had once helped her there a proper salute from the sky. Of course the women would wait for Earhart, they decided, and they staggered back to their planes only when she was ready. It was after lunch when they finally took off for the next stop, Phoenix, and soon they were all bouncing around in turbulence, engines running hot. "Too hot," Thaden thought. She hit a bump so hard at one point that she nearly lost control of the plane. She began imagining sounds in her motor— "disturbing knocks," she called them—and she envisioned her plane slamming into the jagged rocks in the sand down below. But she was flying too fast to worry about it for long. "Have to take a few chances," she believed, passing the other women, making up time by hugging the ground and surging toward Phoenix at 170 miles per hour. "Can't be far now," Thaden thought.

With the crowd at the airfield roaring—seven thousand people in all—Thaden's blue and yellow airplane appeared first on the horizon. She swung low over the trees west of the airfield, banked hard, circled back, and landed, edging out Barnes, the overall leader, by one minute and eleven seconds. Then came the rest: third-place O'Donnell and fourth-place Nichols, fifth-place Noyes and sixth-place Earhart. By the end of the day, every pilot was accounted for except one. Crosson was late. No word from her. By dinner, she was officially missing. Somewhere between Yuma and Phoenix, her plane had gone down. But where and what had happened to Crosson was hard to say. The women, checking in at the Westward Ho Hotel, were concerned but not panicked. Just a week earlier, Nichols had crashed in the desert not far from there and walked miles to get help. Crosson would turn up—and anyway, they had an appointment to keep with the governor of Arizona.

Governor John C. Phillips wasn't sure how he felt about women's rights. "Many of us feel that in the urge to assert themselves they have gone too far ahead of us," Phillips told the women at a banquet that night in the hotel. But he was pleased to meet "the foremost women fliers in the world," "the women of the cross-country race," "these angels," he called them. "They are angels, not myths," Phillips said, "because we have talked with them, shaken hands with them. We know them."

It was the sort of affair it was best not to interrupt with bad news, like a missing flier. So in their speeches, the governor and other men didn't dwell on Crosson, wherever she was. If she was mentioned at all, there is no record of it. But a reporter, moving quietly in the crowd, found an increasingly worried Thaden and told her everything he knew.

"Marvel Crosson is down in the mountains," he whispered.

"Serious?" Thaden whispered back.

It was, for now, just a rumor. All they had were the eyewitness accounts of a few ranch hands and a child near the town of Wellton who all thought they'd seen a plane flying low near a remote stretch of land on the Gila River. In the morning, taking off for their next destination, El Paso, the women still didn't know anything definitive about what had happened. They would have to fly half the day wondering about the fate of their fellow flier before they finally learned the truth.

Marvel Crosson was dead.

THE WRECKAGE OF her Travel Air—found along the Gila River not far from where the witnesses had indicated—offered little insight into Crosson's final moments except that she knew she was going down.

Searchers found the crumpled fuselage of the plane in one spot and her body about a hundred yards away. As best as they could figure, she'd encountered some kind of problem—heat stroke, carbon monoxide poisoning, engine trouble; everyone had a theory—and then sought out the flat riverbed of the Gila to make a forced landing. But coming in fast—her plane could go more than 160 miles an hour—Crosson overshot the riverbed. Realizing she was now headed into the bank or the deep water beyond it, she pulled the ripcord on her parachute, attempting to bail out.

"From my own calculations at the spot, I am satisfied that she made no effort to leave the ship until she was not more than fifty feet from the ground," said C. F. Lienesch, an investigator who inspected the wreckage personally. "She pulled the ring of the chute. And it had started to billow out at the moment she struck." But there wasn't enough time for it to fully open. At midday, at exactly 12:16 and thirty seconds, just twenty minutes after leaving Yuma, Crosson hit the ground, breaking her neck, snapping bones in both legs, and shattering her wristwatch, now frozen in time. "Statements of our witnesses and our own investigation," Lienesch said, "convinced me there was no fault whatsoever with her parachute."

The men wrapped Crosson in the chute's silken folds, carried her out of the desert on horseback, and then put her body, still shrouded in the chute, on a train headed for her home, San Diego. It rolled into town the next morning, and the body was quietly collected at the station by an undertaker who was helping the Crosson family make the final arrangements for their daughter. In three days, they would hold a funeral for her—a simple affair, well attended, with a line out the door of the mortuary and down the street. But as the train arrived in San Diego, there was no scene, no weeping crowds, no impromptu memorial of flowers on the platform, and no hint of the national outcry over Crosson's death that was playing out from Santa Monica to Cleveland.

Some were demanding an investigation into her crash and into the other problems that the women were reporting with their planes. Only fifteen out of the twenty fliers had reached Phoenix on day two. Of the five who didn't arrive, one was dead, one was running late, and the other three were delayed by what they alleged was sabotage. One woman, who'd made a forced landing near Calexico, claimed her plane must have been fueled with "dirty gasoline." "Dirty work," she said, "at the crossroads." Another woman, who also went down in Calexico, reported that two brace wires supporting the wings on her plane had snapped in midflight, a shocking problem for which she had just one explanation. "I am convinced the wires had been tampered with," she announced. "They snapped as squarely as if they had been cut by pliers." Ruth Elder's plane, hobbled by her oil tank filled with gas, had barely made it into Phoenix too. Even though the ground crew cleaned out the tank and filled it properly before she took off in San Bernardino, Elder's plane, once airborne, immediately began coughing smoke. Unable to see in the cloud of vapor and with residue all over her goggles, Elder was forced to circle the airport just in case her plane crashed. The smoke finally cleared and Elder found a handkerchief to wipe her goggles clean. But she lost time, falling behind, well off the lead now. "I must have lost 10 minutes," she said, "flying in circles."

Robert Holliday, the publisher of the *Santa Monica Evening Outlook*, had seen the women off three days earlier. Now he had heard enough. Holliday believed someone must have tampered with Crosson's plane while it sat overnight in San Bernardino, and he made a personal plea to Cliff Henderson to launch a probe into the matter. "If I were in your place," Holliday said, "I would stop the race immediately until those in charge guarantee the proper guarding of ships and the proper inspection before takeoff."

Henderson and the other men in Cleveland refused to stop anything. They had the authorities on their side. The district attorney in San Bernardino questioned mechanics and ground crews, fifteen witnesses in all, and found no basis for any claims of sabotage. The national Exchange Club, the community organization putting up the bulk of the women's prize money, agreed with the district attorney. If anyone was at fault, the Exchange Club claimed, it was Henderson and the other organizers in Cleveland who had allowed the women to fly "unsafe" planes. Still others blamed the women themselves—the exact criticism that Thaden and Earhart had predicted they would face if anything went awry in their derby.

"Women are lacking in certain qualities that men possess," Oklahoma businessman Erle Halliburton announced as the women continued flying east. "Handling details essential to safe flying is one of the qualifications women have not mastered successfully." Halliburton—the president of a small airline and an oil company on the plains, destined to become an American empire—demanded that the women stop flying immediately, not because of any possible sabotage concerns but because they clearly weren't ready to fly. Arthur Brisbane, a nationally syndicated newspaper columnist billed as "the highest paid editorial writer in the world," agreed. "The women's air race from the Pacific Ocean to Cleveland is saddened by the death of Miss Marvel Crosson, a courageous and admirable young woman," Brisbane wrote that week in a column published in papers across America. But to him, her death felt like a waste. A woman as beautiful as Crosson, Brisbane suggested, was here to give life to others—to, literally, give birth—making her a valuable asset. As such, she and other women needed to stay out of the sky—and any air derby. "For the present," Brisbane concluded, "such races should be confined to men."

The women—still flying, through El Paso and onward—weren't listening.

"This is no time to stop," Earhart told a reporter.

Thaden had flown past Barnes into first place. Barnes, slowed by a leaky gasoline tank and then a crash, was soon out. But O'Donnell, the mother from Long Beach, was just behind Thaden, followed by Nichols, who claimed the best time into Pecos and Midland, and then

Earhart, in fourth place. They and the other women had already endured too much: sandstorms and crash landings, the death of their friend, and countless other problems beyond their control. Blanche Noyes had survived a fire that broke out in the luggage compartment of her plane, ignited, it seemed, by a careless mechanic's errant cigarette. Margaret Perry, another female flier, competed for days with a fever of 104 before she finally checked herself in to a hospital in Fort Worth. The diagnosis: typhoid. She was expected to remain hospitalized for weeks. And all the women had weathered the wild winds over Texas and the rowdy crowds on the ground there, surging around the pilots, clawing at them for a piece of history and begging for autographs.

"Hey, Thaden," Earhart shouted amid one such melee after yet another long day of flying in the heat. "Let's go get something to drink."

"Coming," Thaden hollered in reply, drowning in a sea of fans.

She was covered in dust and grease, a filthy flier in what she had to admit was a messy race. "But that is not due to a lack of careful preparation in advance," Thaden said, defending the women. Neither was it the result of any sabotage. Thaden didn't believe any of that. "To be short and sweet," she said, "it is the bunk. Nothing to it."

It was just typical hard flying that any pilot faced when making a transcontinental trip in 1929. Indeed, Earhart agreed, they were doing better than the men. In one transcontinental derby at Henderson's races the previous year, nine planes piloted by men had taken off from New York and only one had reached Los Angeles. The others had been forced down by storms in New Mexico, ice in Wyoming, engine trouble in Pennsylvania, and a crash in Indiana. But the women's newest enemy and vocal critic, Erle Halliburton, said nothing about that.

"Who is this Halliburton?" a defiant Earhart wanted to know. "Who is he to pass judgment on our abilities?" As far as she and the other women were concerned, he was a know-nothing idiot, a stupid man, a fool.

"Stop now?" O'Donnell asked.

Not a chance.

"I have never heard of anything so ridiculous," agreed fellow competitor Jessie "Chubbie" Miller, an Australian pilot flying among the American women in the derby. "Does that man imagine we can't go through to Cleveland?"

The matter was settled in a way that Marvel Crosson would have appreciated. The women—dirty and tired, but together—were in full agreement.

There was no stopping them now.

"Why, we are just getting under way," Earhart said. "And with the worst part of our trip behind us, it is simply straight sailing to Cleveland."

WICHITA WAS WAITING, eager with anticipation, when the women arrived on day six. City officials that week had installed electric lights at the municipal airport, making it possible for planes to land there at night. A local radio station had arranged to broadcast news of their arrivals live to listeners across Kansas and to the assembled crowd of ten thousand people through a system of speakers on the ground. And the Wichita welcoming committee was planning a reception like no other. Each woman would get a personal car for her one day in town, a local hostess to assist her, and a home to stay in overnight, not another hotel room. Thaden, desperate to make a good showing for Jack Turner, Walter Beech, and her family, roared in first, arriving from Tulsa just after 3:17 p.m. and skimming low across the familiar prairie on a straight compass line in what Thaden called "the daily battle for a few precious minutes."

"Atta baby," she told her plane, patting her Travel Air as she rolled to a stop on the field. "You smelled home, didn't you?" She took off her goggles, placed them on her forehead, and then waved to the crowd in her shirtsleeves while the spectators—wild, shouting, and honking their car horns—waved back. That night, the celebration continued at the Broadview Hotel, where locals had honored Beech just three years earlier. The city presented Thaden with a silver cup for winning the leg into Wichita, beating the next plane by ten minutes. With only three days to go before arriving in Cleveland, she was now up forty minutes on her nearest competitor, O'Donnell; an hour and seven minutes up on third-place Nichols; and one hour and twenty-two minutes ahead of the fourth-place Earhart.

"I was glad I was able to come into Wichita in the lead," Thaden told the crowd of three hundred people at the Broadview that night, accepting her trophy. "First, because it seems like home to me, having lived here. And second, because I am flying a Wichita ship."

In the crowd that day were her parents, weeping tears of joy—
"Louise, darling," they said, pulling her close—and Walter Beech,
who wasn't crying at all. He was smoking his pipe and making a plan
to win. Beech had won not just the 1926 Reliability Tour but a host of
other races. First place in Monmouth, Illinois, 1922. First place in Dayton, Ohio, 1924. First place in Tulsa, Oklahoma, 1925, and first place in
Kalamazoo, Michigan, 1926. There was a reason why locals had once
called him the "Knight of the Air." But with his racing days behind him
now, Beech could offer Thaden only two things. First, a mechanic. For
the rest of the race, Travel Air would send one ahead with Thaden, a
perk that almost all the other women had enjoyed since Santa Monica.
Second, some advice.

"You're flying a nice race, Louise," he told her that night at the
Broadview.

"I've been flying the best I know how," Thaden replied.

"You keep on the way you've been going," Beech said, "and you'll
win. Save the motor all you can," he added. "Forget about the laps. Just
win the race."

The next day, in East St. Louis, four hundred miles away, both Noyes
and Earhart finished ahead of Thaden, cutting time off her overall
lead. "Hell's bells," she thought, knowing they were gaining on her.
She had nearly made it worse by almost overshooting the runway, the
sort of mishap that would sink her for sure. With their final destination—Cleveland—now within range, they all seemed to be getting
more competitive. "How much did Blanche beat me?" Earhart asked
as soon as she landed in East St. Louis, wanting to know her time.
No lead was safe, not even Thaden's—a fact that Thaden knew better than anyone. If she crashed at this point, she'd lose, because there
was no time to make up lost ground. If she encountered engine trouble, she could lose too, for the same reason. Finally, getting lost in the
sky remained a definite possibility. Multiple women in the derby had
squandered hours by getting turned around in the air, misreading their
maps, following the wrong railroad into the wrong town, and even
landing at the wrong airfield—all wrong. Thaden knew it could happen to her too. "Ask any pilot," she said, "and he will tell you it is a difficult task to fly almost across the United States without once becoming momentarily lost."

By the end of the night in East St. Louis, exhausted and aware of the stakes, Thaden could hardly speak, grunting her replies to the other women. She laid out her last clean shirt and breeches, clothes she had been saving for the next day's destination, Columbus, Ohio, not because it was the last stop before Cleveland but because her husband, Herb, was coming over from Pittsburgh to meet her there. "Oh, yes," Thaden said, "I am going to meet my sweetheart in Columbus tomorrow night." If she could make it.

Thaden was fidgety in the cockpit in the morning, hot in the eighty-degree temperatures, uncomfortable in her parachute, and fighting fog into Terre Haute, Indiana. Some women got lost; Elder almost crashed. But not Thaden. On the way to Terre Haute, she added three more minutes to her lead. Next stop, Cincinnati—where the waiting crowd at Lunken Airport east of town that afternoon was twice the size of the mob that had greeted Lindbergh two years earlier. "Good luck, everybody," Thaden told the other women as they prepared to leave Terre Haute. Neither she nor the others had ever flown into Cincinnati. Again, some did not fare well. One had mechanical problems, another lost time in a forced landing in Indiana, and a third never found Cincinnati at all, wandering ahead to Columbus, which disqualified her. But Thaden had no issues. She landed first, extending her lead by another five minutes.

"Hey," she hollered on the airfield in Cincinnati after a break for lunch. "Which direction is Columbus?"

There weren't many landmarks between the two cities, and Thaden wanted to be sure she was heading in the right direction as she took off at 4:30 p.m. But soon after getting airborne, she felt lost. There wasn't another plane in the sky. The other women—wherever they were—had apparently taken a different route. More alarming, the railroad on Thaden's map had never materialized on the ground. On a hunch, believing the wind had blown her plane to the east, Thaden adjusted, altering her course a little to the west and flying on. Still, there was no sight of Columbus.

She scanned the horizon for an airfield, breathing hard as her hands began to sweat. It had to be close—she was sure of it. "That airport has just got to be around here someplace," she thought.

And still no Columbus.

She thought of Herb on the ground, studied her compass in the cockpit, and kept flying until, finally, she saw it: a brown field with a newfangled concrete runway just across a railroad track on the Ohio flatlands — Columbus. Thaden nosed down, gaining speed, and crossed the finish line at nearly a hundred and seventy-five miles an hour before banking left in a long, climbing turn, leveling off, and landing.

A wild crowd surged across the field, clambering over one another to greet Thaden, who had stretched her lead by another eight minutes. Up a total of one hour and three minutes over the next closest flier with only an hour's flight to Cleveland the following day, Thaden was now, the reporters said, the sure winner. Fans, wanting a piece of history, pawed at Thaden's plane, climbed atop the wings, and peppered the pilot with questions. "Mrs. Thaden," many asked, "will you autograph this, please?"

Thaden signed everything. But she refused to believe any of this "sure winner" stuff that the reporters were writing. As she saw it, she wasn't beating O'Donnell, Nichols, and Earhart by much. "One little hour." That was still plenty of time for mistakes — or mishaps — to ruin everything. "Take it easy," she told herself the next morning, getting ready to take off for Cleveland and remembering Beech's advice: "Save the motor all you can." There was no need for Thaden to push her engine now. "You can cruise over," she told herself, "and win the race." The day was filled with surprises, as usual.

Elder got lost — again — arriving last in Cleveland but a crowd favorite nonetheless. At the final banquet that night, broadcast on live radio across the country, Elder entertained her fans with stories of all her forced landings in the derby. And on the dusty airfield in Cleveland, she fired playful shots at her old transatlantic copilot George Haldeman, standing there in the crowd. "George," Elder told him, "you're getting fat."

Noyes, despite the fire that had forced her plane down in Texas, managed to finish fourth — a surprising comeback and a big story in Cleveland. Blanche lived with her husband, Dewey, on Clifton Boulevard just two blocks from Lake Erie. By Wednesday that week, the Halle Brothers department store in town had her greeting customers in its new "Aviation Section." Amid racks of goggles, helmets, breeches, and boots for sale, there was Noyes, blue-eyed and petite—a woman who could not only fly, but survive fire. She had even managed to beat Nichols into Cleveland—the biggest surprise of them all, perhaps—after one final mishap.

On a test flight at the airfield in Columbus that morning, just before heading to Cleveland, Nichols smashed her Rearwin into a tractor parked too close to the edge of the runway with the winds that were blowing. The plane flipped over, wheels over wings, and Nichols tumbled along in the open cockpit and then came to a rest in the dirt. She wasn't seriously injured, but her plane was a total loss. Nichols couldn't believe it. She had been in third place for days, one step ahead of the great Amelia Earhart and in line to take home $875, as much as most women made in an entire year. Now her borrowed plane was crushed—"a squashed beetle," Nichols called it. Earhart—not Nichols—would finish third, and instead of giving a victory speech in Cleveland, Nichols was writing apologies to R. A. Rearwin, the man who had given her the plane. She had to hitch a ride just to make it to the finish line and witness the end of the Women's Air Derby, the so-called Powder Puff Derby, and see the crowning of its champion, a new star: Louise Thaden.

Thaden had hardly landed when Cliff Henderson, looking dapper in a shirt and tie, reached up, grabbed her hand, and led her to the microphone to speak.

"I'm awfully glad to be here," Thaden told the crowd of forty thousand. "It was a great race," she added. "I wish everybody could have won."

Officials draped a large horseshoe-shaped wreath over her plane, and photographers began shouting at Thaden, telling her what to do with it. "Put it over your head," they said, hoping to snap her picture with the flowers. Then, after Henderson led Thaden away, the reporters crowded into Henderson's office at the airfield to ask their many questions.

How was the race?

"It wasn't the flying that tired us out," Thaden answered. "It was the banquets and the things we had to go to."

What are you going to do next?

"There's one thing left to be done about the race," Thaden said.

"The cup that goes with first place is going to be inscribed 'Marvel Crosson' and sent to San Diego. Any of the other girls would have done that, too—had they had the luck that enabled me to win."

Someone asked another question, unintelligible to her.

"You'll have to talk louder," Thaden said, temporarily deaf from the roar of her airplane engine. "I can hardly hear out of these ears."

How much do you want for your story of the trip?

"I don't want to write a story."

"You won't have to," a reporter replied. "*I'll* write it."

They were fascinated with Thaden. She had lost ten pounds since leaving Santa Monica, and she looked like it. She was "slim like a boy," one reporter wrote, and wearing a shirt that appeared to be a man's. "Perhaps it was one of her husband's," one person guessed. Had to be. Because Thaden was too "dainty" for it to be hers. "Like a little girl," one woman cried in the crowd. Surely, someone would pay for this story.

"Not interested," Thaden said again.

She claimed that winning wasn't such a big deal.

"Oh, yes, it is," second-place O'Donnell corrected her later.

"It certainly is," fourth-place Blanche Noyes agreed.

By surviving, by making it to Cleveland, the women were real fliers now—or at least they thought they were. Even as Thaden claimed victory in Cleveland, beating Earhart, Nichols, and the other top female aviators in the world, some men weren't convinced, doubling down on their insults. Back in Oklahoma, Erle Halliburton was still blaming Crosson's death on her own stupidity. "If it hadn't been for her fear and confusion regarding the course," Halliburton said, "she would have been leading now." He called the rest of the female pilots a flying joke, essentially. "Women have been dependent on men for guidance for so long," he said, "that when they are put on their own resources they are handicapped." Newspapers around the country weren't sure how to handle the issue. For every editorial that praised the women for the hazards they braved, there seemed to be one that doubted them—sometimes in the same paper, on the same day. Most hurtful, perhaps, the women didn't get public support from the most important man of all: Charles Lindbergh.

The Lone Eagle, as the press liked to call him, weighed in from Cleveland that week on seemingly every possible aviation topic, large and small: the growth of the industry, the usefulness of blimps versus planes, and the need for parachutes on newly established passenger airlines, among other issues. But on the matter of the women pilots— the top story of the week and the most popular attraction at the air races in Cleveland—Lindbergh kept a silence that seemed to speak volumes. In his spare time, he was teaching his new wife, Anne, how to fly. Yet Lindbergh refused to field questions about Anne's flying abilities. "I really can't answer those," he said in Cleveland, brushing off the inquiries. "You mustn't ask me those." As a general rule, he didn't like Anne speaking to the press. "No interviews with Mrs. Lindbergh," he said once. "Positively none. Understand?" And this rule appeared to be in effect that week as well. While Thaden and the other derby fliers gave interviews, Anne stood quietly in her husband's ample shadow, saying little as he dodged reporters' questions. When asked about the women's accomplishments in their first-ever air race—a chance for him to give the female fliers his all-important blessing—Lindbergh, his hair tousled and his face bronzed by the sun, declined to comment.

"Is aviation a woman's game?" one reporter asked him that week.

"I haven't anything to say about that," Lindbergh replied. "I'm sorry."

IN THE DAYS AHEAD, the women kept racing, with Henderson pitting them against one another in a fifty-mile closed-course race. The women climbed back into their planes, took off, and whipped around the pylons placed on the ground. They pushed the speed of their little airships in five-mile laps, just like the men. Then, when Henderson's races were over, three of the women kept going. Thaden, Nichols, and O'Donnell raced on to Pittsburgh—another hundred miles—for fun, a trophy, and $1,500 more in prizes. And when they landed, yet another crowd was waiting, twenty-five thousand fans.

"I am fairly bursting with pride," Thaden told the people in Pittsburgh upon arrival. She finished three and a half minutes behind O'Donnell for second place, a disappointment, but not really, considering that Thaden had beaten O'Donnell in the bigger contest. "Mrs. O'Donnell," she said, "has her revenge." Anyway, it was hard to be upset looking at the crowd. "I can't tell you how glad I am to be home," Thaden said, "or how glad I am to have done something for Pittsburgh."

She had done something for herself as well. In two weeks, Thaden had collected $4,600 in winnings—more than four times what the average American woman earned in 1929. Many of the other women had fared well too. But all the money they had made, all the crowds that had cheered them, and all the miles they had traveled didn't feel like enough. Near the end of Henderson's air races in Cleveland, the female fliers met under a clump of trees on the airfield to talk it over. Earhart was there; Thaden was too. They wanted to discuss the future.

They all agreed: it was time to organize.

11

Good Eggs

CLIFF HENDERSON WAS THRILLED—with the women, with the races, with everything. As the sun set over Cleveland on Labor Day, the last day of the 1929 air races, he squinted into the dust on the airfield, knowing he had been right. The races had been the biggest ever held and, indeed, one of the largest sporting events in American history.

Race attendance, a reported 600,000 people, was roughly double the number that had paid to see the races the year before in Los Angeles. The Labor Day crowd alone, 125,000 fans, nearly topped the entire week's attendance at the races in Spokane two years earlier. That single-day figure was a record for more than just air races; it almost matched the size of the crowd that had turned out for America's last great heavyweight fight: Tunney versus Dempsey at Soldier Field in Chicago in 1927. And it would dwarf the crowds at the World Series later that fall. "There's no question," Henderson said, "about this year's races being the best in history."

He was predicting that, for the first time, the National Air Races would turn a profit—and they did. That fall, the races reported gross earnings of $603,000 and a net profit of almost $97,000. Henderson had helped make the men behind the races rich—or, to be more accurate, richer. But Henderson wasn't lining the pockets of just the race committee. In the wake of the air races, Clevelanders themselves were thriving, and they were beginning to wonder if airplanes were the future. "For nine days, I have been trying to find some adequate language to describe the sound they make — and there is none," one observer at the field noted. "Words simply can't describe it."

By year's end, the number of people with pilot's licenses in the United States had nearly doubled, to almost 9,500. Another 12,000 people were in line to get licenses, flooding flying schools with student-permit requests. Colleges were beginning to teach aviation courses; Boston University that fall enrolled students in a class called Elementary Aeronautics, hoping that one day grammar schools could use the same lesson plan to teach children about planes. And to meet the demand, manufacturers built more planes in 1929 than they had in any previous year in American history. One reason why: the female fliers. "Without women," one pilot said, "there can be no future for aviation." Because women signed off on their husbands going to flight school; women allowed them to buy planes. As Earhart put it: "When mama doesn't want papa to fly, papa just doesn't fly."

But for all their alleged power, many women still felt like "decoration," as one female aviator complained. It had been just nine years since American women had won the right to vote, and many men were struggling to understand these new women. They complained about their short skirts, their bobbed hair, their divorces (too many), and their marriage vows (all wrong). In the revised Book of Common Prayer, published by the Episcopal Church that fall, brides were no longer required to promise to obey their husbands — cause for hot debate. Editors across the country that year sometimes indicated in marriage announcements whether the bride had agreed to obey or not. Either way, at work, American women were getting paid less than their husbands: 30 percent less to kill pigs in a slaughterhouse, 28 percent less to toil in a foundry, and 43 percent less in menial jobs in the aircraft industry, if they were lucky enough to get hired there at all. Still, they went to work — for all sorts of reasons.

"My husband wasn't making enough," one woman reported.

"My husband died."

"He left me."

"I'd rather work."

Swanee Taylor, the announcer at Henderson's air races, found them cute, these working women, especially the 117 American women who had earned pilot's licenses by late 1929. Taylor — a swashbuckling airman, built like a reed and sporting a twirled mustache — considered himself a great judge of character and figured he could classify the flying women into six basic categories.

The Dependent Woman. "This type generally decides to learn to fly after having flown as a passenger with some snappy-eyed aviator," Taylor said. But it never works out because, Taylor said, the Dependent Woman "is so helpless . . . so absolutely powerless."

The Athletic Girl. "She seeks in aviation a certain muscular strain and physical competition," Taylor said. But she ends up battling the controls in the cockpit. "As a result, the ship lurches and heaves about in the sky like a rubber ball gone berserk." And this, too, fails to work.

The Flapper. "She approaches her instructor with a great deal of swagger," Taylor said. But she is "histrionic" and "overbearing" — and ultimately not teachable.

Little Lucy, the Timid Type, is equally lost. "Oh, how she squeals, coos and giggles!" Taylor said. "You are always captain to these babies."

And the *Talkative Woman* is also doomed. "Owing to the fact that she is constantly asking questions and expressing her own opinions."

Which left, Taylor said, just one kind of woman capable of success in the air: the *Good Egg.* "She keeps her chin up and a smile in her eyes . . . There is nothing petty or catty about her." On the contrary, such a woman is even-keeled, hard-working, and, perhaps best of all, Taylor suggested, quiet.

Everybody, he said, loves a Good Egg.

THE WOMEN, well aware of the odds against them, met late that year in New York to organize — not around a single air derby, like McQueen had done, but around a bigger issue. "For our own protection," said one female pilot at the time, "we must learn to think for ourselves, rely on ourselves, and do as much work as possible on our planes." It wasn't about fighting the men, she added. It was about the women sticking together, looking out for one another. "It must be remembered," she explained, "that this club is for all licensed girl pilots. The new girls have just as much rights as those who flew in the derby. We want your ideas. Won't you take an active interest in this and send us your suggestions?"

The group of pilots at the first meeting was small — five Powder

Puff fliers, five mothers, three editors, and two teachers—and they assembled in an unusual spot: a tool bench in an airplane hangar on Long Island. "As a meeting place," the minutes noted, "a hangar has nothing to recommend it." Yet the women were able to sort out a few matters, including, most important, the name of the group they were forming. They were sending invitations to 117 women. Earhart suggested that the number of replies they received—the total number of charter members—should determine the name of the club. At first they were the Eighty-Sixes, then the Ninety-Sevens, and then—when the last reply came in before Christmas—the Ninety-Nines. "We believe," Earhart said, "that such an organization might become influential and powerful."

But they hoped they wouldn't be seen as too powerful. The women knew they needed to be careful around the men. "If we come in modestly," one flier among them suggested, "giving the men credit for all their achievements, they are less apt to oppose us." But it was hard for the women—especially Earhart and Thaden—to hold back. During the formation of the Ninety-Nines in New York, Nichols invited her new friends Earhart and Thaden to stay with her in Rye. One evening there, after dinner, Thaden and Earhart each bragged that they could outwrestle most boys in high school. Before the well-mannered Nichols had a chance to intervene, Thaden had challenged Earhart to a wrestling match, and the two women, both five foot eight and slender, were down on the floor grappling with each other. Nichols refereed until it became clear that Thaden had no chance. Three straight times, Earhart pinned her to the floor. "Her strength," Thaden said later, "was absolutely amazing."

In late 1929, the two women were squaring off together in another arena as well: the court of public opinion. With the Powder Puff fame, Thaden, twenty-four, was becoming a celebrity in her own right. The city of Pittsburgh—Thaden's home for all of eight months—claimed her as a native daughter. Organizations across the city invited her to give speeches. Enamored fans wrote poems about her: "Happy-go-lucky—plum full of fun. Brains plus beauty, all rolled up into one." More impressive to Herb, no doubt, contracts for paid endorsements began rolling in. That winter, McCreery and Company, one of Pittsburgh's premier department stores, launched an entire fashion line around the champion flier: Louise Thaden Sports Dresses—"well fashioned, with simplicity the keynote." Thaden unveiled the line herself, modeling the new styles for customers at the store and showing them off for Earhart, Nichols, and Noyes at an aviation ball they attended in Pittsburgh at the end of January 1930.

Thaden wanted the women to make an appearance and invited them personally to the ball. It wasn't about modeling her new clothing line—Thaden didn't even mention the clothes. It was about the proceeds the ball was generating to help Thaden in the job that really mattered to her: giving flight instruction to women at the new Penn School of Aviation.

By January, more than a dozen women were enrolled at the school and taking lessons with Thaden, because, as any woman knew, it was better than taking flying lessons from a man. Mae Haizlip—a wife and accomplished racer—put it this way: "Have you ever seen a man sew on a button or darn a sock?" Watching him teach a woman to fly a plane was a little like that, Haizlip said, awkward and ugly and hard to stomach. "They usually go at it with the feeling that it shouldn't fall to their lot to do this sort of thing."

Thaden had seen it herself; female flight students were quickly stereotyped by the likes of Swanee Taylor. Now, in her new job, Thaden was not only making $150 a month but giving women the education she believed they deserved, teaching mothers, secretaries, stenographers, lawyers, and college students how to fly. Of course, Earhart, Nichols, and Noyes would come to Pittsburgh for the ball. "Amelia and I plan to come on together," Nichols promised. "If we can wrangle a plane, we will come by air—otherwise, by train." Nichols had just one request.

"You mentioned issuing some publicity." Perhaps Thaden could make sure the local papers didn't use the photos they had snapped of Nichols at the end of the women's air derby the previous summer, the photos in which Nichols believed she looked "more than ever like a picked chicken." "To avoid that possibility," Nichols told Thaden, "I am sending you another one."

The women—rivals in the air—were becoming friends on the ground, the only friends they all had, really. They began spending nights in one another's homes. They coined nicknames for one another too. Ruth Nichols became Rufus, and Amelia Earhart became simply A.E.—the nickname that Amelia's publisher, George Putnam, also used for her. Thaden and Earhart were growing especially close, with Thaden rushing out to greet her friend anytime she flew through Pittsburgh and Earhart inviting Thaden to drop everything and fly with her, to just leave.

"Where are you going, Amelia?" Thaden asked at one chance meeting in early 1930.

"Kansas City."

"Gosh." It seemed like a long way from Pittsburgh. But it was hard to say no to Earhart.

"Come," Earhart begged Thaden, "go along today, we can talk on the way down."

They were the only ones who could understand what they were doing and why; the only ones who appreciated the dangers they faced and how; the only ones who knew what it was like to fly solo into angry headwinds—both figuratively and literally. A decade removed from the fight for suffrage, Earhart, Nichols, and Thaden were at the vanguard of a new battle pushing for true equality. These women wanted more than the right to vote; they wanted the right to be heard and the right to hold any job they wished. Most of all, they wanted respect— a respect that still eluded many women, even those with power. "Of the men I met," said a female elected official around that time, "only one treated me as an intellectual and political equal. None ever welcomed me." Frustrated, the woman finally resigned and walked away. But others now were marching in the streets, and for these women, the female aviators were the ultimate symbols of freedom. Political parties, professional groups, and women's clubs, realizing there was power in these symbols, were soon inviting Earhart, Nichols, and Thaden to attend their meetings, to speak. And off they went, flying across the country, sometimes together, to events in Indianapolis and to Thaden's aviation ball in Pittsburgh that January, all of them walking into the ballroom at the William Penn Hotel together, shoulder to shoulder. That night, they helped raise enough money to give one Pittsburgh woman $750 in flight-school tuition—even though, by the spring of 1930, Herb and Louise could have used that money themselves.

Despite Thaden's winnings the year before, her job at the flight school, her line of clothes at McCreery's, and her freelance newspaper articles at $20 apiece, Herb was worried about the family's finances.

The stock-market crash the previous October had people on edge. Many expected airplane sales to fall in 1930—by just how much, no one could say—and Herb Thaden was no Walter Beech with $2 million in revenue to help cushion the blow. His less established metal airplane company needed every sale it could get, and now those sales were disappearing. With the economy growing worse by the day, Herb was suffering from episodes—"these spells," Louise called them—of darkness. "This company has a lot of pessimists in it," Louise confided to her mother, "and every time they have a conference Herb comes home as downhearted as he can be."

Perhaps it was because Herb knew the full extent of the Thaden family's financial burdens. He needed to support not only himself and Louise but his mother, who was living with them; he had to pay the monthly rent on their house south of Pittsburgh; he knew they were living on credit to make ends meet; and he also knew that Louise was hiding a secret beneath those sport dresses from McCreery's.

She was pregnant.

For a while that spring, the pregnancy didn't change much for Louise. She taught her classes and traveled for talks. She made multiple stops with Earhart, the two of them spending hours together in the sky, and she even survived a mishap in Harrisburg. A gust of wind nearly toppled her plane upon landing, scooping the right wing into the air, throwing the left wing toward the ground, and spinning the plane around. Witnesses said only two things had prevented a disaster: sturdy landing gear and a good pilot—Thaden, then five months pregnant.

By the time she returned from a trip with Earhart in late May, there was no hiding her condition anymore. Thaden had to quit her job at the flight school. "Hate to lose the $150," Thaden wrote to her mother. "But can't be helped." The Department of Commerce didn't think it safe for a woman to pilot a plane while she was menstruating, much less when she was pregnant. She resigned at the end of May and prepared for a long, hot summer, pregnant in Pittsburgh with her mother-in-law looming over her and preparations to be made for the baby. Within a month, both were driving her crazy. Thaden couldn't believe the cost of baby clothes. It didn't help that some magazine editors were slow in paying her for the aviation articles she wrote. Mostly, though, she was mourning what she was missing in the sky: a new

Travel Air plane that Walter Beech promised was "the fastest thing on wheels" and the air races that summer. Thaden was grounded.

"Gosh, I'm anxious to fly," she said. "My hand itches something awful."

The baby came early, at the end of July. And the blue-eyed boy—six pounds and eleven ounces—was so beautiful, so perfect, that he changed everything for Thaden. Neither his wailing nor his crying bothered her.

"He's just impatient to fly," she joked at the hospital. "That's all."

12

Mr. Putnam and Me

I HAVE BEEN HAVING a lovely time here, flying a great deal."
Earhart's reports home to Medford in late 1929 revealed a life decidedly different than the one Thaden was leading in Pittsburgh. Earhart was thirty-two, eight years older than Thaden, still unmarried but seemingly as happy as she had ever been. That fall, she was darting back and forth between Los Angeles and New York, breaking Thaden's speed record on the West Coast and filing articles for *Cosmopolitan* in the East—enjoying the former, not the latter. The day she broke Thaden's record that November—topping it by twenty-eight miles per hour—Earhart wrote to her mother from California that she wished she didn't have to return to New York. Yet she was too busy to avoid it. Earhart was working not only for *Cosmo* but for a new airline and soon for a third outfit, flying passengers between Philadelphia and Washington, DC. The jobs at the airlines didn't include actual flying. Female pilots—even Earhart—need not apply. Her role with the airlines was mostly for publicity purposes. Wherever Earhart went, reporters followed, stumbling over one another in her wake and pestering her mother back in Medford for scoops. Briefly, after the success of her *Friendship* flight in June 1928, Earhart had turned to her fiancé, Sam Chapman, for help, assigning him to protect her family from the press. "Don't worry," Earhart told her mother, "but be careful about seeing people without Sam." Yet by the fall of that year, the engagement was off, and even before that, Earhart was directing her mother to call an-

other man in case of trouble. "When and if reporters come to you," she said, "please refer them to Mr. Putnam."

George Putnam, the New York publisher, influenced almost everything Earhart touched: her jobs, her speaking engagements, and her way of approaching both. For Putnam, no detail was too small to escape notice, and he couldn't stop himself from mentioning these details to Earhart in preachy comments, his letters strewn with exclamation points. He weighed in on what she wore. "Your hats!" he said once. "They are a public menace." He reportedly didn't care for the gap between her two front teeth. "That's why he makes me practice smiling with my lips closed," Earhart told another female flier. Putnam, a decade older than Earhart, especially liked to give her detailed instructions on what he called her "forthcoming platform appearances"—her speeches.

"You are apt to take less time than you think you will take," he told her. Given that, Putnam said, she should have an outline and a pointer—"Get a pointer!"—to help her refer to the photographic slides that accompanied her talks. With the pointer in hand, she would have a tendency to turn her back on the audience. Don't do that, Putnam said. She might also be tempted to speak while away from the microphone. Don't do that either, he told her. "Remember too," he said, "your tendency is to let your voice drop at the end of sentences." She needed to avoid that, Putnam said, and instead speak clearly and end her speech on time because, as everyone knew, the worst kind of talk was a bad talk from a quiet speaker that ran long.

At least a few of the female fliers didn't like him, a feeling that some dismissed as jealousy. They were jealous that Putnam had chosen Earhart for transatlantic glory, not them. Jealous that Putnam was publishing Earhart's book, not theirs. Jealous that Putnam, a powerful man, dark-eyed and handsome, who wore fine suits and had that estate in Rye, would do anything for Earhart—not them.

But perhaps most telling about his character, Thaden wasn't fond of him. She thought him a snob and a schemer, full of naked ambition and willing to do anything to further his own agenda. Thaden worried about his honesty—or lack thereof—and didn't like how he seemed to bask in Earhart's glow, like a moon to her sun, apparently unaware of the difference between the two of them, especially after Earhart's transatlantic feat. "You would think *he* had made the flight," Thaden said. Worst of all, she thought he took a dim view of the other flying women. "Everyone," Thaden said, "except Amelia."

But even Putnam's critics had to admit that he was effective. At Denison House in Boston, Earhart had made about thirty-five dollars a week. Now, the women pilots figured, Earhart was making almost fifteen times that—$500 a week. Even though their envy led them to overestimate and her income was likely lower than they thought, the reality was the same: Earhart was earning more than Thaden, who was pregnant and unemployed in the summer of 1930, and more than Nichols, who was bouncing checks despite her family's perceived riches. In choosing her to fly across the Atlantic and in grooming her to be a spokeswoman extraordinaire, Putnam had created a woman who had many options at a time when most women had few. Earhart paid off the mortgage on her father's home in California. She loaned money to her sister and helped her mother, too, until it became a regular arrangement. "I am enclosing a check for $100," she wrote in early 1930. "Hereafter you will receive it monthly from the Fifth Avenue Bank." While Thaden was living on credit, Earhart was doling out cash. The generosity wasn't for show; it was part of Earhart's character. After the *Friendship* flight, she had agreed to endorse a cigarette brand even though she didn't smoke and knew she would face criticism for her decision. Earhart did it just so she could give the $1,500 endorsement fee to one of the financial backers who had put her across the ocean. There was also little difficulty in what Earhart was doing— and she must have known that too. Writing articles, giving speeches, and listening to Putnam—who was always on her about something— was work, yes. At times, Thaden thought her friend looked exhausted. "Literally gray with fatigue," Thaden told others. But the lecture tours allowed Earhart to do what she loved most: fly. And so off she went in 1930, to Baltimore and St. Louis and beyond, giving the same speech again and again and winning legions of fans along the way.

People of all ages wrote in to newspapers asking how to contact this woman. With the address out there, letters poured in; at times, there were two hundred in a single day. And while she now had a secretary to help answer them, Earhart was forced to address one question personally. People—specifically, the press—wanted to know what was going on between her and George Putnam.

Putnam's wife of eighteen years and the mother of his two boys had filed for divorce over the winter. The official reason: desertion and failure to provide. But among friends, Dorothy Binney Putnam gave a different explanation. "He doesn't need me anymore," she said, packing up her things during a party that Earhart was attending at their home in Rye. The implication was clear. He had Earhart now. The divorce was big news in New York for all the usual reasons: scandal, schadenfreude, and speculation. People wanted to know if Putnam and Earhart were getting married and, if so, when.

Earhart — a media pro at this point — publicly denied everything throughout 1930. "If I were to become engaged or married to anyone," she said, "I should certainly make no mystery of it." Anyway, she wasn't the marrying type. In her personal writings, she had compared marriage to a "plain devoid of vegetation." "To gain the ultimate," she said, "ye throws away life." But now she was conflicted and careful not to concede there was truth in the rumors. Putnam was pushing Earhart hard for marriage, hammering away at her resistance with pleas, proposals, and what one reporter called "cave-man expedients." That November, still nursing her doubts, Earhart boarded a train for Stonington, Connecticut. Putnam met her at the platform and they drove to his mother's house, the Putnam summer estate on the shores of Long Island Sound. Then, a short time later, moving like shadows through the town hall, they applied for a marriage license. The license wasn't marriage itself, but nothing could indicate more strongly that a wedding might be in the offing, and by morning it was front-page news. Putnam quite possibly leaked it to the press himself, forcing Earhart's hand and the question into the open.

Was she really getting married?

"I can't be any more definite than to say that I probably will be married in the next 50 years," Earhart replied. "I'll allow myself that much time."

Was she marrying Putnam?

"I might. But a great many things can happen in 50 years."

Did she know he had obtained the license?

"Let's not answer that," she said.

Putnam was fielding the same questions but in an altogether different manner — with his usual bluster and confidence. He promised to notify the press "when and if" he and Earhart got married. Which would probably be soon. "I've always been partial to the morning papers," he said. "Yes, I'll even promise to get married in time for the first edition."

Earhart was under pressure, "extreme pressure," she confessed to Thaden one night in a hotel stop between flights somewhere along the road that year. Putnam wasn't framing this as love, Earhart said, but as an obligation. Earhart owed him. Unsure what to do, she sought counsel from at least two other people: C. B. Allen, aviation editor of the *New York World Telegram,* and Deacon Lyman, aviation editor of the *New York Times.* "I need some advice badly," she told Allen on the phone one day, "and I need it today, if possible." She summoned Allen to her hotel suite in Manhattan and asked him to bring Lyman. When she greeted the two editors at her door a short while later, she got straight to the point. "It's about Mr. Putnam and me," Earhart said. Should she marry him? "I owe him a lot," Earhart admitted, "and would like to repay him in some way for his help and kindness."

Allen and Lyman stared at her in silence — "mutual disbelief," Allen said later. Only Earhart could say whether she should marry Putnam. "That, I am afraid, is the only answer I can give you," Allen told her when he finally found words. But there was no doubting the role that Putnam had played in crafting the Amelia Earhart brand and no doubting the role he could continue to play if they remained partners. That summer, he had sold his stake in the family's publishing business and left G. P. Putnam's Sons. But he still had the family name — and its connections. "Mr. Putnam is clearly a good promoter," Allen told Earhart. "It may be that you need him as much or more than he needs you."

Lyman agreed, and Earhart thanked them for their input. On February 7, 1931, she finally put the question to rest, marrying Putnam in a private five-minute ceremony in his mother's home that was witnessed by not a single member of her family. Her father had died the previous fall. Her mother was opposed to Amelia marrying a man a decade older than her — and divorced. And her sister was home in Medford that day, tasked by Amelia with a difficult job. "Break the news gently to Mother," Amelia instructed her. None of them got to see Amelia standing before the fireplace, the warm flames aflicker, wearing a brown suit over a tan blouse — no bridal gown, no wedding party.

Even Earhart herself seemed only half in, writing a letter to Putnam just before the ceremony. "Dear GPP," it began.

> There are some things that should be writ before we are married — things we have talked over before — most of them. You must know again my reluctance to marry, my feeling that I thereby shatter chances in work which means most to me. I feel the move just now as foolish as anything I could do. I know there may be compensations but have no heart to look ahead.
>
> In our life together I want you to understand I shall not hold you to any medieval code of faithfulness to me, nor shall I consider myself bound to you similarly. If we can be honest I think the difficulties which arise may best be avoided should you or I become interested deeply (or in passing) in anyone else.
>
> Please let us not interfere with the other's work or play, nor let the world see our private joys or disagreements. In this connection I may have to keep some place where I can go to be myself, now and then, for I cannot guarantee to endure at all times the confinement of even an attractive cage.
>
> I must exact a cruel promise, and this is you will let me go in a year if we find no happiness together.
>
> I will do my best in every way and give you that part of me you know and seem to want.

She signed it, simply, *A.E.* The bride was keeping her name.

13

Law of Fate

RUTH NICHOLS SAW her chance. While Thaden was raising a baby and Earhart was making headlines by avoiding getting married—then by actually getting married—Nichols was planning to shock the world. She was going to be the first woman to really fly across the Atlantic, a female flier in full control of her own plane traveling over the ocean. Unlike Earhart, Nichols was going alone.

She had been thinking about it for at least four years, mulling it over in her usual Nichols fashion: careful and meticulous and, for a long time, patient. "Of course, I'll go," she told people, "whenever I get a good ship." She watched from her parents' home in Rye as Ruth Elder tried and failed, as Frances Grayson tried and vanished, and as her neighbor George Putnam arranged to have Stultz and Gordon ferry Earhart across the Atlantic in June 1928—bold headlines, big news, and grand parades for Earhart. Since then, only one other woman—a Clevelander, licensed pilot, and young widow named Beryl Hart—had tried to cross the ocean by plane, hopping over with scheduled stops in Bermuda and the Azores. But like Earhart, Hart was just cargo; a military pilot was doing the flying. And like Grayson, Hart disappeared somewhere over the ocean, never to be seen again. Still, Nichols was determined to go, clipping articles about ocean-air travel out of the newspapers and making a detailed list of why it was so important for a woman to make such a flight—a solo flight.

"OBJECT," she wrote, typing out her plans. "To show that a trans-Atlantic or Around-the-World Flight can be made commercially safe.

"TIME: To be stated as soon as the equipment can be purchased.

"CREW: Miss Nichols, as organizer and pilot of the ship."

It was, for Nichols, about proving a point — and also about prestige. Not money, exactly. But in order to make a case for the flight to investors, Nichols calculated the financial windfall that could be reaped by getting a woman — her — over the ocean. Book deal: $7,500. Endorsement deals: $10,000. Newspaper and magazine contracts: $15,000. Lecture tour: $23,000. And, of course, a motion-picture contract worth, Nichols estimated, $100,000. The gross total exceeded $160,000, more than double the cost of the proposed flight. Nichols would get a small cut of the profits, "to be arranged," she said, "with backers." But the fame as a real flier would be all hers.

She had begun seeking backers in January 1928, at least four months before George Putnam had ever heard of Amelia Earhart and six months before Earhart became a household name. But without a man like Putnam in her corner, Nichols struggled to make a convincing argument, getting denied by potential backers again and again. "Personally," one wrote in rejecting her idea in early 1928, "I do not feel, at the moment at least, that I want to send any one, either man or woman, for a flight across the Atlantic." Others felt the same and also turned Nichols away. Then Earhart's flight that June, her book about it three months later, and the stock-market crash of October 1929 all combined to make Nichols's ocean-flight proposal even less appealing. Like the animals mounted on the walls of her parents' mansion in Rye, Nichols's flight plan was dead and gathering dust by the spring of 1930. Businessmen, worried about the coming Depression, were looking to save money, not spend it. Most businessmen, that is.

In Cincinnati, radio magnate Powel Crosley Jr. couldn't stop himself. He wanted a plane, and a fast one — a Lockheed. He purchased it that summer for $15,000 and then paid an additional $10,000 for modifications. The plane, dubbed the *New Cincinnati*, would help make the Crosley name famous, he figured — or, to be accurate, more famous. In 1930, Crosley's radio station, WLW, was one of the nation's largest broadcasters, with a signal covering an area almost twice the size of Texas. Listeners almost everywhere east of the Mississippi River tuned in to WLW for the *Crosley Homemak-*

ers' Hour, Crosley Saturday Knights, and, at times, Crosley himself. He was forty-four, tall and lanky, and proud of his new plane, which was bright red, could seat seven, and was able to reach Indianapolis in a swift forty-three minutes. Nichols just had to speak with him about it, pressing her case in a chance meeting on the ground in Cincinnati in October 1930.

She was in the market for a Lockheed, believing she could use it to break Earhart's speed record—and perhaps cross the ocean—if only someone would trust her with such a machine. "Have had eight years flying experience," she said, ticking off her bona fides to potential backers. "Last year solo toured in 46 states without a scratch . . .Would very much like to pick up your ship on my way east."

Crosley, sensing the potential of his name next to hers, their names in the papers, agreed to let her borrow his plane. After years of waiting and watching—passed by, overlooked, and underestimated—Nichols, about to celebrate her thirtieth birthday, finally had a plane capable of setting records like Earhart and Thaden. On November 19, 1930, one week before Thanksgiving, she climbed into Crosley's plane, left Cincinnati, and headed home to New York. The Lockheed's engine was so powerful that Nichols felt like it might jump right out of the nose of the plane, and the modern instrument panel before her was unfamiliar and complicated. But it was a clear day, and Nichols felt good—at least until she ran into the wall of fog five thousand feet high across the Pennsylvania state line, in the Allegheny Mountains. Unable to navigate below it and unwilling to turn around or go through it for fear of plowing into a hidden mountain, Nichols had only one option: a forced landing—in Crosley's brand-new plane. She came down in a rocky field, plunged the plane through a wire fence, and drove the propeller into the hard ground, where it came to a stop. Nichols was alive and uninjured but, as she saw it, an idiot. "What would Powel Crosley think of me?" she wondered.

Once again, she was walking away from a busted plane in search of help, a telephone. At least this time, she didn't have to go far. She had landed in the tiny settlement of Manns Choice, Pennsylvania—a name so ironic that reporters writing about Nichols's crackup couldn't resist a dig. They called it Man's Choice. Nichols found a general store, walked to the old-fashioned crank telephone on the wall, and called the only person she knew within a hundred miles of the godforsaken place: Louise Thaden, at home in Pittsburgh with her baby son, Bill.

"Where are you?" Thaden asked. "I'll come and get you."

Nichols tried to talk her out of it, but Thaden wouldn't listen. She put Nichols up for the night at her home in Pittsburgh, drove her back to Manns Choice a day later, and stayed with her there overnight until her plane was fixed. By that Saturday, three days after the forced landing, hundreds of people from neighboring Appalachian communities were there to catch a glimpse of the women pilots and the plane. It was as if a red spaceship had landed in the rocky field—a spaceship that the forgiving Crosley was allowing Nichols to keep flying. She got off the ground that morning with a wide-eyed crowd and a nervous Thaden looking on. Then, with the forced landing behind her, Nichols was soon flying into the headlines of American newspapers from coast to coast.

In early December 1930, less than two weeks after the circus in Manns Choice, Nichols set a transcontinental speed record, flying from New York to Los Angeles with four overnight stops but a total elapsed flying time of just sixteen hours and fifty-nine and a half minutes—almost nine hours faster than any other woman had previously flown and the second-fastest east-to-west cross-country trip ever completed. Unsatisfied, Nichols turned around, flew back east, and set another record going in that direction—thirteen hours and twenty-two minutes, almost an hour and a half shorter than Lindbergh's fastest transcontinental trip. Crosley was thrilled—and Nichols wasn't finished. A few months later, in March 1931, she climbed back into the red Lockheed on the ground in New Jersey, wearing a green skirt, four sweaters, a plaid scarf, a fur-lined flying suit made of reindeer skin, and tall reindeer boots to match. "The total effect," one witness noted, "was that of a well-padded Eskimo." Not exactly a flattering look. But Nichols didn't care. Weathering temperatures of minus-forty degrees and hundred-mile-an-hour winds that blew her out to sea, Nichols flew nearly six miles into the sky, 28,743 feet—yet another female record. A month later, in Detroit, she claimed one more record: speed. Nichols flew at a sustained 210 miles an hour, almost thirty miles an hour faster than the record Earhart had set in Los Angeles. In the span of just five months, she had proven herself to be arguably the fastest, bravest, and strongest female flier in America, with the best plane — and suddenly people knew it, sending letters to Rye to tell Nichols as much.

From the Crosley Radio Corporation: "What a gal — what a plane — what a record! Congratulations." From George Putnam's ex-wife, Dorothy, already remarried and keenly following the women in the sky: "Hurray . . . You are doing marvelous things. Keep it up." Old friends got in touch with her. New friends heaped praise on her. A gracious Earhart sent Nichols roses, and total strangers sent questions about everything, including the color of the sky when seen from so high in the heavens. Was it dark blue? Indigo, ultramarine, or cobalt? Or was it lighter? Pale blue or perhaps green? By April, after shattering Earhart's speed record in Detroit, Nichols struggled to respond to them all. But she took great care in replying personally to one particular demographic: young girls. June Thames, age eleven, in Brewton, Alabama, whose father had died when she was two and who wore her light brown hair short, wanted Nichols to know everything about her. "My best sports are football, baseball, basketball, tennis and golf." Frances Gunn, age thirteen, in Sanford, North Carolina, told Nichols she hoped to grow up to be just like her. "Many people think I'm a boy," she wrote, "but I'm a girl — a tomboy." Nellie Boich, age twelve, in Bisbee, Arizona, wrote Nichols to let her know she needed help. "Please write and tell me you will be my friend . . . P.S.: Don't forget to write."

Nichols didn't forget. She sent them autographs and advice. She was especially worried about young Nellie in Arizona. "If you are in any sort of trouble," Nichols told her, "I would suggest that you get in touch with a minister or a priest in your own town, as I am afraid I am too far away to be of any help."

Farther away than anyone even knew. In the spring of 1931, Crosley agreed to let Nichols fly his plane in one more feat, one more challenge — the test that Nichols cherished most. She was going solo across the Atlantic.

FULL SECRECY, NICHOLS THOUGHT, was the key to transatlantic success.

"I want to keep the matter entirely confidential," she told a close friend that spring. If news of her plans leaked, other women might try to beat her to Paris. "So, please," she urged the people closest to her, "not a word of it." Nichols wasn't even telling her family about her plans for now, and she wasn't opposed to enforcing other measures to keep these plans under wraps. "As a matter of fact," she told one friend, "it might be well for you to destroy this letter."

There was much work to do, starting with fund-raising. Flying Crosley's red Lockheed cost Nichols about a thousand dollars a month in gas, oil, mechanics' fees, and insurance. Getting to Europe was going to cost twenty times that—or more. Nichols needed cash, and in March, shortly after setting the altitude record, she began raising it, starting with people she knew: moneyed New Yorkers, Wellesley College faculty, fellow pilots, and the same air-minded benefactors who had helped Earhart three years earlier.

"It's been a long time since *Friendship* days," Nichols wrote to one man who had helped Earhart, "but I still feel you must have a corner in your heart for aviation. If so, would you be willing to loan me $10,000 to attain my life-long dream? You know well, for how many years, I have wanted to make an Atlantic hop, and now it really seems as though the door were to be opened."

She had the Lockheed retrofitted for a supercharged 650-horsepower engine that would give her a cruising speed of two hundred miles an hour. She had the support of prominent male fliers, including her old instructor Harry Rogers; the winner of the doomed 1927 Dole Air Race to Hawaii, Arthur Goebel; and, most important, the second man to ever fly the Atlantic, Clarence Chamberlin, who was personally helping Nichols prepare in New Jersey. "All feel I am capable of making a flight from Newfoundland to Ireland or France," Nichols said, "if the winds are favorable." Nichols, flush with recent success, was sure they would be. "There is no possibility of failure," she told potential investors, "except the usual law of Fate, which we meet every day of our lives."

It was a difficult time to be asking for money. The nation was in the grip of an unemployment panic, with jobless rolls in major cities up 150 percent in the past year and an estimated six million Americans out of work. In New York, Cleveland, Detroit, and Chicago, roughly one-tenth of the population was unemployed and not likely to find a job anytime soon. Angry mobs stormed town halls, fighting government officials and one another. Flophouses, which offered beds for twenty-five cents a night, were filled and to be avoided in any case. Those forced to stay there often slept with their shoes tucked under their heads; it was the only way to prevent thieves from taking them. But there was no way to dodge the flophouse filth or their measles out-breaks, both of which pushed the homeless population outside into the new tent cities popping up across America. Here, people slept on cardboard boxes and abandoned seat cushions. They huddled around open fires at night and sought out the bread lines by day, tramping down the road in bedraggled bunches. "We walk up here from Steel-town every day for these breakfasts and suppers," said one desperate man in central Pennsylvania. "If we didn't, we would have nothing to eat."

It was a testament to Nichols and her skills as a pilot that, despite these realities, money began rolling in: $5,000 from Paramount Pic-tures; $5,000 from Columbia Broadcasting; $3,000 from her brother; $1,600 from one of Ruth Elder's former sponsors; and $1,000 from Crosley. Including the personal loan she secured at the bank for $4,500, Nichols had soon amassed enough cash to make the trip possible. But in order to pay off the loans — from the bank and from her friends and family — Nichols needed to make money too. To do this, she needed someone who knew how to organize the business end of such a flight, someone who had helped put a woman over the ocean before, some-one who, in fact, had discovered this woman himself, plucking her from a settlement house in Boston and hand-delivering her to George Putnam. Nichols turned to Hilton Railey.

"Early in May," Nichols told Railey, "I am determined to attempt a flight from St. John's, Newfoundland, to Europe, with Paris as my ac-tual objective." She wasn't seeking his advice. "My decision to make this flight is absolutely definite." She just wanted to hire him.

Railey didn't want the job. In multiple meetings at his office on West Forty-Fifth Street in Manhattan, he resisted Nichols's proposal for all the usual reasons: it was too dangerous. She probably wouldn't make it. Railey didn't want her blood on his hands — the blood of an-other woman sacrificed to the god of the sea. Nichols was infuriated, almost offended, by his explanations. Finally, pacing in Railey's office one day that spring, she snapped.

"All right," Nichols said. "Don't help me."

She understood what was happening here. "If I were a man, you'd help me," Nichols said. "But because I'm a girl, you turn me down.

You're, you're" — she was stuttering now, trying to find the right insult for Railey — "you're mid-Victorian," she said.

As insults went, it was flimsy, and Nichols knew it. But it was out there now, and she let it sink in, staring down Railey. In the end, she told him, it didn't really matter what he thought or said. "I'll sell my car," she told him, "and everything I've got to make this flight possible." She was going across the ocean. "Whether you help me or not, I'm going to make this flight."

Railey, admiring her persistence, couldn't refuse her now. To protect himself in case of calamity, he put his objections in writing, and Nichols acknowledged receipt. If something were to happen to her, the world would know that it wasn't Railey's fault. It wasn't a man pushing a woman onto a plane for a story. It was the woman's idea, Nichols. But he'd take the job — for $13,500. "Since I have not been able to dissuade you from the attempt," Railey told her, "I very earnestly want to help you."

He estimated that she stood to make $215,000 from the flight — a life-changing amount of money, given the jobless masses huddled in the streets outside and the dwindling Nichols's family fortunes, hard hit by the worsening Depression. Within just two weeks, Railey was making good on his promises. He secured her a book deal, two magazine contracts, and an endorsement from a milk company. Just as important, Railey was gathering intelligence on other female aviators who might be considering a solo transatlantic flight that spring and passing it along to Nichols. Most notably, thanks to his relationship with Putnam, Railey knew exactly what was happening with Earhart. Newly married, she was briefly hospitalized that month for a minor procedure, likely to address a sinus problem that Earhart had lived with for years. Bottom line, Railey reported, Earhart was going nowhere. "Definitely not to be considered." Nichols's biggest problem with Earhart, Railey believed, was going to be Earhart's pride. By the end of April, Nichols's proposed flight was probably the worst-kept secret in New York. Earhart had learned of it and was understandably disappointed that it was Nichols, not her, making the first female solo flight across the ocean. But Railey didn't want Nichols to worry about it. "I do not think that Earhart is anything but disappointed in a mild way," he told her. "The best thing to do about this matter is to regard it as a closed issue."

They had a bigger problem on their hands: the newspaper reporters. They were running stories now of Nichols's plans, requesting interviews and trying to find her. "It will be difficult to avoid them," Railey told Nichols. He advised her to make a statement confirming the flight. "And let it go at that." But it wasn't that simple. With the news out there, everyone that spring wanted a piece of Ruth Nichols — a photo for an advertisement, a quote for a story, a moment of her time to make a bold request. "If you consider taking anyone on your proposed flight," a woman in Illinois wrote to her in late April, "would you PLEASE take me?" At least half a dozen other people, all strangers, made the same request. Others sent her personal items — crucifixes, rabbit's feet, and Saint Christopher medals — hoping they would ward off evil winds. One person even offered to send a Boston terrier for her to take to Paris as a mascot. "I have a hunch," the breeder said, "that he will bring you good luck."

Nichols turned them all down, even mailing back the medals and charms. She was trying to focus on the flight itself. Nichols met regularly with transatlantic flier Clarence Chamberlin, who was directing the overhaul of Crosley's plane in New Jersey. She took notes on blind navigation, ran calculations figuring speed and time, and made a list of everything she needed to bring with her.

She had maps of every state in New England, plus Nova Scotia, Newfoundland, and Ireland. She had charts of the stars, the ocean, the moon, and British lighthouses. She knew which way the steamers were going, what they looked like, and what she would eat when she was hungry. She was packing three Thermoses of coffee and soup, plus an emergency knapsack that held six chocolate bars, six packs of gum, two cans of food rations, two fishing lines and hooks, one Bible, one magazine, one pistol, and twelve bullets. Not that she was going to need it. Nichols was packing for Paris too. Amid the tools, equipment, and atlases, she stashed away four hats, four dresses, three pairs of shoes, two different styles of bedroom slippers, and one special item: "Evening in Paris perfume." She made a neat little checkmark next to it on her master list and prepared to leave any day.

"I'll see you on the other side!" she told Railey.

RAILEY SAILED TO EUROPE by steamship on the last day of April. He wanted to be there to greet Nichols when she arrived in France and organize a welcome of Earhartian proportions. Once in Paris, he checked in to a hotel near the Louvre and went to work, securing permissions for Nichols to land, making plans for her to visit the House of Commons in London, managing the press buildup in Paris, and supervising the Paramount camera crew that would film her triumphant arrival. By May 22, everything was in place. "Please advise Miss Nichols," Railey wired his New York office in a coded message, "that we are all set at London and Paris." Then, in his hotel near the banks of the Seine, he waited—and waited.

Back home, the Crosley plane was ready and more beautiful than ever. Nichols hadn't just overhauled the engine and removed the passenger seats to prepare for the flight; she had redecorated. The Lockheed was no longer red, like the Cincinnati baseball team that Powel Crosley would soon purchase, but white with golden wings, and it had a new name dreamed up by Nichols painted across the nose: *Akita*. It was a Dakota Indian word, Nichols explained, that meant "to search, discover or explore." For the moment, however, she was doing none of the above. She was slowed by all the usual delays—test flights, plane-weight problems, bad weather, and then, on June 18, landing-gear failures—which pushed her back for a few more days, maybe a week.

Across the ocean, Railey was growing impatient and, to be blunt, going broke. He had never intended to spend six weeks just sitting in Paris. "The days into weeks," he said, "the weeks into months." He wasn't upset just for his own sake; the lost time was hurting the operation too. Despite his early successes in whipping up excitement for Nichols's flight—the book deal and the endorsements—Railey was forced to admit that with all the delays, prospects weren't looking as great as he had hoped. "In New York," he griped, "one reverse has followed another—cancelled contracts, frozen collections, the utter failure of new business to materialize." Nichols needed to get to Paris and soon, as far as Railey was concerned. At the same time, others around her tried to talk her out of making the flight at all.

The US Weather Bureau was opposed to her flight, in part because Nichols was a woman. "It looks to us," one top meteorologist said, "like personal or sex competition." Nichols's brother, a navy pilot, was worried too, asking her to take more time to prepare. "Might mean your success," he told her, "even though a slight delay." Even fellow members of the Ninety-Nines begged Nichols not to fly across the ocean.

"I guess the reason we don't want you to try is that we know there is no in between," female pilot Mildred Morgan told Nichols while Nichols waited out the delays that spring at a new airfield in Brooklyn. "You will either make it, or you won't. And what in the world is there, anyway, that is worth taking that chance for?"

But Morgan knew there was no stopping Nichols.

"Go to it, if you feel that you must," she said. "But remember that if you do, and when you do, every girl flier in the country will be praying for you every minute of the way. None of us will sleep a wink until we know that you are safe across—and the most famous woman in the world."

On the morning of June 22, Nichols awoke in her room at the Commodore Hotel near the beach in Rockaway, Queens. As soon as she got word that the *Akita* was ready, its landing gear fixed, she reported to hangar no. 6 at the airport in Brooklyn, arriving just after midday. It was hot and cloudy. The city was in the throes of a heat wave, with sidewalks buckling in Manhattan and massive crowds flocking to the beach at Coney Island a few miles to the east. But the weather was clear up the coast all the way to Saint John, New Brunswick, where Nichols planned to spend the night. There was no point in another test flight.

"It is time," Nichols said, "that I got going."

For the long flight across the ocean, Nichols planned to wear a lavender flying suit—a splashy getup, both functional and fashionable. But for the short hop to New Brunswick, she put on a knit sport outfit and, casual and calm, walked toward the gold-winged *Akita* as if she were going on a Sunday drive in the Hamptons. Her mother handed her a bouquet of flowers picked from the family garden in Rye. Nichols climbed into the cockpit, tested the engine, opened the throttle wide, and then, after pronouncing the motor good, waited while a team of mechanics and bystanders pushed the plane to the north end of the runway.

In her preparations for the flight, Nichols, rediscovering her Quaker roots, had scrawled Bible passages in a personal notebook. Psalm 23: "The Lord is my shepherd, I shall not want." John, chapter 14: "If ye shall ask anything in my name, I will do it." And Psalm 121: "The sun shall not smite thee by day, nor the moon by night." Now, with no time left for prayers, Nichols hit the throttle; the propeller spun up, and the *Akita* started to roll—fifteen seconds down the runway, gaining speed, then up into the sky over New York. Nichols briefly flew south over the water before making a steady 180-degree turn and pointing the *Akita* north. She was on her way, flanked by a squadron of US Navy Helldivers that were accompanying her in a grand show at least as far as Connecticut.

The flight up the coast was uneventful, as easy as Nichols thought it would be, and by sundown she spied the tiny airfield in New Brunswick where she planned to stop for the night. It didn't look good. Instead of an expansive field, wide and open, it was more like a small bowl—"a veritable trap," she thought—dropped into a valley in the middle of the hilly Canadian woods. Believing she must be mistaken, that this couldn't be New Brunswick, she circled the airfield twice, checking her maps. But no, this was it. Despite years, months, and weeks to plan, she and her team of consultants had failed to properly investigate the very first stop on the journey, this trap of a runway in the woods. Now it was too late. With the sun in her eyes, photographers waiting on the ground, and darkness coming soon, Nichols decided to land.

She came in fast, at eighty miles an hour, half blinded by the sun. Unable to get a clear view of the runway below, Nichols missed her mark, touching down not at the start of the runway, but in the middle. Realizing now that she wouldn't have enough time to stop the plane before it barreled into the craggy rocks at the runway's edge, Nichols hit the throttle, trying to take off again. And for a moment, it looked like she would succeed. With the *Akita*'s engine shrieking and its tires squealing, Nichols lifted the plane off the runway just before the landing strip came to an end. She was in the air again, but only a few feet up, and still so low that the plane's propeller skimmed the ground, mowing a path through the brush. There was not enough time. There was not enough space. The *Akita* was heading for a rocky ledge, and Nichols braced herself for the inevitable: a crash.

The rocks ripped away the wooden undercarriage of the plane, shattering it like a matchbox. The engine broke apart, the cockpit splintered, and the *Akita* stopped dead in the waist-high bushes, jerking Nichols's body forward with such force that she felt as if the plane's tail were on top of her. People on the ground waited for an explosion; Nichols did too.

Get out, she told herself. *Get out.*

Wincing in pain, she climbed through the jagged wreckage and fell to the ground—free, apparently safe, and suddenly aware she was not alone.

A photographer was already upon her, snapping pictures. Then a half a dozen other men with pickaxes and fire extinguishers arrived. But they found no one to save, no fire to put out, no explosion coming. Just an injured pilot standing there with a request for her would-be rescuers.

"Wire," she said, "for another plane."

IT WAS, FOR NICHOLS, wishful thinking, spoken in a flood of adrenaline. There was no other plane, no other chance, and no way she was going anywhere anytime soon. In the crash, she had broken at least two vertebrae in her back. Doctors at a local hospital in New Brunswick said she could expect to spend the next six to eight weeks in a plaster cast in bed. As terrible as that sounded, it was better, at least, than the alternatives. Nichols was fortunate not to be paralyzed—or worse. "How did she ever come out of it alive?" Nichols's consultant Clarence Chamberlin asked when he finally got a chance to survey the airfield and her busted plane on the edge of it. Even under the best conditions, Chamberlin figured, it would be hard for any pilot to land a fast plane at that little field in the bowl. The sunlight at that time of day had made it even more difficult for Nichols, ending her transatlantic dream before it even started. "It looks as though it's all off now," Chamberlin said.

He had the *Akita* dismantled, piece by piece, and shipped by boat to Detroit, where maybe, with insurance money, Nichols could pay to have it rebuilt. But gone was the book deal. Gone were the magazine contracts. Gone were the endorsements, the lecture tours, the motion-picture plans, and promises of big money—$215,000. At this point, Nichols would be lucky just to pay off her loans.

In the crash, she'd lost everything.

14

Give a Girl Credit

CLIFF HENDERSON HAD a different problem: new money — and lots of it. He rolled down the streets of troubled American cities in 1930 in the back of a limousine, a portrait of wealth in a time when most had none. Thanks to his air-race mastery and big-tent showmanship in Los Angeles and Cleveland, Henderson was making almost nineteen thousand dollars a year — the equivalent today of roughly a quarter of a million dollars. In addition to the limousine, he had a personal driver, memberships to exclusive clubs, enough money to maintain a house for his dead wife's mother in Los Angeles, and a flashy car that he drove himself whenever his chauffeur wasn't on hand. His brand-new 1929 Cord coupe was one of the hottest automobiles in America, with a striking forty-six-inch hood and a powerful eight-cylinder engine vibrating underneath. It was painted pearl white, adorned with red wheels, and equipped with a siren Henderson could use whenever he pleased. But the Cord, which cost more than most people made in a year, wasn't a luxury, Henderson told people. It was a necessity; every turn of the wheels was an advertisement for him, Cliff Henderson, and his air races, big in Cleveland in 1929 and promising to be even bigger in 1930. "The air race crowds will number at least 300,000 people," Henderson vowed that summer, "and many optimists believe it may reach one million at this year's event."

By "many optimists," he likely meant himself; *he* believed the crowds would top one million people. San Antonio and Miami, Detroit and Portland, all competed for the right to stage Henderson's national meet in 1930, but in the end, organizers chose Chicago. Henderson moved into the Hotel Sherman downtown, and began preparing to top himself yet again. In Cleveland, he'd boasted that fans saw a thousand airplanes in the sky. Now, in Chicago, he hoped to double that figure at a new airfield north of the city in leafy, suburban Glenview. Curtiss-Reynolds Airport, unveiled there in late 1929, had it all: a row of hangars capable of housing a hundred airships, an observation deck and promenade with a capacity for five thousand people, a flight school, and a restaurant. There were even plans for a hotel, giving locals reason to boast that Glenview had one of the most modern airports in the world.

Henderson planned to feature Earhart, Nichols, Thaden, and the other women at the races there that summer. But within weeks of Henderson breaking ground for a new grandstand at Curtiss-Reynolds field—he dragged the ceremonial plow behind a plane he piloted himself—the women were in full revolt. Earhart told Thaden she was furious about what she called "unauthorized promotion publicity." Henderson was using their names—"selfishly exploiting us," Earhart said—claiming they would be competing in the Powder Puff Derby again that year when, in fact, neither Earhart, nor Thaden, nor Nichols planned to participate. They were upset over rules that prevented women from competing in any race against men. They were also frustrated over new proposals requiring that a doctor and two US Army planes escort the women in the female derby across the country and about new restrictions limiting the power of their engines. "They naturally dislike the idea of going back to kindergarten," a race official said in a statement about the women. But the reason for the rule was simple. "Without power restrictions," officials noted, "the prettiest flier would probably get the biggest plane of the best manufacturer, and if her luck and her flying skill held out she would probably reach Chicago first." The implication: men with powerful planes had them because they knew what they were doing. Women with powerful planes had them because they knew how to flirt.

Earhart, in particular, was incensed. "Quite perturbed," Thaden told Nichols. The men were acting like they were taking care of the women—"we poor little women pilots," Thaden said—and soon Earhart, Thaden, Nichols, and other women of the Ninety-Nines made a decision. They wouldn't fly in the derby or in any other race Henderson was planning in Chicago. "Rather see no race," Earhart said, "than a poor one." They were out.

The races that August—for men and women both—went off as scheduled, boycott or not, attracting a crowd of forty thousand people on the first day and an estimated four hundred thousand more over the next week. It was well short of the million people that Henderson had suggested would attend, but thirty thousand cars filled the parking lot every day, another thirty-five thousand spilled into nearby neighborhoods, and the new grandstands were crammed with spectators. Here were heroic male aviators diving their red-winged planes from two thousand feet in the air and peeling away just before slamming into the ground. Here were the Lindberghs, Charles and Anne, escorted around the field by Henderson himself. Here were the races, including a new one: the Thompson Trophy race. In it, men whipped their planes around pylons placed across the field in a five-mile course, twenty laps, a total of one hundred miles, for a trophy made of marble, gold, and silver and a prize of $10,000, the largest sum ever posted for an airplane race.

Still, for all the crowds and attractions, the 1930 races made headlines mostly for one reason: flaming disasters. A well-known engineer who was trying to demonstrate the safety of an experimental plane went down in full view of the crowd, plunging into a cluster of parked airships. Rescuers sawed away a wing to free the man from the wreckage. But it was too late; the engineer was dead. A US Navy captain fared no better. He was winning the inaugural Thompson Trophy race, cruising to victory around the pylons in front of seventy thousand fans, when, for unknown reasons, the plane crashed, killing him. But the worst crash involved the spectators. A showboating airman inverted his plane as he crossed the finish line on day four of the races "as a salute to the crowd," one observer said. In doing so, he lost control. The plane cartwheeled into the ground and burst into flames, killing not only the pilot but a man working at a concession stand and injuring a dozen other people as plane parts flew like shrapnel and hot oil spewed everywhere.

It was like a bomb had fallen from the sky—not good for business. The races in Chicago barely broke even. And the prospects for 1931, with the event returning to Cleveland, looked even worse. Bread lines were growing, flophouses were full, and tent cities were becoming more common by the day. There was no spinning this. Henderson needed a new idea, more money for a different race, and something to distract from the disasters in the air as well as the ones on the ground, seemingly everywhere in 1930s America.

He needed Vincent Bendix.

THE HOUSE ON East Jefferson Boulevard in South Bend, Indiana, was so big that it had a name: Elm Court. The grounds, two miles south of the University of Notre Dame football stadium, encompassed twelve acres in all and featured an in-ground swimming pool —South Bend's first—as well as a three-hole pitch-and-putt golf course. But it was the structure itself, with multiple wings and a central courtyard laid out like a French palace, that made the estate notable. Visitors approached on a brick driveway, stepped out into the courtyard, and then walked through the main entrance, under a glass ceiling, into another world: three stories, thirty-four rooms, and fifteen fireplaces, all under a slate roof with copper fixtures. There was a smoking room with oak-paneled walls; a parlor with three chandeliers; two sunrooms, west and east, with limestone fixtures; a dining room with a marble fireplace; a freight elevator large enough to hold a car. And for guests, there was no reason to get up. Servants could be summoned to deliver drinks or food to almost every room using call buttons built into the wall.

But it wasn't enough for Vincent Bendix, a wealthy South Bend manufacturer of Swedish descent with dark eyes, meaty jowls, a big waist, and a rack of patents—reportedly 5,500 in all. Shortly after buying Elm Court in 1928, Bendix began making it bigger, better. He ripped out the swimming pool in the front of the house and replaced it with a new one out back, this one lined with aqua tile, decorated with ceramic crabs and fish, and illuminated by underwater electric lights. He added six more holes to the golf course. He built a bowling alley where a horse stable had once stood. And he hired crews to dig at least thirty feet beneath the main house to add what he felt the mansion really lacked: an air-conditioned ballroom with a bar. The bar was stocked with an illegal stash of booze locked up in a secret passageway, down yet another flight of stairs, and through at least three heavy doors—a level of detail that revealed something important about the man and his desires. Bendix—once described as a "round, roly-poly, humorous looking Swede"—was serious about a few things: his work, his drink, and his parties, the last of which were legendary in South Bend. Rumors said champagne laced with cocaine flowed from the fountains at the mansion, and it hardly mattered whether or not the stories were true. People in town knew that anything was possible at the house on East Jefferson Boulevard. But they weren't to call it Elm Court anymore. After Bendix bought it, he changed that too, giving the estate a name he thought more fitting: Chateau Bendix.

It was a mansion almost entirely for entertaining. Bendix spent most nights back in Chicago, where he lived with his wife in another famous and equally opulent home, the Palmer House on Lake Shore Drive. But his factory, churning out parts for cars and planes, was located in South Bend, and the business was Depression-proof, or so it seemed at the time. Bendix stock prices increased by 1,600 percent between 1924 and 1929, and even with the value falling in early 1931—plummeting from $120 a share to about twenty dollars a share in the span of just two years—his products were in high demand. Manufacturers couldn't build cars or planes without his drive belts or brakes. People speculated that Bendix, despite everything, was still on track to become the wealthiest man in Chicago.

His days often began with a deep massage from a hulking Norwegian. As the masseur went to work kneading Bendix's fleshy body in the morning light of his bedroom, a secretary moved in to take dictation for a flurry of new telegrams and letters. While the masseur and secretary did their jobs, an art dealer sometimes appeared to do his, showing Bendix new tapestries that the manufacturer might want to add to a collection that soon numbered 357 pieces valued at an estimated $600,000. Then there was breakfast with a second secretary, followed by a train ride to South Bend, followed by meetings with engineers, then a dinner party at Chateau Bendix or the Palmer House back in Chicago, whichever Bendix preferred. He had options both highbrow and lowbrow—evenings with Hollywood actresses, nights at the opera, and ringside seats at wrestling matches. One night he'd be applauding the work of Verdi or Puccini, and the next night he'd be imploring "Jumping Joe" Savoldi or Ed "Strangler" Lewis to beat the brains out of the "Golden Greek," Jim Londos. Either way, whatever he did, Bendix liked to end his days the same way he started them, by

summoning the Norwegian masseur to his bedroom for another rub-
down.

But Bendix didn't use his money solely to satisfy his own whims.
He was generous with it, giving it away to others for projects that
meant little to him, winning awards and press adulation just for being himself: a rich man. Bendix, in short, was Cliff Henderson's kind
of people. Henderson just had to meet him. Despite the deadly mishaps marring the national air meet in Chicago, Henderson had a plan
to boost interest in the races that involved even more danger: a transcontinental speed dash, a true test of endurance, smarts, flying skill,
and courage, with a purse that would dwarf the Thompson Trophy
jackpot. Henderson had even gone so far as to draw a picture of what
he thought the silver cup for this elite cross-country speed race should
look like. All he needed was someone to finance it: Vincent Bendix. In
a dark time, few others had the money that Henderson needed. "But
how could I meet him," Henderson wondered, "and where?" Bendix
wasn't the sort of man a stranger just called, even a stranger like Henderson. The famous air-race promoter couldn't get past Bendix's sec-
retaries.

Finally, in early 1931, he got lucky. On a train ride from Chicago to
New York, Henderson spotted his prey through the smoky haze of
the club car. Bendix had his nose in a newspaper. Henderson gathered
himself and then eased into the empty seat beside Bendix. He was a
small man next to a big man, and, apparently, he went unnoticed.

Bendix didn't look up. Henderson—nervous, for once—spoke first.

"Mr. Bendix," he said, "my name is Clifford Henderson and I've
been trying to meet you for some months."

"Yes," Bendix replied. "Is there something I can do for you, young
man?"

Henderson explained everything, that he was director of the National Air Races, that he was seeking a new sponsor for a grand new
race, and that he wanted Bendix's money—and name—to make it
happen because, to Henderson, the Bendix name meant progress. "To
me," Henderson told the manufacturer now, "the National Air Races
mean the same thing."

Bendix was interested enough to keep listening. But he didn't like
the sketch of the trophy that Henderson had drafted. A simple silver
cup would never do for Vincent Bendix. He asked Henderson to draw

something better, something bigger, and get back to him. The result was a pedestal topped with a cresting wave and crowned with a streamlined aviator's head—the logo of the air races—and then, above that, a globe flanked on either side by a naked deity reaching out with one hand beneath a plane emerging from the top of the miniature Earth. The trophy was more like a statue, really, weighing almost a hundred pounds and standing nearly three feet tall, a prize of prizes for a race of races, the sort of mad grandeur that a man like Bendix could support. He approved a transcontinental race with a $15,000 purse—50 percent bigger than the Thompson Trophy jackpot the year before and the largest prize ever offered at the air races.

AT THE NATIONAL MEET in August 1931, two months after Nichols's crash in New Brunswick, Bendix took center stage in Cleveland and spoke via radio broadcast to the first Bendix race contestants sitting with their planes on the ground in Los Angeles.

"To you out there in California, at the starting line, two thousand miles away, I can almost hear your motors roaring as you'll be getting ready to give them the gun and this big field roars away in the dim hours of the night," Bendix said. "What a thrill! Cleveland is alive with excitement . . . They're gathering literally by the tens of thousands to welcome you here . . . And the whole nation will be following you through the radio and press."

He wished the eight men good luck on their journey across the nation. Then, in the predawn darkness on the first Friday of September, the eight planes took off. One ran out of gas in Nebraska. Another made a forced landing in Indiana after his engine briefly caught fire. But the other six made it to Ohio, with a green-and-yellow airship the first to appear over Cleveland, a dot on the southwestern horizon.

"He's coming!" someone in the crowd shouted. "Doolittle's coming!"

Jimmy Doolittle was a father of two, an army veteran, and a well-known racer from St. Louis—short, stern, and scrappy. He had once held an amateur bantamweight boxing title and had twice saved himself by leaping from a doomed plane with a parachute, the second time that very summer. After that incident, he had vowed to retire from racing—news that seemed to please his wife. "I'm through with

Louise McPhetridge was determined to fly airplanes and once she arrived in Oakland, Calif., in 1927, with D. C. Warren, left, she quickly made headlines. *Thaden Family Collection*

FÉDÉRATION AÉRONAUTIQUE
INTERNATIONALE

NATIONAL AERONAUTIC
ASSOCIATION OF U. S. A.
INC.

Certificate No. 7559

The above named Association, recognized by the Fédération Aéronautique Internationale, as the governing authority for the United States of America, certifies that

Ruth Rowland Nichols

born 23rd day of February, 1901 having fulfilled all the conditions required by the Fédération Aéronautique Internationale, for an Aviator Pilot is hereby brevetted as such.

Dated June 12, 1930

CONTEST COMMITTEE

Orville Wright
Chairman

Executive Vice-Chairman

(SEAL)

Signature of Pilot:

Ruth Nichols's pilot's license — signed by pioneer Orville Wright — was just the beginning for Nichols, who wanted to set records in the sky. *Courtesy of Jeff Nichols*

Ruth Elder, wearing one of her signature "Ruth ribbons" around her head, took New York by storm in 1927. *Smithsonian National Air and Space Museum (NASM 82–702)*

Ruth Elder and George Haldeman, on Long Island, before their historic transatlantic flight attempt that October. *Photo by George Rinhart / Getty Images*

Frances Grayson — with the original crew of the *Dawn,* pilot Wilmer Stultz, left, and navigator Brice Goldsborough, right — hoped to beat Elder across the ocean.
Bettmann / Getty Images

Herbert von Thaden, Louise's future husband, knew two things in the late 1920s: he wanted to build planes and he wanted to marry Louise.
Thaden Family Collection

At her homecoming in July 1928, Boston turned out to greet transatlantic heroine, Amelia Earhart, center, and the men who flew her across the ocean, Wilmer Stultz, right, and Lou Gordon, left.
Courtesy of Purdue University Libraries, Karnes Archives and Special Collections

Cliff Henderson flew an airplane to help advertise his first business: a Nash automobile dealership in Santa Monica, Calif. *Courtesy of the Historical Society of Palm Desert*

Henderson wanted to hold the 1928 air races in a bean and barley field, an airport initially called Mines Field and later known worldwide by three letters: LAX. *Courtesy of the Historical Society of Palm Desert*

Shortly after her marriage in 1928, Louise Thaden began setting a slew of female flying records, intent on becoming the best woman pilot in America. *Thaden Family Collection*

An exhausted Thaden gets a hug from her mother-in-law after setting the female solo endurance record in 1929. *Thaden Family Collection*

Roughly 20,000 people watched the start of the National Women's Air Derby in Santa Monica in August 1929 — the beginning of a historic, momentous, and fatal week that would make the women pilots famous. *Thaden Family Collection*

Some of the competitors in the first-ever women's air derby, stopping in East St. Louis, Ill., in August 1929. From left to right: Mary Elizabeth von Mach, Jessie "Chubbie" Miller, Gladys O'Donnell, Thea Rasche, Phoebe Omlie, Louise Thaden, Amelia Earhart, Blanche Noyes, Ruth Elder, and Vera Walker. *St. Louis University Libraries*

Cliff Henderson was among the first to welcome Thaden to the finish line in Cleveland in 1929.
Thaden Family Collection

With the birth of her first child, a son, in 1930, Thaden quit racing—for a while. *Smithsonian National Air and Space Museum (NASM 9A14419–017B)*

Other female pilots doubted the motivations of George Putnam, right. But everyone agreed that he helped make Earhart famous. *Courtesy of Purdue University Libraries, Karnes Archives and Special Collections*

By 1931, Nichols had everything she wanted: funding, a reliable plane, the *Akita,* and a chance to be the first woman to fly solo across the Atlantic Ocean. *Courtesy of the International Women's Air & Space Museum, Cleveland, Ohio*

Famous airmen—like Clarence Chamberlin, left, and Wiley Post, right—believed Nichols would succeed in her transatlantic attempt, seeing her off in New York. *Courtesy of Jeff Nichols*

While Earhart and Nichols chased records—and each other—Thaden had to turn to freelance writing to help make ends meet, selling stories at $20 a piece. *Thaden Family Collection*

Henderson's work with the National Air Races made him a star in his own right, introducing him to moneyed men and glamorous women, like actress Jean Harlow, at the air races in Los Angeles. *Courtesy of the Historical Society of Palm Desert*

Everything about manufacturing tycoon Vincent Bendix was larger than life: his mansion, his ego, his pocketbook—and the air race named after him, the Bendix Trophy race. *Courtesy of The History Museum, South Bend, Indiana*

The Bendix Trophy stood more than three feet tall, weighed roughly 100 pounds, and initially came with a purse of $15,000—almost $250,000 in today's money. *Smithsonian National Air and Space Museum (NASM 83–2126)*

Florence Klingensmith — nervous before her first flight here, around 1928 — soon emerged as the woman to beat in the sky. *Historical and Cultural Society of Clay County*

When Klingensmith won the Amelia Earhart Trophy at the 1932 air races in Cleveland, Earhart herself was there to congratulate her. *PhotoQuest/Getty Images*

Zantford Granville's fast and dangerous Gee Bee Super-Sportster could fly 300 mph, a marvel of its time—the perfect race plane for Klingensmith. *Courtesy of the Lyman & Merrie Wood Museum of Springfield History, Springfield, Massachusetts*

Rivals in the sky, Earhart, Nichols, and Thaden became friends on the ground, helping the female pilots organize against the men. *Thaden Family Collection*

While the women protested, Benny Howard, left, and Roscoe Turner, right, kept flying, establishing themselves as two of the fastest pilots in America. Unbeatable, many believed. *Smithsonian National Air and Space Museum (NASM A–5194–B)*

Thaden felt the pressure of many modern working mothers: she wanted to fly, but had responsibilities at home.
Thaden Family Collection

Blanche Noyes, left, Thaden, second from left, and two other female aviators were lucky to get hired as "air-markers," making flying safer. *Thaden Family Collection*

By 1935, crowds surged around Earhart wherever she went, including this landing in Oakland. *Courtesy of Purdue University Libraries, Karnes Archives and Special Collections*

Olive Ann Beech started as Walter Beech's secretary in Wichita, Kan., but was soon instrumental in running his start-up airplane company, Beechcraft. *Courtesy of Mary Lynn Beech Oliver*

In July 1936, Walter and Olive Ann Beech took their newest Beechcraft to Denver to compete in the regional air races there. A month later, Olive Ann decided to enter it in the Bendix. *Courtesy of Mary Lynn Beech Oliver*

Mister Mulligan, Benny Howard's plane, swept the 1935 air races and was the heavy favorite to carry Howard to victory again in 1936. *Smithsonian National Air and Space Museum (NASM 0056879)*

Thaden, before the 1936 air races, at the controls of her borrowed Beechcraft, a plane she described as a "trim, blue princess." *Thaden Family Collection*

Thaden wanted to spend more time with her children, Bill and Patsy, and would ultimately make a difficult choice. *Thaden Family Collection*

stunts to thrill crowds," he said. "That's a bit of foolishness that I won't indulge in anymore."

But the big-money Bendix race apparently fit into a different category. Sure, he told reporters, he had considered retiring. But this race was about science. "If there's any reasonable project that will advance the science of aviation," Doolittle declared, "I'm ready for it, any time." So he was in. He would race. And when Doolittle won the trophy — beating his rivals into Cleveland by a full hour and then hustling on to New York to set a transcontinental record on the same day — Bendix and Henderson had the headlines they wanted.

Science was often cited by the women as well for why they flew and why they needed to race in both Henderson's air meets and across the ocean. The female fliers believed that their record-breaking flights — and even their failures — contributed something, "furthering," Nichols said, "scientific aeronautical knowledge." They also believed they could defeat the men if given the chance, and now they had statistics to prove it. With three years of air-race data to analyze, the Ninety-Nines pointed out that the women were, in some cases, flying faster than the men, recording higher average speeds, and, twice in small affairs, even beating their male counterparts to the finish line. "It is believed the figures, as such, may be of real value from the standpoint of flying history," the Ninety-Nines noted in a newsletter that was mostly ignored by everyone other than the women themselves. The men, the newsletter continued, needed to "sit back and take notice." But Nichols would have been happy with just a little more respect and recognition. As she put it, "Give a girl credit."

In the summer of 1931, still reeling from the crash that doomed her failed transatlantic attempt and recovering from the broken vertebrae in her back, Nichols was struggling even to get sympathy.

"There, little girl, don't cry!" one patronizing man wrote her while she was still hospitalized. "You aren't the first pilot ever to trade a Lockheed for a basket of chips and you won't be the last one . . . Only the next time you start transatlantic, please be frank and call your ship the *Flying Squirrel* if you intend to use it for climbing trees, scaling cliffs, and what have you."

Friends like Thaden tried to make her feel better.

"If it was in the cards for you not to go," Thaden told Nichols, "perhaps it is better so, as something worse might have happened." She promised to come visit Nichols in Rye while she was laid up that summer and offered to help her pass time by sharing juicy gossip about aviators they knew and reading to her. "I'm not very good at entertainment," Thaden told her injured friend, "but I can read books aloud for some time without losing my voice."

"Please come soon," Nichols begged in reply. But she couldn't help correcting Thaden. Her crash wasn't "in the cards," and it wasn't going to prevent her from attempting another transatlantic flight. "Because it can't!" she told Thaden. Within hours of her crash, in fact, Nichols was already planning to rebuild her plane for a second attempt. She knew the fuselage was firewood. "The rest of the ship, however, is perfectly OK," she said from her hospital room. It could be fixed quite easily, she figured, if she could solve one problem: funding. "You can do anything," she said, "if you can get the money."

Insurance helped cover the cost of replacing the fuselage on Crosley's Lockheed. The Cincinnati radio magnate was even willing to finance a second transatlantic attempt. But in mid-August, back in Rye, Nichols was still in her plaster cast and $3,000 short of the money she needed to finish repairing the plane. August came and went — and there was no flight. Labor Day passed in New York and the air races ended in Cleveland. Doolittle won the Bendix. Henderson had his glory. And still, for Nichols, nothing. "The spine is recovered," she assured friends. "Ship is all ready." In mid-September, however, she pulled the plug for the season, citing US Weather Bureau warnings that the time for flying the Atlantic had ended for the year. It was too cold over the ocean now, too stormy. Unlike Ruth Elder and Frances Grayson before her, Nichols was listening to the reports. "It would be suicide," she said, "to attempt flying over either the Pacific or Atlantic, with winter weather approaching."

The decision could not have been an easy one. Thanks to her crash, the plane repairs that followed, and now the second flight shelved until spring, Nichols the wealthy socialite was now mostly just a socialite, struggling like most Americans that autumn and hoping for a living wage. She was $20,000 in debt, unable to pay her bills, and requesting patience from those who had loaned her money. "I am forced to ask you to allow me to postpone the return of your so generous contribution to the ocean flight until some other time in the near future,"

Nichols told her supporters in late 1931, "when, I trust, the flight will take place as planned, or that I shall have earned the money to repay you through other efforts."

That October, Nichols devised a plan to help make that possible — or at least keep her in the news. More than six hundred gallons of gasoline consigned to "Miss Nichols" arrived in Oakland, stirring up interest in what reporters were calling a "special stunt." Two days later, Nichols herself arrived on the West Coast, landing in her refurbished *Akita* and declaring her intentions to the world. "The only record I do not hold at present," she said, "is the women's distance record." A female French pilot had set it the previous year, flying 1,810 miles across Europe. Now, Nichols said, standing on Thaden's old airfield, she intended to break the Frenchwoman's record by flying across America. "To do it, I must fly 1,900 miles non-stop."

That Saturday, near sundown, she climbed into the cockpit of the *Akita*. "With less fuss," one reporter noted, "than a college girl makes about attending a prom." She was wearing a purple leather coat over a purple wool dress over a steel corset to support her injured back. It was going to be cold overnight, flying at fifteen thousand feet and riding a strong tailwind east — to Cleveland or, maybe, with luck, New York. Yet she wore no goggles, no helmet. This was, Nichols said, "just another flight," and she had only a few supplies on board: two bottles of Coca-Cola, one quart of hot coffee, a box of cookies, and six caviar, tomato, and mayonnaise sandwiches that the press described as "man-sized." "If I get there," Nichols said, "I won't need anything more."

She took off at 5:15 as airport officials sounded a siren to bid her farewell — Nichols was on her way. She rose above the bay with the moon behind her, darkness ahead, and the continent laid out before her beneath a blanket of stars — perfect conditions. By one a.m., she was over Cheyenne, and by dawn, she was over Des Moines, making good time. Then, inexplicably, in the daylight, Nichols got lost. She missed Chicago. Missed Cleveland. Wandered around in the sky for two hours and then stumbled on Louisville, Kentucky — way off course. Low on fuel and fearing bad weather in the Alleghenies, where she had faced trouble before, Nichols opted to land in Kentucky — short of her goal but a record all the same. She had flown nearly two thousand miles, and the next day, she hoped to set yet another mark: a new speed record into New York.

"Clear sky all the way," officials informed her in the morning. "Good," Nichols declared.

With a crowd gathered to see her take off, she climbed up onto the golden wing of her plane and paused there to accommodate the photographers, then she smiled at them and waved them off. "Don't stop me again," she told them. "I must go."

Moments later, with the plane engine in full roar and Nichols taxiing away from the crowd, a faulty valve on the *Akita* dumped fuel out of the right gas tank and onto the ground, splashing it everywhere. A spark ignited the river of fuel. And suddenly, the *Akita* was engulfed in flames. Nichols, moving quickly, clambered back out onto the wing and jumped to safety with the plane's engine still running—a feat that witnesses at the field credited to her athleticism. Yet there was no saving the Crosley airship. Loaded with two hundred gallons of fuel, it burned for twenty minutes, the paint peeling off and the metal melting away, until the gold lettering on the plane's nose chronicling Nichols's many record flights was gone, and all that remained was the charred carcass of a star-crossed bird.

For the second time in just four months, Nichols—already up to her eyes in debt—needed a new plane or significant repairs to fix this one. The estimated cost: ten thousand dollars—money that Nichols didn't have.

15

Grudge Flight

AMELIA EARHART SAW her chance. With Ruth Nichols grounded and Louise Thaden refusing to fly the ocean—she thought it too dangerous now that she had a baby son at home —Earhart was planning to shock the world. She, not Nichols, would be the first woman to fly across the Atlantic in full control of her own plane. Unlike she'd been in 1928, Earhart would not be cargo transported by men while she sat on a heap of flight suits in the back. She would be in the cockpit, flying alone.

C. B. Allen—the New York aviation editor who Earhart once summoned for marriage advice—thought he understood why the world's most famous female aviator would assume such a risk. For one thing, at the end of 1931, Allen believed, Earhart was a fading star, "gradually slipping," he said, "out of the public eye." The story of the year had been Ruth Nichols—for better or worse—setting her records and trying to get across the ocean. Even when she failed, Nichols did so in spectacular fashion, cracking vertebrae or leaping from burning airplanes while reporters watched. Since marrying Putnam, Earhart was living a far more pedestrian life, it seemed. In 1931, while Nichols was trying to conquer the sky, Earhart was trying to master a new, experimental airship called the autogyro. Part plane, part helicopter, it had both wings and a giant rotor over the cockpit, giving it the appearance of a giant prehistoric insect. The press, not knowing how to describe the contraption, often called it a "windmill plane."

But some aviation experts believed the autogyro to be the future. Harold Pitcairn, America's top builder of these windmill ships, saw a day when people would commute to work in them, as he did from his home near Philadelphia. He argued that flying the autogyro was 90 percent physics, 10 percent skill, so it basically flew itself, and even an inexperienced pilot could handle it. By late 1930, Pitcairn had convinced Earhart to give this easy-to-fly airship of the future a try. In December, she took it up several times near Pitcairn's factory. In April 1931, she set an altitude record in the machine. Then, two months later, sponsored by the Beech-Nut Company and accompanied by a mechanic, Earhart set off across the country in the autogyro to shill for both Pitcairn and Beech-Nut chewing gum. "I'm advertising the stuff," she said at one stop, "so I have to take my own medicine."

The autogyro, however, proved less foolproof than advertised. Earhart crashed it in Abilene and again in Detroit, marring the end of the state fair there in September 1931.

"Are you hurt?" two police officers shouted when they arrived at Earhart's downed chopper-plane.

"Only my pride," she replied.

The autogyro was turning Earhart into a traveling sideshow, puddle-jumping across America in her windmill ship—today Binghamton, New York, tomorrow Zanesville, Ohio. She showed up for air fairs and state fairs and annual conventions of such glamorous groups as the Ohio Grocers and Meat Dealers Association. There was seemingly no town too small, no gathering too insignificant, for Earhart to visit in the curious flying machine, offering rides to the masses. "Here," an official said at one fair that summer as he handed liability waivers to Earhart's would-be passengers. "Sign your death warrant."

From the moment Putnam put Earhart on the *Friendship* back in 1928, skeptics, both male and female, had questioned her flying abilities, crediting the publisher, not Earhart, for her success. "Probably saved her," one critic said, "from becoming a nice old maid." When she flew across the country, her antagonists wanted to know what mechanic had flown with her. When she set the speed record, they wondered if maybe a man had done it for her. And whenever she suffered a mishap such as a forced landing or a crash, the skeptics were there, sprinkling doubt in Earhart's footsteps. Her year in the autogyro had likely done little to dissuade them in their thinking. But quietly that winter in Rye, Earhart—now president of the Ninety-Nines—was planning her rebuttal: a transatlantic trip slated for the spring of 1932 that Allen called her "grudge flight."

It had all the hallmarks of a Putnam operation. In the months before she took off for Europe, Earhart penned a new book but left the last chapter unwritten; her new transatlantic tale would go there, if she made it across. In the meantime, Earhart prepared in total secrecy, just as she had in 1928, relying on two men, famed Arctic pilot Bernt Balchen and trusted mechanic Eddie Gorski, to get her Lockheed ready for the journey. As Balchen and Gorski worked on the plane in Teterboro, New Jersey, Earhart stayed away—out of the spotlight and, for once, almost entirely out of the newspapers. She was finished hopping from town to town in her autogyro. In the late winter and early spring of 1932, Earhart said almost nothing at all, while across town in Rye, Nichols was all but screaming for money, for help, for relevance once more.

Between January and May, Nichols reached out to a long list of major corporations—Bendix and Studebaker, Kellogg's and Wrigley, B. F. Goodrich and Firestone—begging for funding to renew her transatlantic dream and laying out all the reasons why they should support her. "The possibilities of pictorial and verbal advertising are manifold," she insisted, noting her still-existing contracts with Paramount and Columbia Broadcasting. All she needed was $10,000— or, if they couldn't afford to spend that much, just $5,000. "In return for this sum," Nichols argued, "your company would have the benefit of all the publicity outlets as outlined." The corporations could make headlines while she made history, but only if they acted soon. "As you well realize," Nichols told one potential donor, "it takes about two months to complete preparations for long distance flights, and in order to take advantage of possible Atlantic flying weather in May, I am most anxious to begin preparations on the ship immediately. May I hear from you, therefore, at your earliest convenience?"

It was no different than what Earhart was planning at the same moment, but the press gave Putnam's wife a pass while they savaged the cash-strapped Nichols. That winter, the magazine *Inside Stuff* put a smiling picture of Nichols on the cover under the sarcastic headline "Flying to Paris—with What?" The gist of the article was that Nichols had ruined Crosley's plane and wasted Paramount's money trying to satisfy her "Lindbergh complex." "Miss Nichols," *Inside Stuff* declared, "is obsessed with the delusion that she is the 'Woman Lindbergh.'" But she would never get across the ocean, the article suggested, seeing as she hadn't even been able to find her way to New York on her ill-fated trip the previous October that ended with the fire in Louisville. "Imagine what such navigation would do on the Atlantic!"

Nichols still hoped that someone would sponsor her new flight, making her pitches not only by mail but in person and traveling long distances at times with money she didn't have in order to prove she was worthy of a corporation's investment. But one by one, the companies rejected Nichols. Phil Wrigley, the Chicago chewing-gum magnate, personally declined her request in February. "As under the present conditions," he told Nichols, "it will be impossible for me to be of any assistance to you." A spokesman for B. F. Goodrich sent Nichols a rejection letter a month later. "We are interested in the splendid work you are doing," the letter noted. "However, we are not in a position at this time to participate in your project along the lines you propose." In May, Kellogg's turned her down not once, but twice, even after executives met Nichols at company headquarters in Michigan. "It was indeed very thoughtful of you to have called on us," a Kellogg's executive told her, "and a real pleasure and honor to have had the opportunity of meeting and talking with you." Still, Kellogg's was out for the same reasons as the others. It had no money for airplane flights — even historic ones — but at least the company sent Nichols some parting gifts: a care package of Kellogg's cereals.

Nichols received the last rejection during the third week of May, the same week she and Earhart sat down for lunch in Rye. She knew Earhart was up to something. Rumors of Earhart's transatlantic preparations had leaked to the papers. But publicly, Putnam was still denying everything, and newspapers were running planted stories that Balchen, not Earhart, was planning a major adventure with the Lockheed in New Jersey. At their lunch in Rye, Earhart revealed nothing, or perhaps only enough details to mislead Nichols.

The same week, Earhart was equally cryptic with Thaden, writing her a letter that said everything and nothing at the same time. "As Vice President of the Ninety-Nines," Earhart told Thaden, "you will succeed to the Presidency, if anything happens to me. To make your job easier — in case — I am listing what you will find in the club files and making some suggestions for future conduct of its affairs." She told Thaden where she could find the old correspondence files and archived newsletters, about her plans for the next annual meeting, and of her hopes that the Ninety-Nines, in the future, would help women become true individuals. "Industrially, mentally and spiritually," Earhart told Thaden. "This they should strive for despite failures which might tend to discourage them." But Earhart didn't say goodbye to her friend or even hint at what she was about to do.

Forty-eight hours later, Earhart's red Lockheed took off from New Jersey and headed toward Canada, following the Great Circle route north. Her secret was finally out and picked up by newspapers around the globe: Earhart was flying the Atlantic solo. Except that initially, she wasn't flying the plane at all. Bernt Balchen—her consultant, a Norwegian adventurer with more ocean-flight experience than almost any man—would be at the controls of the Lockheed while Earhart rested in the fuselage behind an auxiliary gas tank. He was piloting the plane into Saint John, New Brunswick, and then Harbour Grace, Newfoundland, some eleven hundred miles in all, so she could conserve her energy. There would be no Nichols-like failure before Earhart got out to sea, in part because Balchen, blond and handsome in a three-piece suit, would see to it—a key detail omitted later from many stories and from the breathless film footage that helped create the Earhart legend.

"Please don't forget to phone just the minute you get there, eh?" Putnam told his wife as he stood beside the plane in what appeared to be a carefully crafted farewell scene staged for a Movietone camera crew and likely filmed sometime before she left New Jersey.

"I will," Earhart said, her head sticking out of the cockpit.

"Goodbye," Putnam said.

"So long," Earhart replied.

With that, Putnam moved in. He shook her hand and planted a kiss on her lips that was so awkward and apparently so unexpected that Earhart hardly kissed him back. Then she smiled, stole a knowing glance at the camera, and, with a deep breath, retreated to the place where she was always most comfortable: the cockpit.

Now, in a scene that wasn't staged at all, Earhart walked to her red plane on the ground in Harbour Grace, calm before a crowd of excited Canadians. Balchen had taken her as far as he could. From here, Earhart would have to go alone. "To all my friends, both far and near," she announced, "let me say that you will hear from me in less than fifteen hours."

The goal was Paris—and perhaps beyond. "If my fuel holds and I am not too fatigued," Earhart vowed, "I will fly farther." But a worried Balchen told reporters he would be happy if she made it to one place: "Dry land," he said.

It was 7:20 p.m. on May 20, exactly five years to the day since Lindbergh had left New York for Paris. Earhart shook Balchen's hand, climbed into the cockpit, waved to the crowd, opened the throttle on the 500-horsepower engine, and let it roar.

"Good luck," Balchen shouted.

His words were drowned out by the sound of the plane rumbling away. Loaded down with 420 gallons of fuel, twenty gallons of oil, one quart of warm soup, and one woman, traveling light with only a toothbrush, the unnamed Lockheed used two thousand feet of runway before easing into the sky with no drama, no panic, and no problems. Then, with the crowd watching, Earhart banked the plane over an inland lake, buzzed low over the town of Harbour Grace, and flew out over the sea. In less than a minute, she was gone.

It was about eighteen hundred miles to the coast of Ireland, twenty-five hundred miles to Paris. And for the first couple of hours in the sky that night, Earhart felt like Nichols had the year before when she'd left Oakland: like she was making any other flight. The winds were calm and the weather fair. There was a lingering sunset at her back and a full moon rising over low clouds. She was flying at twelve thousand feet—and then, suddenly, according to the instruments, she wasn't. The plane maintained altitude, but the altimeter in the cockpit failed, its hands swinging wildly, useless. With no way to for Earhart to know her altitude, her plane bounced around, carved through a storm, ran off course—Earhart knew it—and began picking up ice on the wings, a problem Ruth Elder had faced years before. Trying to find warmer air in the dark, Earhart nosed the Lockheed down so low that she could see the ocean waves breaking—dangerously close to the water. But exactly how close, Earhart couldn't say. Then, around midnight, new problems. Leaking fuel began dripping down her neck, and blue flames started burning through a broken weld in the exhaust manifold— a worrisome development that Earhart couldn't fix and half wished she hadn't noticed. The blue flames looked angry in the dark. But with nowhere to land, alone in a small plane over the North Atlantic in the middle of the night, Earhart kept going. By dawn, she knew Paris was out of the question. She was hoping for Ireland—if she could find it.

Back home in America, it was Saturday morning. Flight fans were turning on radios for updates, and Earhart's loved ones were sitting by their phones.

No news.

In Medford, Earhart's mother busied herself caring for her two young grandchildren, Amelia's sister's kids. In Rye, Nichols surely pondered the future, including the public statement she would have to make that day no matter what happened with Earhart. Nichols would have to say something, and so would Putnam. As morning dawned in New York, he paced inside a suite on the eleventh floor of the Hotel Seymour on Forty-Fifth Street, waiting with Hilton Railey. It had been fourteen hours, and there was still no word from Earhart.

Finally, around nine thirty that morning, the phone in Putnam's suite rang.

"London calling," Railey said, handing the phone to Putnam.

"Yes, yes," Putnam said into the phone, his eyes narrowing. Then, turning to Railey, he whispered the news: "A.E. is all right."

Her plane had landed in Northern Ireland in a farmer's field and rolled to a rest not far from a cottage near the town of Londonderry. She was covered in oil, smelling of fuel, and almost deaf from the roar of the plane engine, but she was alive—a true transatlantic heroine this time.

"You have done an amazing thing," the mayor of Londonderry told Earhart when he greeted her a short time after she landed. He wanted her to know she could have anything she wanted—a warm meal, a bath, a bed for the night, even a fresh supply of gasoline, free, so she could fly on to London or Paris. But Earhart—the fourteenth person ever to pilot a plane east across the ocean, the first woman ever to do it, and the first person to do it solo since Lindbergh himself—was finished. For once in her life, she felt no need to go farther.

WHATEVER BITTERNESS NICHOLS might have felt because a man, Balchen, flew Earhart eleven hundred miles to Newfoundland and whatever regrets she might have harbored because her own attempt had failed the year before, she kept to herself. The last rejection letter from Kellogg's had just arrived at her home in Rye, and with the sting of that news still fresh in her mind, and now this, Earhart's success, Nichols sat down that Saturday morning and prepared a telegram congratulating her rival. "You beat me to it for a second time," she told Earhart, as gracious as ever, "but it was a splendid job."

Cliff Henderson thought so too. "Hurry back," he told Earhart. There was money to be made, lectures to be given, and that new book to complete. Putnam, working at another publishing house now, would hustle it onto the shelves in only a month. These were the spoils of victory that any woman who crossed the Atlantic first would have enjoyed but perhaps Earhart most of all. Even Thaden was jealous. "Little envious," she conceded to Earhart. There was nothing Thaden or any other woman could do in 1932 to top what Earhart had just accomplished. "But you can have it," Thaden told her friend.

In flying the ocean alone, Earhart had proven a point that each of them had been trying to make for years: women belonged. They *should* belong. Even their harshest male critics had to agree now. The women deserved to be included in any air race, over any distance, at any speed, in any plane. "This is the year," Henderson said, "for women's suffrage in aviation."

PART THREE

16

Spetakkel

SHE WAS BLOND and young—three and a half years younger than Ruth Nichols, seven years younger than Amelia Earhart. Just twenty-seven in the summer of 1932 and lying about her age, saying she was just twenty-five. Most notable, as far as the men were concerned, Florence Klingensmith was a darling of the northern plains: born in rural Minnesota, part Swedish, part Norwegian, and alone. Unlike Earhart, she had no husband to look after her, and unlike Thaden, she had no child underfoot.

"Let's pause for a moment to look at Florence Klingensmith," said one male pilot who admired her golden hair, her blue eyes, and her fair skin. It was over-the-top ogling, perhaps. But even friends liked to joke that Klingensmith had "dangerous curves"—a comment on her flying, her figure, and the general notion that she was and had always been hard to ignore, seemingly destined for a perilous act that would have ramifications for female pilots everywhere.

At the very least, she was restless. As Earhart returned to America by ocean liner in June 1932—finished with record-breaking ocean flights for a while and preparing for her book tour—Klingensmith felt like she was just getting started, and she was willing to do almost anything to make a name for herself in the sky. Stunts, races, maybe even flying the ocean.

"I want to go," Klingensmith said, "if I possibly can."

It was like she was chasing the others—Earhart, Thaden, and Nichols—stalking the pack, coming from behind.

THE GUNDERSONS — Gustav and Flossie—had known early on that their daughter Florence was different than most kids in Kragnes Township, a farming community in western Minnesota across the Red River from Fargo, North Dakota. She was filled with what the Old-World folks called *spetakkel*. "That's Norwegian," explained one local woman. "Means 'rambunctious.'" There was no containing Florence, not in the neat rows of desks in the tiny structure where she attended elementary school and not on the Gunderson family farm. The flat land, hugging a bend in the Red River, should have given Florence the space she needed. But life there was hard. She and other kids walked for miles to get to the closest schoolhouse. The winter frosts came as early as September and lingered long into spring. In between, it was often freezing—a fact noted by the local farmers in their diaries: "34 below zero this morning . . . Frozen." "Cold wind from the north." "Cold storm from the north." "It will be a Big Snow Winter."

August in Kragnes Township was for threshing the alfalfa or wheat —if it had not been ruined by the floods. September was for digging up the potatoes—if they were any good this year. Sundays were for rest. The other days of the week were for work: plowing fields, hauling coal, delivering the harvest to the nearby town of Moorhead, and counting their many losses: the old horses that had to be shot, the young horses that died unexpectedly, the cows that escaped, never to be found again, and the crops that died, devoured by grasshoppers or consumed by fungus. "Same as ever," one neighboring farmer noted in late 1916, when Florence was twelve. "Still another year without making Debts any smaller."

Florence's father tried to make life easier for the kids. In Kragnes Township he was both the barber and the school-bus driver, taking children to the little schoolhouse in a horse-drawn wagon and, later, his car. But by 1918, the Gundersons had left the farm and moved into Moorhead, east of Fargo, where Florence enrolled in high school and soon developed a reputation for her *spetakkel*. While the other girls at Moorhead High joined the debate team, the glee club, the class play, and the yearbook staff—the only activities available to female students—Florence busied herself elsewhere. She impressed local boys with daring feats on the town ski jump. She raced motorcycles and she hitched rides on the streetcar in town, traveling in a way that suited her best: she clung to the cowcatcher up front as she rode the rails, just inches off the ground.

Perhaps not surprisingly, Florence didn't finish high school. She dropped out and began to drift. She chopped wood in the northern forests of Minnesota, herded sheep on a ranch in Montana, and clerked at a five-and-dime somewhere in between before finally moving back home to Fargo, where she got hired at the Pantorium, a dry cleaner, near the river. The job was filled not with *spetakkel* but humdrum tasks and it was, within a short time, the dim sun around which Florence's entire world revolved. She worked at the Pantorium. She lived three blocks away in an apartment building, and she married one of her co-workers: Charles Klingensmith, four years her junior and only eighteen at their wedding in July 1927.

Their union lasted less than two years. In fact, if there was a defining moment for Klingensmith in the summer of 1927, it wasn't her marriage, of which she never spoke, but what happened six weeks later: Charles Lindbergh's visit to Fargo on his goodwill tour of America in the *Spirit of St. Louis*. The town stopped everything for "Lindbergh Day." Banks and stores closed. Thousands of people got up early and turned their eyes to the sky, straining to see Lindbergh's plane. Then, once he landed, they lined the streets to cheer him in a grand parade that moved at a fast clip, an attempt to keep the hordes away from the Lone Eagle, who was sitting atop the trunk of a convertible, his feet planted on the back seat. The car hustled down Thirteenth Street, turned east on Front toward the river, and then rolled up Broadway, right past the Pantorium.

Klingensmith, just five foot four, pushed through the crowd to see him and waved to Lindbergh as the convertible rumbled past. When Lindbergh didn't wave back—as he often didn't, since he surely couldn't wave to everyone—Klingensmith didn't shrug it off. She was personally offended. She'd show him, she said, that he wasn't so important, that he wasn't the only one who could fly a plane. "Show him," she said, "a woman can handle one of these things, too."

Within months, Klingensmith enrolled in electrical school, the only woman among four hundred men, working her way up to mechanic's apprentice. By March 1928, she was happy to be covered in grease, mingling with male pilots, and working on plane engines at the new airfield in Fargo. At times, she even cajoled pilots into giving her flying lessons. But realizing she didn't have the money to be a pilot herself, Klingensmith took the only aviation job that could get her into the sky on a regular basis: stunt girl. She began leaping from planes with a parachute on her back or standing on a wing high in the sky wearing only a bathing suit and smiling to thrill the crowds down below.

"It has been a hard ladder to climb," she admitted to another woman at one point. But in early 1929, after a year of sacrifices, it all paid off for Klingensmith. Businessmen in Fargo gave her $3,000 to help her buy her own plane, unable to say no to the daring, persistent, and persuasive blonde who kept asking for money. "If you're willing to risk your neck," one man finally told her, "I'll risk my money." Her marriage was falling apart, and her time at the Pantorium was over. But Klingensmith had what she wanted: a plane, which she called the *Miss Fargo,* and a pilot's license, the first ever issued to a woman in North Dakota. In the local phone book in 1930, she described her occupation with one word: *aviatrix.* As if to prove it to the folks back in Kragnes Township, one afternoon she flew her plane low over the farm where she'd grown up, over her old schoolhouse, and over the pioneer cemetery nearby and landed on the prairie for everyone to see. "You'll enjoy a chat with this famous woman flier!" advertisements began promising across the upper Midwest. "Attraction Extraordinary: Florence Klingensmith."

She was soon setting records for flying loops in the sky, getting hired as a flight instructor in Minneapolis, earning the nickname Tree Tops, and cleaning up at the 1931 air races in Cleveland. With the $4,300 she won that summer, Klingensmith bought herself a new plane, a Waco, and prepared to return to the air meet in 1932, the first year of Henderson's "women's suffrage" races — the races where men and women would be equals.

Klingensmith was, no doubt, thrilled at the chance to race after everything she had overcome. "I have had to be my own mechanic, and my own ticker seller," she said, "in addition to flying my own plane." Yet Henderson's "equality" races didn't exactly play out as advertised. "The men have connections with plane manufacturers. They are able to find backers and obtain planes that are fast enough to offer competition," one female flier complained. "But where are you going to find anyone to furnish a fast plane for a woman? It just isn't done."

The women that summer ended up racing against one another yet again, with Klingensmith leading the pack, hitting nearly two hundred miles an hour in qualifying rounds, weathering a dangerous thunderstorm to finish third in an eighty-mile free-for-all, and winning the first-ever Amelia Earhart Trophy race: six laps around a three-and-a-half-mile course in the sky over Cleveland. The race was something of a comedy of errors, mocked by the male announcer on the ground because many of the women flew around the wrong pylons and in the wrong direction. But there was no doubt among those who saw Klingensmith fly that she was a real contender. "The men," one reporter said, "should be on guard against Florence Klingensmith."

All she needed to compete was a faster plane.

THE YOUNG INVENTOR stood on the airfield in the dark, a shadow in the night—exactly how he wanted it. For the first test flight of his airplane, he didn't want people around. He was no accomplished aviator, no Walter Beech. He was just a Yankee tinkerer whose name was a mouthful: Zantford Delbert Granville. Most people called him Granny.

Granny, the oldest son of New Hampshire farmers, had a mustache, a tidal wave of thick hair, and a mind that was always calculating something. As a boy, he'd invented a number of contraptions to improve life on the family farm on the edge of the White Mountains. By age twenty-one, he had his own garage on Massachusetts Avenue in Arlington, on the outskirts of Boston, just two miles from Amelia Earhart's home. And by age twenty-seven, he had graduated from automobiles to airships—or at least he hoped he had. He had repaired a lot of broken airplanes by then, anyway. "We have seen where a plane fails and why," Granny said. Surely, he could do better. At nights and on weekends, there was Granny, leaning over a sheet of brown wrapping paper, marking it up with calculations and designs for a ship that soon had a name. Unlike his own, this one would be short. Granny was calling his new plane the Gee Bee.

The test flight in the predawn darkness in East Boston in May 1929 was a success. The little two-seater biplane—just over twenty feet long and twenty-seven feet across the wings—flew as well as Granny could have hoped. Boston newspapers hailed the airship, the first one ever built in the city that actually managed to get airborne, and Granny made plans to build more. But it wouldn't happen in Boston. Investors in Springfield, Massachusetts, ninety miles west, swooped in and lured Granny away with promises of financing and space, a new airfield in the Connecticut River valley for him to use if he wanted it. By the summer of 1929, he and his four brothers were building Gee Bees there, working out of an old dance pavilion and preparing to unveil their new line at the national aviation shows that winter. It was big news back in Springfield when they sold a plane at a show in New York and even bigger news, perhaps, when the market for that plane disappeared overnight. In the deepening Depression, most people had no appetite for any kind of big purchase, but especially not a new, unproven recreational airplane.

Granny needed a pivot, and with Henderson's air races, he found it. The new Gee Bees wouldn't be for lazy weekend flights but for high-stakes racing—silver cups and trophies. In a new design, unveiled in 1930, Granny and his brothers changed everything. They stripped away the biplane look, opting instead for a monoplane with shorter tapered wings built with spruce ribbing and coated with lightweight fabric reportedly strong enough to withstand any stunt, flip, roll, or dive. The fuselage was shorter too, by almost ten feet, while the engine was nearly twice as powerful, a combination that, with other modifications, helped give the second-generation Gee Bee a top speed of 150 miles an hour. "The Gee Bee Sportster," Granny called it. "Note its low landing speed, its facilities, exceptional maneuverability, and the unusual power in takeoff and climb!"

That summer, Granny chose a trusted local pilot for the job of racing the new machine: Lowell Bayles. He was everything Granville could have wanted in a pilot. Bayles didn't drink. He was always focused. He was small enough to fit in the cockpit of the little plane —just five foot seven and 128 pounds—and intense. Bayles, a former coal miner from downstate Illinois, knew there were harder jobs in life than flying a plane, and he jumped at the chance to pilot Granville's new Gee Bee. In his first effort in 1930, he finished second in a cross-country, multistop derby and brought home $7,000. With the money, Granny made the 1931 Gee Bee even faster. Bayles continued winning, collecting still more checks. Finally, just before the air races that year,

Granny rolled out his most powerful Gee Bee to date: the Super Sport-ster, with a 535-horsepower engine, almost ten times more powerful than Granny's first plane, and a design like no one had seen before. The plane was a stubby cylinder, just fifteen feet long, painted black and yellow, and it swooped toward an enclosed cockpit situated, not in the middle of the fuselage, but just a few feet from the tail. And with the design, Granny's planes had left the past behind. Originally crafted for novices, with dual controls and two seats side by side, the Gee Bee now had room for just one pilot, and it had just one purpose—to win.

In Cleveland in September 1931, Bayles entered it in the Thomp-son Trophy race. He climbed into the airship before a crowd of eighty thousand people while, back in Springfield, hundreds gathered at the local airfield, waiting to get the results by telephone. This was their race too—their plane too. Many had personally invested in the Gee Bee, buying shares for a hundred dollars each. Finally, just before five thirty that evening, the phone at the airfield rang with the news. Bayles had won, racing at an average speed of 236 miles per hour over the hundred-mile course.

The people in Springfield erupted in celebration. They honked car horns, beat oil drums, threw their hats in the air, and then marched down Liberty Street in an impromptu parade as if they themselves had won the trophy and the purse that came with it. Then, to welcome Bayles home a few days later, they scheduled a real parade and a dinner with speeches. Standing before the crowd that night, Granny already knew what he wanted to do with the $13,500 that the Gee Bees won in Cleveland. He would use the money to help Bayles break the air-speed record flying the victorious Super Sportster, because, it seemed, the Gee Bee could do anything: slow rolls and snap rolls, races and stunts, upside down and right side up. "Anything you want," Granny said. "The motor roars, but you feel no breeze. It seems as if you were stuck on a cloud."

The heavenly feeling, for Granny, would not last. In early 1931, seven months before Bayles's success at the air races, the first Gee Bee fell from the sky. A well-known airmail pilot, Johnny Kytle, was flying in Atlanta, doing stunts at a low altitude, when he lost control and plunged the brand-new Gee Bee nose-first into a swampy creek bed, hitting it at an estimated 180 miles an hour. The pilot, who died from his injuries, had a fractured skull, two broken arms, and two snapped femurs. "Nearly every bone in the popular young flier's body was broken," one report declared. Kytle was dead at age twenty-five. "One of our most valuable men," a fellow aviator said in mourning, "a pilot of extraordinary capability." As one witness put it, "I could see him frantically fighting the controls."

It might have been easy to write off Kytle's death as accidental, the cost of doing business in a fast plane flying low. But in the months to come, Gee Bee engines caught on fire. Gee Bee wings clipped pylons. Gee Bee planes, including both of Granny's entrants in the 1933 Bendix race, went down, resulting in the death of one of the pilots. In the middle of the Bendix race, after refueling in Indianapolis, famous transatlantic aviator Russell Boardman somehow lost control of his Gee Bee. The plane inexplicably nosed upward on takeoff and then rolled over, crashed to the ground, slid on its back for six hundred feet, and then came to a stop, leaving Boardman unconscious and seriously injured with a cracked skull, a punctured lung, a broken neck, and other injuries unknown. He slipped into a coma, and, like Kytle, he was soon dead, leaving a widow and a four-year-old daughter.

But the biggest loss — for Springfield, anyway — came in early December 1931, just a few months after the city's greatest aviation moment. Lowell Bayles was attempting to break the speed record in Detroit. His goal: three hundred miles an hour. And on his second attempt, Bayles seemed to have it. Witnesses watched in awe as the black-and-yellow Gee Bee descended from the winter sky, smooth and controlled, like a shooting star on a string. He was going to set the record, flying at an estimated 310 miles an hour. Then, about 150 feet from the ground, the plane suddenly dipped to the right and began to spin in a violent corkscrew. Once around, twice, three times — and down. On impact, the Gee Bee exploded into a sheet of fire, then rolled across the airfield for some four hundred feet. There was no need to call for an ambulance. Bayles was dead, burned in the flames.

Witnesses on the ground blamed the crash on a faulty right wing. They claimed they'd seen it break away under the strain of the speed, snapping at the point where the brace wires were attached. Some even said they heard the wood cracking or the fabric tearing as the wing shredded. "A ripping noise," one person described it. "I saw something let go on the right wing," another said. "Then came the crash."

Granny initially offered a different explanation for the incident that absolved him of any guilt. Maybe, he said, Bayles had become incapacitated in some way and simply lost control of the plane. But investigators, walking elbow to elbow at the field, found evidence of the broken wing on the ground. There was splintered spruce long before impact and ripped fabric from its coating. Worst of all, for Granny, there was newsreel footage of the plane in midflight, making it clear that the wing fell off in the air, dooming Bayles and finally prompting a confession from the man who had put him in the cockpit.

"We are forced to admit that the wood in the spar, which failed, was very poor," Granny told investigators nearly a month after the crash. "The excuse for this was that it was the only piece available, and there was not sufficient time to obtain any more." It was a terrible excuse, he said now, and he claimed to have fired the man who'd made the decision. But that didn't change the outcome. Bayles was dead, Granny said, "due to an inferior part, subjected to tremendous strain, for which it was never intended." Manufacturer error.

Granny headed west to Illinois for Bayles's funeral. He was saying goodbye to the famous airman but not to the famous plane that had ferried him to his death. The Gee Bee was soon returning to the sky, as difficult and as fast as ever. "To fly that plane," Jimmy Doolittle once said, "is exactly like the task of balancing an ice cream cone on the tip of one's finger."

In short, the aircraft was impossible—the perfect plane for Florence Klingensmith.

CLIFF HENDERSON PERSONALLY invited Klingensmith to the 1933 air races in Chicago. He couldn't spell her name correctly, sending the invitation to Florence *Klinginsmith*. But Henderson wanted her there that September at a time when he was beginning to believe that the hard years were behind the air races. "No doubt you have plans to participate," Henderson told Klingensmith. "If I can help you," Henderson added in a personal note, "let me know."

He and other air-race officials were finally making good on their promise to offer "women's suffrage" in the sky. That summer, both Earhart and Nichols had gotten approval to compete for the Bendix

Trophy, hoping to beat four men from New York to Los Angeles—
or, at least, each other. The two women were, by then, "friendly enemies," as one newspaper called them, and winning the Bendix that
July certainly would have gone a long way toward proving one's worth
over the other's. Neither did well. Nichols couldn't get her plane off
the ground in New York at first, starting a day late, which disqualified
her, and Earhart was hobbled by an overheating engine. She fell hours
off the pace in the Bendix and finally opted to turn around near Ama-
rillo and land in Wichita for the night, knowing she was, in her words,
"hopelessly out of the race."

Klingensmith hoped to do better in Chicago, a metropolis that she
didn't particularly like. On a visit there that spring, she groused about
the city—a hard place in a hard time, with its unemployment lines and
roving gangs of bandits holding up pedestrians for their jewelry, cash,
and, at times, the coats right off their backs. But thinking big, as usual,
Henderson wasn't just holding a race there; he had plans to save the
city. He was staging these races to coincide with another attraction
in Chicago that summer, the World's Fair, giving his show global importance. It would be called the International Air Races—the World's
Fair of the Air. "Admittedly, a thrilling spectacle and a masterpiece of
pageantry," Henderson boasted. "A significant story of tremendous interest to everyone."

Tickets went on sale that August at every department store in the
Loop, ninety post offices, local candy stores, and Henderson's headquarters at the La Salle Hotel, all targeting the crowds going to the fair.
Since the end of May, nearly thirteen million people had visited. They
attended operas at Soldier Field. They marveled at the 218-foot neon-
gas-powered thermometer recording the daily temperatures, and they
cheered the selection of beautiful women. "Wanted: 51 girls!" said ads
for a pageant to select an official queen for the fair, sponsored by the
Chicago Tribune. "Only unmarried girls are eligible," the *Tribune* stipu-
lated. "Judgment will be based on charm—loveliness, gracefulness,
and character."

The crowds brought Chicago's streets back to life. But without
question, the single biggest weekend of the summer was expected
to be Labor Day, with the fair and the air races happening at once.
The city was preparing for a crush of nearly four hundred thousand
visitors, and Henderson spared no detail to make sure they found his

races, twenty miles north of the fair at Glenview's modern gem of a field: Curtiss-Reynolds Airport. From his office at the La Salle, he wasn't recruiting just pilots but also cashiers and gate captains, bus drivers and donors. Despite all the hype, Henderson had only $35,000 in prize money to hand out. But at least he had convinced oil tycoon Frank Phillips to donate $10,000 for the last race of the weekend, the new Phillips Trophy race, open to both men and women who were willing to fly twelve laps around the eight-and-one-third-mile course laid out with large pylons at the field.

"You will perhaps be asked by your clients what pilots will be seen at the races," Henderson told his salesmen as they got ready to line up advertisers for the weekend. He instructed them to make it clear that the list of aviators in Chicago would be unforgettable. "The racing program," he said, "will represent the greatest galaxy of national and international flying aces ever seen in the United States." A galaxy that would include, among others, the rising star of Florence Klingensmith. She had accepted Henderson's invitation to come to Chicago, intent on flying in the women's speed race as well as in one other event that weekend.

"We have a surprise for you," the race announcer told the crowd on Labor Day, the last day of the races, building up the drama, on the sun-kissed airfield. "Florence Klingensmith of Minneapolis has just filed her entry in the Phillips Trophy race."

In doing so, the announcer informed the crowd, she would be the first woman ever to compete against men in a pylon speed race of such importance, the only woman to try. It was a decision she made, no doubt, based on her skill and her confidence. But lots of women — Earhart, Thaden, Nichols, and others — had loads of each. Only Klingensmith had a plane that could compete with the men's. It was on loan, a borrowed airship, red and white and blazing fast.

It was a Gee Bee.

"Florence," the announcer said, turning to her, "step up to the microphone and say hello to the crowd."

KLINGENSMITH GLIDED PAST the men on the airfield, wearing light green riding pants, a brown jacket, a beret, and a smile. At the microphone, she shrugged off the accolades. "I'm going out to try to give the boys a race," she said, modest and demure. That was all. "I'll tell you more about it after it's over." But away from the microphone and the crowd, Klingensmith had to admit she felt good — she had reached a pivotal moment in her life, and she knew it. She was ready.

"I'm feeling lucky today," she said, flipping a quarter to an attendant outside the women's restroom. She expected to challenge the men for the three-foot trophy and the money: $3,600 for first place, $2,000 for second, $1,200 for third, $800 for fourth, and $400 for fifth. Maybe she wouldn't win, but she would place. "The plane is fast enough," Klingensmith said, "and I can fly it."

All that weekend at the airfield, the men had been having fun at her expense. The day before, the announcer broadcast rumors of her love life over the public address system. Klingensmith was forced to show him her ringless left hand to prove she was not married. Reporters had also needled her, questioning whether she truly thought women were equal to men in aviation. Sure, the women could fly, one reporter said. But none of them really understood how an airplane worked. None of them had ever taken apart an engine.

"Ah, but I have," Klingensmith shot back. "Ask the men if I don't know all about planes. Ask them if I don't do all my own mechanical work. I learned planes from the ground up. I'm as good with a plane as any man."

Now, settling into the cockpit of the Gee Bee with a parachute strapped on her back, a tan leather helmet on her head, and goggles pulled down over her eyes, she set out to prove it. Klingensmith placed her left hand on the throttle, her right hand on the stick, and both feet on the rudder pedals, fixing her eyes on the instrument panel before her. As the engine roared to life, she could feel its strength — 670 horsepower. "Souped up," the boys on the ground said, "beyond any reasonable factor of mechanical or structural safety." It shrieked to get into the sky, and in no time at all, Klingensmith was in the air.

From the cockpit, she could see the three steel pylons laid out in a triangular course in the northwest corner of the field — far enough from the grandstand to keep the crowd safe in the event of a crash but still close enough that the fans could watch everything: the moves, the dips, and the whipping turns that required the utmost coordination and experience. To make each turn, Klingensmith and the six male pilots had to fly fifty to a hundred feet off the ground at speeds exceeding 220 miles an hour, using both the stick and the rudder pedals to cut each corner. They had to go low, but not too low; tight, but not too tight; fast, but in control, avoiding the other planes, the pylons themselves, and the ground—any of which could kill the pilots. It was the aviation equivalent of *spetakkel*—and there was no stopping it now. Just after six o'clock, with the sun starting to dip on the horizon, Klingensmith's Gee Bee and the six other planes competing for the Phillips Trophy crossed the home pylon, roaring to the north in the air. They were off.

On the ground below, people were everywhere—sitting in the grandstands and standing on the floorboards of their parked cars, watching from official seats they'd bought for a dollar each and from unofficial viewing spots they claimed for free on nearby roads and golf courses. They watched as two male pilots quickly shot to the front of the pack, flying close to 250 miles an hour. And they watched as Klingensmith fell in somewhere behind them. At the end of the first lap, back at the home pylon closest to the grandstand, the crowd could finally see exactly where she was; her red-and-white Gee Bee was challenging for third, flying nearly 220 miles an hour and banking so hard that she tipped the plane vertically on its wing and seemed to kiss the top of the fifty-foot pylon. "Just look at that girl make that perfect bank," the announcer cried for the crowd to hear. "Did you ever see such a beautiful race?"

She was for real; they knew that now. "With that turn," one pilot on the ground said, "Florence Klingensmith stole the show." She was surely going to make some money, as she had promised, winning third place and its $1,200 prize or better. Then, at the home pylon on the eighth turn, roughly sixty miles in, her Gee Bee faltered, buckling under a familiar problem. The right wing—the same wing that doomed Bayles's Gee Bee—was failing. Fabric ripped away in chunks and fell to the ground like confetti, and with the air now whistling through the holes in her wing, Klingensmith peeled off course. She was flying away from the crowd in the grandstand, over the spectators in their parked cars at the edge of the safety fence, beyond the railroad tracks heading south toward Chicago, and then out over the streets of Glenview, in trouble.

"Bail out," one pilot on the ground said, pounding his fist into the back of the man standing in front of him. "Jump, Florence. Jump NOW!"

In the cockpit, thinking fast, Klingensmith pulled back on the stick, tipping up the elevators on the tail and gaining altitude, maybe 250 feet. She needed to get higher in the sky before attempting to jump. She also needed to get away from the Labor Day race crowds beneath her. A jump near the airfield at a decent altitude might save her, but it could lead to the death of scores of others on the ground. Without Klingensmith at the controls, her Gee Bee would no longer be a plane but a missile flying at almost two hundred miles an hour, unguided and indiscriminate.

Ten seconds passed. Fifteen, maybe twenty. Everyone near the airfield was tracking the red plane, hoping to see it turn back toward the field or to spot the white canopy of her parachute floating above it. But there was no turn and no parachute either.

Without warning, the Gee Bee dipped to the right, leaning on the wounded wing, then dived, nose-first, into the ground.

FROM ACROSS GLENVIEW, people came running: police officers and farmers, race fans and gawkers. They discovered the busted heap of the aircraft in a tree nursery, and after pulling the limp body of the pilot from the cockpit, they dragged her five feet away and laid her on the ground. She was tangled up in the strings of her parachute, bleeding profusely, and probably already gone. "Dead," one man at the scene confirmed, "absolutely."

But they called for an ambulance anyway, and, finding a pulse, medics hustled her to a hospital ten miles away. The short drive was, like the race itself, a disaster. The ambulance broke down en route. With no way to transport the patient, police officers hailed a passing sedan, placed the wounded pilot in a stretcher on its roof, and then stood on the floorboards and held her there while someone drove the car as fast as one possibly could with a person lying on top.

Most likely, none of it mattered. Doctors at the hospital in nearby Evanston declared Florence Klingensmith dead on arrival, with a list of injuries that would have killed any pilot. Her upper left arm and multiple ribs were broken, as were both of her femurs, each snapping at almost exactly the same spot, just above the knee, and breaking through her skin. But the worst of her injuries were to her chest and head. Her sternum and the right side of her skull were crushed. On impact, Klingensmith had broken nearly every bone in her face.

The cause of death was easy to determine—"injuries sustained due to external violence," according to the coroner's report. The cause of the crash should have been easy to determine as well. People at the field had seen the fabric tearing away from the wing of Klingensmith's Gee Bee. "A large piece of fabric," one witness said. "Several pieces," said another. "Once the wind was able to catch an edge, it was torn off clean." Klingensmith's death was just another Gee Bee crackup with a relatively simple explanation: the structural failure of a powerful plane traveling at a high rate of speed at a low altitude. The pilot had done everything possible to save herself and others. She flew away from the crowd. She tried to gain altitude to make a parachute jump, and the plane had crashed either as she let go of the stick to make that jump or before she had the chance, due to the faulty wing.

But local investigators—special air deputy coroners assigned to probe plane crashes—weren't satisfied with that answer. At a pro forma inquest to determine the cause of Klingensmith's crash just one day after it happened, they called eleven witnesses to testify, including fellow pilots, mechanics, race fans who had seen Klingensmith go down, and Cliff Henderson's quiet brother Phil, his trusted sidekick, rolling out her body for the witnesses to see.

Many at the hearing praised Klingensmith: her racing qualifications, her finely honed skills built up over years of flying, and those beautiful turns that impressed the crowd during the Phillips Trophy race. One deputy sheriff testified, "The girl has had quite a bit of ability. She has had a lot of experience." But the same deputy in the same breath wondered if Klingensmith had made a mistake. The shredded wing fabric, in his estimation, wasn't enough to cause the plane to crash. Maybe she was physically or mentally overwhelmed. Maybe she panicked. "I believe that she possibly fainted and leaned forward into that there stick," the deputy speculated, "throwing the plane into a dive."

In this scenario, the dangerous Gee Bee wasn't to blame. The whole affair was quite possibly pilot error, an explanation that seemed to make sense to the coroner's investigators, who questioned everything about Klingensmith: her limited experience with the Gee Bee, her minimal knowledge of the plane, and even her body. The aeronautics branch of the US Department of Commerce had strict physical standards that every pilot needed to meet to be licensed. An aviator had to have strong eyes, functioning eardrums, good balance, and a healthy heart. Unrepaired harelips and stuttering speech could be cause for disqualification, as could a history of asthma or pneumonia. In general, government inspectors frowned on any imperfection, but especially troubling were disorders of the brain—phobias and worries, amnesia and insomnia. The successful candidates would be cheerful, stable, self-reliant, and aggressive, yet also modest, fond of people, sharp, and resourceful. They would not be, as the government put it, depressed or hypercritical, submissive or irritable. And they would absolutely not be menstruating when sitting in the cockpit at the controls of an airplane. *"All women,"* the rules noted in italics, *"should be cautioned that it is dangerous for them to fly within a period extending from 3 days prior, to 3 days after, the menstrual period."*

"Was this pilot examined before these races, as to her physical condition?" the coroner's investigator asked Phil Henderson when he took the witness stand at Klingensmith's inquest.

"I do not believe that she was," Phil said. "I would not say positively, no."

"You do not know that positively?"

"No."

Phil testified that a doctor typically examined pilots at the races only in one scenario. "If they had been out drinking," Phil said, "the night before." If they were hung over or, worse, still drunk. "And we know pretty much," Phil said. "We know pretty well how the boys are conducting themselves." By this measure, he suggested, there was no need to examine Klingensmith. But by failing to do so, Henderson's men had missed something.

"Did any official or doctor there know that this woman was having her periods at this time, monthly periods?" the investigator asked Henderson.

"No, sir," he said.

The verdict, in the end, reflected the reality. "A Gee Bee monoplane," the coroner concluded, "went into a nose dive apparently due to fabric tearing off the right wing." But reporters fixated on Klingensmith's physical state at the time of the crash, with the *Chicago Daily News,* the main sponsor of the air races and the newspaper with the most access to Cliff Henderson, leading the charge. The paper reported that Klingensmith "wasn't well," that she lacked "stamina," and that she had died due to her "weakened condition"—a condition she had known about prior to the race and disregarded. "For fame," the *Daily News* declared the next day, "for prize money, and to prove that girl fliers can 'take it.'" Instead, the *Daily News* suggested, Klingensmith had proven the opposite.

Officials shipped her body by train back to Minnesota, naked and wrapped in newspaper, inside a cheap casket, with her blond hair unwashed and her clothes unaccounted for—an insult, as far as the folks in Kragnes Township were concerned. "She had given her life for the show," the local mortician pointed out. And for her sacrifice, she got nothing. Not even the most basic human respect. "I've had hundreds of bodies shipped to me," the mortician said much later, "and I've literally shipped thousands." But never before and never again did he see another case like this one.

The locals tried to make it up to her parents with a proper funeral, well attended. Her Fargo sponsors bought the family a bronze casket to replace the shabby box sent from Chicago. They purchased a black dress for the morticians to put on Klingensmith's body, and they arranged for services in which she could be honored, first at a church in Fargo and later at her gravesite in the cemetery near the little school she had once attended. "The girl we knew as a pilot has come to an untimely end in one sense," said the presiding minister, who was a pilot himself in Minneapolis and had known Klingensmith personally. "But in a larger sense, there is no such thing as an untimely end." Her pioneering spirit, he hoped, would live on forever. "Florence Klingensmith would say she did not regret giving her life for aviation, were she able to speak here," the minister added. "She would say she found it all worthwhile—her only regret being that, while still young and healthy, she could not further enjoy a world that she found good."

Then, in the southwest corner of the cemetery, they lowered her casket into the ground soon to freeze in the coming frosts of winter, burying her beneath a pile of flowers—yellow marigolds and pink carnations, white daisies and orange sword lilies. Frank Phillips, the oil executive who'd financed the fatal race, sent a floral arrangement shaped like wings. Friends, not to be outdone, sent an arrangement in the shape of a small plane, purple and pink. Cliff Henderson sent flowers too, cut red roses. But he couldn't attend the funeral or the coroner's inquest into her death in Chicago. Henderson had other plans. While Klingensmith's body was wrapped in newspapers and shipped north,

Henderson was in Indiana dedicating an airport for his friend Vincent Bendix and then attending a raucous party at Bendix's mansion for all the pilots who'd flown in for the affair.

Flying home to Chicago the next morning, three of Bendix's guests disappeared in a green airship over Lake Michigan. It would be five days before their bodies washed ashore. And that fall, a government official in Washington wrote an internal memo warning that planes would continue to fall from the sky. They would crash into homes, businesses, and city streets, "in many cases resulting in damage to property and life," and there was little that authorities could do to prevent that from happening. But they could stop the women—and they would. Henderson would see to it himself. The man who took credit for inviting the women to fly in the Powder Puff Derby, the man who hyped the female pilots every chance he got and who had personally invited Klingensmith to participate, now proclaimed himself opposed to the very concept of their inclusion. "Miss Florence Klingensmith's fatal crash in Chicago in 1933, in a closed-course race, only proved what I already knew," he declared.

Women didn't belong in his races.

They were out.

17

All Things Being Equal

Louise Thaden bolted upright in bed, screaming in the dark —another flying nightmare, another tortured vision of death in the sky, her own. Thaden was having a lot of these nightmares lately. They were always the same: the airplane was going down, spinning below the rooftops, out of gas or out of control or both, with a shoddy wing shorn off at the brace wires or a faulty engine engulfed in flames and Thaden shrieking in the cockpit.

"Pull it out!

"Put it out!"

She awoke in tears sometimes to find herself in bed next to her husband, Herb, in a new house, in an unfamiliar city, chasing work yet again, another aviation job for Herb, anything to pay the bills. In the past seven years, Herb had held down jobs in five different cities in three different time zones and Louise had always followed him: first to Pittsburgh, then Baltimore, and now Kansas City, where they lived in a squat, two-story stucco home.

Somewhere down the hall, their son, Bill, almost three, was surely asleep, oblivious to his new surroundings, his parents' increasingly nomadic ways, and his mother's growing anxiety. At least Thaden understood the reason for her troubled dreams. In the months between Earhart's transatlantic success and Klingensmith's disaster in Chicago, Thaden had returned to the sky herself in an aviation feat sure to grab headlines. She wanted to set a new female endurance record, flying nonstop over Long Island for a week or longer—twenty-four hours a day, refueling in the sky via a hose dropped from another airplane. For the job, Thaden would need a copilot. Organizers paired her up with the likable Frances Marsalis, an experienced pilot from Texas five years older than Thaden. And together, not long after Earhart's ocean flight, the two women took off over New York in a modified six-seater cabin plane that reporters dubbed the *Flying Boudoir.*

No matter what the reporters might have thought, no matter how they described it, the endurance airship was no posh feminine retreat. By night, Thaden and Marsalis froze in the cold, huddled beneath a thin wool blanket. "Frightfully inadequate," Thaden said. By day, they struggled to stay awake, making circle after circle around the airfield about two thousand feet off the ground. They were taking turns at the controls, but neither woman got much sleep. Their air mattress sprang a leak almost as soon as the flight began. With no cushion, they had to curl up between the auxiliary gas tanks, feet toward the cockpit and head toward the tail, lying downhill, a near-impossible angle to find rest. Both unable to sleep and almost incapable of staying awake, they passed the time by singing, whistling, sticking their heads out the cockpit window into the wind, and pumping fuel by hand into the tanks—220 gallons every twenty hours, funneled in with little drips of fuel, a fourth of a pint with every hand stroke, more than seven thousand strokes to do the job. By the time they finished pumping, Thaden felt like they almost needed to start all over again, heaping monotony on top of tedium, with a side of fatigue and fear. The nightmares set in almost immediately. Anytime Thaden managed to doze off during the endurance flight, she dreamed that the *Flying Boudoir* was spinning, stalling, skidding, or crashing—only to awake to the same tasks as before. "Pump gasoline, eat, pump gasoline, check oil, sleep, fly," she wrote in her log at one point. "Pump gasoline, pump oil, check strainers, eat, fly."

In the end, Thaden and Marsalis broke the female endurance record after five days and then flew on—into the headwinds of exhaustion. Male organizers on the ground were so giddy that they suggested the women keep flying all the way to Cleveland to open Henderson's annual air races starting later that week. "Of course, there would be a lot of risk," one of the men informed the women in a note dropped into the plane during one of the midair refueling visits. "Bad weather, motor failure, etc., and we would not attempt it unless everything looks perfect." But, he added, "newspapermen think it would be a knockout."

The two women couldn't help but laugh.

"Why don't they come up here," Marsalis said, "fly a couple of hundred years and see how it feels!"

The *Flying Boudoir* was coming down.

"It's over, gal," Thaden said, reaching over and rumpling Marsalis's dark hair on the morning of the eighth day. "We're going to land."

On the ground that night, to celebrate the new endurance record— 196 consecutive hours in the sky—Thaden had a Scotch and soda. "Doctor's orders," she said. But she couldn't shake the nightmares that had begun in the sky over Long Island or the reality of her life back on the ground: the new job for Herb, the move to Kansas City, the stucco house on the quiet street there, and the demands of motherhood. While Nichols and Earhart were pushing each other across oceans, and while Klingensmith was challenging the men, Thaden was sitting in the sandbox with her young son or lying on the grass next to him, staring up at the sky and wondering if her days of flying, real competitive flying, were over. She was turning twenty-eight in the fall of 1933—and, after the endurance flight, she got pregnant with her second child. This time, reporters wouldn't be coming to visit her in the hospital. They were slowly forgetting Louise Thaden. "Torn between two loves," she conceded. Her flying and her family, her career and her children. She was trying to have both. Because that's what she wanted. She wanted it all. "To a psychoanalyst," Thaden wrote, "a woman pilot, particularly a married one with children, must prove an interesting as well as an inexhaustible subject." She was, she admitted, "emotionally confused," and yet determined.

The second child, a girl, was born in Kansas City less than three weeks after Klingensmith's death in Chicago. She was golden blond like Klingensmith, tall like Thaden, and "supercharged," the Thadens reported in a lighthearted mock press release. "Announcement of the Thaden Avigating Outfit, Inc.," the release began. "The management of the T.A.O., Inc., take pleasure in announcing the acquisition at 3:30 AMC time, September 22, 1933, of additional equipment to their fleet of modern streamlined Aviats."

"Name," the memo continued, "Patricia (Pat to you!) . . . High speed: Very high . . . Cruising speed: Still higher . . . Range: 4 hours . . . Fuel: Mammary, Grade 'A' . . . This addition," the Thadens wrote in conclusion, "has been acquired at no small cost in time, money or energy and represents the very latest results attained in aesthetic art and scientific engineering skill."

Louise Thaden had a family of four, two healthy children, a boy and a girl — a good life. Still, she was unsettled inside the stucco house in Middle America, itching to fly again.

Herb could feel it.

THE WOMEN MOURNED the death of Florence Klingensmith that month. She was one of the original Ninety-Nines, a charter member of the organization. "Only Viking stock, America, the twentieth century could have produced Florence Gunderson Klingensmith, the woman transport pilot who died proving that women can fly on an equal basis with men," read the obituary in the Ninety-Nines' newsletter. Her story, the obituary continued, deserved to be remembered, with Klingensmith given a heroic place in American history. "More particularly," the Ninety-Nines said, "in the history of feminism." It was a moment — their moment — and they were not going to let the male aviators and Henderson hijack it and use it to ban them from the air races. In late 1933, women had enough problems as it was.

That September, as Klingensmith climbed into the cockpit of her doomed Gee Bee outside Chicago, there were an estimated 250,000 unemployed women clattering along in dirty boxcars and hitchhiking from town to town, a bedraggled feminine army. "One of the strangest armies this country has ever known," one female writer noted. "A nomad army, penniless or nearly penniless." Relief workers were stunned at the sight of these lost American women. "Thin, emaciated girls," one government report declared, "overwhelmed at the sight of a simple supper." Many had contemplated suicide, despondent about not working. Others found jobs but got paid far less than men — a fact not lost on cash-strapped employers. It was, one employer said, the only real reason to hire women: "They produce more and demand less."

The story in the aviation industry that fall was different in only one way: women usually couldn't get hired at all, the Ninety-Nines believed, a hypothesis that they set out to prove. With Earhart and Nichols leading the way, the organization mailed surveys to almost every plane manufacturer, supplier, and commercial airline in the country requesting information about the women they employed, the types of jobs they held, and their worth to the company compared to men. Question: "What jobs if any do you feel that women are better fitted for than men?" Question: "Would you keep a woman in a job that you feel a man could do equally well?" Question: "Why do you not use women in larger numbers?"

Most companies simply didn't reply. But those who returned the surveys, mailing them directly to Nichols at her parents' home in Rye, didn't hold back. Women, aviation executives reported, were best suited for "routine perfunctory duties" — answering phones or taking dictation. They had no place flying a plane or holding any other job on board an airliner unless they were acting, one vice president explained, "as hostesses." As a result, the companies saw little need to hire many women, passing them over for a whole host of reasons. "Limited positions . . . Our business calls for more men . . . All things being equal, prefer men." One parachute manufacturer put it this way: "Our experience," he said, "has disclosed the fact that most women have insufficient mechanical ability and little desire to observe and learn." They could really do only one job at the parachute company: operate a sewing machine.

But that was still more than they could do elsewhere. At the Waco Aircraft Company in Ohio, the personnel director had no interest in hiring women at all. They just created problems around the factory, he said. "Further might add that if women spent more time making homes pleasant and less time trying to get men's jobs there would be less domestic trouble," he opined. "More men would be employed. The world would be happier."

Waco Aircraft wanted the women's money; it wanted them as customers. The Ohio plane builder was soon advertising in *Ninety-Niner* magazine, a publication written by women pilots for women pilots. The company just didn't want the women in the workplace.

"I WANT TO WARN YOU," Nichols told anyone who asked, "that opportunities for work, for women in aviation, have become almost impossible."

The situation had been bleak before the Depression; it was worse

now. The surveys confirmed it, and Klingensmith's death only complicated matters. Already blocking women from jobs on factory floors,
the men could now argue that women didn't belong in a cockpit either. Didn't belong in the races. Didn't deserve a stake of the prize
money. As it was, there wasn't enough money to go around. Nichols
didn't need to read the surveys to understand the depths of their disapproval. She wasn't riding the rails, like many other American women
that year. She wasn't emaciated or going without food. But she was
just as lost.

Since her mishaps of 1931 — crashing her white-and-gold Crosley airplane on the runway in Canada and then burning it up on the
ground in Louisville in a span of just four months — Nichols was, in
her own words, "freelancing." Mostly, she wasn't working at all.

Crosley wasn't interested in backing her anymore. Times were
too hard, he informed Nichols in late 1933, two months after Klingensmith's death. He was cutting everything "to the bone," he said. "I do
hope that you find something that will appeal to you and be profitable to you," Crosley told Nichols. "But there just isn't a chance in the
world of our going into such a thing at this time."

It wasn't the only source of income drying up for her. Just a few
years earlier, awash in the glow of her aerial success, Nichols had been
in demand on the lecture circuit, receiving invites to speak and charging as much as five hundred dollars to appear. At times, she was so
busy that she turned down opportunities. Now the money and the invites were gone. She was lucky to get fifty dollars for an appearance
or even to be invited at all. The rejection letters piled up in her mail-
box — and still, Nichols was dreaming, vowing to do something big.
"A long over-water record next summer," she said. Maybe even something unprecedented for a woman. She wanted to be the first female
pilot to go around the world. "This is," she said, "the last important
news flight left."

But as with her lectures, Nichols's around-the-world flight plans
spurred little interest. One by one, major American corporations
passed, making it clear, if it wasn't already, that Ruth Nichols, like the
other women, was going nowhere. By 1934, there was perhaps only
one woman with enough power to convince moneyed men, race organizers, and Henderson to listen.

AMELIA EARHART STEPPED into the church to the delight of the crowd, fifteen hundred people in all, sitting in the pews, spilling into the chapel, and even crowding into the basement, where they couldn't see Earhart but could still enjoy the sound of her voice emanating from loudspeakers. The large Tuesday-night crowd in the fall of 1933 was unusual for Mason City, Iowa; it felt like half the town was there. But to Earhart, it was just another night. As soon as her talk was finished, she would head to Minneapolis, then Emporia, Kansas, and Maryville, Missouri, covering nearly nine hundred miles that week alone. After that, she would loop back to Iowa again to hit Des Moines, where she was getting three hundred dollars to appear—the sort of money that Nichols didn't dare ask for anymore but that clubs paid Earhart knowing they could recoup her exorbitant speaker's fee with ticket sales. People happily paid fifty cents or a dollar to hear Earhart repackage the same comments she had made the night before in some other town's junior high school, church, tearoom, or auditorium. "Don't miss it," ads declared in the small towns she visited across America. "What she has to say will be as be interesting to men as it is to women, for Miss Earhart is an authority on aviation as well as an entertaining speaker and one of the most famous persons her sex has produced."

Her talk—"Flying for Fun"—was almost always the same. Like a well-practiced candidate running for office, she took the stage in navy blue chiffon or brown tweed and delivered her stump speech with an ease that made her audience feel as if she were speaking the words for the first time, as if she had crafted the words just for them. Earhart wanted people to know that flying was safe and getting safer; that they had nothing to fear; that "the fear business," as she called it, was illogical; and that one day soon, everyone would travel by plane. "It is coming much faster than we realize," she said, making it clear that, yes, flying was more dangerous than traveling by horse and buggy or ox cart. "But," Earhart liked to add in one of her oft-repeated lines, "I didn't see any ox-carts around this building this evening."

In her speeches that fall, she made no obvious reference to Klingensmith's death or the brewing controversy with the men at the air races. But anyone who attended her talks understood exactly how Earhart felt. For years now, the former social worker had been pointing out the hypocrisy of the system—in this case, the aviation world and the reporters who covered it. "When a man cracks up, no one pays any special attention," Earhart said at one point. "But oh, when a girl does . . ." Here came the questions and the criticism, fair or not.

It bothered Earhart, who had long ago developed a keen sense of justice. Women, Earhart argued now, had just as much reason to fly as men. Just as much ability too, if they trained and got experience. "Women," she said during one stop at Yale University that November, "should be treated no differently from men." Earhart, a pacifist, even advocated that the government should make women eligible to be soldiers. "They should be drafted," she argued, "made to do the dirty work, and real fighting instead of dressing up and parading up and down the streets." If nothing else, she said, it would discourage old male politicians from pushing the country into battle. "They are the ones," she said, "who start war."

Henderson didn't exactly fit the description of an old male politician. He was just thirty-eight that winter, only two years older than Earhart, and he was an air-race promoter, not an elected official in Washington. But he was as smooth as any carpetbagger and increasingly at the center of the war between the men and women. As the air races resumed in early 1934, Henderson wasn't backing away from the idea that women shouldn't race. At the first national air meet after Klingensmith's death, scheduled to take place in New Orleans during Carnival in early February 1934, he and other race organizers banned women, writing three words beneath every competition listed in the race program: "Men Pilots Only."

The reason, Henderson told curious reporters, was simple. "There is no more place for women pilots in the high-speed, free-for-all air race game," he said, "than there is a place for women drivers on the speedway at Indianapolis." Or on a football field. He claimed that the women had no interest in such racing anyway, having turned past events into "a farce," he said. But he conceded there was one other factor behind the new rules. "Obviously, the unfortunate death of Florence Klingensmith contributed to this decision."

Local leaders in New Orleans didn't raise a single public objection to Henderson's ban. The city had a new $4 million airfield on the shores of Lake Pontchartrain to open and dedicate. Henderson's races were going to be perfect for the occasion, and civic clubs placed advertisements encouraging New Orleanians to support the races, support Henderson. "Do your part," they were told.

He blew into town not long after Klingensmith's death with his brother Phil, set up shop in a suite at the elegant Roosevelt Hotel near Bourbon Street, and quickly earned invites to mingle with the city's Uptown elite. He lounged under the towering oak trees on Palmer Avenue after Saturday-afternoon football games at Tulane University. He spoke at downtown luncheons, making all his usual bold declarations, promising thrills. He convinced a local radio station to give him a fifteen-minute weekly radio show to spread the word, and he helped find a job for at least a few young women at the races. The city's debutantes, he said, the refined daughters of local wealth and privilege, could christen the airplanes of the great aviators soon to be zipping into New Orleans for this grand event. All of the top men were coming. Zantford Granville, the crafty builder of the Gee Bee, was flying in from Springfield, Massachusetts. Captain Merle Nelson, a Pennzoil airman famous for performing "night fire rides," spewing a trail of fireworks from his airship while flying three hundred miles an hour in the dark, was coming too. Henderson had appointed Nelson to be his chief of acrobatics, demonstrating inverted flight, inside loops, inverted outside loops, spins, and barrel rolls for the crowd. Big Lee Miles, a husky Californian and record-holding speed racer, would be there, folding his 194-pound, six-foot-two-inch frame into the cockpit of his fast plane, or any plane. Miles would be racing every day, Henderson promised, and two other famous aviators were expected to be jousting with him in the sky: Roscoe Turner, a Los Angeles pilot built like a middle linebacker, and Turner's polar opposite, Benny Howard, a Chicago airman with all the girth of an egg whisk. Together, Turner and Howard had more speed records, race wins, and Henderson-made trophies than almost any other two pilots combined. Better still, they were colorful creatures cut from iconic cloth and thus easy for Henderson to market to the masses. If any man epitomized American machismo in the sky in 1934, it was Turner—or Howard.

Turner, who got his start flying in the army and later in Hollywood movies, burst onto the air-race scene in 1929 when he attempted to set a new transcontinental speed record. He fell short by two hours but returned to claim the record in 1930. He then bettered his mark in 1932 and won both the Bendix and the Thompson trophies in 1933, making him the fastest flier in the sky. "Speed with safety—that's what I wanted to demonstrate," he said after his Bendix victory. "And I believe

I carried out my purpose." If he sounded sure of himself, it was only because he was, proving it with his skill in the sky and his flair on the ground. Turner usually wore a full military-style uniform, blue and imposing and designed by Turner himself. He took great care grooming his mustache, using wax to spike it up at the tips. And to make sure that people remembered him — "He loves to be a big-shot," reporter Ernie Pyle once wrote — Turner flew with a pet lion named Gilmore.

"He likes an airplane better than crowds," Turner said of Gilmore. But the famous lion had to deal with both. Turner would walk the big cat on a leash down the streets of Los Angeles or New York, Cincinnati or Cleveland. He'd take him to banquets and feed him steaks at the table, and Gilmore even stayed with him at hotels until the animal's size made it impossible to accommodate him. By 1934, Gilmore was four years old, four hundred pounds, and living on a steady diet of horsemeat in a large zoo-like enclosure not far from the Turner home at a major intersection near the Hollywood Hills.

Benny Howard paled in comparison to Turner — anybody would have. He had no lion or swashbuckling uniform, and his dark mustache seemed small and plain next to Turner's waxed creation. Howard looked more like a door-to-door vacuum salesman than a pilot, more huckster than aviator. But the Texas native had one thing Turner lacked: engineering know-how. With no degrees and no formal education beyond elementary school, Howard had gotten a job working in Houston as an airplane mechanic when he was a teenager. Hanging around the airfield there, he took lessons and earned his pilot's license that winter, and he soon had a reputation for flying unusual cargo across the South: contraband, bootlegged alcohol, and, on at least one occasion, a seven-hundred-pound bull that the Carnation Milk Company needed moved from Chicago to Texas in a hurry. "It is not likely that we will all ever fly again with a bull," a thankful Carnation Milk man told Howard afterward. "But if we should leave the ground, I am sure that we would want to place ourselves in your care."

Airlines soon hired him, putting the reliable Howard in the cockpit of their new passenger planes. It wasn't just that he could fly well; it was his innate understanding of why it was possible, the physics of it all. He built his first plane at age twenty-two — the Howard Flyabout, it was called — and by age twenty-six, he was the story of the air races: this Texan now living on the South Side of Chicago building his own planes in his yard and flying them to victory, an everyman's hero. "Others carried off larger sums in money," one fan noted after Howard's first showing at the races. "But Howard carried with him the admiration of the crowds." He had ditched the whole Howard Flyabout business. The name was too boring. He was now calling his home-built airships DGAs—Damn Good Airplanes. "I've sunk everything I own into these planes," he grumbled, forty thousand dollars or more. A small fortune for planes that put him in debt and worried his employer, United Airlines. The airline banned him from racing the DGAs himself. Too dangerous.

But Howard refused to be denied. For pylon racing, he employed a team of pilots to do the flying for him. And he managed to convince his bosses at United to let him personally fly his DGAs in transcontinental races like the Bendix. It wasn't that Howard didn't trust his team of pilots to do the job; he just knew he could do it better, with his knowledge of the machinery, his feel for the controls, his long-distance flying experience racked up at United, and a certain intangible quality that Howard called "Go-Grease." In simple terms, Howard wanted it more, wanted to win, flying with a combination of ease and recklessness. In the air, he often kept a bottle of whiskey at the ready, while on the ground, Go-Grease Benny enjoyed the company of his young blond wife. When he landed, she was often waiting for him, greeting him with a kiss as the photographers snapped their picture, urging them on.

"Come on, Mrs. Howard," they pleaded. "Kiss him again."

With brave airmen like these on hand, Henderson could live without the women in his races in 1934. And proving him right, a large crowd turned out for opening day in New Orleans. The debutantes were there to christen the aviators' planes, as requested. The Louisiana State University marching band came too. Tulane football players helped usher the fans to their seats, and the governor spoke to them all, bringing glad tidings from President Franklin D. Roosevelt. "The president expressed to me his regrets that pressing affairs in the national capital prevented his attendance," the governor told the crowd. "But asked me—and I deem it a signal honor on my part to be able to deliver to you—his greetings and blessings on this occasion."

The governor had hardly finished addressing the crowd before the mishaps began. Rounding a pylon on a test flight that afternoon, a pilot banked his plane too hard, too low, clipped the ground with one wing, and rolled in a deadly somersault across the brand-new airport with its modern concrete runways. The pilot survived—a miracle. The races almost didn't. For the next four days, heavy rains, black clouds, and a torrent of bad weather—including hailstorms, freezing temperatures, and even snow in some parts of the South—made flying impossible, forcing Henderson to do something he'd never done: cancel. The Mardi Gras races would have to begin on Ash Wednesday, he announced, promising to honor any tickets purchased in advance.

But those coming to the races that Wednesday didn't get a chance to see Zantford Granville in his famous Gee Bee. On his way to New Orleans for the races, Granny was attempting to land in Spartanburg, South Carolina, when, for reasons unknown, he lost control of his blue-and-yellow Gee Bee. He was flying roughly as high as Klingensmith had been at the time of her Gee Bee malfunction, about seventy feet off the ground. But no one questioned whether Granny should have bailed out, recovered, or saved himself or the plane. The pioneering airman surely did everything he could before plowing his Gee Bee, nose-first, into the ground, cleaving off the engine on impact and smashing his body inside the tiny cockpit. He was dead, with a list of injuries almost exactly like Klingensmith's. "A tough break," one man back in Springfield said. "There is no comment we can make at a time like this," said another. At his burial that week near Boston, a squadron of small planes dived low over the cemetery and scattered flowers on Granny's grave—a fitting tribute that nearly ended with another funeral. One pilot in the aerial procession had to make a forced landing on a frozen pond after his engine sputtered and stopped in midflight without warning. Luckily, the ice held.

That same morning, back in New Orleans, Henderson's all-male races resumed, with similar good fortune. The skies were clear after days of bad weather, and Henderson had a perfect finale in store for fans who stayed until the end. That night at the races, Captain Merle Nelson, Henderson's handpicked chief of acrobatics, took to the sky for his "night-fire ride" spewing a stream of fireworks from his comet plane and performing loops and spins.

The show didn't last long. At exactly 8:52 p.m., twenty minutes after taking off, Nelson crashed his looping plane into the ground just two hundred feet from the grandstands, in full view of the crowd. Laden with explosives, the aircraft burst into flames on impact, skidded across the ground like a rolling fireball, and came to rest, flipped over, with its burning cockpit pressed against the ground. Inside, Nelson was on fire — alive and screaming. The first person to reach the wreckage, hearing the yells of the desperate aviator, tried to push the plane over with his hands. But in doing so, the would-be rescuer burned himself. There was nothing to do but stand there and wait and watch in the flickering glow of the burning plane on the lakeshore until the fire burned through the pilot's seat belt, dropping the lifeless body of Merle Nelson to the ground — uninjured, the coroner ruled later, but for the extensive burns.

Even Henderson, who had witnessed his share of air deaths, was shaken by the scene. "This is," he said that night, "one of the greatest surprises of my life. If we feared for any of the fliers, we feared least of all for Captain Nelson's safety." Nelson himself, apparently, had thought differently. Well aware of the dangers associated with the air races, the pilot had left written instructions were he to die in New Orleans. He wanted to be cremated, sent back into the sky once more on the shores of the lake, and scattered across the field by another pilot — a tribute that Henderson helped organize. The man who had skipped Klingensmith's funeral set aside time to honor Nelson during the races. He placed his ashes in a silver urn on a flag-draped table on the airfield, then had them scattered by plane, as directed. He arranged to have three buglers play taps as the ashes floated back to the earth and also secured, for good measure, the Louisiana National Guard to fire off a three-volley salute with a massive seventy-five-millimeter gun.

But before all this, air-race officials were grappling with yet another calamity. That Saturday, just three days after Nelson's crash, a veteran parachute jumper got hung up on the tail of a plane two thousand feet above the grandstand. The chute had opened too early and the man was just dangling from the moving plane while the panicked pilot tried to shake him loose. There were twists and turns — and then, finally, a spiraling dive that could have been mistaken for more thrills had everyone on the ground not known the truth. In his effort to shake off the tangled parachute and save the jumper, the pilot had lost control and plunged his plane into the lake about a hundred yards off the beach.

Boaters motored to the crash site within moments to find the parachute jumper dead, still tangled up on the tail, his chest wall having been crushed upon impact. The pilot was missing, thrown clear from the plane, just gone. It would be almost a month before his body washed ashore in the tattered remains of his aviator's jacket, rotting after weeks in the warm water. And by then, Cliff Henderson was long gone. He had moved out of his suite at the Roosevelt Hotel and returned to Cleveland, where he settled in at a different hotel, a horse-shoe-shaped castle known for its views of Lake Erie, its thick walls, and its wealthy guests: movie stars and mobsters.

Henderson was neither, but he was perhaps just as powerful. He was already planning his next show, the next air races, set to take place over Labor Day weekend in Cleveland, where, once again, the women were not invited to compete because, of course, they didn't know how to fly.

18

That's What I Think of Wives Flying

THE PROBLEMS IN New Orleans—the fires and the funerals, the crashes and the bodies floating in the lake—were just that: problems in New Orleans. As Henderson set up his office, once again in Cleveland, he seemed to bear no scars from the time he'd spent down south alienating the women and watching men die. He and his brother Phil were still getting rich, anyway. They were on pace that year to earn more than forty-three thousand dollars from the air races alone, roughly eight hundred thousand dollars in today's money.

But his income—and his customary bravado—belied the challenges he faced. The National Air Races had been losing money or barely breaking even for three years now. It wasn't Cliff and Phil's fault, exactly. "If there are better men than the Hendersons to direct this racing circuit," one aviation expert said, "where are they?" Still, the fact was that the Henderson brothers were making money while others were losing it—or dying. All the death was making even the bravest pilots wonder if it was worth it. Yet in order to keep the public interested in the races, Henderson was under pressure to make the events faster and, therefore, more dangerous, more likely to result in yet another death. "The public will not continue to pay large sums of money to watch commercial planes race," *Aero Digest* magazine declared around that time. The people wanted speed and stunts—thrills, no matter the outcome. "They pay only to see fast stuff."

Now there was the problem of the women, who were not accepting their banishment from the air races in silence. "Hell hath no fury like a woman scorned, you know," one Ninety-Niner told a reporter, preferring to remain anonymous to avoid reprisals from the men. "And it sure looks as if Cliff Henderson and his gang are holding us up to scorn." In the races that he was planning to put on in Cleveland in September 1934, the women would be allowed to do only one thing: parachute-jump. No flying. For the second air meet in a row, they would be relegated to the grandstands—a rule that the women would not accept. Earhart got on the phone with organizers; others wrote letters. In late July, one month before the Cleveland races were to begin, the new president of the Ninety-Nines, Margaret Cooper, pleaded with both the National Aeronautic Association in Washington and Henderson in Cleveland, demanding inclusion for the women—now. "The '99' girls are up in arms," Cooper said. "We feel it is only fair to recognize our presence as contestants."

Years earlier, at the first meeting of the Ninety-Nines in New York, Earhart had dreamed that one day the group would be, as she said at the time, "influential and powerful." But there were limits to what they could become. Dues to join the group remained small by design, just a few dollars per year. At this price, many women struggling in the Depression could afford to join. Yet at the beginning of 1934, only 625 women in America had a pilot's license—and not all of them joined the Ninety-Nines—making the club small by definition, with a limited budget and limited reach. It almost didn't matter if the women were, as Cooper said, "up in arms." Race organizers could overrule them.

On the defensive now, Henderson fired back at Cooper, refusing to be made the villain in this now public drama of his own making. "If any individual has championed women's participation in competitive aviation during the past six years," he told Cooper, "it has been myself. And I have done so in the face of protest and ridicule of all types." Apparently, Henderson said, they had forgotten the Powder Puff Derby of 1929. "The fact of the matter is, I developed and championed this event." He couldn't stop himself from taking credit for the landmark race again, even though it wasn't his idea in the first place. He also couldn't resist blaming the women in general for their current predicament. Perhaps, he said, if they had participated in past races in greater numbers, they wouldn't be in this situation. He had been their advocate, Henderson added, but he would no longer be, in part because he claimed to be haunted by a ghost.

"I shall never forgive myself," he told the women, "for not reacting to my personal 'hunches' in protesting against permitting Florence Klingensmith to enter the mixed competition in Chicago last Labor Day." Others had approved Klingensmith's participation, of course, including the contest committee, the officials on the field in Chicago that day, the emcee with his glowing pre-race remarks about the intrepid flier, and, by extension, Henderson himself. But it had all been a mistake, Henderson claimed now. "To this day," he said, "I am endeavoring to answer to my own conscience for not inaugurating definite protest against her participation."

With the women's prospects looking grim for Cleveland — and the top pilots, Earhart, Thaden, Nichols, and others, planning to boycott yet again — a small group of female fliers met instead in early August in Dayton, Ohio, for a weekend of all-female racing in the first-ever women's national air meet. The crowds there were expected to be much smaller than usual — a few thousand race fans per day, at most. The prizes would be smaller too. Some races paid just $175 combined for the top three finishers, a meager windfall that barely covered gas money. Even the racecourse itself seemed small, stitched together in an almost haphazard fashion. In place of fifty-foot steel pylons with B-E-N-D-I-X written down the side in large letters, the women in Dayton would have to whip their planes around other items: a truck in a farmer's field, a barn in a nearby town, flimsy thirty-five-foot poles, and a local landmark, the Waco Aircraft factory, where the personnel director had recently encouraged women to stay in the kitchen "making homes pleasant."

Only about a dozen pilots showed up to compete, smaller names, mostly, or those in need of money. Frances Marsalis, Thaden's copilot in the endurance record for eight days over New York, counted herself among the latter. In recent months, Marsalis had struggled to cover even basic expenses, reaching out at one point to Earhart for help with a long-distance phone bill she had racked up making calls for the Ninety-Nines. She was unable to pay the $8.63 herself. "I wouldn't say one word," Marsalis told Earhart, "excepting I am not so wealthy here of late." Earhart did what she could to help Marsalis, even sending her a flight suit so that the endurance record co-holder would have something to wear while flying. But life in August 1934 was presumably about to get even harder for Marsalis. As she left Long Island for Dayton, she and her husband, airline pilot William Marsalis, were officially divorced. Just a week earlier, a judge had granted them a decree.

Her registration paperwork in Dayton reflected the change. Frances had dropped the Marsalis from her name, flying now as Frances Harrell and finishing just outside the money in the first major race of the weekend: a twenty-mile sprint around the improvised pylons that Saturday. But Marsalis—everyone was still calling her that—wasn't disappointed. From the beginning, she was focused on the big-money race of the weekend, Sunday's fifty-mile free-for-all around a triangular course with $1,000 for the winner. "And boy, how I need that $1,000," Marsalis admitted to others in Dayton.

The city was suffering through a spell of simmering heat, which was killing livestock and turning the Great Miami River into a bed of sand, and Sunday morning brought more of the same conditions. The day dawned hot and bothered. Another afternoon of ninety-degree temperatures was coming. But it wasn't enough to keep six thousand locals away from the biggest race of the weekend, the fifty-miler, featuring ten pilots and Marsalis, who was rested and ready. She was so confident of winning that a friend tossed her some reading material as she climbed into her plane, an open-cockpit Waco. "Here's a book for you to read," the friend said, "on the last lap."

Marsalis came from behind, stalking the pack from the rear and picking off her competitors in a slow, methodical march to the front. By the fifth and final lap, she was only sixty seconds off the lead and gaining, closing in on the leaders at pylon no. 2, which was in a potato field about four miles from the starting line. Several planes were soon bunched up together, each of them banking hard and low at the undersized pylon. They needed to stay low so that the judges on the ground wouldn't disqualify them for cutting the corner. But Marsalis, seeking an opening, pushed her Waco airship even lower than the others and then stayed there, skimming across the ground—dangerously low—to avoid slamming into two of her friends in the planes above her. Perhaps she misjudged her plane's ability to dart into the lead or her distance from the ground. Maybe it was impossible to hold the vertical-banked turn for as long as she did, turning hard to the left at 150 miles an hour. Or maybe there were just too many planes in the sky flying too close together. All eyewitnesses could say for sure was what happened next: the left wing on Marsalis's plane dug into the ground, carving a three-foot gash into the potato field and driving her down into a cloud of dust.

The plane began to roll, tumbling across the field a dozen times before finally skidding to a halt two hundred feet away. Plane parts were scattered everywhere, strewn across an acre of Ohio flatlands. And while Marsalis's competitors roared on—racing for the third pylon, the finish line, and the $1,000 prize—judges and farmers ran across the potato field, hoping to save the woman inside the airplane.

They hacked away at the busted fabric and wood of the fuselage, trying to free her. She was injured and unconscious, yet, for the moment, alive. They needed to get her to a hospital. But by the time the ambulance arrived, it was too late, and the medics drove her body to a local funeral home. Someone would have to notify her husband, or ex-husband, or whatever he was: Marsalis was dead.

Thaden, with her two children in Kansas City, read the news in her morning paper and was stunned. Another Ninety-Nine down, another friend dead in the races, another funeral in the offing. Marsalis, at least, was getting first-class treatment, an indication, perhaps, that the times were changing. No one was going to let Marsalis be shipped home wrapped in newspapers in a cheap box. At dawn on Tuesday morning, thirty-six hours after Marsalis's death, airmen in Dayton loaded her coffin into a plane bound for her home airport on Long Island, Roosevelt Field, where Charles Lindbergh and Ruth Elder had started their historic flights. A convoy of planes—three army, three navy, and three civilian—flanked the funeral ship for hundreds of miles, and at least fifty more were circling in the air in homage to Marsalis when her body arrived in New York. After the plane landed at Roosevelt Field, the mourners delivered her coffin to hangar C and placed it in front of a Waco airship framed by piles of flowers. Then two thousand pilots and mechanics, friends and loved ones, crowded into the hangar to remember Marsalis—*Your gal, Frances,* she liked to sign her letters—in a brief ceremony.

Thaden and Nichols comforted themselves with the idea that Marsalis would have wanted to go this way: in a plane, at the controls, with the engine roaring wide open. She had told Thaden as much. "When my time comes," Marsalis said, "I hope it's in a plane where I can crack up in one grand splurge." Now, inside the hangar in New York, they honored her for this sacrifice. "Mrs. Marsalis," Earhart said at the funeral, "was one of the friendliest and most likable women I have ever known, and also one of the best pilots."

But the women amid the crowd of mourners knew that Marsalis's death would hurt them all. Henderson, in Cleveland, was already using it against them. He had told the women they couldn't race. He had told them they weren't cut out for it. They hadn't listened—and now another one of them was dead.

"Everyone knows that it's not that I have anything against women fliers because they are women," Henderson said after Marsalis's crash, appearing unusually nervous before reporters in Cleveland. He claimed just to be speaking the truth, doing what was best for aviation and the air races. Just doing his job. "And Frances Marsalis's death has again proved my theory is right."

LOCAL LEADERS IN CLEVELAND, starting with all three of the city's daily newspapers, fell in line behind Henderson. He wanted the papers' approval—needed it, really—recruiting them to be cheerleaders for his cause: the 1934 air races. "Obviously," he told one top editor, "the pledged editorial support of the Cleveland metropolitan newspapers, plus their financial underwriting, is the leadership necessary to guarantee the success of this enterprise."

The *Plain Dealer,* the *News,* and the *Press* all gave Henderson what he wanted: glowing, positive, wall-to-wall air-race coverage, focused not on his increasingly bitter feud with the women but on the glory of his planned program of events. No prose was too purple, no adjective too outrageous, and no phrase too florid for the Labor Day weekend air races that year. Clevelanders were told to expect them to be "hair-raising" and "soul-stirring," ten days of thrills packed into just four days, and cheaper than ever so that more fans might enjoy "the splendor of 1934's aviation display." Finally, to make their positions perfectly clear, each of the three newspapers published stories suggesting Henderson was right to exclude the women. They quoted pilots saying as much. "Flying is a man's business," one male aviator said. And to prove they were being fair to the female pilots, the newspapers also quoted women on the subject—women who agreed with Henderson.

"I do not believe women, as a rule, are equipped for racing," said

Gertrude Chester, a licensed pilot and wife of a pilot from Illinois who had come to Cleveland for the races. "My husband wouldn't think of me entering an event against him, and doesn't think I should do any racing at all. And I quite agree." Women, she argued, didn't have the mechanical background required to make it possible. Or planes fast enough to really compete, forcing them to borrow airships from men. "If they crack up," she explained, "it sometimes causes hard feelings." No one wanted that, especially because, as another woman in Cleveland pointed out, women were too weak to fly in the first place. "Imagine a jockey's wife being a jockey just because her husband is one. Or a truck driver's wife riding around with him on his deliveries." It was an absurd notion, the woman argued, a laughable idea—insanity, even. "That's what I think of wives flying."

The races kicked off that Friday with star power in the form of Hollywood actress Mary Pickford. Unable to convince Earhart to fly Pickford in from California—Earhart refused, given the no-female policy—Henderson tapped old friend and hero Jimmy Doolittle for the job. And the reliable Doolittle made sure to get Pickford to Cleveland before the Bendix racers came screaming in from Los Angeles that afternoon. The crowd—thirty-eight thousand in all—had been hoping to cheer on Roscoe Turner and Benny Howard, who had both entered the Bendix race. But after mechanical failures and mishaps knocked them out of the cross-country speed dash before the race even began, fans had to settle for Doug Davis, a decorated flier, airline pilot, husband, and father of two young children. It was the tie-wearing Davis, not some colorful character, who showed up first in the Bendix, covered in grime and telling stories about how he had almost crashed during the race—twice.

"I took an awful beating," Davis admitted, working on no meals and almost no sleep. But the trip had earned him a $4,500 prize. And fans in Cleveland knew they hadn't seen the last of him. After posing for photos with Pickford, the mayor, and Vincent Bendix himself, reveling in the moment, Davis turned his eye to the next big race: Monday's twelve-lap, hundred-mile Thompson Trophy free-for-all around pylons positioned at the field in the same triangular layout as Klingensmith's fatal race one year earlier.

The race worried Davis. Roscoe Turner was going to be there for this one; his plane had been repaired and he was zooming in from Los

Angeles in record time. Benny Howard would make it too. He wasn't flying, but he was going to send his most trusted pilot up in one of his Howard racers. "I've half a notion not to enter at all," Davis admitted that Saturday. "Someone's going to get killed." The planes were too fast and the pylon course too treacherous. But the winner was going to take home another $4,500, and Davis couldn't help but remember what his six-year-old son had said to him before he left Georgia for the races: "Bring home some money this time, Dad. We've got enough trophies."

One of the largest crowds in air-race history turned out for the event that Monday, an estimated quarter of a million fans, paying and non-paying, watching from seats and from the hoods of their cars, parked on nearby highways. Top officials that weekend had already declared the races the most successful ever held, and now, with the historic Labor Day masses, they had further proof that Henderson knew what he was doing. "Attendance today and the first two days of the races shows what the public thinks," the chief of the National Aeronautic Association said, marveling at the size of the crowds.

It was almost sundown at the end of the long weekend when those crowds finally got to see the Thompson Trophy race, with eight pilots competing for the prize, all bunched up together in the sky. Right away, Doug Davis shot to the front of the pack, flying 250 miles an hour in his red monoplane with black wings. With his children at home, Davis was intent on flying a careful race, seeking, as Turner once called it, "speed with safety." "Not going to take any chances," Davis said before climbing into the cockpit. But if he had open air lanes, open sky—"clear sailing," Davis said—he was going to push the plane as he always did. "I'll sure push her hard," he said, "and set a new record."

By the fifth lap, about forty miles in, it was a two-man race: Davis and Turner—no other plane was even close—with Davis leading Turner by just a few hundred feet, and the rest of the field out of contention, far behind. The two leading planes buzzed along together, banking left around the home pylon and flying west into the setting sun. It was their eighth time around the course now, with four more to go, and Davis and Turner were lapping other planes. One of the two men was going to win the trophy. Most likely, it would be Davis; he was still leading. Then, at pylon no. 2 in a farmer's field, Davis made a mistake. He cut the corner, darting inside of the pylon. Knowing he had to circle back and go around the pylon to avoid disqualification, he banked his plane hard, shot five hundred feet into the sky, and prepared to turn, dive, and pass outside of the pylon this time. But at the apex of its steep, hasty climb, Davis's plane began to tumble, spiraling toward the ground.

"He's going to crash," the race announcer calling the play-by-play said with a gasp. "His plane shot straight up in the air and then disappeared behind the trees."

The race was effectively over. With Davis crashing and the other planes lagging behind, Turner cruised to victory, claiming the $4,500 prize without any finish-line drama. The crowd was now focused on Davis and his crash, four miles to the west. Most people, including Henderson, were too far away to have seen it, so instead of news, people relied on rumors and hearsay. And for almost an hour, these early reports relayed back to the grandstands were good: Davis had escaped from the spiraling plane. His parachute had opened in time to save him. His injuries were only minor—Henderson was sure of it, finally agreeing to have the miraculous news announced to the crowd.

"I had the message checked," Henderson said.

Of course Davis had survived. The man knew what he was doing. Speed with safety. Not going to take any chances. Wife and kids at home. Pushing his plane hard, bringing home money, not trophies. But Turner, who had seen Davis go down from the air, as he darted beneath Davis's falling plane, didn't believe it and pressed for more details.

"Are you sure?" Turner kept asking at the finish line. "Are you sure that Doug is all right? I didn't see him get out."

"I don't think he got out," Doolittle agreed.

No one had seen the white flutter of a parachute on the horizon. And no one was seeing Davis strolling across the field now, alive and unscathed, in his overalls, shirt, and tie. Those close enough to the crash site were watching instead the actions of a mob—thirty-five hundred people "mad with excitement," one police officer said, running through the bramble to reach Davis's plane. They arrived at the wreckage before race officials could, and then fought one another at the scene. They weren't looking to rescue the pilot. Davis was killed on impact, crushed and mangled, with one arm apparently ripped away from his body. They just wanted souvenirs from his remains, his clothes, and his red-and-black airplane, claiming anything they could carry away.

One woman pulled a brass button off his overalls and sold it on the spot for five dollars. Others went after the plane, stripping it clean. By the time police officers, national guardsmen, and field mechanics arrived and linked arms in a circle around the wreck to keep the mob at bay, almost all that was left of Davis's airship was the bare motor, glistening in the twilight. Still, the souvenir hunters kept coming, trying to steal the plane's instrument panel and the leather helmet right off Davis's head. Women fainted in the crush of humanity with the corpse on the ground, and the police just watched. "But what could we do," one officer asked later, "with several thousand apparently insane people?"

To honor Davis, the air races booked thirty minutes of local airtime the next night on Cleveland's WHK radio. "Ladies and gentlemen," the announcer intoned, "this station takes time to pay humble tribute to a great man in aviation—Doug Davis." Henderson himself said a few words on the program honoring Davis, and then he flew out to Atlanta for the funeral. He wanted to personally attend, going to Davis's grave in the hillside cemetery overlooking the airfield there and hearing the eulogies for the pilot. "One of the very best pilots we had." A good man. "Everybody wanted to fly with Doug."

The crash wasn't Davis's fault. A chunk of wing, four feet wide and eighteen inches long, had ripped away under the strain of the speed, sending Davis to his unavoidable death. "It's a wonder there aren't more racing pilots killed," one official said afterward. The case was simple—and it was closed. "It was an experimental plane, flying at a fast speed, on a bumpy day. There's no doubt that something gave way. There's nothing further to investigate."

19

They'll Be in Our Hair

AMELIA EARHART LOOKED OUT on the crowd—three thousand women packed into a ballroom at the Waldorf Astoria hotel in New York City. It was late September, three weeks after Davis's death in Cleveland, and Earhart wished she had better news for her audience, a better report to give the crowd interested in hearing Earhart's thoughts about women and their place in the sky. "Two capital Ts stand in the way of their progress," she told the women in the room. "One is Training—or lack of it. The other, Tradition."

Her talk was supposed to be directed to young women, a task that gave Earhart pause. She had celebrated her thirty-seventh birthday that summer with an automobile trip to Wyoming with her husband, Putnam, and she didn't feel so young anymore. She was joining, she joked, the ranks of "the ancients." But if anything, she was becoming more radical with time, refusing to believe in the notion of a "woman's place" and increasingly willing to say so in public, whether the crowd before her was composed of liberal New York socialites or conservative Kansan housewives. "Her place," Earhart said, "is wherever her individual aptitude places her." Or it should be, anyway. "And the work of married men and women should be split," she added. "She should taste the grind of earning a living—and he should learn the stupidity of housework."

Six blocks away from the Waldorf Astoria on the afternoon of Earhart's speech, a small army of dedicated women were at work inside the Fifth Avenue office of the Ninety-Nines, mounting a campaign against Cliff Henderson, his races, and his rules. The women weren't stopping at personal letters pleading with Henderson. They called him out publicly late that summer, in a two-page editorial under a headline that surely punctured the showman's oversize ego: "Cliff Henderson Turns Back the Clock."

In the editorial, the women pointed out they had been flying in the races since 1929, and if they'd been good enough to merit inclusion then, they were certainly good enough now, no matter what had happened to Florence Klingensmith or Frances Marsalis. Men died in the races all the time, the editorial pointed out, yet no one talked about canceling because of the deaths in New Orleans or Cleveland. No one talked about banning the men. "Women are invited to cooperate," the editorial declared, "by sitting in the grandstand." But they weren't going to listen. They wanted the same chances the men had—the same shot at living or dying in the sky. "We who fly cannot recognize sex," Nichols said. "Women have the same inherent right to be killed in airplane races as men have." The women, meeting late that summer, even voted on it.

"Be it resolved," they declared in a formal statement, "that we protest the discrimination against women fliers, eliminating them from the schedule of events of the 1934 National Air Races" . . .

"Be it resolved," they said, "that we protest the name 'National Air Races' being applied to any event in which women do not have fair representation."

And "be it resolved" that they would oppose any future efforts to keep them out of the races because "such action is prejudiced, unjust, and without any foundation whatsoever."

Even the reporters friendly to Henderson—almost all men—could no longer defend his banishment of the female aviators. He had made it about Klingensmith; she was, one reporter noted, "his star example" of why women shouldn't race. But the circumstances around Doug Davis's death—a wing tearing away under high speed and a pilot who couldn't bail out in time—had rendered that example worthless. Everyone could see the truth: Klingensmith and Davis had died in almost exactly the same fashion. "More and more veteran patrons of the National Air Races are swinging to the belief that if a little of the energy expended on eliminating women were devoted to tightening up restrictions on the air-worthiness of participating planes American air meets would be attended by fewer fatalities," C. B. Allen wrote in the *New York Herald Tribune*. "The best pilot in the world, when all is said and done, can do very little with a ship that starts to disintegrate in the air—else both Doug Davis and Florence Klingensmith might still be alive."

Allen and other aviation editors from America's biggest newspapers met in September 1934 and voted to support including women in the races. And into the summer of 1935, the pressure continued to build around Henderson, threatening to derail the air meet that year. "Cliff Henderson," one female flier said, "is a brave man."

She was being sarcastic. Really, she thought Henderson misguided, there alone in his hotel room on Lake Erie, with all the charm of one of the rising tyrants making news in Europe. "Mr. Henderson's autocratic ruling," the woman continued, "sounds dangerously like Herr Hitler's or Signore Mussolini's ideas on women's place being in the home."

IT WAS UNSEASONABLY COLD and wet in late August 1935 when they all—the men and the women—arrived in Cleveland for the races, with a hard rain falling across the lake and the male aviators still kicking up a fuss over the women. In private conversations, away from the field, Roscoe Turner supported the female fliers, befriending them and even speaking before their clubs. "It is my belief that a man or woman, provided they have no serious handicap, can do almost anything they make up their minds to do," he told one woman, "if they keep trying." But Turner made no such proclamations to the press, choosing instead to twist his mustache and keep his silence. Benny Howard stayed quiet too, making clear his feelings on the topic with the choices he made at home. He taught his wife, Maxine, how to fly, and fly fast. But racing was out of the question. "I wouldn't let her," Howard said. He seemed to prefer that she wait for him on the ground and greet him with one of her kisses. In a men-only pilots' meeting in Cleveland, other airmen agreed. The women, they suggested, were only playing dress-up. "They just like to show up on the field with helmets and goggles on," one pilot said.

In agreement, they voted to maintain Henderson's ban, preferring that the women hold their own races somewhere else—a result that didn't surprise anyone. One male pilot had already previously proclaimed the women pilots to be "notoriously inefficient and dangerous." If given the choice, he said, he'd rather fly with a winged dragon than a woman. But Howard's star pilot, Harold Neumann, pointed out a flaw with the men's plans. "I'm afraid there will be trouble," he said, "unless the women have at least one race."

Henderson apparently agreed and quietly gave the women more than just one. He offered them three in 1935: an all-female pylon race; a mixed-gender, multistop cross-country derby; and, finally, a chance to compete in the Bendix if they wanted, a compromise that Henderson hoped would put an end to the women's bitter editorials and angry comments about him. Forget about everything he had said in the past or how he had treated them in 1934; 1935 was going to be different. "The women," Henderson told reporters, "will be in the foreground of the picture."

That was one way of putting it. Veteran racer Lee Miles put it a different way. The women, Miles suggested after the pilots' meeting in Cleveland, were about to ruin the picture. "The first thing you know they'll want to borrow our planes," Miles griped, "and some of them are so good looking it's hard to say no." He spoke for most of his fellow airmen when he announced that he wished the women were out of the air races for good. "If we let them in," Miles said, "they'll be in our hair and become pests."

CLIFF HENDERSON WAS all smiles as the races began that weekend in Cleveland. He had brokered a truce with the women. He had contradicted almost everything he'd been saying about them for almost two years in order to do it, and yet, somehow, Henderson was spinning the story his way. He was acting as if including the women was just him giving folks one more reason to attend his air show. "The world's most spectacular presentation," he was calling it this year, "a combination of the Indianapolis Speedway, the Kentucky Derby, a New Orleans Mardi Gras and a cross-section of Hollywood." He pointed out that Amelia Earhart was sponsoring the all-women's speed race and he suggested that other big-name female fliers would attend too. "Again," Henderson said, with his usual dramatic flair, "the eyes of the world are to be on Cleveland."

Thaden was listed among the pilots expected to be there. But it was false advertising — or wishful thinking. As the air races opened, Thaden was home, far from Cleveland, looking for a job. She and Herb were struggling financially; not broke, exactly, but close. Her best hope was getting hired at the US Department of Commerce as an air-marking pilot. In 1935, aviators could still easily get lost flying across the country, especially in bad weather, and they crashed and sometimes died as a result. Air-marking pilots helped to prevent that by identifying barns or factories with roofs at least a hundred feet long and twenty feet wide on which the government could paint large letters spelling out the name of the nearest town to help confused aviators determine their location and land safely. It wasn't glamorous work; there were no cheering crowds. But it was important. More to the point, it was almost the only job a female aviator could get in 1935 — and Thaden needed it. She didn't have the luxury of dreaming about racing anymore. With two children at home, she was hoping to air-mark, and, finally, she got hired. As Henderson's races opened in Cleveland, the government approved her application at a salary of $2,600 per year. "To take effect," she was told, "upon entrance on duty."

Thaden wasn't going to Cleveland; she likely couldn't afford to make the trip. Nichols wasn't going either. In August 1935, she felt fortunate to have a regular job. A longtime aviator friend and consultant had purchased three Curtiss Condors, a large passenger plane with a ninety-three-foot wingspan and seats for twenty-eight people, to start a new East Coast airline. He wondered if Nichols would agree to come on as a copilot. "And he didn't have to ask twice," Nichols said. "I would have taken the job for nothing." For the first time in almost two years, she was flying again. Nichols assisted a male pilot at the controls of the large Condor in a promotional tour across the Northeast, giving joy rides, essentially, to help generate interest in the new airline — "$1 per passenger," ads said in the small towns they visited. It wasn't racing or setting records, and it was a long way from the transatlantic glory that Nichols had come so close to enjoying. But it was flying, and, after her long exile from the sky, that was enough for her. "This," she said, recalibrating her dreams as Thaden had, "was living."

Only Earhart could take Henderson up on his challenge in 1935. While her friends and rivals were pulled from the sky by the challenges of life on the ground, Earhart was flying farther and faster than ever, adding new records all the time yet again. Eight months before the

Cleveland air races that year, she arrived by luxury ocean liner in Hawaii accompanied by her husband, Putnam, a Hollywood pilot named Paul Mantz, and her red Lockheed, which was lashed to a tennis court on the deck of the SS *Lurline*. Islanders were curious about the woman from the moment she stepped onto Pier 11 in Honolulu. Local reporters pressed for interviews and noted every detail about her, right down to her manner of sneezing—dignified and "ladylike." Hawaiians attended her usual lecture and cheered at the usual lines. "I didn't see any ox-carts parked out in front this evening . . ." They also wondered what she was doing in Hawaii with her plane and this other aviator, Mantz. He was intent on testing the new radio on Earhart's red airship. In a marvel of modern science, the device was said to be able to connect all the way to the US mainland. If everything worked as Mantz hoped, Earhart could speak to America from the middle of the ocean.

She went sightseeing on Maui like any tourist, only she was flown around by the president of a local airline. Also, this was no vacation. While Earhart toured, granted interviews, and gave her talks, Mantz was flying the Lockheed, testing the equipment, and delivering reports directly to Putnam. "Notify Mr. Putnam," he declared in early January, "that we are now in two-way communication with the coast." It was time for Earhart to leave Hawaii for California, alone again in an airplane, with plans for another historic flight. The world's transatlantic heroine now hoped to be the first woman to fly solo across the Pacific.

The flight was roughly twenty-four hundred miles—more than three hundred miles longer than her solo transatlantic trip two years earlier. And for the first time, she was facing criticism for her "foolhardy" plans. One newspaper dismissed her proposed flight as a "publicity stunt," alleging that Earhart was doing it only for money. Critics figured the motivation had to be money, not science, because, as one pointed out, "there is nothing to be gained by flying solo from Hawaii to the mainland in a single-engined land plane." Indeed, there was much to lose, a great chance of crashing and dying; everyone knew it. Just a month earlier, a plane with a crew of three men who were attempting to make a similar transpacific flight crashed into the sea near Oahu and were never found. "The American public is devoted to Amelia Earhart because she is an excellent type of woman, sensible and wholesome," one Hawaiian reporter wrote, but this time she had gone too far.

Putnam, as usual, came to Earhart's defense, denying she was making the flight for money and scoffing at his wife's other critics. "Go ahead," Putnam said, "and say what you like." But the criticism—"the unwarranted criticism," Earhart called it—weighed on her. "As you know," Earhart told Putnam in a letter before leaving, "the barrage of belittlement has made harder the preparation in many ways. So malicious does some of it seem that I suggest you search for evidence of sabotage in case of an unexplained mishap."

Still, she was going. On a Friday afternoon two weeks after she had arrived in Hawaii, Earhart and Putnam drove in a blue sedan to the muddy airfield on Oahu where Mantz had been preparing her plane. With no fanfare and no public goodbyes, she stepped out of the car, climbed up a ladder leaning against the Lockheed, and settled into the cockpit of the plane. The engine was already running and the ground crew outside was ready.

"Not yet," Earhart told them.

Then, a minute later, she waved to the men outside. They removed the blocks in front of the wheels of the thundering red plane and Earhart began to taxi to the runway, toward the fire truck and ambulance waiting at the far end—just in case. She gunned the engine once, twice, then opened the throttle up, needing only half a mile to get her plane, loaded down with two tons of gasoline, into the air. She was up and away just before five p.m., going first to Diamond Head at the tip of the island, then banking northeast toward the open ocean and the long, moonless night ahead of her, filled with squalls, clouds, fog banks, and the unknown.

The radio didn't work at first; there was nothing but garbled static.

"Speak louder," Putnam begged Earhart from the ground more than two hours into the flight. They couldn't hear her through the scratchy fuzz. But soon the messages were coming in, not exactly loud or clear, but intelligible. There was Earhart's voice in Putnam's ears and in the ears of ordinary Americans leaning into their radios inside their West Coast living rooms.

9:47 p.m.: "All is well."

12:45 a.m.: "Everything okay."

3:45 a.m.: "I am becoming quite tired."

Finally, dawn broke over the ocean—she was close to her goal. Or she hoped she was. Honestly, Earhart wasn't totally sure where she was as she skimmed over blankets of fog and wondered if her compass was working. "I should be near, if the course is correct," she said. "Heading for Oakland."

On the ground, at the East Bay airport where Thaden had once gotten her start, ten thousand people had been waiting for hours. When Earhart's red plane finally appeared, low in the sky, they could wait no longer. The crowd pushed past police barricades, ran onto the field, and swarmed around the plane, its propeller still spinning, in a dangerous stampede. Some people fell and were nearly trampled in the scrum. A field truck had to plow a narrow path through the crowd just to get the plane into a hangar. And once inside, Earhart relaxed, leaning against a wall and chatting with reporters that police officers kept trying to shoo away. "The police think I am very frail," she joked with the press. "But I'm not an invalid."

Earhart didn't even plan to stick around long enough to see her husband, who was arriving by ocean liner from Hawaii. In the morning, she was flying to Los Angeles. But for the moment, tired and covered in grime—"I feel dirty," she said, "and *I am* dirty"—she retired to the majestic Hotel Oakland, slipping in through a back door, and napped that afternoon in her suite with detectives standing guard outside. Earhart had now conquered both oceans, and five months later she would add still another feat to her list of accomplishments: flying nonstop from Mexico City to Newark in record time. Surely, in 1935 she could compete against the men in that great American transcontinental air race: the Bendix.

THE PURSE FOR THE BENDIX that August was $10,000—four times Thaden's new annual salary—and it drew the usual group of hopefuls, nine aviators in all, to the starting line at a small airport in Burbank on the outskirts of Los Angeles. On the day of the race, the pilots gathered at midnight for a final meeting and weather bulletin and then headed back to their airships in the dark to prepare to take off in a staggered start. Fastest time to Cleveland would win.

Roscoe Turner was there with his waxed mustache and his gold plane—"The game little fellow," he called it—boasting that it could hit speeds over three hundred miles an hour and expecting to win, as usual. "So I am looking forward to this year's races," he said with his typical confidence, "to new conquests of the air." But to prevail, Turner was going to have to beat Benny Howard, who was also expecting victory in his crisp new plane that he was calling *Mister Mulligan*. The plane—all white, with a simple 40 painted on the fuselage—had cost Howard $17,000 to build and then, after a minor mishap in late 1934, $5,000 to repair, putting him deep into debt. Taking a look at the simple plane, critics wondered why he had bothered. *Mister Mulligan* wasn't a single-seat racer like Turner's golden airship but a four-passenger cabin plane, the sort of stock model that one might find at any airfield. Competitors figured *Mister Mulligan* would max out at around 180 miles an hour—certainly not fast enough to beat Turner or Cecil Allen, another man competing in the Bendix. Allen—a square-jawed adventurer and washing-machine salesman—attended the midnight pilots' meeting, too, with his own plans to win. He was flying a fast and familiar airship, a red Gee Bee, one of Granville's notorious death planes, against the wishes of his mother. And there, among the men, stood two women, each looking to make history. Earhart was preparing to fly to Cleveland in her now famous red Lockheed, while another woman, Jacqueline Cochran, almost a decade younger than Earhart, was vowing to get to Cleveland without a single stop.

Cochran barely even made it off the ground in Burbank. She nearly crashed her plane on takeoff, almost plowing it into a fence at the end of the runway, and then quit just three hundred miles in. She'd been forced down in Arizona by radio problems and chose to stay there—finished. If a woman was going to win the Bendix, it would have to be Earhart. And she got away first, taking off just before 1:00 a.m. in a dense fog and banking hard for Cleveland, 2,046 miles away, a perfect takeoff cheered by five thousand people in the dark. But Earhart quickly fell off the pace, which she blamed on the size of the Lockheed—"the family bus," she joked, as it was ferrying her, Mantz, and another man, a motor manufacturer. By the time they reached Albuquerque, their first refueling stop, at 5:25 that morning, Earhart was two hours behind Turner, already out of contention for the Bendix Trophy, and she knew it. But at least she was still flying, pushing on to Cleveland, no matter her time. Two other men in the Bendix had been forced down with engine problems; they were out. And Cecil Allen, with his red Gee Bee, struggled even to get off the ground in California.

"Let's go," he said, grousing in the dark.

The motor on his Gee Bee was coughing for reasons unknown—not a good sign. Aviators often chose not to take off over smaller issues, training their ears to catch even the slightest imperfection in the thrumming growl of their machines, knowing that it was better to hear it on the ground than in the air. But Allen had accepted $2,000 from a religious New Jersey woman in order to prepare the Gee Bee for the Bendix. He had named the red plane the *Spirit of Right* in her honor. He needed the prize money. He expected to win it. "And nobody," Allen's girlfriend said, "could dissuade him."

Allen took off last, four hours after Earhart, chasing the other planes over the San Gabriel Mountains. But he never came close to them, much less Cleveland. His Gee Bee went down just three miles from the runway, plowing into a field while residents of North Hollywood watched in horror. They could see the red plane was out of control, wobbling, falling, then cartwheeling across the farmer's field. "A vicious cartwheel," one witness said, "that tore it to pieces." When the *Spirit of Right* stopped rolling, there was a five-foot hole in the earth, a crumpled plane on the ground, and a dead pilot inside, crushed between the engine and the gas tanks.

At her home nearby, Allen's mother collapsed at the news. Howard and Turner just kept flying. Unaware of Allen's death, they flew on, streaking toward Cleveland in some of the worst weather they had ever experienced. "Hell," Turner called it bluntly. He hated flying in the rain. The wet weather fogged up his goggles, made it difficult to see and hard to fly. Each raindrop felt to Turner like a small needle piercing the fabric of his plane's wooden wings and throwing it off balance. "If one unavoidably gets in a storm of this kind," he advised others, "there's nothing to do but power down and sacrifice speed for safety." But neither Turner nor Howard was sacrificing anything that day, dashing into Cleveland, despite the heavy rains east of Albuquerque, the headwinds across the plains, and the storms into Ohio.

Howard—flying with the engineer who helped him build the *Mister Mulligan* and a bottle of whiskey, just in case—went high to dodge the worst of the conditions. They knew the plane had been designed for higher altitudes and Howard pulled back on the stick now, guiding it to smoother air well above the weather. Turner did the opposite to get out of the soup. While Howard climbed to twenty thousand feet and stayed there, sucking oxygen through a tube and freezing in the cold, Turner hugged the earth for two thousand bumpy miles, never more than twenty-five hundred feet off the ground and often screaming just a thousand feet over farms, highways, and homes. The golden plane was averaging 238 miles an hour. The white plane was too. Turner and Howard had no way of knowing it—separated as they were in the sky—but they were effectively wingtip to wingtip coming into Cleveland, in a dead heat for the Bendix Trophy and the prize money.

On the ground, the weather was as miserable as Henderson had ever seen it at the air races. He had planned for a day of thrills across the city, with marching bands and parades, but the cold, torrential rains forced the bands to seek shelter in firehouses, hotel lobbies, and stores, sopping wet with their instruments in hand. Henderson had no choice but to scrap the bulk of the afternoon festivities, canceling almost everything, which left just a couple of thousand wet souls in the stands when the first Bendix racer appeared in the sky, dropping out of the gray mist like a white dart.

It was Howard.

"Where's that man, Roscoe?" he asked as soon as he hit the ground and climbed out of *Mister Mulligan*, weary from eight hours, thirty minutes, and sixteen seconds of travel.

Howard had arrived in Cleveland first, coming in at 1:40 p.m. But Turner had left Los Angeles one hour and forty-three minutes after his rival, meaning he had until 3:23 p.m. to get there and beat Howard, forcing everyone sitting amid the puddles on the ground to watch the electronic timer—and wait.

Two o'clock came and went. And there was no Turner.

Three o'clock came. No Turner.

Reporters began to tell Howard that he could start celebrating, snapping pictures of him and his wife, Maxine, and urging them to kiss, as usual. "Oh, she is who I flew through the rain for," Benny cried. But he refused to accept victory. "Wait," he cautioned, "until Turner gets here."

Finally, at exactly 3:23 p.m., the last possible moment, Turner came in low from the west in his golden plane, sending officials scrambling for the timer. They needed to make sure they had their calculations right before announcing the winner to what was left of the soggy crowd. They ran the math and made their announcement.

Howard had won the Bendix by twenty-three and a half seconds.

"The closest shave I've had," he said, "in ten years of flying."

On the field, in celebration, Howard held up his bottle of whiskey for the fans to see — still mostly full, evidence that he'd hardly drunk anything on the flight to Cleveland. "Are you sure you didn't stop for a refill?" someone shouted. Howard bounded up to Turner, smiling at him. And Turner, gracious in defeat, smiled back, shaking Howard's hand. With the rain still falling, he claimed to be more worried about his waxed mustache than anything else. "Hurry up," Turner instructed photographers snapping pictures, "before the rain melts it."

He hoped to do better in the pylon races that weekend in Cleveland. But the Howard race team swept those events too, proving that *Mister Mulligan* was the fastest plane not only over long distances but also in short bursts. An amazing little ship, everyone agreed, unbeatable, perhaps and, better yet, for Howard, profitable. Over the course of the four-day weekend, Howard collected more than seventeen thousand dollars in winnings, arguably the single greatest haul in air-race history, flying quite possibly the fastest, most versatile airplane ever built. "*Mister Mulligan*," Howard declared afterward, "will fly rings around any current commercial ship in America."

It had easily defeated Earhart, anyway. The world's most famous female pilot finished last in the Bendix, fifth place — more than five hours slower than Howard's white airplane — landing in Cleveland at dinnertime, long after most fans had gone home. If women were ever going to win in races like this, they would need better planes and better luck.

They would need a miracle.

20

Playing Hunches

H E WAS ANGRY AGAIN. Walter Beech, focused on success, was always getting upset about something at his airplane factory on the prairie in Wichita.

The cost of entertaining clients bothered him. "I find that we are spending too much money on this item," he complained. Long telephone calls bothered him too. "Please limit your conversations to five minutes," he snapped at employees, "regardless of what the call is about." He also really hated repeating himself about these and other matters and threatened to fire employees who didn't follow directions the first time. "I do not intend," he liked to say with an icy detachment, "to call this to your attention again."

But in early 1936, the problem at his factory was hours. Beech was pretty sure that the men in the machine shop, the workers in the fittings section, and the employees in the fuselage department weren't putting in a full day's work for a full day's pay. He thought they were arriving late, skipping out early for lunch, or leaving at the end of the day before cleaning up their workstations. So he typed up a pledge and then had his employees sign it so he could be sure they understood that they owed him every minute of the workday. "I also understand," Beech's pledge concluded, "that I will not be advised of this again."

Beech — now forty-five and putting on weight — had reasons to be ornery. His racing days were long over, and his good fortune at the once-thriving Travel Air company was over too. In the span of just three years, Beech's aviation outfit had gone from two million dollars in annual sales to zero sales. It made no money except the cash it generated by selling off its equipment, then it terminated its employees and abandoned the factory, leaving the old Travel Air water tower standing in the tall grass east of town like a crumbling castle from a bygone era. Beech, at least, was spared most of the pain. He'd sold Travel Air to a New York manufacturer just before the Depression set in and taken a top job with the new company. But he got tired of the bureaucracy of it all—no one listened to his ideas there—and he'd returned to Wichita in March 1932 with a new plan and a young wife. It was an unlikely development that had begun in a typical way. Beech had fallen for his secretary Olive Ann Mellor.

The relationship had not started well. From the moment Mellor stepped into Beech's office at the old Travel Air building, she had been subjected to harassment, stares, and leering—and that was just from her prospective boss, Beech. As she interviewed for her job there, he seemed less interested in her work experience than in her physical attributes. She was about twenty-two at the time, more than a decade younger than him, with blue eyes, blond hair, full lips, and, as far as Beech was concerned, one other notable feature. "You got pretty good-lookin' legs," he told her before offering to hire her. "I guess you'll do."

The comment stung Mellor enough that she never forgot it. But she took the job anyway. At twenty dollars a week, it paid better than anything she'd done before. For years, her family had blown across Kansas with the wind, moving from Waverly to Paola and finally to Wichita, chasing the jobs that Mellor's father landed as a carpenter. By 1920, they had settled into a home in a humble neighborhood that would one day be plowed under to make way for Interstate 135. Mellor got work as a cashier, then as a stenographer and a bookkeeper, running numbers, something she enjoyed. She had been paying the family bills since she was eleven years old, balancing the books and writing checks. She knew enough about math, anyway, to realize that at the weekly wage Beech was offering at Travel Air, she could put up with him and his rules. The first one, he told her, was to leave the married men alone.

"Don't worry," Mellor replied. "I'm not going to bother you, either."

Her job, in the beginning, was to answer the phones, report to

Beech, ride the waves of his impatient sea, and help get the people of Wichita excited about his planes by selling rides in them for a dollar apiece. Yet over time, things changed—both in the workplace and between Beech and Mellor. She began taking on greater responsibilities while he continued to flirt with her. She ignored him while he grew lonely. She went flying with him, and he tried to scare her with stunts, flipping his open-cockpit plane in the air—yet another tactic that didn't work. Mellor was unflappable, seemingly perfect for Beech. In 1930, the couple got married, and the secretary soon took on a new title. She was increasingly known as O. A. Beech, a powerful and mysterious woman who could be both warm and tough, friendly and calculating; the sort of woman who would never forget a person's birthday but could also fire someone on the spot. As one friend later put it, "Nobody knows Olive Ann Beech."

It was—from a business perspective, anyway—an ideal match for Walter. He could build his planes and maybe even see the future, but he hadn't even finished grammar school as a boy in Tennessee, drifting away, as drifters do. Olive Ann would have to fill in the gaps in his knowledge, serving in whatever capacity he might need. Bookkeeper and head of payroll, bill collector and distributor liaison—she could do it all. She would have to now, given her husband's crazy plans. At a time when airplanes weren't selling—when even famous names like Travel Air were disappearing from the landscape—Walter was planning to launch a new aircraft company in Wichita, using his own money and his own name this time. He was calling it Beechcraft and he was sure it would succeed. The key, he thought, was building planes that were more reliable—safer, but also faster. "The field," he said, "lies in speed."

He and Olive Ann returned to Kansas in the midst of a freak early-spring snowstorm and were greeted by gusty winds, four inches of snow, and drifts piled high enough to maroon cars on the highway. The homecoming celebration was warmer, at least. The mayor, the chamber of commerce, and members of the local flying club all turned out to greet the Beeches, throwing them a dinner party at a downtown hotel a few weeks after they arrived and begging Walter—"the creative genius," they called him—to speak about his dreams of building a fast commercial plane there in Wichita.

"We have killed people—yes," Walter said, looking out on the crowd in the ballroom and acknowledging the dangers inherent in any fast airship. "But mark this," he told them, "there was never a faster method of transportation offered to the world that failed."

Railroads (dangerous) had replaced horse-drawn wagons. Cars (even more dangerous) were replacing railroads. In the end, despite all the financial struggles and tragic deaths, Beech predicted the aviation industry would prevail too, in part because of the financial risk he was taking right now by returning to Wichita to build something new.

The Beeches, joined by savvy engineer Ted Wells and a few others, quickly got to work building this new flying machine inside an abandoned factory east of town. The airplane in question was to be known as the Model 17, and the design, dreamed up by Wells, was notable for one reason in particular. The wings on the new biplane were staggered—that is, the top wing was positioned almost two feet behind the lower. Beech and Wells had no idea if the design would work. They just liked the concept. With the top wing staggered back, the pilot would have unfettered visibility from the cockpit.

They began building the new Beechcraft on a Monday morning in April as reporters milled around outside. By June, the press had caught its first glimpse of the airship, this Staggerwing: sleek and futuristic, with seats for five, landing gear inside aerodynamic sleeves, and a 420-horsepower engine in the nose. And that November, eight months after arriving back in Wichita, the Beeches unveiled their new plane. Fifteen hundred people came to the local airfield to watch it sweep low over the ground, deep red, graceful, and going two hundred miles an hour in the autumn sky.

The red plane was the only Beechcraft built in 1932, and it wasn't for sale. Walter was using it for demos. The following year was hardly more profitable. In 1933, Beechcraft reported net sales of about seventeen thousand dollars—the rough equivalent of a single airplane. While Walter and Olive Ann were settling into their new home east of town, their new company was dying—"starving," engineer Ted Wells conceded. They needed a breakthrough.

With Olive Ann in her office at the factory helping to oversee operations in Wichita, Walter hit the road, bouncing from Oakland to Indianapolis, Cincinnati to Miami, spreading the gospel of Beechcraft until, finally, a trickle of sales began to come in. In 1934, the company had enough resources to build eighteen planes. The following year, it produced twice that number, and the Beeches had reason to be hopeful about 1936 too, despite all those lazy employees loafing in the machine shop and the fuselage department. Their newest Staggerwing—a C17R—had enough speed to compete in races. That summer, Walter entered the new Beechcraft in a regional meet in Denver.

Olive Ann was thinking bigger. She wanted to win the Bendix, pitting their Wichita airship against Roscoe Turner's golden plane and Benny Howard's seemingly unbeatable *Mister Mulligan*. She just needed someone to fly it, and Olive Ann had an idea for that too.

Perhaps they should enter a woman, she suggested. A female pilot.

RUTH NICHOLS WAS the kind of woman deserving of consideration for the job: a veteran pilot who was both famous and calm in the cockpit. This is what passengers told investigators in late 1935, anyway. Nichols was cool, even after it became clear that the giant Curtiss Condor that she was copiloting across the Northeast was going down in Upstate New York.

The promotional air trip had, until that moment, been exactly like all the others in recent weeks. The Condor crew—consisting of Nichols, pilot Harry Hublitz, one mechanic, one ticket taker, and the latter two's girlfriends, enjoying the weekend tour—had thrilled the people of Troy, New York, the day before with hours of airplane rides under perfect conditions. Nichols figured they had flown a thousand people in a single day, some forty takeoffs and landings, exhausting work but lucrative for the new airline at a dollar a ride. They all stayed overnight and boarded the big Condor the next morning to head back to Newark, feeling good about the trip and themselves. Then the problems began. The plane's left engine, sputtering on takeoff, died with an unsettling boom as soon as the Condor climbed into the air. The large plane, shaking now and wobbly, flying with just one of its two engines about fifteen hundred feet off the ground, immediately began to lose altitude and sag to the left. Hublitz, circling back to the runway, quickly realized it was worse than he'd thought.

"We're not going to make it," he told Nichols quietly.

"I know it," she replied, also quietly.

Through the windows of the cockpit, she could see what was coming: the forest, the eighty-foot trees, and the suddenly inevitable—this crash on a beautiful autumn morning. The cockpit, holding Nichols and Hublitz, was going to be crushed. "They could have jumped clear," the ticket taker recalled later in amazement. But instead, they remained in their seats, fighting for control of the wounded Condor until the last moment. When the plane hit, the cockpit cracked open like an egg, and the plane's four-hundred-gallon gas tanks burst into flames, turning the machine into a fireball amid the trees. Hublitz — suffering a compound fracture of one leg but still conscious — crawled to safety through a jagged hole in the busted cockpit. The crew in back, mostly unharmed, did the same, and then the ticket taker returned and saved Nichols by dragging her unconscious body, still belted into the copilot's chair, away from the growing inferno.

She was a mess, with broken bones in her arms, legs, and face and serious burns on her skin. Newspapers across the country reported that Nichols had been rushed into surgery in Troy and might not live. Might not make it. But it was Hublitz who died from his injuries at the hospital that night, about twelve hours after the crash. Nichols, the ultimate survivor, had managed to evade death again. She was giving interviews from her hospital bed by the end of the week.

"I'm not a thing of beauty," she said, apologizing for her appearance. Most of her face was covered in bandages. But Nichols wished to thank the ticket taker who saved her life. "It was a grand, heroic thing," she said. She wanted to pay tribute to Hublitz, a good pilot, and she needed the world to know that she would soon be flying again, maybe even before she was walking. "Wherever the air trail leads," Nichols declared, "I will be there with bells on."

The air trail, for now, was unfortunately leading to a public inquest, the details of which were splashed across the front pages of the New York newspapers. The local coroner and district attorney wanted to question Nichols, the only pilot to survive the crash, about what had happened and why. Nichols was happy to answer their questions once she was healthy enough to sit up in bed. She just didn't want photographers there. But at least one got into her hospital room anyway, and he snapped pictures of Nichols fielding questions from a wheelchair next to her bed wearing a powder-blue suit with a red scarf long enough to hide her hands, still wounded and swollen.

She was clearly self-conscious about her hands and her appearance in general. She realized none of it looked good. But there wasn't much Nichols could do to help investigators, she informed them at the inquest. She had no idea what might have caused the crash. No memory of it at all, actually. Just Hublitz turning the large plane around, the Condor going down, the prayers in her head—*Oh, please, God, not yet*—and then nothing.

"From then on," Nichols reported, "it was darkness."

She was talking about the ill-fated flight, but she might as well have been referring to her lifetime of bad luck, her six-week stay in the hospital, her Thanksgiving dinner off a tray, her flight home on a stretcher that December—her second such flight in recent years—and then her long, slow recovery back in her parents' house in Rye, stuck in the mansion yet again. For all the miles she had traveled, for all the places she had gone, Ruth Nichols was right back where she had started.

"Dear Rufus," Earhart wrote her from a lecture stop in Michigan not long after her crash. "I am so sorry. Do get well as soon as possible as we women pilots can't afford to have you sitting on the sidelines for long."

But Nichols was almost thirty-five years old, and she could feel it. She was finished.

EARHART WASN'T FEELING well either.

That December, while Nichols returned home to Rye on a stretcher, bandaged and broken in more than one way, Earhart was laid up in New York as well. She was suffering from a bad case of laryngitis, which had forced her to cancel three lectures in the first week of December alone, and was having Putnam reply to her mail. Earhart's illness, at least, was temporary. By the middle of the month, she was back on the road, speaking to high-school students in Binghamton, New York, one of 136 lectures that Putnam had scheduled for her that winter. She needed to be out there talking and preparing for the new year, 1936; a big year, they hoped.

Olive Ann Beech had always admired Earhart. But the famous American flier had no need for the Beeches' fast, new Staggerwing rolling out of the hangar in Wichita. Putnam was working every angle to get his wife an airship that was all hers, one that was fast enough to set transcontinental speed records, large enough for long flights, and reliable enough for an ambitious plan that she and Putnam were secretly hatching—a trip around the world.

At first, they spoke about this potential new airplane to no one. Earhart said she was taking a break. "Right now," she said, "I've stopped being a personality in order to be a person." She did the talks that Putnam had scheduled for her—fine; it was her job, she'd do it. But she was also making time to decorate the new house they had just purchased near the airfield in Burbank, California, and settling into an unlikely job in an even more unlikely place. The president of Purdue University, a college in rural, northern Indiana, had hired Earhart to be a consultant—a visiting professor, effectively—in a new department he called the Center for the Study of Careers for Women. He offered her $2,000 for a few weeks of work on campus, and he had people prepare a corner room for her on the first floor of the college's new dormitory for female students. "All of the women of the university," the residence hall director informed Earhart, "are looking forward to your coming."

It was, relatively speaking, a tiny number of women. Purdue was lucky to enroll two hundred women every year, meaning the vast majority of the 4,677 students on campus in the fall of 1935 were young Midwestern men—people who had very little in common with Earhart. But the university, which focused on science and engineering, did have its own airfield, built for students ("You're Always Welcome at the Purdue University Airport"); a training plane that they could use for five dollars an hour; and a president, Edward C. Elliott, who was so interested in aviation that he not only crafted the rules for student pilots at the university but recruited Earhart to come.

Earhart was thrilled to be there. She pulled up on campus in a large brown car—not a plane—and impressed the young women from the start with her first, and possibly only, rule: no one was allowed to call her Mrs. Putnam, not ever. "Even my own husband," she told the students, "would call me Miss Earhart." She ate with them in the dining hall, walked with them to class, and encouraged them to ask her any questions they wanted, about anything at all, while she asked them some questions of her own. "Are you planning to seek employment after you leave college? . . . How did you choose your career? . . . Do you plan to continue working after marriage?" And the kicker: "What do you think a married man's part in running the household should be?"

When Earhart left campus, at the end of November, hustling off to talks in Dayton and Zanesville, she announced the findings of her survey. "Some of the men think it's baloney," she reported, but 92 percent of female students at Purdue told Earhart they planned to work after college, and almost half the freshmen women already knew what they wanted to do. "This is a large proportion, I think, when you consider how little education does along the way to trace talents or analyze desires," Earhart said.

She seemed excited about her findings, but she was probably not as giddy as Putnam, back in New York. He had convinced Elliott and other Purdue officials to help buy a new Lockheed Electra for Earhart, making his pitch at the peak of Amelia Earhart fever in northern Indiana: just a couple of days after his wife arrived.

"I play my hunches," Putnam told Elliott, "and your cooperation is exactly what is needed in this project."

Elliott agreed, enamored with the bright aura of Earhart on the cusp of another long, bleak Indiana winter. "She has," Purdue's president told Putnam, "the entire campus on its toes." Just listening to her speak had rich men swooning. At a dinner party at Elliott's house that fall, they began lining up to give her money for this plane that she wanted, and by the spring of 1936, Putnam had hammered out an agreement: the Purdue Research Foundation, a nonprofit closely associated with the university, would put up $40,000. Vincent Bendix was chipping in another $5,000, and other money poured in until Earhart had amassed the small fortune she needed to buy her new Lockheed, a state-of-the-art modern airship she called her "Flying Laboratory." She was trying to suggest to the press that the plane would be used to further scientific knowledge, to do something academic. But privately, Putnam was more candid, assuring Elliott of great publicity for the university as Earhart used the new plane to pursue history, records — important flights.

"Several outstanding flights," Putnam promised.

Starting with the Bendix race.

She collected the plane in July 1936 and began to prepare.

THADEN AND EARHART were drifting apart and had been for a while. It wasn't just that Thaden didn't like Earhart's husband or understand their relationship; it was that, increasingly, she didn't understand Earhart. While Thaden was trying to be a wife, a mother, and an aviator — a balancing act that didn't always work, keeping her out of the sky and close to home — Earhart seemed to be pushing herself harder than ever, almost to the point of recklessness. The breaking point for Thaden was Earhart's solo flight from Hawaii to California, across the open water of the Pacific for almost eighteen hours. It was by far the longest flight Earhart had ever attempted over water. A fifty-fifty gamble, officials said at the time. Far too risky, Thaden thought, and she told Earhart as much, giving her a dressing-down after the successful flight, in a teasing tone, while others cheered her.

"Maybe I'm getting old," Thaden confessed to Earhart. "But darn your hide, I could spank your pants! Would you mind telling me sometime in strict confidence why the heck you DO things like that? I'd really like to know."

Because to Thaden, the Pacific flight seemed not only dangerous but shortsighted. "Dimmit," she scolded Earhart, coming close to cursing, "you're worth more alive than dead, and what profit fame when you are not here to reap the benefits, presupposing there are benefits."

It was almost as if Thaden, a mother of two, couldn't stop herself from mothering her friend. She wanted Earhart to cool it. "I wish you'd rest on your laurels," Thaden told her. And she wanted Earhart to know how she felt, even though she realized that Earhart might resent her for saying it. "It's just the way I feel about you." She considered Earhart one of her best friends—one of her only friends—and an enigma. "When it comes down to brass tacks, I don't know you at all," Thaden told Earhart. "I doubt anyone does."

Thaden, by comparison, lacked the slightest hint of mystery. By 1936, in fact, she felt almost ordinary, a terrible feeling. In order to make ends meet, she had returned home to Arkansas and moved in with her mother, who had never really approved of her flying, and father, who seemed to revel in it. She'd come full circle, just like Nichols. She was a grown woman, thirty years old, and living at home with her parents. There was, for Thaden, no way around it.

Herb's time in Kansas City had come to an end. In his new job—yet another in a long line of short-term aviation gigs—he was traveling too much. Then Louise had gone and gotten hired as an air-marking pilot, meaning she, too, would be traveling now, flying across the country to convince local officials to let the federal government paint city names on the roofs of barns and warehouses. Thaden needed her parents to look after her children while she was gone, and that winter she was gone a lot, dispatched to Montana, Texas, and elsewhere to make the government's case. "Even experienced fliers get lost," Thaden said in town after town, noting the importance of air-markers. "The proposed system of markers will reduce accidents."

She was thinking a lot lately about crashes—and it wasn't just because of her new job or Nichols's mishap in Upstate New York. That winter, while Thaden was on an air-marking trip out west, a plane went down in a snowstorm near Buffalo, New York. It crashed into a wooded hill, shearing off both wings on impact, demolishing the plane—a Beechcraft—and killing the two men on board. The crash would have gone unnoticed by Thaden had it not been for the man flying it: Dewey Noyes. He was a jolly, redheaded airman, the first pilot to fly the mail run from Cleveland to Pittsburgh, and an experienced aviator who had once landed a hobbled plane on the Monongahela River. More notable, Dewey wasn't the most famous pilot in his own house. He was married to Blanche Noyes, the fourth-place finisher in the 1929 Powder Puff Derby, one of the original Ninety-Nines, and a friend to Thaden and the other women.

Dewey had taught Blanche how to fly, how to land, how to handle a plane in bad weather, and how to race, pushing her into the 1929 derby. "It was always his idea," Noyes said. "Up until the time he was killed, it was his idea, always." Even when Dewey wasn't flying with her, Blanche felt like he was there, over her shoulder, speaking in her ear, on her mind.

"Dear Dewey," she wrote him once from the road. "The Lord is my pilot. I shall not crash. He maketh me fly in clear skies. He leadeth me down to smooth landings. He keepth my charts. Yea, though I fly through the storms and tempests of life, I shall dread no danger. For Thou art near me."

Now, without him, Noyes was lost, crying all the time. "She is pretty well shot to pieces," Earhart said, lobbying the Department of Commerce to give her old friend an air-marking job alongside Thaden. At least then Noyes would have something to keep her occupied. "I can vouch for her integrity," Earhart said in a letter of recommendation to the department's top man, a good friend, "and would be glad to pay her fare to Washington (without her knowledge) should you feel it worth while to interview her."

Noyes joined Thaden on the air-marking circuit that summer, and

Thaden was glad for the company, happy to reunite with Noyes in a lonely and fragile time. Thaden was far from home, away from her husband and children, and also grieving that summer. Her father, Roy—a traveling salesman who had always treated Louise the same way he would a son—had died that June in a car crash north of Bentonville on a road he had traveled countless times. Just lost control of his vehicle somehow. Driven off a bridge somehow. Plunged his car into a lake and drowned. A search party dragged the lake bottom and found his body. The man who had taught Louise how to work on engines, who had taken her on sales trips and encouraged her unusual interest in aviation while others had scoffed, was gone. "Gone to heaven," Thaden said. Or hoped. All she knew for sure was that she felt her father's presence. "I feel him close to me."

It was a dark summer, a hard year. But instead of disappearing into sadness, Thaden was putting herself back out there, emboldened, it seemed, in the face of despair. In July, she went to the air races in Denver with her mother and young son. Ten days later, for the first time in years, she climbed back into a plane, intent on setting a new female record. She flew a pylon course in Virginia at an average speed of 109 miles an hour—surprising speed for a lightweight plane. Her airship that day weighed barely nine hundred pounds. Then, late one night that summer, back on the air-marking trail with Noyes in Texas, Thaden got a phone call from Olive Ann Beech offering her the chance of a lifetime—a spot in the $10,000 Bendix race, with an additional $2,500 to be awarded to the first woman to finish.

"I think we might as well have that money," Olive Ann said, "don't you?"

21

A Woman Couldn't Win

THADEN ALMOST SAID NO.

At first, anyway, she considered turning down Olive Ann's offer to fly in the Bendix, fearing disaster or defeat — or both. The race was dangerous. Cecil Allen's death the year before, crashing on takeoff in Burbank, had proven that. Russell Boardman's death at a refueling stop midway through the Bendix in 1933 had proven it too. The statistics made it clear that the odds were stacked against anyone, man or woman, flying across the country at high speed. In five years of Bendix races, almost half of the thirty-five pilots who had competed had failed to even finish.

Three pilots had never gotten off the ground; three others arrived horribly late, lost and slow and forgotten; and ten — roughly a third of all Bendix pilots — had gone down, littering the countryside with disabled planes, hobbled by a host of unpredictable problems. Fires, empty gas tanks, broken fuel lines, busted radios, and, of course, horrific crashes. Thaden, with her children at her mother's home in Arkansas, had to pause and weigh the potential outcomes of any Bendix flight. But in the end, she accepted Olive Ann's offer — and her challenge. She requested a leave of absence from her air-marking job to make the Bendix trip possible and asked one of her coworkers, Blanche Noyes, to join her.

For the aviation-beat reporters, it was a cute story. A year earlier, race officials had allowed Earhart and another woman to fly in the

Bendix, but only if they were accompanied by a man who knew what he was doing in the air. The idea that two women—two former Powder Puff Derby pilots—might fly together with no man at all was almost a joke. Some went so far as to suggest that this year's Bendix should be organized into two divisions: one for the men, who were actually trying to win it all, and one for the women, who were clearly just trying to claim Vincent Bendix's $2,500 consolation prize set aside for the female competitors.

They weren't going to prevail, these women. Not Thaden and Noyes in their Beechcraft awaiting them in Wichita. Not Earhart, joined in her new Flying Laboratory by female copilot Helen Richey. And not Laura Ingalls either. Ingalls, a dark-eyed Brooklyn native who was the third female flier to enter the race, held the new female transcontinental speed record. She would be flying a souped-up, coal-black plane that was far more powerful than Thaden's. Still, no one thought Ingalls had a chance. Everyone knew this year's Bendix was a two-man affair, Turner versus Howard, or Howard versus Turner, head to head once again, perhaps for the last time, after finishing a mere twenty-three and a half seconds apart in the Bendix the year before.

Even Louise's husband, Herb, believed the race would be a contest between Turner and Howard. Herb wasn't a pessimist by nature, and he certainly never doubted Louise. He was just an engineer surveying the field, running the numbers, and trying to be objective. At best, he told Louise, she might finish third and take home the women's prize—if she could beat Earhart.

Earhart's new Lockheed Electra was no speedster with a cruising speed of 215 miles an hour. But with a price tag of $64,000, the Electra was four times more expensive than the Beechcraft waiting for Thaden in Wichita. And it was loaded with features: twin 550-horsepower engines, retractable landing gear, and enough gas reserves to fly nonstop for forty-five hundred miles, an impressive range that already had reporters talking. Maybe, they said, Earhart's Bendix entry was a warm-up for a flight around the world—a suggestion that she denied. "Somebody invented that," she said. "I have no immediate plans except that we are remodeling our home in North Hollywood."

Just a few miles away, in the hills overlooking Los Angeles, Roscoe Turner wasn't thinking about the interior design of his impressive house; he was thinking about his fast and golden plane. He had waited a year, feeding his caged lion and twirling his waxed mustache, to avenge his losses of 1935. "Roscoe maintains silence," one observer said, "and a poker face." But rumors swirled around the airfield in Burbank, rumors that his golden plane in the hangar there was faster than ever before—"sensationally fast," one person declared; that it was equipped with a new 1,000-horsepower engine; and that he hoped to use it to not only win the Bendix, but break his own transcontinental speed record. In secret, he was testing it, saying nothing of note in his radio interviews and divulging no details to anyone, especially not to the man who had swept him at the air races the year before: Benny Howard.

Half a continent away, in his humble shop on West Sixty-Fifth Street near the airport southwest of Chicago, Howard was ready—and so was his speedy plane. *Mister Mulligan* was no mere machine; it was, by the summer of 1936, a legend with a devoted following. *Popular Aviation* magazine splashed the sleek white plane on its cover, using pre-publication advertisements to stir up excitement for the image, a collector's item. "A fine color drawing of Benny Howard's famous plane," the magazine declared, "which will be prized by all air-race fans." People across America sent away for model kits, paying fifty cents each so they could build their own miniature *Mister Mulligans*. "Only a limited number," ads said, "so act quick. See your dealer at once." Most important, perhaps, aviation experts were equally passionate about the white plane and the man flying it. "Howard won in 1935," one prognosticator said on the eve of the Bendix, "and looks like a good bet to repeat with *Mister Mulligan*." The plane was too fast and Howard too talented not to win. "He is," said one reporter, "the acknowledged master of all race pilots."

Not even Walter Beech thought Thaden could beat Turner and Howard. When Thaden arrived in Wichita to pick up the plane—painted teal blue, Olive Ann's favorite color, with two white pinstripes down each side of the fuselage—she found Walter stewing. He was upset that Olive Ann had entered the plane in the Bendix race at all. If it failed, it could hurt business. At least one male pilot at the factory was angry too. He didn't like that Olive Ann had chosen a woman to fly the plane. And Thaden, though impressed by the beauty of the airship—"a trim blue princess," she called it—had her own problems with it. The radio on board was all wrong; the compass was too. She and Noyes needed to get to New York, where Herb was waiting to inspect the plane himself, and they were running out of time—time to get the maps they needed, to study the course they would fly, and to answer their many critics in the press, who were asking the usual questions.

Thaden knew what she was up against. Earhart, for starters, and then Turner and Howard, of course. Herb was probably right; third place would be great. Maybe finishing first among the women was the best she could do. But when reporters talking to Thaden suggested as much, it sounded like an insult and Thaden refused to let it pass. She wasn't trying to win the "women's division," she declared, because, after all, there was no such thing. She was thinking bigger.

"We are going to fly in the Bendix," Thaden told reporters, "and unless some of the other pilots do better flying or show better speed, we will win it."

She vowed the plane would make it, coast to coast, in fourteen hours. "We will put it over the route," she said. With that, Thaden climbed into the blue Beechcraft, pointed its nose into the hard prairie wind, and pushed east. She was heading for the starting line in New York City.

EARHART WAS ALREADY on the ground at Floyd Bennett Field in Brooklyn when Thaden and Noyes arrived. Her new Lockheed had performed well in its first long trip, flying from Burbank to Brooklyn that week with a crew that included not only Earhart and a mechanic but, for half the trip, her technical adviser Paul Mantz.

She was still acting like her goal was scientific advancement, not transcontinental races or, as Putnam had put it, "outstanding flights." She was also still denying the rumors that she was planning an around-the-world flight. "My plane, you see, is equipped for the research work I am to do for Purdue University." But Earhart couldn't help but gush over the new twin-engine airship. "The kind," she said, "you could write poetry about." She was thrilled to announce that the Lockheed had made it from Cleveland to New York in just two hours and twenty-five minutes.

That time sounded good until Benny Howard blew into Brooklyn, along with his wife, Maxine, in *Mister Mulligan*. Just for fun—a warmup exercise, really—the couple had made the trip from Chicago to

New York in a record-breaking two hours and forty-five minutes. That was fourteen minutes faster than the previous top time set two years earlier and further proof that *Mister Mulligan* was ready to defend its title as the fastest plane in America.

Howard intended to fly the Bendix race in a tweed suit, something dashing to greet the fans in when he stepped off the plane in Los Angeles, arriving first. He was allowing his wife, who had earned her pilot's license, to join him this year, and she was dressed in tweed as well. Together, the Howards could greet the adoring fans at the finish line — a nice photo for the papers — and perhaps share a celebratory swig from the flask of whiskey they planned to bring aboard the plane. Benny already knew what he wanted to do with his Bendix prize money. He would prepare a modified version of *Mister Mulligan* for mass production: "We intend to build this airplane for private owners who want airline performance and reliability."

Airfields on both ends of the continent were abuzz with excitement. And in Los Angeles, Henderson had already won, no matter the outcome. He had a $35,000 contract to put on the air races, an office in the swank Ambassador Hotel, a sprawling home in Brentwood among the houses of Hollywood stars that he dubbed Chateau Avion, and a beautiful woman on his arm seemingly every night at the Cocoanut Grove night club or at supper dances at the West Side Tennis Club. Today an actress, tomorrow a baroness. According to the gossip columns, "Cliff Henderson always escorts the most attractive bits of femininity." Vincent Bendix, looking as thick as ever, signed the wall in Henderson's trophy room in Brentwood that week, and the two men, feeling good about themselves, met at old Mines Field, the site of Henderson's original races, to await the pilots soon to be screaming in from New York: Howard and Earhart and Thaden. But in a stunning development, there would be no Roscoe Turner.

The mustachioed Hollywood showman had problems with his plane long before reaching the starting line in New York. In Burbank the week before the race, Turner could barely get the airship off the ground to fly east. Twice, he aborted on takeoff, swerving onto rough ground near the runway to keep his $35,000 machine from plowing into a hangar. Not good. He ordered mechanics to work through the night to make adjustments; Turner was worried about getting to New York in time for the race. Finally, with just a few days to spare, mechanics pronounced Turner's plane ready to fly. He took off before dawn the next morning, rose over Los Angeles in the dark, climbed to ten thousand feet, and pointed his plane toward the glow on the eastern horizon. He planned to hit Albuquerque by lunchtime; New York, surely, by nightfall.

But three hours into the journey, the throttle cut out, jiggling in his large hand, disconnected and worthless. As the plane began losing altitude, Turner, who had never crashed in nineteen years of flying, began scanning the ground for a place to make a forced landing amid the jagged canyons and lonely mesas of western New Mexico. *Malpais*, locals called it. Bad country.

One option was bailing out. Turner had a parachute on his back, and he could have used it. But he hated the idea of parting with his beautiful golden plane. "Too much good airplane," he thought, "to leave flying around by itself." And it almost felt like giving up. If he found a way to land safely, perhaps he could get the mechanics back to work and still enter the Bendix, still get to New York. So despite the risks, Turner stayed with the broken plane, identifying from high in the sky what appeared to be mostly flat ground and coming in for a landing at around ninety miles an hour.

A smooth touchdown, it was not. On impact, the plane bounced fifteen feet in the air, spun on its side, and began to cartwheel across the desert floor — once, twice, maybe more. It was impossible to keep track; Turner wasn't thinking clearly enough to count. Then one wing — the left wing, maybe — dug into the rocky earth, which flipped the plane, snapped it in half just behind the cockpit, and brought it to a lurching halt.

The nearest city was sixty-five miles away; the nearest Indian settlement, the Zuni reservation, eighteen miles. The region was so remote that an airliner that had crashed nearby years earlier had gone missing for five days, eluding an extensive search party led by the federal government. By the time the searchers found the wreckage, everyone on board was long dead.

But Turner was only battered and dazed, with fractured ribs, maybe, an aching neck, and perhaps a concussion, nothing more — a miracle. He stirred inside the twisted plane, crawled from the cockpit, gathered himself, and, in his high boots and signature uniform, began to walk, hoping to find help and looking preposterous in the desert. It was three hours before he stumbled upon a Zuni farmer with a couple of horses and several more hours before the two of them arrived at the reservation on horseback, the famous pilot following his unlikely guide and feeling broken, as if the bones in his injured neck might snap with each step of the horse.

At 6:45 p.m., more than thirteen hours after takeoff, when he should have been in New York, Turner finally reached a telephone in New Mexico. He picked up the receiver and called his panicked wife back in Hollywood to let her know he was alive. He was okay.

"It looks like I'm out of the running—flying, I mean, this year," he said. He sounded nervous, like a different man. "I'm pretty shaky," he admitted.

Roscoe Turner was returning to Los Angeles by train, leaving the wreckage of his golden plane in the desert. A pile of glinting metal and wood. A trash heap.

"Splinters and a grease spot," Turner said. "It's a wonder I'm not, too."

THADEN'S SIX-YEAR-OLD SON, Bill, had been praying at bedtime. Every night, for the past few weeks, the same prayer: "Bless Mother," the little boy said, "and please let her pass all the others in the race . . . Bless Mother, and please let her pass all the others in the race . . . Bless Mother . . ."

The boy, staying with his newly widowed grandmother in Bentonville, understood the stakes; Thaden had taught him well. But even with Turner out, few people thought she had a chance in her Beechcraft. It was Howard's race now, people agreed, eyeing the speedy *Mister Mulligan* on the field in Brooklyn. And if not Howard, then perhaps one of the other men: young Joe Jacobson, with his own flying school in Kansas City and his name painted on the fuselage of his record-setting, low-wing Northrop Gamma; George Pomeroy, from Washington, flying a modern Douglas DC-2 transport plane with four beds and a telephone switchboard; or Buster Warner, a navy lieutenant and local hero from Brooklyn with twenty-eight hundred hours of flying experience and a crew of three men flying with him, a mechanic, a copilot, and a US Coast Guard navigator. A man like that would certainly have a good shot at Bendix's trophy and his cash. "An excellent chance," one reporter said, "of winning."

The night before departure, the fliers mingled together at a pre-flight dinner at the Half Moon Hotel on the boardwalk in Coney Island and then returned to Floyd Bennett Field in Brooklyn for the final pilots' meeting at ten thirty. The meeting room there was small, and Thaden was distracted, thinking about everything: the plane, the compass, the route, the weather—perhaps the weather most of all. Some of the competitors had private weather services churning out reports, but not Thaden. She and Noyes would have to make do with the ten-thirty advisory handed out to everyone that promised "generally good" conditions at least as far as Wichita, the site of Thaden's scheduled refueling stop, halfway across the country.

Walter Beech was waiting for her there. Olive Ann was in Los Angeles at Henderson's finish line, and a large crowd was pushing to get close to the fliers at the airfield, even now in the dark, with midnight coming in New York. Peanut vendors fought to make sales; hot-dog merchants hustled along next to them. Thaden and Noyes found beds and tried to get some sleep. Then airplanes began roaring into the air, bound for the West Coast in a staggered start.

Buster Warner, the Brooklyn flier with the crew of three, got off first in his silver plane at 1:37 a.m. George Pomeroy, in the large Douglas transport ship, took off next, followed by Earhart with her copilot, Helen Richey, in her new Lockheed, and then Jacobson, the Kansas City flying instructor determined to defeat Benny Howard. Jacobson was so confident of success that he was prepared to leave Brooklyn with a parachute that he hadn't checked or repacked in six months—a dangerous plan, which the airport manager overruled. He gave field attendants permission to break into a private plane in the middle of the night, steal a newly packed parachute, and give it to Jacobson, who—ready now—waved to photographers in the moonlight and bounded into the sky, rising over Brighton Beach and Staten Island, going west.

Thaden felt like she was losing already. "I can't stand this," she said in the dark. And finally, after five thirty a.m., restless and tired of waiting, she and Noyes walked toward the blue Staggerwing on the airfield beneath the morning stars.

Most race fans had gone home by then, leaving just a few hundred people on the ground. But Herb was still there, standing by his wife's plane.

"Goodbye, darling," Louise told him. "And try not to worry about us, will you?"

"Goodbye, dear," he told her, kissing her farewell.

An old friend was there too: Ruth Nichols was still recovering from the many injuries suffered in her plane crash in Upstate New York. But race officials had asked her to help out on the ground. Always loyal, never bitter, she had agreed and waited all night for this moment.

"Good luck," she told Thaden.

"Well, so long," Thaden replied, waving from the cockpit.

Now, close to six a.m., she taxied her Beechcraft past the still-waiting *Mister Mulligan,* angling the nose of her blue plane into the wind near a wall of race officials — timers and starters — at the end of the runway.

"One minute," a starter hollered, holding a handkerchief in the air.

Thaden pushed the throttle and waited.

"Fifteen seconds," he said.

She pushed it a little more.

Then, at exactly 5:56 a.m., the starter dropped his handkerchief. The timers hit their stopwatches. And Thaden and Noyes's plane sped down the concrete runway and took to the sky just as the soft morning light began creeping over the eastern horizon. They had a long flight ahead of them, a course to chart, and competitors both ahead and behind. Benny Howard and his wife, Maxine, were soon in the air, too, stalking Thaden's Beechcraft with *Mister Mulligan* — thirteen minutes off the pace at first, but coming on fast and soon rocketing past the women. Thaden and Noyes had barely left New York, and they were already falling behind.

Howard was particularly motivated to fly fast that day. In addition to offering $2,500 to the first female finisher, Bendix, feeling generous, promised to give an additional $2,500 to any flier who broke Turner's transcontinental speed record — yet another blow for Turner, who was out of the race and resting at home in Hollywood on doctor's orders. Howard wanted both the money and the speed mark, Turner's record and his fame. Just imagine what it would do for the sales of the DGA — Howard's Damn Good Airplane — that he was preparing to mass-produce. With his wife at his side, the Chicago airman, dressed in tweed, pushed the nose of *Mister Mulligan* toward Kansas City, traveling at a seemingly unbeatable 245 miles per hour, chasing the remnants of the night and picking off his competitors one by one.

Pomeroy's Douglas transport plane was big and modern but slow. Buster Warner's airship was too. No Coast Guard navigator could make up for its inherent lack of speed. And Earhart struggled to make good time due to other problems. Shortly after takeoff, the hatch over her head inside the cockpit of the Flying Laboratory blew open, nearly sucking out Earhart and her copilot and throwing them into the night. Even after it was clear that she and Richey wouldn't be ripped from their seats, Earhart worried that the flapping hatch would tear away, smash into the tail, and make the Lockheed impossible to fly. "A very serious predicament," Earhart called it, with her usual understatement.

By Earhart's estimation, they lost forty minutes fighting the flapping door before finally tying it down with a rag—a backyard fix on an expensive airship, but the best they could manage. They limped into Kansas City, their one refueling stop, trailing Howard by almost two hours and then losing still more time, another twenty-three minutes, waiting for mechanics to remove the rag and wire down the busted hatch for safety. Meanwhile, back east, it was beginning to look like Herb's calculations were right. Third place might be the best Thaden could do. Howard and Jacobson were simply too fast, with Jacobson the first to arrive in Kansas City.

The morning skies there were stormy, hot and unsettled, with showers in the forecast and thunderheads on the horizon. But Jacobson knew this territory; Kansas City was his home. And taking off with a fresh load of fuel on board, the flier quickly guided his Northrop Gamma to an altitude of six thousand feet, dodging, he thought, the worst of the stormy skies by climbing through two large clouds. Suddenly, the left wing ripped away; it just folded back on the fuselage, severing a fuel line and causing an explosion that tore the plane to pieces. Jacobson was unconscious and falling now—blown not only from the disintegrated plane but somehow from his safety belt and his seat. He was just a body tumbling in the sky, closing in fast on the prairie below, finally regaining consciousness maybe five hundred feet off the ground. He pulled the ripcord on the stolen parachute and twisted the lines with his hands to make it open quicker. He was coming down fast, too fast, in the worst possible spot: the fiery wreckage of his own exploded plane. It was only the wind that saved him — a breeze blew him away from the flames at the last moment, and, somehow, Jacobson emerged from the crash with nothing but a wrenched ankle. Stunned but alive, he limped to a nearby farmhouse for help.

"Few men ever come as close to eternity as Jacobson did and survive," the *Wichita Eagle* declared the next day, "and he was able to dismiss, with a smile, the loss of the valuable ship." He planned to take a TWA airliner to Los Angeles in the morning. Jacobson was out of the Bendix, clearing the skies for one man.

BENNY HOWARD WAS THRILLED by his fast time into Kansas City: just four hours and fifty-four minutes, definitely on pace to break Turner's record. It was a big moment, a great morning. "Everything's lovely," Howard reported on the ground in Kansas City, refueling *Mister Mulligan* in a quick sixteen-minute stop and then returning to the air. He headed southwest in a straight shot for the finish line, fourteen hundred miles away, at Mines Field in Los Angeles.

On the ground there, the day had begun with a parade starting at city hall downtown. Massive floats rolled up Broadway to Wilshire Boulevard and then went on to the airport, carrying fifty airplanes representing, Henderson said, the history of aviation. While these gleaming airships rumbled to the airport, army fliers and race pilots dived low overhead. And starting at noon, fifty thousand people, including the city's elite — movie stars and politicians — began gathering at the field to see the stunt pilots flying upside down, the parachute-jumping contests, the first races of the weekend around the tall pylons with B-E-N-D-I-X written on the sides, and the arrival of the transcontinental fliers.

At the rate they were going — 245 miles an hour — the Howards should have been there no later than midday, arriving in *Mister Mulligan* just before Henderson's typically grandiose opening ceremonies with an afternoon fireworks display to follow. It would be perfect timing, a real showman's arrival. Howard would land with a Hollywood ending that Henderson and Benny's rival Roscoe Turner could have appreciated.

But one o'clock came and went — and there was no white plane in the sky. The opening ceremonies unfolded, and the fireworks too, and still nothing. No Howard. He was late, maybe lost — or worse. People knew only one thing for certain: Howard wasn't breaking Turner's transcontinental record that day. The overdue *Mister Mulligan* was still six hundred miles east, somewhere in western New Mexico's *malpais.*

Benny, in the cockpit, was the first to detect a problem: a slight vibration in the plane's spinning propeller. Something was off. He leaned toward the dashboard to tinker with the propeller controls and get a better listen to the odd sound when, without warning, *Mister Mulligan*'s propeller hub failed. One of the prop's two blades ripped away, snapping off in midflight — with a jolt — and then falling to the earth from four thousand feet in the sky. Benny, caught by surprise, slammed his head against a bracing tube, momentarily knocking himself out and slicing a nasty gash over one eye. Blood was everywhere. And the plane was spinning, following the lone propeller blade around and around, until the engine coughed and died. Benny quickly regained consciousness and, also, control of the airplane. He took the stick in his hand, righted *Mister Mulligan,* and then, together, with his wife, flew on in eerie silence.

Maxine went to work on her husband's forehead, mopping up the blood with a handkerchief, while Benny surveyed the desert wastes below through cockpit windows covered in oil spewing from the busted prop hub. He was weighing their options. Like Turner less than a week earlier, the Howards had only two. They could bail out and parachute to safety, sacrificing the plane, hoping their chutes would work and, if they did, that they wouldn't break their legs on impact — a sure way to die in the desert. Or they could stay with the plane and make a crash landing — on flat ground, if they could find it.

The Howards, like Turner, chose the latter. Gliding down toward the earth, Benny thought he spied the exact sort of improvised runway he needed: a dry creek bed, flat and wide. But with the blood in his eyes and the oil on the windows, visibility was terrible. As they got closer to the ground, Benny realized this creek wasn't dry. It wasn't even a creek. It was a shallow lake. A good place to flip the plane and drown. "No place to land," Benny said. Running out of options now, he swung the airship around, hoping to land near one of the small streams feeding into the lake. But this was no landing. *Mister Mulligan* was crashing. "Too hard," Benny said.

The plane bounced and settled, plowing into clumps of sagebrush and hidden rocks that cleaved off the landing gear, first the left wheel and then the right. Skittering along now on its white belly, *Mister Mulligan* was out of control, ripping across the hard clay. It nosed into the ground and finally came to a rest with such fury that the half-ton engine at the front of the famous plane blew back through the firewall and into the cockpit. The motor that Benny had installed with his own hands at his shop in Chicago was now sitting in his lap—and the lap of his wife—smashing the bones in their legs and feet. There was dust and silence and then darkness.

Both Benny and Maxine lost consciousness, waking some time later to the fresh horrors of their new reality. They were covered in gasoline, pinned beneath the engine, trapped inside the plane, and forty miles from the nearest town, with compound fractures in their legs. Benny could see his wife's shinbones sticking out through her tweed pants, his own leg bones had pierced through his skin, and his left foot was almost severed at the heel. They were going to die there, he figured. This was how it would end, the two of them trapped and wounded. They ate ice chips from a canteen, their only comfort, until that, too, was lost, rolling away just out of their reach when they opened a door to get some fresh air. It was then that they spotted him: a Navajo just standing there, looking at the Howards in curious silence.

They cried for help. He did not come. They wailed and cursed, and the man just walked around, circling the ship. Finally, they wrote a note and somehow convinced the man to take it. He delivered it to a nearby trading post. But instead of help, the Howards just got more spectators—a dozen more Navajo afraid to approach the crumpled white plane on their reservation near the town of Crownpoint, New Mexico. One of them, a forty-year-old man, had seen the bird come down, and he thought it a bad sign—a notion with which, apparently, everyone agreed. *Sky chindi,* they called the couple who had fallen from the heavens. Sky ghosts.

For almost three hours, the Navajo just stood there, eyeing the machine and the bloody couple inside, observing their odd behavior. They watched the thin man drinking whiskey from a flask and the blond woman not drinking at all. They watched the man finishing the contents of the flask—"If this isn't an emergency, what in the hell is one?" he said—and the woman just sitting there. And most of all, they listened to the man raging. He was screaming at the Navajo, at the engine on his legs, and at the world while the woman bore her pain in near silence.

"Don't worry," Maxine told Benny. "Everything's going to be all right."

Finally, around three p.m., townsfolk who'd been alerted about the crash arrived. They brought axes to free the Howards and pickup trucks lined with mattresses to carry them to the nearest hospital. Benny was still coherent enough at that point to help direct the would-be rescuers and he instructed them not to hit the gas lines with their axes. "Don't do that," he warned, "you'll start a fire."

But at the hospital later that day, he descended into what doctors considered delirium.

"How is my plane?" he kept asking.

He went on and on about *Mister Mulligan* and his wife and Roscoe Turner's record—some kind of speed record. It could have been his, Benny said. It should have been his.

"IRRATIONAL," nurses wrote in his chart at the hospital. And then doctors moved in to amputate his left leg, saving his life but ending his racing career. It was a month before he and Maxine were well enough to go home to Chicago, flown there not in a glamorous race plane but a more pedestrian machine: a medical-transport aircraft.

BEFORE TAKEOFF, THADEN had worried about a crash just like the Howards', playing out the possibilities in her head and talking it over with Noyes in the dark in Brooklyn while the two were trying to sleep.

"Blanche," Thaden said at one point, "are you awake?"

"Yeah," Noyes replied, "are you?"

As the pilot, Thaden wanted Noyes to know that in the event of a mishap, she would stay with the controls while Noyes bailed out. "It's to be understood," Thaden said, "that you jump first."

Noyes wouldn't hear of it. "You have two children," she told Thaden, "so *you* jump first."

They left it like that, undecided and, hopefully, unnecessary. Still, it had been worth discussing. Thaden knew anything could happen in the Bendix, and by morning, a couple of hours out of New York, she was already staring down the first problem. Her blue Beechcraft was somewhere over the dangerous Allegheny Mountains, bouncing along at eight thousand feet—and lost. A thick fog, white and gray, blanketed everything. Thaden could make out only the highest peaks beneath her, giving her little to use for navigation. Worse still, the plane's radio had been reduced to static — "useless," Thaden called it — making it impossible for the two women to check their position. Finally, after ninety minutes of blind flying, they broke clear of the fog and began scanning the ground for a landmark that corresponded with something on their maps or, even better, for an air-marker.

"Look!" Noyes said, spotting a sign.

Thaden guided the plane down to four thousand feet and circled. The sign was indeed an air-marker. Noyes used it to fix their position. "We are only ten miles off course!" she shouted a moment later, pounding Thaden on the back. The women were back on track. But they lost time near St. Louis, fighting storms and crosswinds. "Tighten your belt," Thaden told Noyes. And when they reached Wichita, Walter Beech was upset again — of course.

"What the hell do you think you're in?" he asked Thaden, meeting her amid the fuel trucks on the airfield. "A potato race?"

He and the women had no way to know what had happened to the Howards in New Mexico. And until they landed in Wichita, Thaden and Noyes couldn't have known about Joe Jacobson exploding in the skies over Kansas or about Earhart's blown hatch tied down by a rag. Regardless, Beech didn't think Thaden was going fast enough, imploring her to push the Beechcraft engine to its limits.

"Open this damn thing up," he demanded.

It was hot and sticky on the ground, closing in on ninety-four degrees. Too miserable outside to argue. Thaden had no time for it, anyway, focused on refueling the plane with 165 gallons of gas — enough to make it to Los Angeles — and fixated on getting back into the air.

"Yes, sir," she told Beech.

But really, Thaden was only humoring him. It might have been seven years since she won the Powder Puff Derby, but she remembered why she had prevailed in that long, grueling race: by not getting lost, by not rushing and making mistakes, and by not crippling the engine by forcing it to run beyond its capabilities over thousands of miles. "Speed with safety," the men liked to say, though they often seemed to be primarily interested in the speed. Thaden intended to have both. She took off into the unsettled skies over Wichita after an eleven-minute stop — she and Noyes hadn't even gotten out of their seats—and flew west into the storms, the rains, and the angry head-winds fighting them all the way to California.

The two women did not speak of winning the Bendix. They just flew: over the flatlands where Thaden had gotten her start selling coal a decade earlier and the jagged mountains that the men had once warned were too dangerous for female pilots to cross; over the deserts where Turner had crashed and the Howards had, too, and the *malpais* that had claimed the lives of so many other aviators, some of them good friends.

They flew for Marvel Crosson, who'd died in that kind of country trying to land her disabled plane in a creek bed, and for Ruth Nichols, who had nearly died too many times to count in deserts and forests and flames. They flew for the insulted Florence Klingensmith, her naked body wrapped in newspapers and shipped back to Fargo in a box, and for the failed Frances Marsalis, killed while racing in Dayton, desperate to win that $1,000 but getting no credit for her efforts, only blame. And they flew for the others who had paid a price over the years: the missing Frances Grayson, her secrets held by the sea; the underestimated Ruth Elder, her secrets known by all; the scrappy Olive Ann Beech, waiting in Los Angeles; and Thaden's son, Bill, with his prayers in Bentonville. It was almost six p.m. in Los Angeles when the little blue plane appeared in the eastern sky, coming in low and fast, as Walter had wanted, at speeds exceeding two hundred miles an hour. Thaden was flying right into the setting sun and trying to get her bearings amid the fruit orchards and the crowds below, the people coming to the airport, it seemed, from every direction: La Tijera Boulevard and Manchester Avenue, Imperial Highway and Vista Del Mar—large and busy streets that meant nothing to Thaden except that she and Noyes had made it. They had arrived in Los Angeles, crossing the continent in fourteen hours and fifty-five minutes—slower than Roscoe Turner's record, yes, but almost four hours faster than any woman had previously flown from coast to coast. A new female record.

As the Beechcraft taxied across the field, race officials began running along next to it, flagging down the tired women inside and hollering nonsense, it seemed, to them. "I wonder what we've done wrong now," Thaden said to Noyes.

Then, after the plane rolled to a stop, Henderson stepped up.

"I'm afraid you've won the Bendix," he said.

Thaden didn't believe him at first. "If we win the Bendix race," she told the crowd outside her plane, "we'll be more surprised than anybody." But climbing out onto the wing, she and Noyes soon realized that maybe it was true. They could see it in the photographers pushing toward them, flashbulbs firing. They could see it in Henderson's face—he looked "crestfallen," Thaden thought—and they saw it, too, in the eyes of Olive Ann Beech, pressing forward to greet them on the ground. She was fighting back tears as she threw her arms around Thaden, pulled her close, found the words she was seeking, and spoke them into her ear.

"So," Beech said, "a woman couldn't win, eh?"

THADEN HAD BEATEN her nearest competitor, Laura Ingalls, by almost forty-five minutes, the closest man by fifty minutes, and Earhart, in her expensive Lockheed, by almost two hours. In doing so, she claimed more than $9,000 in winnings—$7,000 for first place and $2,500 for being the first woman to land. Vincent Bendix personally signed the check for the woman's prize while telegrams began pouring in on the West Coast, congratulating Thaden on her victory.

"Congratulations from your home town."

"You deserve the honor."

"All Arkansans are proud of you."

Even Walter Beech was pleased for once. "Splendid," he exclaimed, boarding a plane bound for Los Angeles to take part in the celebration that had already begun. Thaden had collected the massive Bendix trophy. She had given a speech she could hardly remember and she had traveled by police escort downtown where the aviators' ball, the social event of the weekend, was about to begin at the Ambassador Hotel.

But somewhere in the night, Thaden slipped away, ducking out on an errand. There was something she needed to do. She found a Western Union office and prepared to send a telegram of her own to her mother back in Bentonville, who was looking after her two children.

There were so many things Thaden could have said, so many stories to tell and ways to tell them. But it was almost midnight back in Arkansas. The kids were surely fast asleep, and Thaden decided to keep the telegram short. "We won," she wrote, and left it at that.

22

The Top of the Hill

THE WOMEN ON THE GROUND in Los Angeles were the first to cheer Thaden.

Gladys O'Donnell—second-place finisher in the 1929 Powder Puff Derby—couldn't stop praising her old rival's showing against the men. "With Louise first in the Bendix," O'Donnell said, "we have established ourselves in open competition." Ruth Elder was also there, looking beautiful, the men thought, in brown jodhpurs, a matching brown shirt, and a yellow beret, and she, too, was thrilled. "I think it's grand," Elder said, "that the girls have done so well." Henderson, in particular, got an earful about it.

"At last, the races have gone feminine," one woman told him.

"More power to the women," another informed Henderson.

"Ladies first!" said still another.

The jabs—playful, yet sharp—reminded Henderson that the women had not forgotten the past. But if Henderson was disappointed about it all—as Thaden and Noyes suspected he was—he did a good job of hiding it. On the ground beside the victorious Beechcraft in Los Angeles that Friday night, Henderson smiled, knowing that Thaden's unlikely victory in the Bendix was similar to her victory in the Powder Puff Derby in 1929. As he noted years later, "It immediately had news value."

The story of Thaden's flight made headlines that week in every major American publication: *Newsweek, Time* magazine, the *New York*

Times, the *Los Angeles Times,* the *Chicago Tribune,* and almost every other newspaper, large and small, from coast to coast. Only death, near-death, and disaster in the Bendix—and the National Air Races that weekend in general—prevented the women's underdog tale from becoming an even bigger story.

Of the eight aviators who had planned to fly in the celebrated transcontinental race that year, one had crashed and nearly died before even making it to the starting line in New York (Turner) and two others had gone down en route to Los Angeles (Jacobson and Howard). Reporters, understandably, fixated on the epic failure of Benny and Maxine Howard, nearly bleeding to death for hours in the desert in New Mexico inside the crushed remains of their legendary plane, *Mister Mulligan.* There were actual deaths to cover that day too. Not long before Thaden landed in Los Angeles, a young parachutist competing for a hundred-dollar prize jumped from a plane with a chute that did not open and slammed into the ground before fifty thousand fans, snapping his neck. He died fifteen minutes later. A second jumper was injured that afternoon, cracking his skull and slipping into a coma. And aviation reporters were also scrambling to cover another surprise involving a woman. The same day that Thaden won the Bendix, British pilot Beryl Markham took off from England in an attempt to become the first woman since Earhart to fly solo across the Atlantic and the first to do it flying east to west. She made it—just barely—crashing her plane into a muddy swamp in Nova Scotia and stealing still more headlines from Thaden.

Still, Markham's achievement underscored the significance of Thaden's triumph. Both proved that female pilots had all the skills and courage their male counterparts did. That weekend, Earhart, always the most outspoken of the women on the subject of her gender's airworthiness, predicted a day in the near future when men and women would stand as equals, judged not by their gender but by their abilities. "If a woman wishes to enter important competitions," Earhart told reporters, "the question will be, 'Is she a good enough flier?' instead of primarily a matter of whether she wears skirts or trousers." That's all the women had ever wanted, and now they had proof they could compete if only they had the chance. "Look," Earhart gushed, "at the Bendix!"

Thaden went on tour, posing for photos at aviation shows, giving radio interviews, signing autographs, and even signing walls. The Mission Inn in Riverside, California, invited the world's top aviators to press ten-inch copper wings into its Famous Fliers' Wall. After winning the Bendix, Thaden and Noyes got their invitations—and their Bendix trophies too. Vincent Bendix personally presented the golden hardware to the women—to "you girls," he called them.

Perhaps just as important, Thaden's win in the race paved the way for other women. Two years later, in 1938, Jacqueline Cochran won the Bendix race in a time almost seven hours faster than Thaden's, then parlayed her victory into fame of her own and a crusade to make female pilots eligible for military duty. Had Thaden and the other women failed in 1936—had they crashed their planes like Roscoe Turner and Benny Howard or, worse, had they given up long before that—Cochran might never have gotten that chance. From the beginning, all the women had been connected, whether they liked it or not, building on one another's successes, saddled with one another's failures, and pressing on together. As Earhart said once, the women had to keep fighting, keep knocking on the door, if they ever wanted to be accepted in this male-dominated world. "As more knock," Earhart explained, "more will enter."

EARHART WASN'T WORRIED about her poor finish in the Bendix, claiming just five hundred dollars for all her transcontinental troubles. She just laughed it off. "Please keep the air races going," she told Henderson after the 1936 event, "until I can get something better than fifth place in the Bendix." In the meantime, Earhart and Putnam were turning their focus to her still-secret around-the-world flight, finally admitting her plans four months later, in January 1937. Earhart was, indeed, flying around the world, leaving from Oakland, heading west across the Pacific, as early as March 1.

"Well, I guess you're right," she admitted to a crowd of reporters in a press conference in New York. "I have wanted to do it."

She just had one request.

"Please make it clear that I am not out to 'demonstrate' anything about the scientific aspects or future possibilities of aviation. The flight isn't meant to prove anything."

Still, it would be a challenge, flying twenty-seven thousand miles in as little as three weeks and finding tiny refueling points, like Howland

Island, a speck of sand and coral about two miles long and no more than fifteen feet above sea level in the middle of the Pacific Ocean. "Howland itself is kind of a nightmare," one correspondent reported, noting its desolate landscape, treeless and sunbaked; its large population of rats and birds scurrying everywhere; and its lack of fresh water.

But as hard as it was for the US government to build three runways there—using tractors in early 1937 to tame the wild beach into an ocean pit stop for American military interests—it might be even harder to find the island by air. To do it, experts said, a pilot would have to be perfect. And for that reason, Earhart was glad to be making the trip with accomplished navigator Harry Manning. Without him, Earhart said, she felt she'd be unable to find a place as small as Howland Island. "He will be the navigator on the flight across the Pacific," she explained, adding: "The course we have chosen gets the water jumps out of the way at the beginning."

Thaden didn't like the idea, and that February she told Earhart as much.

"You have nothing to gain," Thaden said, "and everything to lose."

It was a quiet moment away from the press, inside Earhart's hangar in California. The two friends were sitting on the side of an inflatable raft that would be part of Earhart's emergency supplies and talking about the future, Earhart's flight. Thaden just didn't understand it. Too much could go wrong too fast, she thought, and out over the ocean, with no way to solve the problems high in the sky, even the best pilot was doomed to fail.

Thaden begged Earhart not to take such a flight. But sitting on the edge of the raft, Earhart just smiled, squeezing Thaden's hand. Thaden squeezed back and the two women stood up to say goodbye, wisecracking to break the tension.

"If I don't see you before you shove off for Hawaii," Thaden said, "what flowers should we send?"

"Water lilies seem appropriate, don't you think?" Earhart joked.

She understood the risks. "Please know I am well aware of the hazards of the trip," Earhart wrote in a note she gave Putnam before leaving. Still, she was going. "Women," she explained, "must try to do things as men have tried. Where they fail, their failure must be but a challenge to others."

The failures for Earhart began almost immediately. After making a successful hop from Oakland to Honolulu in March 1937—with Manning; a second navigator, Fred Noonan; and Paul Mantz on board, assisting with the flying—Earhart crashed her Lockheed while trying to leave Hawaii on the second leg of the trip, piloting it on her own. Both propellers were crumpled in the crash, and both wheels ripped away. Instead of making a historic flight to Howland Island that morning, she was headed back to California—by boat. "Well, boys," Putnam told a roomful of reporters back in Oakland, "she's crashed in Honolulu."

Mishaps like this one were enough to end many ambitious flights; Ruth Nichols had certainly learned that lesson. But Earhart had better connections and a bigger name—the biggest name of all. Before she'd left Oakland, thirty thousand people had come to the airport to see her, driving in on a boulevard that bore her name: Earhart Road. There was no stopping this flight. Even as she hurried up the gangplank of an ocean liner headed for Los Angeles on the afternoon of her crash in Hawaii, Earhart vowed to find a way to continue her around-the-world plans. "I'll be back," she said, and it didn't take long.

Two months later, she was ready to go again, with just a few changes to the plan. She would be flying this time with only Fred Noonan; Harry Manning was out. They would be going east, not west, to adjust for seasonal changes in global weather. "Heading into dawns," Earhart said, "not sunsets." And they would be leaving over the objections of not just friends like Thaden but government officials who wanted to stop her. For a month, she and Noonan seemed to prove the skeptics wrong. They traveled some twenty-two thousand miles, jumping from Oakland to Miami, Brazil to Senegal, Sudan to India, Burma to Australia, and finally to Lae, New Guinea, overlooking the warm blue waters of the South Pacific. Next stop: Howland Island, 2,556 miles to the east. "Lockheed stands ready," Earhart reported, "for longest hop, weighted with gasoline and oil to capacity."

She and Noonan took off from Lae at ten a.m. on July 2, barreling down a primitive runway carved into the jungle at the edge of the sea and then rising into the sky above the waves inside their silver plane. Trips of late had been relatively short and easy for a flier as experienced as Earhart. This one would last almost twenty hours with no land in sight most of the way and Earhart and Noonan flying through the day and night and into the next dawn.

Somewhere up ahead and down below, the US Coast Guard cutter *Itasca* was waiting, charged with tracking the plane. The 250-foot ship had been bobbing in the water near Howland Island for days, the crew passing the long hours by watching movies, fishing, and catching large and voracious sharks—"man-eaters." Now, finally, with Earhart en route, at least one man on board—the *Itasca*'s thirty-year-old radio operator Leo Bellarts—had something to do. Starting at 2:45 a.m., Bellarts began hearing from the Lockheed in a series of brief and scattered reports, clouded by static at first and then loud and clear: Earhart's voice in his ears.

5:15 a.m.: "About 200 miles out."

5:45 a.m.: "About 100 miles out."

And then, at 7:30, a problem: "We must be on you," Earhart reported to the *Itasca*, "but cannot see you. Gas is running low. Have been unable to reach you by radio. We are flying at 1,000 feet."

Outside, the sky was blue, ceiling unlimited, with visibility as far as twenty miles. Still, the tiny island would have been easy for Earhart to miss. She was working on no sleep and flying directly into the blazing equatorial sun. Bellarts was worried she had passed the island or had never reached it at all, maybe gotten turned around in the cloud banks to the west. But due to a preflight miscommunication between Earhart and the Coast Guard, the Putnam team in Oakland and the government in Washington, the *Itasca* struggled to get a bearing on Earhart's plane. In Miami a month earlier, Earhart had decided to scrap the antenna for one of her radio's frequencies—the frequency typically used by ships at sea and, more important, the frequency the *Itasca* believed she still had. Earhart hadn't felt knowledgeable enough to use it; Noonan apparently hadn't either. "The antenna would be just one more thing to worry about and we've got plenty of things to keep us busy," Earhart told a reporter at the time. She would rely instead on two other frequencies to communicate.

Now, somewhere near Howland Island, these frequencies were failing her. She was circling.

"But cannot see island. Cannot hear you," she reported.

"Earhart calling *Itasca* . . ."

At 8:44 a.m., Bellarts heard from Earhart one last time. Her tone, firm and tense an hour earlier, was now frantic, desperate even. "That of a frightened woman," Bellarts thought, "in a voice close to breaking." But it was loud—so loud he believed that she had to be close to Howland, a belief that Earhart herself seemed to hold until the end.

"We are on a line position of 157-337," she said, giving the plane's location in her final transmission. "Will repeat this message . . . Wait, we are running north and south."

And then there was nothing. The voice—loud and clear for so long, then panicked and garbled—was gone.

The legend of the lost flier began almost immediately, inspiring rhapsodic poems about Earhart's life and spawning great myths about her death. Ship captains and sailors, engineers and businessmen, psychics and seers, crackpots and kooks from across the world sent news, often to Putnam himself, declaring that Earhart was alive. They were sure of it. She was safe on a reef. She was in a small boat. She was two hundred miles northwest of Howland Island. She was on a rock in the water. She was waving her arms on the sand. She was crawling along like she was trying to catch something. She was dragging Noonan's limp body ashore.

"She is very weary," one wrote.

"Haste is necessary," said another.

"This dream was so starkly clear I felt it my duty to tell you."

"Please get this information to George Putnam."

Putnam, initially, was confident she was alive, not because of the psychics or the seers, but because of the strength of the plane, the temerity of the woman flying it, and the radio operators reporting, in the early days, that they heard her; they thought they heard Earhart's voice or her plane's call letters, KHAQQ, crackling through the static from somewhere in the Pacific.

The radio reports might have lifted Putnam's spirits, but the alleged contacts kept the *Itasca* and US Navy warships on the run for days as they chased down leads that were very likely just hoaxes. If the plane had been on the water—floating like a boat—the plane's radio likely could not have worked. The salt water would have fried the batteries. And if Earhart had somehow managed to land, without crashing, on high ground—on a beach, say, or a coral reef somewhere—the radio generator would last only as long as the fuel supply. By Earhart's own admission, the plane's fuel tanks were almost empty at 7:30 on the morning it disappeared, and it had continued to fly for at least another hour and fifteen minutes. Meaning that, even if the Lockheed was on a reef and undamaged, its gas was all but gone.

Still, one radio report did draw the interest of searchers. "Two Eight One North Howland," a transmission reportedly said. "Don't hold with us much longer . . . Above water . . . Shut off . . ." Experts at the time doubted both the source and the contents of the message. For starters, it was garbled and fragmented—a "ragged transmission," the *Itasca* said—that could have been incorrectly transcribed or misheard altogether. In the blue waters 281 miles north of Howland, there was no place to land, no islands, and no plane. The Coast Guard looked there and found nothing. If genuine, the code "Two Eight One North Howland" might have been indicating a different location where islands did exist. Putnam, studying maps, began to believe that this location had to be 281 miles to the southeast—the Phoenix Islands, a small chain of coral reefs. So the search party—now including the US Navy, the Japanese navy, the US Coast Guard, and passing freighters— shifted its focus to there. "Please note," Putnam informed the Coast Guard, "all radio bearings thus far obtained on Earhart plane approximately intersect in Phoenix Island region."

Putnam, by this time, was short on sleep, exhausted. He had spent days hovering over the shoulders of Coast Guard radio operators in a government office in San Francisco, sometimes staying there until five a.m. But with the search moving to the Phoenix Islands, and an aircraft carrier, the USS *Lexington*, streaking in from San Diego to help, he was feeling more confident than ever that the navy would find his wife. Earhart knew of these islands, and Putnam believed she would have turned south in that direction along the line position of 157-337 after not finding Howland. "The news," he said, "is very encouraging."

The search, however, turned up more of the same. "Nothing discovered," the navy reported, leaving some officials to wonder whether any of the radio transmissions after Earhart's disappearance had been authentic. As one expert at the time said, "I personally am very much afraid that all of the calls reported from the plane since it was forced down are 'phonies,' much as I hope otherwise."

On July 18—more than two weeks after Earhart disappeared—the US government ended its search. Three thousand people in 102 airplanes and ten ships had combed roughly 250,000 square miles of remote ocean—a search area the size of Texas—flying low over islands so small that, at times, even the navy airmen struggled to see the tiny spits of land below them. They, too, missed islands altogether, circling back and checking their maps and finding no evidence of Earhart's plane anywhere—a reality that even Putnam finally accepted. In January 1939, he secured a court order to have Earhart declared dead. He was moving on, or trying to. It was the others—the well-meaning and the hopeful, the writers and, as one reporter said, "the weirdies"— who refused to let Earhart go.

In the 1940s, with America at war with Japan and stories filling newspapers every day about the hated "Japs," rumors spread that Earhart had crashed in Japanese-held territory, that the Japanese had taken her captive, and that they'd later killed her. These rumors took no account of the fact that Japan had assisted in the search for her, sending its own ships to help, or that at the time of her disappearance, the country was on the cusp of war with its own hated adversary: China. The Japanese military, mobilizing ground troops that month to fight the Chinese, was, if nothing else, seriously distracted in July 1937, a bad time to begin holding one of the world's most famous women captive. In September 1945, just weeks after signing a peace treaty with the United States ending World War II, the Japanese government, under pressure to respond to the rumors, denied any knowledge of Earhart's death. And yet the rumors persisted, bubbling up through the muck every couple of decades, including, most recently, in 2017, when a documentary rehashed the old story, overlooking one key reason why it had ever gotten traction in the first place: xenophobia, racism, hatred for the "Japs."

At the same time this documentary aired, in July 2017, a team of modern-day Earhart searchers had just finished diving off the coast of a small reef in the Phoenix Islands that they believed to be the location where Earhart landed and sent her radio messages. It's a compelling idea, and certainly plausible; Putnam had always thought his wife was on a coral reef like this one. But in July 1937—just eight days after Earhart disappeared—a navy pilot from the USS *Colorado* reported flying low in his plane over this very island and finding no trace of Earhart and Noonan or their silver airship with its fifty-five-foot wingspan. If they were there, the navy pilot must have missed them.

Still others chasing the ghost of Earhart over the years pursued theories so outlandish as to be insulting to everyone involved. In 1970, two former US Air Force officers wrote a book, *Amelia Earhart Lives,* suggesting the following chain of events: the Japanese found Earhart in the Phoenix Islands, took her prisoner, held her for eight years in Tokyo, and then released her in 1945, with the approval of the US government, to secretly integrate back into American society. The authors identified her as an aging widow living under the assumed name Irene Bolam in Jamesburg, New Jersey — a clever cover that had gone undetected until they revealed it.

Such sensational theories soon loomed larger in the public consciousness than the most likely explanation behind Earhart's disappearance: that she simply missed Howland Island, crashed her plane into the water, and died. At the news that she was missing, fellow aviators immediately shook their heads in dismay, knowing the odds against her. Could the plane be floating on the water, buoyant and seaworthy, the fliers awaiting rescue? Sure. But likely not for long. Or could they have landed on a reef somewhere? Of course. But even if Earhart had stalled out her plane before impact, they said, it would have hit the water going roughly fifty miles an hour — the equivalent of slamming into a hillside. Thaden, for one, believed that's how it ended. Her friend had just missed the little island. "To find that in the Pacific Ocean, with the poor navigational aids they had then," Thaden said late in life, "would be like telling a pilot today to fly from New York and land on a handkerchief in Los Angeles." Perhaps more important, the man who heard Earhart's final verified radio messages never wavered in his belief that she and Noonan had crashed into the Pacific and died.

Leo Bellarts, the radio operator aboard the *Itasca,* was haunted by Earhart until his death in 1974, unable to shake her from his mind. "I'll never forget her voice in that final transmission," he said. To him, it didn't sound like it belonged to a woman who was about to find salvation on a coral reef; it sounded like a woman who was staring out at a vast and unforgiving ocean, knowing she was about to crash into it.

"This is just a letter from me to you, I am just speaking for myself," an officer aboard the *Itasca* wrote one of the highest-ranking US aeronautics officials shortly after Earhart disappeared, summarizing the radio contacts and his personal beliefs. The facts, he said, were clear. "I am firmly convinced that she crashed upon going down and went right to the bottom."

It could have ended there. But the story was so impossible and so tragic that it lived on, and still lives to this day, dwarfing the bravery, the sacrifices, and the achievements of the women who flew with Earhart in that exciting decade between 1927 and 1937, a time later remembered as the golden age of flying.

They outlived Earhart, these women, but each was forgotten in her own way.

RUTH NICHOLS MADE GOOD on her promise to keep going "wherever the air trail leads." She recovered from her many injuries, returned to the sky, and, when war broke out in Europe in the late 1930s, she jumped into the fray. Nichols established Relief Wings, a humanitarian air service, and in 1942 marched with ten thousand nurses, Red Cross workers, and defense volunteers in New York City's first all-female parade showcasing war-readiness. Her relief plane, a donated Beechcraft, rolled along just behind the Salvation Army, wowing the crowd and Mayor Fiorello La Guardia at the reviewing stand on Fifth Avenue. "Peace is not a popular word these days," Nichols said, "but surely there can be nothing controversial about the desire to help sufferers."

Nichols herself claimed to be doing just fine, as strong as ever. In 1958, at the age of fifty-six, she flew a US Air Force supersonic jet at speeds exceeding a thousand miles an hour nearly ten miles above the earth—a feat no woman, even Earhart, could have imagined two decades earlier. Nichols boldly declared that women would have a future in another nascent field: space exploration. Women, she said, were better suited than men to be astronauts, being as they were calm in emergencies, with "a greater ability than men to summon up their forces to meet a challenge." And she predicted that she would be among the first female space pilots. "When spaceships take off," she said, "I shall be flying them."

Nichols was half right, as it turned out. Women would indeed go to space—a Soviet cosmonaut went in 1963 and an American, Sally Ride, an inexplicably long two decades later aboard the space shuttle *Challenger* in 1983. But Nichols wouldn't survive to see either accomplishment. Despite her appearances—her bold statements, her news-making flights, and her humanitarian work—Nichols was struggling, and had been for a long time, living in a dark cloud of regrets, disappointment, and failure.

In employment applications, she claimed the Relief Wings work paid her $5,200 a year—decent money. But she was desperate for something better, something bigger, and she couldn't find it—not even from sources that, seemingly, could have helped. In July 1938, one year after Earhart disappeared, Nichols reached out to her alma mater, Wellesley College.

"Will you kindly place my name and qualifications on file," Nichols asked, "for any administrative or organizational position which may arise that can use the experience I have acquired." The college's personnel bureau charged Nichols two dollars for the favor of taking her application and said it would be back in touch soon. But Nichols was advised not to get her hopes up. "I know you realize that there are very few positions coming to us, particularly at the present time, that would offer remuneration equal to that which you received in your last employment."

Her job search continued into the 1940s and didn't fare any better. At one point, Nichols had applied to be a pilot, copilot, or employee of some kind at almost every single major air carrier: United, American, Pan American, Eastern, Colonial, Northwest, and Northeast. With most male pilots off at war, Nichols hoped to fill the void by flying one of their planes. "I am writing," she said, "to inquire if I could be of service in that capacity." Yet the airlines had no interest in hiring Nichols, sending her rejection letters that Nichols saved in a tidy folder.

"I think women have done an outstanding job in the promotion of aeronautics," United's director of personnel informed Nichols in one of those letters. But he couldn't hire her. "You, no doubt, are more familiar than I am," he told Nichols, "with the many controversial issues arising over the eligibility of women for first and second pilots on air transport services."

With nowhere to go—Nichols couldn't even get hired as a flight instructor—she finally did the unthinkable: she took a job that had nothing to do with aviation. Around 1945, she began working in the public relations office of a hospital in White Plains, New York. "The hospital is interesting," she told friends. But really, the best part was that she got a month's vacation every summer. And even the vacation wasn't always ideal. Sometimes, Nichols had to go by herself, though at one point she reached out to invite a friend to join her: Thaden.

The two fliers remained close, calling each other by their pet names, Rufus and Louisa. Sometimes, Nichols visited Louise, Herb, and the kids wherever they were living: Maryland, Pennsylvania, New Jersey, and, finally, Roanoke, Virginia, where the Thadens ultimately settled. "You will note," Thaden once wrote Nichols when Herb got a new job, "we have MOVED AGAIN." Other times, Nichols invited the Thadens to come spend the weekend with her in New York. "You have been hostess so often and so grandly that it is now time for you to come to Rye," Nichols told Thaden. "Please say that you will."

Nichols's mother was still alive, and Nichols had other relatives who would visit her from time to time. But almost fifty years old in the late 1940s, she was increasingly on her own. She attended Ninety-Nines dinner dances, only to realize the scene had passed her by. The great Ruth Nichols didn't know most of the other women there. Her job at the hospital ended, forcing her to look for work—again—with little luck. And she longed for what Thaden had: a husband, a family, and children—yet another joy that had eluded her. "Not being married or having any children of my own," she said once, "I am quite envious of those who have."

Thaden began to worry about her friend, who seemed increasingly trapped in the claws of a dark depression. In the late summer of 1951, she began offering Nichols not only empathy but advice. Everyone has to fight off the darkness, Thaden told Nichols. "I do all the time," she said. "The best panacea I've found is to keep busy—keep occupied." Then, about a month later, just to make sure Nichols knew how much she cared, Thaden paid Nichols a personal visit. She went to New York and, when their time together was over, reluctantly said goodbye with a twinge of fear and sadness in her heart. "I just wish you didn't feel so alone," Thaden told Nichols. "You aren't, you know."

Nichols just needed to remind herself of a few things, Thaden told her. That she was still the same courageous woman who had tried to fly the Atlantic before Earhart and, indeed, dreamed up flying around the world before Earhart too. That she should be proud of everything she had accomplished, wearing it as a coat of armor against whatever enemy she was fighting now. Above all, Thaden wanted Nichols to know that she would always be there for her.

"Know my thoughts are with you, for whatever that is worth," Thaden told Nichols. "And sometimes my prayers, too. Have you ever felt me reaching to you across the miles? I do, you know."

Nichols finally seemed to catch a break a few years later. A publisher agreed to print her memoir, *Wings for Life*, briefly putting Nichols's name back in the newspapers and on a new and exciting medium: television. In early 1958, as part of her book publicity tour, Nichols appeared on the show *To Tell the Truth*, a game of deliberate misrepresentation. Three middle-aged women, each claiming to be Ruth Nichols, sat before a panel of stars who asked questions in an attempt to determine which one of the women was the real Ruth. Almost twenty-five years removed from her flying career, Nichols managed to fool them all. Not a single star on the panel correctly identified her, choosing instead contestant no. 1, a housewife. Nichols left with parting gifts, at least. "As you can see," the host crooned, "the panel was completely wrong. So that means, ladies, that, from Geritol, you receive a thousand dollars!"

None of it, however—not the book, the publicity, or the limited money she made off the project—changed much in Nichols's life. In her private journals, she revealed how much she was struggling, fighting, drowning. She felt guilty for not having achieved more in her life. She couldn't stop herself from dwelling on her failures, the crash in New Brunswick in particular. And she was hurting—both mentally and physically, possibly from all her injuries over the years. "Aching," she said. Unable to sleep one night, then sleeping too much the next, and taking a cocktail of sedatives to stop the pain.

Journal entry: "Taking red and blue pills."

Journal entry: "Scared, guilty, and depressed . . . occasionally all at once."

Journal entry: "Very depressed all day."

In late September 1960, a relative became concerned that Nichols wasn't answering the phone at her apartment on East Forty-Ninth Street in New York City. The building's superintendent was dispatched to investigate. He unlocked the door and found Nichols inside.

She was dead. And based on the notes discovered inside her apartment, officials determined that her death was no accident. Ruth Nichols—the famous flier and survivor—had committed suicide at age fifty-nine, overdosing on her pills.

＝＝＝＝

IN DEATH, AS in life, the other Ruth—Ruth Elder, always more interesting and more beautiful—was one step ahead of Nichols, drifting away first, her fame forgotten and the fortune she had reaped from it long gone. "The money slipped through my fingers," she said, "and soon there was nothing."

No more movie deals. No more airplanes. No more standing around at the air races in a yellow beret. And no more reporters showering her with attention, just mockery and criticism. Life got so hard for Elder that by 1950 she changed her name to hide from the world. She was now Susan Thackeray, wife of George Thackeray, her fifth husband, an artist and art dealer in San Diego. The pair lived in a nondescript home on a nondescript street, and Ruth—or Susan—was apparently miserable about all of it.

One night that year, in early July, she dipped across the Mexican border to Tijuana and returned home with a boxful of sleeping pills, the same kind of pills that would later prove fatal to Nichols in New York. Chugging whiskey and grain alcohol, Elder, the once-beloved American Girl, the Miss America of Aviation, downed sixty-one pills and capsules. "Enough to kill a person," local police reported, "but luckily was discovered in time."

Elder survived. But with her secret out—Mrs. Thackeray was far more interesting than anyone knew—Elder's marriage to the art dealer didn't last. She was soon divorced and called one of her previous husbands, Ralph King, a Hollywood cameraman, to ask him a question.

"Daddy," she said, "are you married again?"

"No," he replied.

"Can I come home?"

Yes, he told her.

"A real love story," King called it later—a moment of peace at the end of a difficult life. Elder was finally happy, it seemed, living with King in San Francisco and content, maybe for the first time, to just be herself: Ruth Elder, for better or worse, with her feet on the ground.

"Flying in the sky is nice," she said at age seventy-three in 1976, "but the earth has so many wonderful things in it to make people happy." At that point, Elder said, she just wanted to enjoy those things: the cool Northern California summers, the long walks that she and King shared along the water, and the view of the sailboats floating on the bay. "We are living," she said, "a lovely life."

Elder died in her sleep fifteen months later, slipping away without any farewells. She had prepared for this moment, at least, instructing her husband on how to handle her remains: Ruth Elder wished to be cremated and have her ashes scattered from an airplane into the sea.

"DISAPPOINTMENTS," THADEN SAID with a sigh late in life. For the women pilots along the way, there were so many: the banishment, the discrimination, the snide remarks and the insults. Thaden knew what the men thought of the women and it was hard, at times, to keep going, to keep flying. "It took dedication," Thaden explained. "And the courage to accept defeat, after defeat, after defeat."

Ruth Nichols's suicide was, for Thaden, the hardest defeat of all. She could handle Earhart's disappearance and the violent plane crashes that had killed Florence Klingensmith, Frances Marsalis, and others. "But when someone you love takes their own life," Thaden said, "it's different."

She thought a lot about Nichols and about the other female pilots who struggled emotionally, mentally, and financially after their time in the sky was over, never finding their footing on the ground. Thaden stayed in touch with many of them. But then, Thaden — a prolific writer with motherly instincts — stayed in touch with almost everyone from the time of the air races.

She and Cliff Henderson became pen pals, writing back and forth to each other into the 1970s. By then, the air races were long over and Henderson's aviation connections were too. He left the air races in 1939, scooped up fifteen hundred acres of sand near Palm Springs, California, and then did a very Cliff Henderson sort of thing. He built a town, Palm Desert. It was, arguably, his greatest show. Between 1948 and 1980, Palm Desert grew from a population of zero to ten thousand people — and then it kept on growing. Today, more than fifty thousand people live there, many of whom don't know the first thing about Henderson — the man who let the women fly in the air races and then kicked them out, stirring up outrage in the 1930s, an outrage that he never really apologized for causing except, sort of, once.

"There was a time in my growing up years when I looked upon women as just wives and mothers," Henderson wrote in a never-published memoir unearthed decades after his death. "I took motherhood as a woman's supreme ambition." And, he admitted, "some of this tag end of tradition still clung to me when women insisted on flying. To me, it was unthinkable that mothers and grandmothers would ever want to become part and parcel of air racing."

But the women he met on the airfields in the 1920s and '30s helped change his mind, Henderson said, and his marriage in 1960 to actress Marian Marsh helped change him personally. Cliff realized that he and Marian were true equals, man and woman living together in the desert. From his home there, he wrote often to Thaden, and Thaden wrote him back, seeming to forgive Henderson for all his past transgressions before his death, at age eighty-eight, in 1984. "Cliff is just a lovely gentleman," Thaden said. "He's just a peach of a guy."

Thaden also stayed in touch with Olive Ann Beech, an aviation promoter in her own right. By the early 1940s, with Walter's health failing, Olive Ann was effectively running Beechcraft in Wichita. Sales, by then, had jumped 4,000 percent. The little aviation outfit on the prairie was now among the most profitable airplane companies in the world, and the company continued to grow under Olive Ann's leadership after Walter's death in 1950. She was officially in charge now, serving as president—the only female president of a major airplane-manufacturing company. Her estimated worth at the end of the 1950s was $7 million. Yet it was a pittance, really, compared to the paydays still to come. In 1979, she sold her husband's plane company for $615 million. "Take it easy, Kiddo," Thaden told Olive Ann at one point, speaking to the powerful Mrs. Beech in a way that only Thaden could. "It distresses me to see you so tired." But Olive Ann couldn't stop herself from working and working hard. "Unfortunately," she told Thaden, "I keep busy." The aviation executive often didn't even have time to write. Still, Thaden was there for her, sending Olive Ann—her "Annie"—notes and encouragement and even love. "I love you, Ann Mellor Beech."

Finally, Thaden stayed in contact with Blanche Noyes, her companion in the 1936 Bendix. The race had changed life for Noyes too. She was no longer a grieving widow in need of Earhart's help; she was a sensation all her own. And Noyes knew how to play it up. A little too much, Thaden thought. In interviews that Noyes gave over the years discussing the Bendix, she often didn't mention Thaden at all, acting as if she, Noyes, had flown the Beechcraft—as if she had won the race by herself.

For more than a decade, Thaden kept her silence on the matter. "Always too big-hearted for her own good," Nichols once said. But finally, in 1949, Thaden could stay quiet no more, personally asking Noyes to stop taking credit for the Bendix victory. "I do insist you refrain," Thaden said. "Sorry, but that's the way it is."

Noyes, knowing they needed to talk, paid a visit to Thaden in Roanoke. The two women sorted out their differences behind closed doors, away from Herb and the children, and then never spoke of it again. There was room enough for the both of them, and anyway, Noyes still had a job to keep her busy, air-marking for the federal government—a job she held for some thirty-five years, earning awards of her own and the gratitude of wayward fliers saved by her air-markers on the ground.

"I still remember the July afternoon in the 1950s when an American barn might have saved my life," pilot William Smith once wrote. Smith was flying a small plane from Des Moines to Kansas City one day when he got lost in a violent thunderstorm. "Just as the gauge on our fuel tank indicated we were about out of fuel, we spotted a barn through a break in the clouds—with the name TARKIO on the roof."

Tarkio, Missouri. Way off course. But the town wasn't far away. Smith and his two passengers could make it in time, and ultimately they did, landing safely in the nowhere town of Tarkio, population 2,200.

"I recall many barns in Missouri with painted signs," Smith said. "But I best remember that one very special barn near Tarkio."

And he also remembered the person who was most likely responsible for making sure there was a sign on that particular barn in that unremarkable stretch of vast American farmland.

"For our safe landing," he said, "we were thankful for Blanche Noyes."

PEOPLE WERE THANKFUL for Thaden, too, cheering her not just at aviation shows and banquets but at an especially notable appearance at the Advertising Club of New York in April 1937.

The club, at Thirty-Fifth Street and Park Avenue, was essentially just for men—powerful men. But on this afternoon, the men were thrilled to host Thaden and present her with the Harmon Trophy—the annual prize awarded to the best male and female pilots. A radioman, broadcasting the affair, greeted listeners on the airwaves. Then the emcee stepped to the microphone in front of the room packed full of women and introduced Thaden to the crowd. "I now present to you," he said, "our guest for the day, Mrs. Louise Thaden."

Then, after a pause, he ceded her the stage.

The crowd roared its approval, applauding her, cheering her, and finally settling down to hear her speak. If they were hoping for Thaden to tell boastful tales of air conquest, about risking her life to beat the men in the Bendix, they left disappointed that day. Thaden was self-deprecating and modest on the stage, giving credit to others.

"The full significance of all that is represented in this Harmon Trophy," she said, "has brought the realization that I cannot accept it for myself alone." She needed to thank Walter Beech, and his engineers in Wichita, and the woman who had trusted her with everything. "Olive Ann," she said, "whose faith in the plane—and in me—was responsible for my entry into the Bendix."

Thaden spoke for just a few minutes. But the emcee wouldn't let her off so easy, keeping her onstage after her speech to pepper her with questions that were played over the amplifiers and the airwaves. He wanted to know what kind of bedtime stories Thaden told her children, Bill and Patsy. "Instead of Donald Duck and Peter Rabbit," she joked, "they hear airplanes all the time." He wanted to know who gave her kids their baby bottles all these years while she had been flying around the country. "Mr. Thaden," Louise said, drawing laughter from the crowd. Finally, he pressed her to be honest. "You won that Bendix race," the emcee said. "Please forget your modesty for a minute and tell me why you think you won it against these other crack pilots."

"Oh, dear," Thaden said, again to laughter in the room.

It was difficult to say, she explained. But speaking in general, she said, racing success was a simple equation: 25 percent the plane, 25 percent the pilot, and 50 percent luck. Thaden suggested she was lucky and had been for some time—a luck that she hoped would continue to hold. In just a few weeks, she would shatter Earhart's speed record, flying almost two hundred miles an hour in the skies over St. Louis, and she planned to do even more at the 1937 air races later that summer.

"Will you enter the Bendix race this year?" the emcee asked her.

"Yes," Thaden said, "I think so."

She had no reason not to enter. At the time, she was touring the nation in her Wichita-built airplane, making several stops in a single day. Breakfast in Hartford, Connecticut. Lunch in Boston. Dinner in Providence, Rhode Island, and asleep that night in Albany, New York— always on the move, drawing large crowds, smiling for photographs next to her massive Bendix trophy, and giving interviews to the press. With Earhart having left the country to fly around the world in June 1937, reporters turned their attention to the champion air racer and mother of two who was still in their midst: Thaden. As one legendary military pilot, Major Al Williams, put it that spring: "Louise Thaden is one flying woman every American should know."

Life at home, however, was hard that year—with a working father and a working mother and two children growing up fast. Bill was almost seven; Patsy, almost four. The kids, by 1937, were left in the care of a nanny, and one day Thaden returned home from one of her trips to learn that the nanny had punished her daughter, Patsy, by repeatedly striking the little girl on the back of her legs with a branch from a forsythia bush growing in the yard. Thaden, furious and horrified, confronted the nanny and fired her on the spot, a parenting moment that a guilt-ridden Thaden never discussed and that Patsy never forgot. It was possibly one of her first memories. Her mother was there for her. Her mother was coming home.

In June 1937, just three weeks after breaking Earhart's speed record and one week before Earhart disappeared, Thaden made a sudden announcement: she was quitting aviation, retiring, walking away from flying at the peak of her fame. She knew Earhart—halfway around the world, preparing to take off in Java—wouldn't approve. She also knew what she was giving up. The following week, Thaden was scheduled to sit down with the governor of Pennsylvania, after which she was supposed to fly on to meet with even more important politicians in Washington—fun and meaningful work. But she had no other choice.

She wanted to be with her kids, to really know them. Take them to the beach in summer. Go sledding with them in winter. She wanted to be a mother, a job that she knew wouldn't be easy. In the mid-1940s,

Thaden, now a stay-at-home mother in Roanoke, began to struggle. Like Ruth Nichols and Ruth Elder, she was increasingly lost, far from the sky and the spotlight that had once shone on her there. Instead of sleeping pills, Louise was drinking too much, cause for arguments between her and Herb and, finally, one night, an incident inside their home. Louise had been drinking and broke a glass bottle in the kitchen, slicing open her hand so badly that a doctor had to come to the house.

It was the wake-up call she needed. Thaden never drank again, willing herself to get better, feel better, where others could not, climbing out of the valley of her despair through sheer determination, trying to reach what she called "the top of the hill." "Is it close now?" she asked Nichols in 1951. "I hope so." But whether it was or wasn't, Thaden planned to keep climbing because it was worth it. "Worth the climb," she told her troubled friend. "Never seen a panorama yet from a valley."

Thaden, of course, had motivation that Nichols lacked. She wanted to play tennis with Patsy and attend Bill's football games at high school in Roanoke and later Georgia Tech. She and Herb, never rich, traveled far at times to see Bill's games, and they splurged on Patsy too. Thaden liked to take her daughter shopping, refusing to let Patsy go to her high-school dances in old dresses, and she even took her flying. In 1950, the mother-daughter duo participated in a revival of the Powder Puff Derby, flying in a borrowed plane from Montreal to West Palm Beach, Florida. The Thaden women, Louise and Patsy, finished third.

But it was Thaden's son, Bill, who really took after his mother, growing up to serve in the US Air Force and then working as a pilot for Eastern Airlines—a job that one day led to an unlikely encounter. On a flight from New York City to Greensboro, North Carolina, Bill learned that his mother was one of his passengers, clicked on his intercom, and introduced her to everyone in the cabin. "Ladies and gentlemen," he said from the flight deck, "I have just been informed that I am enjoying the rare experience of having for the first time my mother on board . . . Welcome aboard, Mom."

She and Herb lived the last two decades of their lives in High Point, North Carolina, celebrating forty years of marriage in 1968 as grandparents. Herb died just months later in early 1969, and Louise kept going, struggling with heart problems but pushing on just long enough to be rediscovered. In the 1970s, a small group of Beechcraft enthusiasts tracked her down, reviving interest in Thaden's long-forgotten story, inviting her to speak at their meetings in Tennessee, and giving her a victory lap near the end of her life. In 1976, the airport in Bentonville was rededicated Louise Thaden Field. The governor in Arkansas declared that Sunday "Louise Thaden Day," and it felt to locals like most of Bentonville turned out to hear her speak. "Louise Thaden," Olive Ann Beech declared that day, "one of the best." Still, the news of Thaden's death a few years later, just before her seventy-fourth birthday in 1979, didn't travel far, ignored by the national newspapers that had once followed her everywhere. By walking away from racing at the height of her popularity, Thaden had pulled off a vanishing act of her own.

But she didn't regret it. Thaden was satisfied with the life she had lived and the decisions she had made, at peace, in the end, with who she was, who she had always been, and where she was going.

"I have never been far away, nor will I ever," she told Patsy once. And nothing, not even her death, could change that. "Will you remember that—always?" Thaden asked her daughter. "Wherever I am, I will be with you."

She would be, she said, in the rustling of the leaves on the trees and the lazy drift of the clouds across the sky. She would be in the whispers on the wind, in the great blue horizon, and in the falling rain.

"The hues of sunset will be a part of me," Thaden said, "and the smell of flowers in the air. Contrails cut across God's heavens will be the paths along which I walk—the drifting snowflakes, my caress—the morning sun, my confidence."

All her children had to do, she said, was close their eyes, and they would find her. They would feel her presence in the air.

Acknowledgments

In writing this book, I was faced with an obvious challenge: the primary characters were all dead. And almost everyone who knew them was dead too, or they were too young in the 1920s or '30s to have a detailed memory of important events in this narrative. In order to bring these characters back to life — and reconstruct their world with details, dialogue, internal thoughts, feelings, and quotes — I had to rely almost exclusively on primary and secondary source material, including but not limited to diaries and journals, memoirs and oral histories, newspaper and magazine articles, private letters held in archives, unpublished manuscripts unearthed from boxes held by distant relatives, and public records documenting plane crashes, deaths, and disappearances.

As a journalist, I have always loved a great library. But after writing this book, I have a new and fervent appreciation for librarians and archivists and the work that they do preserving history. Without them, this book would not have been possible, and I need to thank several of them in particular: the archival staff at the National Archives and the National Air and Space Museum, including Elizabeth Borja, doing great work in the shadows for researchers everywhere; Ann Sindelar at the Western Reserve Historical Society in Cleveland; Mary Nelson at Wichita State University's Special Collections and University Archives; the entire staff at the Schlesinger Library at the Radcliffe Institute for Advanced Study at Harvard University; Tracy Grimm, Neal Harmeyer, and others in the Purdue University Libraries, Archives and Special Collections, who not only look after the Amelia Earhart archives there but years ago gathered important documents related to Cliff Henderson that I could not find anywhere else; Richard Sanderson at the Springfield Science Museum in central Massachusetts, who opened the Gee Bee archives for me; Brandon Anderson at the History Museum in South Bend, Indiana, who not only opened the Bendix archives for me but arranged for me to get a tour of Vincent Bendix's mansion, now converted into a private school; Merilee Colton and Brett Romer at the Historical Society of Palm Desert, who for years have kept Henderson's personal papers well organized in a back room and accommodated me for days; Denise Neil-Binion at the Ninety-Nines Museum of Women Pilots in Oklahoma City, who culled through historical files for me and sent me countless documents; Mark Peihl at the Historical and Cultural Society of Clay County, who, decades ago, interviewed people who knew Florence Klingensmith, preserving their memories of her and keeping these memories, along with hundreds of detailed documents related to Klingensmith's life and death, at his archive in Moorhead, Minnesota; Bill Barrow and others in the Cleveland State University Michael Schwartz Library's Special Collections, who saw fit to preserve the *Cleveland Press* clip morgue — an invaluable resource — and opened their doors for me in blizzards and driving snow, the worst of the Cleveland winter; Heather Alexander and Michael Sharaba at the International Women's Air and Space Museum in Cleveland, who fought the same winter weather to stay open for me and, more important, preserved for decades one of the greatest discoveries I made in this project — Ruth Nichols's personal papers, kept in several file cabinets in a back storage room and opened to me again and again; and, finally, the understanding supervisor at Chicago's Harold Washington Library who allowed a stressed writer (me) to fly home with several reels of microfilm from defunct Chicago papers after the library's scanner ate an entire day of digital images taken from the film.

I was able to find what I needed to tell this story only because these archivists — and countless others who are not named here — found the information first, realized its historical significance, and then held on to it. They have more than my gratitude; they have my respect.

But locating the material was only the beginning. For the writing — the crafting of the actual story — I need to thank, first of all, my literary agent, Richard Abate, at 3 Arts Entertainment, who saw value in this book idea from our very first phone call about it. Richard helped me make the idea better, refused to accept a good book proposal when a great one was possible, and then worked his magic to sell it. This book doesn't happen without Richard, and it also doesn't happen without Eamon Dolan, my editor at Houghton Mifflin Harcourt. From our first discussion about this book—before he even agreed to buy it—Eamon was pushing me to make the book better and asking insightful questions that forced me to focus my story, make it sharper. In working with him, I found not only an editor but a writing coach, a sounding board, and a fellow storyteller; his edits made this book stronger, from beginning to end. Finally, I am eternally grateful to three other people who offered detailed feedback on early drafts of the book: my wife, Eva, for picking me up, helping me find the way, and helping me understand these characters; my friend Andrew Bauer, for his courage to save me from myself; and my longtime editor at National Public Radio Russell Lewis, for his dedication to this story—and to me. Throughout this process, Russell not only edited early drafts but also e-mailed or called late at night or on weekends to offer suggestions that helped make the book better—not because he stood to gain anything by it, but because he cared.

There were many others who helped along the way and I would be remiss not to thank them. They include editorial associate Rosemary McGuinness at Houghton Mifflin Harcourt, for fielding my many requests and making things happen; the extraordinary Tracy Roe for her careful, thoughtful, and detailed read; designer Martha Kennedy for crafting this beautiful book jacket; Rachel Kim at 3 Arts for always taking the call; Erin Hardie Hale for her invaluable insights; Michelle Betters in Boston, Brian Welk and Lara Altunian in Los Angeles, and Sydney Soderberg in Kansas for their research assistance; my family, especially Cormac, and Cal, for their unwavering support; and finally Dan Crow, Tom Haines, John Lilly, Ian McNulty, Dan Wenner, Steven and Jennifer Serio, and the entire Goldscher family—Jeff, Kristin, Jack, and Kate—for their counsel, advice, and title suggestions.

Last, I need to thank the relatives of some of the characters in this book, the handful of people I was fortunate enough to track down who had personal connections to this story. I am indebted to all of them, including Ruth Nichols's nephew Norman Nichols, his son Jeff

Nichols, and their relative Richard Hechenbleikner for their memories and their photographs of "Aunt Ruth"; Florence Klingensmith's great-nephew Wayne Chapman, who sent me Florence's letters and other personal effects, saved by family members for almost eighty-five years; Cliff Henderson's stepdaughter Cathy Scott, who found for me in storage Cliff's completed and never-published memoir, a 268-page document that she never threw out, despite the fact that Cliff died more than thirty years ago; Mary Lynn Beech Oliver, Walter and Olive Ann's daughter, who still lives in Wichita and welcomed me there; and, finally, the entire Thaden family, especially Louise's daughter, young Patsy—now Patricia Thaden Webb—who was eighty-two years old and still going strong when I first met her at her home in Maryland in October 2016.

Like a lot of the other family members of the long-ago aviators, Pat had documents, letters, photos, and even poems written by her mother that I couldn't have found anywhere else. But that's not why she was important to me. In Pat—tall and slender, warm and bright—I felt like I was sitting with Louise Thaden, or at least a piece of Louise, the only real piece left. In my long conversations with Pat over several meetings, I came to understand her mother—her motivations, fears, hopes, and dreams—in ways I never could have by just reading old letters and news stories. And it seemed that Pat came to understand me too. In time, she began calling me "kid"—a term of endearment.

"Okay, kid," she'd say in parting. "Good luck."

It was what my grandmother had called me before her death years ago, and it was, for me, a subtle reminder of how quickly things change, how quickly time passes. I feel fortunate to have met Louise's daughter, Pat, and will always remember the afternoons we got to spend in her kitchen, talking about the old times when a few bold women dared to fly.

Notes

LAT	*Los Angeles Times*
"LITHW"	Janet Mabie, "Lady in the High Wind" (unpublished manuscript, Schlesinger Library, Harvard University)
NYDN	*New York Daily News*
NYHT	*New York Herald Tribune*
NYT	*New York Times*
OT	*Oakland Tribune*
PEE	*Portland Evening Express* (Maine)
PP	*Pittsburgh Press*
PPH	*Portland Press Herald* (Maine)
"STF"	Louise Thaden, "So They Flew" (unpublished manuscript, LTC, box 4, NASM)
SW	George Palmer Putnam, *Soaring Wings* (New York: Harcourt, Brace, 1939)
WB	*Wichita Beacon*
WE	*Wichita Eagle*
WFL	Ruth Nichols, *Wings for Life* (Philadelphia: J. B. Lippincott, 1957)
20 Hrs.	Amelia Earhart, *20 Hrs., 40 Min.* (Washington, DC: National Geographic Society, 2003)

CHC	Cliff Henderson Collection
FKC	Florence Klingensmith Collection
HCSCC	Historical and Cultural Society of Clay County
HSPD	Historical Society of Palm Desert
IWASM	International Women's Air and Space Museum
LTC	Louise Thaden Collection
NASM	Smithsonian National Air and Space Museum
RNC	Ruth Nichols Collection
SHLA	Springfield History Library and Archives
SLRC	Schlesinger Library, Radcliffe College
WEIU	Women's Educational and Industrial Union
WIAA	Women's International Aeronautic Association
WOABC	Walter and Olive Ann Beech Collection
WRHS	Western Reserve Historical Society

Introduction

xi   *"such a crisis"*: Paul Collins, *Tales of an Old Air-Faring Man* (Madison: University of Wisconsin Foundation Press, 1983), 65.

      "the only discriminable object": "Night Flying in Bad Weather," *Aviation,* March 7, 1927.

xii   *"wood fuselage ships"*: Bertram W. Downs, *The Modern Airplane* (St. Paul, MN: Roth-Downs Airways, 1928), 59.

      240 people: Aircraft Year Book, Aeronautical Chamber of Commerce of America, 1927.

      "no place for slovenly": Aircraft Year Book, Aeronautical Chamber of Commerce of America, 1926.

      "Would you ride": "What Pilots Think About Air Legislation," *Aviation,* March 29, 1926.

      unable to explain: Investigator reports come from the following: US Navy crash records and investigations, report on accident of airplane A.S. 23-691, wrecked at New Salem, PA; report on accident of airplane A.S. 22-100, wrecked at Dayton, OH; report on accident of airplane A.S. 22-1196, wrecked at Lore City, OH, National Archives, College Park, Maryland.

      "It has become": Miscellaneous race clippings, CHC, HSPD.

xiii *"swat the fly": Eau Claire Leader,* June 1, 1924.

xiv *colorful planes:* Ninety-Nines Museum, *Women in Aviation* 42 (July 20, 1930).

Chapter 1: The Miracle of Wichita

3   *five foot eight and a quarter inches:* NASM, LTC, box 1, license application.

      "boyish pursuits": "Beautiful Wichita Girl Flies! And How! Sells Travel Airs," *Wichita Evening Eagle,* December 31, 1927.

4   *joined him on his trips:* "Former Bentonville Girl Wins Fame by Sale of Commercial Planes in California," *Arkansas Gazette,* September 4, 1927.

      "where last employed": "Help Wanted—Female," *WE,* June 30, 1927.

      seven dollars in his pocket: "Life of Jack Turner Reads Like Page from Horatio Alger Novel," *WB,* February 27, 1931.

      "metropolis of the plains": Ibid.

      as early as 1922: "Should Women Draw the Same Pay as Men?," *Wichita Beacon Sunday Magazine,* November 12, 1922.

      "Everything in Coal": *WB,* October 28, 1921.

"Coal Is Scarce": "To Wichita Coal Users," advertisement in ibid., August 11, 1917.

5   *in a boarding house*: Wichita City Directory, 1922, Wichita State University Libraries.

He drank: Interview with daughter Mary Lynn Oliver, also confirmed by photographs and paintings, often depicting Beech with a pipe; Louise Thaden's recollections in her unpublished manuscript in her collection in the NASM, LTC, box 4, titled "So They Flew"; and transcript of an oral history of aviation and Wichita, interview with Wade Albright, WOABC, Wichita State University Libraries.

"I want to stay in Wichita": "$30,000 Airplane Factory," WE, August 22, 1926.

two airplane factories: "Wichita a City of Air Fans," WE, August 12, 1926.

"untiring zeal": Letter of recommendation for Sergeant Walter Beech, June 1, 1920, scrapbook, 1919–1932, box 2, FF 1, WOABC, Wichita State University Libraries.

Ford Reliability Tour: "Beech in Travel Air Wins Second Reliability Tour," *Aviation*, August 30, 1926, and "Navigating the Airplane Reliability Tour," *Aviation*, September 6, 1926.

"is Wichita's chance": "Now," WE, August 8, 1926.

6   *invested $12,000*: Ed Phillips, *Travel Air: Wings Over the Prairie* (Eagan, MN: Flying Books, 1982), 25.

"A loose nut": "75,000 See Beech Take Trophy," WE; n.d. Beech recounts his feats in this first-person article.

"Don't save this motor": "Great Epic of the Air," WE, October 3, 1926.

"to be back home again": "Beech Makes Average of 128 MPH on Wichita Hop," WE, August 14, 1926.

thirty thousand people: Accounts of how many people witnessed the end of the race vary wildly from fifteen thousand (*Detroit Free Press*) to seventy-five thousand (*WE*). With this account, the author took the number in the middle, thirty thousand, reported in *Aviation*, August 30, 1926.

with its propeller: "Beech Winner of Ford Tour," *Wichita Sunday Beacon*, August 22, 1926.

7   *"Wichita's Own"*: WE, August 13, 1926.

At the Hotel Broadview: Details of the event at the hotel celebrating Beech and the speeches made there all come from "Great Epic of the Air."

McPhetridge once jumped: "A Girl Flies to Fame," *Pacific Flier: Magazine of Air Commerce*, n.d., box 1, NASM, LTC.

her father's car: Some stories say she began driving at age nine, others say eight; box 1, news clippings, NASM, LTC.

Once, to impress: Thaden's daughter Pat Thaden Webb, interview by the author, October 8, 2016.

8   *"Warren has agreed":* HWF, 12.

"competition with men": "Beautiful Wichita Girl Flies!"

"Oh, Louise": HWF, 12.

"the one thing": "Beautiful Wichita Girl Flies!"

April 1927: HWF, 13.

almost freezing: "Weather," WE, April 2, 1927.

Chapter 2: Devotedly, Ruth

9   *no street number:* The official address for the Nichols family, according to US Census records, was 265 Grace Church Street, but in all of Nichols's correspondence, she listed no number, just the street name.

scary for children: Nichols's nephew Norman Nichols, interview with the author.

three of them: New York State Census, 1925.

expected to marry well: In her memoir *Wings for Life,* page 22, Nichols wrote that she was not following "the prescribed course for a delicately reared sub-deb."

10   *"Daddykins":* Letter sent home by Nichols from steamship, dated December 7, Family Correspondence, 1924–29, RNC, IWASM.

"Motherkins": Letter dated "Thursday," in Family Correspondence, 1919–21, in ibid.

"the blessedest girl": Letter to Nichols from her mother, sent October 26, 1920, in ibid.

"our Heavenly Father": WFL, 20.

"live my own life": Ibid., 36.

her eighteenth birthday: Résumé and biographical details, RNC, IWASM.

Every fiber: Nichols wrote in *WFL* that she climbed into the plane with "a feeling of panic," 16.

five foot five: Résumé and biographical details, RNC, IWASM.

"as if my soul": WFL, 19.

"College life": Letter home from Nichols dated September 29 [1919], Family Correspondence, 1919–1921, RNC, IWASM.

11   *"So late, in fact":* Ibid., undated letter.

"Devotedly, Ruth": Ibid., letter home from Nichols dated September 29 [1919].

mother and father pressured her: WFL, 23.

"flying lessons, Captain Rogers": Ibid., 24.

to pay Rogers five hundred dollars: Ibid., 25.

machinist's son: US Census records, 1910, for Harry's father, Silas W. Rogers.

"For Pete's sake": WFL, 31.

"numbskull speed": Ibid., 30.

"I'm a flier now, Harry": Ibid.

12   *in the fall of 1922*: Wellesley College records relating to Ruth Nichols.

"more men per person": Letter sent home from Nichols from steamship, dated December 7, 1924.

Chapter 3: Real and Natural, Every Inch

13   *six high schools*: 20 Hrs., 1.

possibly drinking: In her memoir *Courage Is the Price*, page 83, Earhart's sister, Muriel Earhart Morrissey, wrote about her father's drinking.

her parents' marriage: Ibid., 131.

classes at Columbia University: Columbia University records.

14   *job as a tutor*: WEIU files, SLRC.

the Yellow Peril: 20 Hrs., xxii.

kept a scrapbook: AOE Papers, SLRC.

"to financial difficulties": AE, letter to friend, October 1925, Marion Stabler Collection, IWASM.

August 18, 1926: WEIU files, SLRC.

"I have had five": Ibid.

"anything connected": Ibid.

15   *five foot eight*: LT interview, 1971, PTW Family Files.

"extremely interesting": WEIU files, SLRC.

"sky pilot's license": Ibid.

The first time: 20 Hrs., 6.

The second time: Ibid., 11.

"I want to fly": Neta Snook Southern, *I Taught Amelia to Fly* (New York: Vantage Press, 1974), 101.

one inch: Ibid., 112.

Christian Science church: CITP, 117.

taking in boarders: Ibid.

on credit: Southern, *I Taught Amelia to Fly,* 102.

16 *"whenever I can":* CITP, 128.

"Unskilled labor": 20 Hrs., 22.

Pooling together: CITP, 129.

for about two thousand dollars: George Putnam and Earhart's sister, Muriel, later wrote that the plane cost just five hundred dollars. But in her first memoir, written in 1928, Earhart said it was two thousand (*20 Hrs.,* 22).

"All in all": Southern, *I Taught Amelia to Fly,* 122.

Twice, she and Earhart: Both Southern and Earhart wrote about these crashes, with different details, in their respective memoirs.

"done the same": Southern, *I Taught Amelia to Fly,* 126.

"have to look nice": Ibid.

in air rodeos: "Pasadena Air Rodeo," *Ace,* December 1921, 7.

falling in love: Earhart herself almost never spoke of Sam, but her sister recounts what she knew of their relationship in her memoir, and Sam himself spoke about it to reporters from the *Medford Mercury.*

tall, redheaded: "Interesting Sidelights on Big Welcome to Flyers," *Medford Mercury,* July 13, 1928.

17 *"A Lady's Plane":* advertisement, *Ace,* June 1922.

plane had been sold: 20 Hrs., 32.

"In the near future": "Reporter Learns That Amelia Has Sweetheart," *Medford Mercury,* June 8, 1928.

"Real and natural": Ibid.

"is all right": WEIU files, SLRC.

18 *neighborhood was filled:* Boston City Directory and ward 3, plate 14, Norman B. Leventhal Map Center, Boston Public Library.

"I'll never go back": AE, letter to friend, October 1925, Marion Stabler Collection, IWASM.

Chapter 4: The Fortune of the Air

19 *the dare began:* "Puts Up $25,000 for Paris Flight," *NYT,* May 30, 1919.

20 *"see what you can do":* Biographical details about Orteig's early life come from the obituary "Raymond Orteig, Hotel Man, Dies," *NYT,* June 8, 1939.

padlocking the doors: "Brevoort Hotel Accepts Padlock on Dining Room," *NYHT,* March 9, 1926.

"greatest feats": "Fonck to Fly American Plane Across the Atlantic,"
NYHT, March 31, 1926.

"Dashed to pieces": "Wings of Uncertainty," *NYT*, February 20, 1927.

21 *"caught myself nodding"*: Ernie Smith recounted the troubles on his
Pacific flight and with ocean flying in general in "Ocean Flights Are the
Bunk," *Popular Aviation* (January 1931), and "Ernie Smith Says, 'I Was a
Hero,'" *Flying* (October 1939).

22 *looking dapper*: Fonck's flight and failure were covered by the national
press, including these detailed accounts: "Fonck Plane Burns, Two Die,
at Start of Paris Flight, Ace and Curtin Escape," *NYT*, September 22,
1926; "Two Die When Fonck's Plane Falls in Flames," *BG*, September
21, 1926; and "Fonck's Plane Burned, 2 Die, But He Plans to Try Again,"
NYHT, September 22, 1926.

23 *"Too much news"*: "Nungesser to Take Off for New York May 10, Paris
Hears," *NYHT*, April 20, 1927.

Hussar of Death: "Nungesser Has Skull and Bones for Ocean Luck,"
NYHT, May 8, 1927.

"Warmest congratulations": "How the Airmen Arrived," *Guardian*, May
10, 1927.

"see you soon": The details of Nungesser's flight and takeoff can be found
in a number of places, among them "Nungesser and Coli Missing in At-
lantic Flight Attempt," *Aviation*, May 16, 1927; "Nungesser Off on Paris–
New York Hop," *NYT*, May 8, 1927; "Davids of the Air Brave Goliath of
Elements," *NYHT*, May 9, 1927; and "Nungesser Flying Over the Atlantic
Hops Off at 5:19 A.M.," *NYHT*, May 8, 1927.

24 *ballroom of the Hotel Astor*: "Throng to Greet Nungesser at Battery Today," *NYHT*, May 9, 1927.

pressing against the wall: The wait for Nungesser and Coli was chronicled
in stories by the New York papers, among them "Beacons Flood Battery
in Vigil for Nungesser," *NYHT*, May 10, 1927, and "Nungesser, Hours
Overdue, Believed Down at Sea," *NYHT*, May 10, 1927.

25 *"My prayers"*: "Nungesser Seen Leaving Ireland, British Assert," *NYHT*,
May 11, 1927.

"greatly deplore": "Orteig Expresses Regret," *NYT*, April 28, 1927.

"five sandwiches": Russell Owen, "Lindbergh Leaves New York at 7:52
A.M.," *NYT*, May 21, 1927.

"No coffee": "Lindbergh Arrives After Record Hops," *NYT*, May 13,
1927.

Didn't chew tobacco: "Lindbergh Is Noted for Practical Jokes," *NYT,* May 21, 1927.

"death chamber": "Lindbergh Risks Disaster on Field to Force Plane into Air at Start," *NYHT,* May 21, 1927.

26 *"Ready, Slim":* Ibid.

Lloyd's of London: "Lloyd's Refuses to Quote Odds on Capt. Lindbergh," *St. Louis Post-Dispatch,* May 20, 1927.

jammed the switchboard: "10,000 Telephone Inquiries on Lindbergh Answered by the Times in 11 Hours," *NYT,* May 22, 1927.

At a boxing match: "44,000 Join in Prayer That Lindbergh Wins," *NYT,* May 21, 1927.

27 *"Defeat and death":* Owen, "Lindbergh Leaves New York."

"hokum": "Lindy Likes Lack of 'Hokum' at Reception Here," *Indianapolis Star,* August 10, 1927.

"down the gangplank": Lindbergh sound files, San Diego Air and Space Museum.

"Lighter by $25,000": "Raymond Orteig, Hotel Man, Dies."

Chapter 5: The Fairest of the Brave and the Bravest of the Fair

29 *barely flying anymore:* FOI, 57.

in the women's department: Business letters, 1927–1929, RNC, IWASM, contain details about her job.

30 *"Gas bought":* "Girl, 23, Flies Here for Paris Jump Sunday," *NYHT,* September 15, 1927.

31 *"Perfectly powdered":* "Miss Elder Insists on Flight to Paris," *Philadelphia Inquirer,* September 15, 1927.

"What is this you're doing": "Smile of Ruth Elder Causes Many Guesses on Her Flight," *AS,* September 22, 1927.

"here to fly": "Girl, 23, Flies Here."

Noble Street: All details about the Elders' homes, J. O. Elder's jobs, and his sources of income come from US Census records and Anniston city directories.

golf and schemes: Details related to the Florida and West Virginia backers of Ruth Elder's flight and how they came together comes from "Who Will Share Ruth's Glory?," *PP,* October 16, 1927.

32 *"doesn't seem right":* United Press, September 15, 1927.

"bravest of the fair": Picture caption, *Defiance, Ohio, Crescent News,* September 14, 1927.

were insured: "Who Will Share Ruth's Glory?"

hated instructing women: "Movies Make Her Nervous," *LAT,* September 2, 1928.

"plugged nickel": "Explaining Ruth Elder," *BG,* November 30, 1927.

33 *especially busy:* "Summer Visitors Bring Maine Best Season for Four Years," *PEE,* October 23, 1927.

Visitors there: Descriptions of life that summer in Old Orchard Beach come from the *Biddeford Daily Journal* in the following stories: "Old Orchard" town report, August 17, 1927; Town at a Glance, August 12, 1927; "Miss America," August 25, 1927; Town at a Glance, August 26, 1927.

Great Circle route: "US Experts Suggest Better Routes For Trans-Atlantic Air Heroes," *PEE,* October 19, 1927.

"fully confidential": Letter from Frances Grayson to Harry Jones, Harmon Museum and Old Orchard Beach Historical Society, Old Orchard Beach, Maine.

"into the 'movies'": "Two Women Plan Overseas Air Expedition," *NYHT,* September 3, 1927.

"give my life": "Will Fly from Paris to New York," *Muncie Evening Press,* September 7, 1927.

34 *botched hysterectomy:* Indiana certificate of death, no. 310, for Minnie May Wilson, November 10, 1910.

The society pages: Details about Grayson's life as an entertainer come from stories and briefs in the society pages of the *Muncie Evening Press* on the following dates: May 2, 1907; August 6, 1909; September 29, 1910; October 19, 1910; and August 22, 1911.

white and yellow roses: Grayson-Wilson wedding announcement, *Muncie Evening Express,* September 16, 1914.

at suffrage events: "Warrenton Turns Out to Hear Suffragists," *Richmond Times Dispatch,* August 17, 1915.

"make that atom": "Gave Up Society for the Theater," *Boston Post,* April 4, 1921.

sold $2 million: "Frances Grayson Sacrificed a $2,000,000 Realty Business to Make 'Safe and Sane' Flight," *Brooklyn Daily Eagle,* December 27, 1927.

give her $38,000: "Will Fly from Paris to New York."

"Don't worry": Ibid.

S-36 Flying Boat: "The New Sikorsky Flying Boat," *Aviation,* September 5, 1927.

35   *"child of destiny"*: International News Service, "Fulfillment of Dreams Near, Says Mrs. Grayson," October 15, 1927.

"in the cockpit of an airplane": "Miss Elder Up in Tests Today for Her License," *NYHT,* September 17, 1927.

"bluffer or faker": Ibid.

a host of new rules: "Ruth Determined," *PP,* September 15, 1927.

36   *"cannot rise here"*: "Old Glory Passes Over Cape Race on Flight from Rome to Maine," *NYHT,* September 7, 1927.

"Making good time": Ibid.

chunk of wing: "Old Glory Dived Head On in Sea, Wreck Indicates," *NYHT,* September 22, 1927.

"fine young men": "Hoover Averse to Flight Ban as Unfair to Youth," *NYHT,* September 11, 1927.

37   *"asking too much"*: "Stinson to Refuse Planes for Solo Oceanic Flights," *NYHT,* September 3, 1927.

"publicity" purposes: "Lindbergh Talks Generally on Sea Hops—Silent on Elder Attempt," *NYT,* October 12, 1927.

"They shall not stop me": "Ruth Elder Has Been Flyer but Two Years," *BG,* October 12, 1927.

38   *morning of Elder and Haldeman's departure:* Most details of Elder's takeoff from New York come from two accounts: "Flapper Wings for Paris," *NYDN,* October 12, 1927, and "Ruth Elder Takes Off on Paris Flight, Soars with Haldeman into Ocean Dusk," *NYHT,* October 12, 1927.

"Ruth ribbon": "Miss Elder Trailed by Throng at Field," *NYT,* September 19, 1927.

39   *In the cockpit:* The details about Elder and Haldeman's flight over the ocean come primarily from Elder's four-part, first-person account, published that fall in the *AS* and other newspapers under the headline "Ruth Tells of Atlantic Flight." Additional details related to the SS *Barendrecht* saving Elder and Haldeman come from the ship captain's own first-person account via the United Press story published around the world on October 15, 1927.

41   *blowing up the beach:* "Heavy Frost Weather Forecast for Today," *PPH,* October 11, 1927, and "Cold Snap Due to Break Today," *PPH,* October 12, 1927.

"*Prayers of women everywhere*": "The Dawn Due to Hop Thursday," *PPH*, October 12, 1927.

"*a pioneer flight*": "The Dawn Takes Off from Curtiss Field," *PPH*, October 11, 1927.

going broke: "Mrs. Grayson's Entire Fortune Used Up on Fateful Ocean Flight; Wouldn't Cancel Attempt Because of Duty to Money Backer," *Brooklyn Daily Eagle,* January 8, 1928.

42   "*glory enough for both*": "Flapper Wings for Paris."

by the fireplace: "The Dawn Plans to Hop Today," *PPH*, October 14, 1927.

"*prayers followed you*": "Grayson Plane Escapes Storm, Starts Today," *NYHT,* October 14, 1927.

called his temperament: "Chamberlin Refuses to Fly Dawn," *PEE*, October 28, 1927.

wagon maker's son: US Census records for the Goldsborough family, 1880.

a miserable time: "Forty-Mile Gale Rages at Eastport," *PPH*, October 20, 1927; "So. Boston Lads Are Near Death Off Maine Coast," *PPH*, October 20, 1927; "Record Rainfall Throughout State," *PPH*, October 21, 1927; "Thousands Damaged by Torrential Downpour in Washington County," *PPH*, October 21, 1927.

43   "*all is gray*": In October 1927, while stuck in Old Orchard Beach, Grayson wrote a pondering letter that reads almost like a diary entry. She gave it to a *NYT* reporter, saying he could publish it "if something happen[ed]" to her; "'Still Small Voice' Led Mrs. Grayson," *NYT,* December 26, 1927.

crew had argued: "Mrs. Grayson and Navigator in Row," *PEE*, October 18, 1927.

planning a mutiny: "Thea Rasche May Pilot the Dawn Across Atlantic," *PEE*, November 1, 1927.

Snow was already: "Snowfall at Moosehead Proves Aid to Hunters," *PPH*, October 25, 1927.

"*is obvious*": "Stultz Asks Release as Dawn Pilot," *PPH*, October 29, 1927.

Goldy was shaken: The intimate details of Brice Goldsborough's final nights with his family in Brooklyn come from an affidavit written by his wife, Gertrude, and included in Grayson's administrative file at Surrogate's Court in New York declaring her legally dead in 1928; file no. A1928-4635.

44   "*for Miss Grayson's plane*": "Mrs. Grayson and the Dawn Heard from by Radio," *PPH*, December 25, 1927.

speculate wildly: Reports of various radio messages swept up and down the US coast and through the Canadian maritime provinces for days after the *Dawn* went missing. Accounts of these reports can be found in the following articles, among others: "Five Destroyers to Continue Hunt for Missing Plane," *PPH*, December 29, 1927; "Dirigible Back at Hangar After 31 Hours' Vain Hunt," *PEE*, December 28, 1927; "'Plane Down—Can't Last Long'; Mystery Message Upsets Island," *PPH*, December 30, 1927; and "Plane Heard Late Saturday Evening Over Newfoundland," *PPH*, December 30, 1927.

"all off now": "Father Fears for Safety," *Muncie Evening Press*, December 24, 1927.

45 *"absolutely correct":* "Five Destroyers to Continue Hunt."

an impossibility: Several reports placed the *Dawn* over Cape Cod around 7:30 the night it went missing; see "Dawn Crew Plunged to Death Off Cape Cod in Howling Storm," *PEE*, January 2, 1928; "Last Known Dispatch," *PEE*, December 29, 1927; and "Mrs. Grayson and the Dawn Heard from by Radio," *PPH*, December 25, 1927.

"any hope": "Fear Chokes Queries of Lost Pilot's Wife," *Philadelphia Inquirer*, December 25, 1927.

"our objections": Associated Press, December 24, 1927.

46 *in late October:* Details of Elder's arrival in Paris can be found in the following stories: "Thousands Greet Miss Elder as Plane Arrives in Paris," *NYT*, October 29, 1927; "Paris Welcomes Ruth Elder and Aide as Sky Conquerors," *NYHT*, October 29, 1927; and "Throngs at Paris Greet Ruth Elder," *BG*, October 29, 1927.

like "Cinderella": "Movies Make Her Nervous."

"my boy is alive": "Ruth Elder May Hunt for Nungesser, Coli," *PP*, October 30, 1927.

2,623 miles: "Flew 2,623 Miles, New Oversea Record," *NYT*, October 14, 1927.

$400,000: "Coolidge Presents Medal to Lindbergh; 6,000 See Ceremony," *NYT*, November 15, 1927.

"Ruth Elder Day": The details about Elder's homecoming come from the *AS*'s coverage of the events in the following stories: "Anniston Expects Huge Crowd Ruth Elder Day," December 19, 1927; "Hometown Gives Ruth Big Reception," December 20, 1927; "Ruth Elder Resting Today After Hectic Welcome Activities," December 21, 1927; "City Prepares to Bid Famous Guests Goodbye," December 22, 1927; "Kiwanis Club

Honors Ruth and Haldeman," December 22, 1927; "Ruth Elder, Haldeman Depart from Anniston After Three-Day Visit," December 23, 1927;
and "Dinner Party at Club for Miss Elder," December 25, 1927.

47   *"the American Midinette"*: "Throngs at Paris Greet Ruth Elder."
      every chance he got: Stories of Womack's frustration about his wife's ex-
      ploits and their ultimate divorce can be found in multiple papers in 1927
      and 1928, including "Ruth Elder's Mate Bars Flying," *NYHT*, November
      5, 1927; "Mate and Aunt Here at 'Outs' to Greet Miss Elder," *NYHT*, No-
      vember 8, 1927; "Curious Throngs Greet Ruth Elder Mid Sirens' Blast,"
      Brooklyn Daily Eagle, November 11, 1927; "Return to Dishes? No, Vows
      Ruth," *OT*, November 12, 1927; "Ruth Elder's Husband Charges Cruelty
      in Suit," *NYHT*, September 7, 1928.
      "to do such things": "Ruth Elder May Hunt for Nungesser, Coli."
      "to enter the lion's cage": "Today," *AS*, October 15, 1927.
      most hurtful: "Women Criticize Elder Attempt," *NYT*, October 14, 1927.
48   *"ten thousand thanks"*: "Elder, Haldeman Depart from Anniston."

Chapter 6: Flying Salesgirls

49   *"old hat"*: The details of Nichols's state of mind at New Year's Eve 1927
      come from *WFL*, 41–42, in which she describes the night as "one of the
      dismal points of my life."
      handy list: Loose pages, RNC, IWASM.
50   *"foolhardy"*: "Women Criticize Elder Attempt," *NYT*, October 14, 1927.
      newspaper editors: "Miami's Story Is Youth, Say City Guests," *Miami
      Herald*, January 5, 1928.
      headed to Rockaway: WFL, 42.
51   *before 8:00 a.m.*: Flight log of the journey was published in detail in the
      Miami Herald under the headline "Log of New York–Miami Flight,"
      January 6, 1928.
      "personal things": "Woman Passenger on Miami Flight Evades Lime-
      light," *Miami Herald*, January 6, 1928.
      "interesting way to travel": "Ruth Nichols Is Impressed by Her Flight,"
      Miami Herald, January 6, 1928.
52   *"his stenographer"*: "Ruth Nichols Urges Commuting by Air," *NYT*, Janu-
      ary 9, 1928.
      sixty dollars a week: Canceled checks, Fairchild Aviation folder, RNC,
      IWASM.

"relatives, of any sort": Telegram home, January 5, 1928, album no. 1, May 15, 1916–January 6, 1928, RNC, IWASM.

"like a rooster": "Athletic Accomplishments," loose in book, in ibid.

around her neck: Thaden chronicled these stops, the crowds, her efforts to fly, and a flight home from Bakersfield in an undated letter home, NASM, LTC.

"and avoid the rush": "Fly High and Avoid the Rush, She Says," *OT*, January 12, 1928.

53   *hangar no. 3 in Oakland:* "Oakland Aviatrix Weds Plane Designer," *Oakland Post Inquirer*, July 27, 1928; "Local Girl Aviatrix Weds Captain Vo. Thaden," *Benton County Herald*, July 27, 1928.

her grit: "'Round San Francisco Bay," *Western Flying* (June 1928).

at $12,000: "Former Bentonville Girl Wins Fame by Sale of Commercial Planes in California," *Arkansas Gazette*, September 1, 1927.

twenty-nine million: "Woman Vote Plays Big Part This Year," *NYT*, July 9, 1928.

official figures: Bureau of Labor Statistics, "Statistics of Industrial Accidents in the United States to the End of 1927," August 1929, and the US Department of Commerce, "Statistical Abstract of the United States," 1928–1933, specifically table 78 in 1931, "Deaths: Number and Rate Per 100,000 Population," and table 49 in 1933, "Gainful Workers 10 Years Old and Over: By Occupation and Sex, Continental United States."

"sell airplanes": "Oakland Girl Sells Planes," *OT*, January 12, 1928.

54   *Hattie moved:* US Census records and Cincinnati city directory, 1903.

gravitated more toward: Herb Thaden résumé, PTW Family Files, and "Who's Who in Aeronautics," *Aviation*, February 26, 1923.

knew what he wanted: "The Thaden 'Argonaut,'" *Aviation*, February 13, 1928.

55   *invited one person:* "Local Girl Aviatrix Weds Captain Vo. Thaden."

corral her: Pat Thaden Webb, interview by the author.

spinning to the ground: "Flier Killed in Alameda Field Crash," *OT*, August 5, 1927.

headed there too: Thaden's crash with William A. "Sandy" Sanders was covered in detail in Bay Area newspapers including the following stories in the *OT*: "Probe Is Begun of Plane Crash That Hurt One Man," March 14, 1928; "Alameda County Has First Flying Deputy," July 6,

1927; "Aerial Officer Himself Jailed," July 8, 1927; "Aerial Officer Forfeits Bail on Drunk Charge," July 15, 1927; "Oakland Flier Killed in Crash," August 20, 1928; "Planes to Soar Over Rites for Oakland Flier," August 21, 1928; "Coroner's Jury Finds Death Accidental," August 28, 1928. Additional details related to the overheating engine and Thaden's feelings about the crash come from her memoir, *HWF*, 25, 27.

56 *stealing away to Reno:* "Oakland Aviatrix Weds Plane Designer."
"notorious like we are": Herb Thaden, letter to Louise, July 25, 1928, PTW Family Files.

Chapter 7: The Right Sort of Girl

57 *"right sort of girl":* Hilton Howell Railey, *Touch'd with Madness* (New York: Carrick and Evans, 1938), 101.
"adequate standards": GPP, "Lady with Wings: The Life Story of My Wife, Amelia Earhart," *Liberty*, n.d., AE Papers, SLRC.
"sporting-scientific adventure": "Putnam Says Flight May Start at Anytime," *BG*, June 5, 1928.
impervious to obstacle: "Reminiscences of GPP," GPP Papers, box 1, Purdue University Libraries, Archives and Special Collections.
bluer than most: Colonial Families of the United States, 1607–1775, 428; *New England Historical and Genealogical Register, 1847–2011,* 226; US Sons of the American Revolution Application for Worcester Putnam, George's cousin, descendant of Joseph Palmer, May 21, 1928; US Census records.

58 *became just Putnam:* George Palmer Putnam obituary, *NYT*, December 21, 1872.
blood pressure: GPP, *Wide Margins* (New York: Harcourt, Brace, 1942), 62.
within a hundred miles: "First Bend Daily," *Bend Bulletin*, December 14, 1916.
"boy mayor of Oregon": "Early Days in Bend," *Bend Bulletin*, April 14, 1942.
his father's death in 1915: "John B. Putnam, Publisher, Dies," *NYT*, October 9, 1915.
saves the day: "Book Written by Local Man," *Bend Bulletin*, March 25, 1918, and "Would Make Hit as Movie Play," *Bend Bulletin*, July 23, 1918.
park rangers personally: "The Yellow Stone Park," *Bend Bulletin*, September 1, 1925.

to the Arctic: For the Putnam Greenland Expedition, Putnam himself wrote a series of first-person stories for the *NYT.*

"prizes": "Putnam Party Back with Arctic Prizes," *NYT,* October 2, 1926.

pair of polar bears: Several stories in the *NYT* chronicled the specimens the Putnam expedition brought home; see "Putnam Bags Birds Under Midnight Sun," July 22, 1926; "Explorers in Fight with Walrus Herd," August 19, 1926; and "Putnam Party Gets Three More Narwhals, Completing Collection of Polar Animals," August 22, 1926.

pure sport: "Putnam Party Bags Large Polar Bear," *NYT,* August 31, 1926.

out of necessity: "Cowboy Lassos Two Polar Bears," *NYT,* September 7, 1926.

Putnam looked on: "Putnam Party Back with Arctic Prizes."

59   *"wear shadows well":* "Reminiscences of GPP," GPP Papers, Purdue University.

"Pull your chair over": Putnam and Railey each have different recollections of how they learned about the *Friendship* flight and who was in charge of finding a woman to replace Guest, and they each render their dialogue about it with different phrasings. Earhart, too, has slightly different phrasings of the conversations she had with Railey. But overall, the sentiment is the same. The exchanges rendered here between Putnam and Railey come from Railey's account in his memoir *Touch'd with Madness,* 100.

answers he needed: Reporter Janet Mabie, who knew Earhart personally, wrote for the *CSM* and *NYHT* and remained close with Earhart's family after her disappearance, interviewing many people who knew Earhart in the 1940s and attempting to write a book she titled *Lady in the High Wind.* Publishers turned down Mabie's manuscript and it was never published, but her many drafts of the manuscript, filled with her reporting, remain in her collection at the Schlesinger Library at Radcliffe College, in Cambridge, Massachusetts. The details about the Scotch come from vol. 9, 6.

60   *"undesirables":* "Immigration Discrimination," *NYT,* October 4, 1925.

immigrant smuggling: "Quota Law Parts Families," *NYT,* October 14, 1926.

"hard to believe": "Big Swindles Bared in Alien Smuggling," *NYT,* June 29, 1925.

immigrant men and women: 20 Hrs., xxii.

around their tables: "Interview in South End Kitchen Where She Often Sat," *BG*, July 11, 1937.

"after a year's friendship": 20 Hrs., xxii.

61   *"It is nothing":* Details of Rasche's crash and Earhart's response were carried in two stories in the *Boston Herald*, "Thea Rasche Escapes Injury as Plane Crashes in Swamp," September 29, 1927, and "Aviation Sidelights," October 2, 1927.

"women who fly": Letter from Amelia Earhart to Ruth Nichols, September 15, 1927, AE Papers, Purdue University.

"as Chairman pro tem": Letter from Ruth Nichols to Amelia Earhart, in ibid.

"more women flying": "When Women Go Aloft," *Bostonian* (May 1928).

62   *"ask for Amelia Earhart":* Railey, *Touch'd with Madness*, 101.

children scampered around: FOI, 58.

"Captain H. H. Railey": Ibid., 59.

"fly the Atlantic": Ibid.

as mechanic: "Lady with Wings."

the second meeting: The best descriptions of Earhart's meeting in New York come from three places: *20 Hrs.*, 42; "Lady with Wings"; and *CITP*, 141–42.

"a crisis": 20 Hrs., 42.

"too fascinating": Ibid.

63   *nor memorable: CITP*, 141.

one of his moods: By his own admission, George was "cross" that day and "harassed with business complexities," "Lady with Wings."

"home, either": CITP, 142.

"ride a horse": Mabie interviewed Amy Guest's lawyer, David T. Layman, in 1944, who recalled for her his meeting with Earhart; the story is recounted in "LITHW," vol. 9, 7a.

$60,000: Ibid., 3.

"for summer school": "Lady with Wings."

64   *too foggy:* 20 Hrs., 51.

rumors were beginning: Boston Evening Transcript, June 4, 1928.

high-laced boots: "LITHW," vol. 9, 15.

"50-50 bet": "Lindbergh's Success," *PEE*, October 26, 1927.

"midst of it": SW, 56.

"I wish we might": Ibid., 55.

"were opening for me": AOE Papers, SLRC.

the flight was troubled: 20 Hrs., 54, and AE, flight log, Seaver Center in Western History Research, Los Angeles County Museum of Natural History.

five tons: FOI, 64.

65 *into the sea:* This near disaster is recounted in multiple places, including *20 Hrs.*, 53, and AE, flight log.

"selected this port": F. Burnham Gill, "First Woman to Cross the Atlantic in a Flying Boat," *Newfoundland Quarterly* 60, no. 4 (Winter 1961–62).

"are you doing here": "LITHW," vol. 10, 3.

"in store for us": AE, flight log.

a lost fortune: Details about Earhart's time in Trepassey in the next two paragraphs come from her flight log; additional details related to Stultz's drinking come from *SW*, 63, and "LITHW," vol. 10, 6.

66 *"We're going today":* Details of takeoff in Trepassey come from "Monoplane Friendship Lands Safely," *St. John's Evening Telegram*, June 18, 1928; "LITHW," vol. 10, 7; and Gill, "First Woman to Cross the Atlantic."

one last time: "Monoplane Friendship Lands Safely."

Sixty: FOI, 73, and "Lady with Wings."

67 *to shed weight:* AE, flight log.

"Miss Earhart now": 20 Hrs., xxiv.

"Two boats": AE, flight log.

68 *"that's out":* "Miss Earhart Predicts Great Airport at Trepassey for Transocean Flights," *NYT*, June 21, 1928.

a "mess": AE, flight log.

"Let's leave it that way": "Miss Earhart and Aides Get City's Salutes," *NYHT*, July 7, 1928.

250,000 people: "Boston Shouts Joy to Amelia Earhart," *NYT*, July 10, 1928.

two thousand social workers: "Big Throng of Women at Reception in Hotel," *BG*, July 10, 1928.

in song: "Picks 'Em Out at Lincoln Fields," *Chicago Daily News*, July 20, 1928.

greatest celebration: "Thousands Pay Tribute to the Friendship Flyers," *Medford Mercury*, July 13, 1928.

69 *Chapman too weak:* CITP, 135.

"all-right girl": "Miss Earhart's Homecoming," *NYHT*, July 8, 1928.

"a little lady": These quotes about Earhart come from multiple sources including "Miss Earhart's Smile and Poise Capture Huge Throngs in

Boston," *BG*, July 10, 1928; "Miss Earhart Feted, Companions Beg Off," *BG*, June 21, 1928; and "Secret Flight Miss Earhart's Original Plan," *Brooklyn Daily Eagle*, June 10, 1928.

"Aren't you excited": "Chance Sent Amelia Earhart on First Ocean Venture," *Philadelphia Evening Bulletin*, September 10, 1938.

"gasoline supply": "What Has Miss Earhart's Flight Accomplished?," *Boston Traveler*, July 8, 1928.

Chapter 8: City of Destiny

73 *trim and compact*: El Rodeo, USC yearbook, 1917, 85, listed Henderson as weighing 137 pounds in 1917; by World War II, twenty-five years later, Henderson listed his weight at about 170 pounds.

74 *quagmire*: "Muddy Field Mars Races, Many Mishaps," *Philadelphia Inquirer*, September 7, 1926.

if the pilots were safe: "20 Planes Long Overdue at Sesqui Air Meet," *Philadelphia Inquirer*, September 6, 1926.

"Polish Day": "'Polish Day' Draws 85,000 to Exercises in Sesqui Grounds," *Philadelphia Inquirer*, September 4, 1926.

"tossed rocks with the other": "Spokane Thrills to Airplane Derby," *NYT*, September 20, 1927.

"heaps of Indians": Ibid.

"in Los Angeles County": "Los Angeles County Spreads Her Wings," 1928, CHC, WRHS.

"not silver ones": "FWTF," 19. Before his death, Cliff Henderson began working on a memoir that was never published. Two chapters of one version of this memoir exist in his collection at the Historical Society of Palm Desert; the complete account was found in 2017 by Cliff's step-daughter Cathy Scott in her home in Arkansas and graciously given to the author. Titled "From Wasteland to Fairyland," this 268-page account offers detail and insights about the key points of Henderson's life, including his early years.

"best kind of dollar": Ibid.

75 *"a Shetland pony"*: Ibid., 21.

"Two hundred dollars": Ibid., 22.

muskrat: Ibid., 22–23.

a better life: US Census records, 1910, for Nelson Henderson, Cliff's father.

coyotes for pay: "FWTF," 38.

E. L. Ferguson: The story of the Alco truck's trip west was covered by newspapers in every town it visited that summer. In his unpublished writings Henderson said he was fourteen when he went west, but news coverage shows that Ferguson made the trip in 1912, when Henderson was seventeen.

76 *delivery by motor truck:* "Motor Truck to Cross Continent," *Philadelphia Inquirer,* June 23, 1912.

"see it my way": "FWTF," 44.

"a good boy": Ibid., 56.

"my word, Mother": Ibid., 45.

eighty miles a day: "Alco Truck Cuts Its Own Trail for 70 Miles in Wyoming Wilds," *WE,* August 11, 1912; "Alco Truck Making Long Trip," *Salt Lake Tribune,* August 21, 1912.

prostitute of his own: In the unpublished "FWTF," page 55, Henderson writes about the brothel experiences at length, declaring the men "permitted me to witness everything that took place."

77 *"building roads":* "Pioneer Freighter Ends Ocean to Ocean Journey," *San Francisco Call,* September 21, 1912.

left behind in Colorado: "FWTF," 59.

grape juice: Ibid., 63.

At Manual Arts: Education folder, CHC, HSPD.

"Rah": Song list, in ibid.

"among the USC players": El Rodeo, USC yearbook, 1918, 73.

78 *"Each Used Car":* "FWTF," 94.

"Babe Ruth of Motor Row": "Cliff Henderson Named Swat King of Auto Row," publication source unknown, January 1924, Employment folder, CHC, HSPD.

twenty thousand dollars: "FWTF," 101.

satisfy their demands: Audit, September 21, 1927, Employment folder, CHC, HSPD.

"have these races here": "What Happens in the World Above Terra Firma," *LAT,* January 1, 1928.

"in recommending him": Letter from Lieutenant Governor Buron Fitts, February 6, 1928, CHC, WRHS.

They hired Henderson: Air-race contract, May 17, 1928, CHC, WRHS.

"municipal airfield": "September Set for Air Races," *LAT,* January 24, 1928.

some six thousand: "Turning Out a Factory Record," *Southern California Business,* January 1927.

"city of destiny": Ibid.

79   *in nearby towns: Aircraft Year Book,* Aeronautical Chamber of Commerce of America, 1928, 162.

downtown LA: Mines Field site selection papers, March 16, 1928, LAX historical archives, Flight Path Museum.

"geographical position": "Why Local Air Field Is Choice," May 29, 1928, race scrapbook, CHC, Purdue University.

barbed-wire fencing: Interview with Dudley Steele, February 9, 1966, LAX historical archives, Flight Path Museum.

80   *twenty thousand people:* There are varying accounts about how big the grandstand was, ranging from twelve thousand (*LAT*) to thirty thousand ("FWTF"). In this case, the author went with the number in between, which the author found in "Shipload of Lumber for Mines Field," *Inglewood Californian,* July 20, 1928.

284 booths: Exposition hall map, 1928, CHC, WRHS.

Italian sculptor: "Mines Field in Readiness," *LAT,* September 4, 1928.

$200,000 in prizes: "Elaborate Plans for Air Exposition," *NYT,* September 9, 1928; "Program Fixed for Air Races," *LAT,* August 5, 1928.

three hundred thousand watched: "City Declared Flying Center," *LAT,* September 17, 1928.

frightened fans: "Air Stunt Hero Hurt in Crash," *LAT,* September 11, 1928.

missing only one thing: Ruth Elder and Amelia Earhart were both invited to the 1928 races; Elder flew some sort of exhibition but did not race. Earhart didn't fly at all.

one of his stages: "FWTF," 112.

"the most beautiful girls": "Aerial Ballet at Mines Field," race scrapbook, 1928, CHC, Purdue University.

Chapter 9: If This Is to Be a Derby

81   *"Yours for America":* Air-race letter from Henderson, 1928, CHC, WRHS.

hoping to compete: In the days before the races, multiple stories reported that Rogers hoped to enter a plane and would bring Ruth Nichols along with him, but they never got off; see "All Derby Fliers Report," *LAT,* September 14, 1928.

Famous Fliers: "Notables of Air Due at Dance," *LAT,* September 13, 1928.
new friend: According to *NYHT* coverage, they first met in person that
July.

82   *Avro Avian biplane:* "Earhart and Companion Crash Here, Escape Injury," *Pittsburgh Post-Gazette,* September 1, 1928, and AE, flight log.
"hidden ditch": Details from Earhart's crash in Pittsburgh come from
"Earhart and Companion Crash Here" and AE, flight log.
busted plane: "Plane Fixed, Miss Earhart Hops for West," *Pittsburgh Post-
Gazette,* September 3, 1928.
"just an amateur": "Miss Earhart Flies to Town," *LAT,* September 14,
1928.
access to Mines Field: LTC, NASM.
"on the Pacific Coast": "Planes to Soar Over Rites for Oakland Flier," *OT,*
August 21, 1928.

83   *on Sanders's grave:* HWF, 27.
"not a good pilot": "Five Miles Up," *Motormates,* December 1928.
"very careful": HWF, 19.

84   *to go higher:* "Oakland Aviatrix to Set Women's Altitude Record," *OT,*
October 11, 1928.
to think about anything: "Woman Finds High Flight Is Safe, Irksome," *OT,*
December 11, 1928.
higher into the fog: "Five Miles Up."
"American women pilots": "Woman Finds High Flight Is Safe, Irksome."
"I'm tired": "Woman Flier Breaks Record," *OT,* March 18, 1929.

85   *"World's Leading Woman Flier":* San Francisco Examiner, March 27,
1929.
a big success: "Thaden Concern Sold to Pittsburgh Group," *Aviation,*
February 16, 1929.
"you were here": Telegrams from Herb to Thaden, March 1929, LTC,
NASM.
"any more records": "Fair Pilot Holding Two Records Living Here," *PP,*
April 28, 1929.
by airmail plane: "FWTF," 115.
inflammatory rheumatism: Ibid., 105.

86   *by early March:* California Death Index, 1929, 4738.
"my everything": "FWTF," 105.
a storeroom: Ibid., 117.

"every possible way": "Women Organize Association to Boost Aviation," race scrapbook, 1928, CHC, Purdue University.

of many talents: "Breathless Pace Set by Airwoman," *LAT*, February 16, 1933.

87 *"first in the air"*: Letter from McQueen, March 23, 1929, WIAA records, University of Southern California Libraries, Special Collections.

"the entire United States": Letter from McQueen, February 18, 1929, WIAA, USC.

"any of the Los Angeles airports": Letter from Earhart to McQueen, undated, WIAA, USC.

"officially entered": Letter from Thaden to McQueen, April 11, 1929, WIAA, USC.

"in opposition": Letter to McQueen, March 9, 1929, WIAA, USC.

"on the ladies": Ibid.

"trip into Cleveland": Ibid.

"pink tea affair": Letter from Thaden, May 18, 1929, WIAA, USC.

"'to do anything'": Ibid.

88 *"trying to ride"*: "Women Fliers Balk at Easy $10,000 Race; Don't Want Men's Aid in Flying over Rockies," *NYT*, June 12, 1929.

strike a compromise: "No Men to Fly with Women in First Air Race," *CSM*, July 15, 1929.

"Oklahoma City and Tulsa": Telegram to McQueen, June 14, 1929, WIAA, USC.

89 *"not to tell anybody else"*: Letter from Turner to Thaden, February 16, 1929, LTC, NASM.

Chapter 10: There Is Only One Cleveland

90 *most famous fliers*: Associated Press, August 17, 1929, and Associated Press, October 7, 1929.

sell $2 million: "Many Contracts for Travel Air," *Aviation*, December 22, 1928.

Wichita in summer: Details about the city that summer come from several local stories, among them "Eagle's Corn Calendar," *WE*, August 20, 1929; "Stiff Wind Fails to Keep Wichitans from Feeling Heat," *WE*, August 21, 1929; "Usual and Unusual," *WE*, August 22, 1929; and "Colored Movies Make Hit Here," *Wichita Beacon*, August 20, 1929.

91   *all across the country:* HWF, 43.

"fighting performance": Lockheed advertisement, *LAT,* July 8, 1928.

plane of her own: Letters from Nichols to plane owners and manufacturers requesting a plane can be found in her personal correspondence related to the Powder Puff Derby, folder FL-01, National Women's Air Derby, RNC, IWASM.

92   *"get mad":* Letter to Nichols from Curtiss Flying Service, dated August 6, 1929, folder BU-05, RNC, IWASM.

"nothing but first": Telegram from Rogers to Nichols, dated August 21, 1929, folder FL-01, National Women's Air Derby, RNC, IWASM.

beginning to wonder: HWF, 43.

along the way: "Strain Is Telling," WE, August 22, 1929. According to Thaden, only three of the women didn't have a mechanic: Blanche, Pancho, and herself.

"Where are we": Details about Ruth Elder's preparations come from "Flies Again," OT, June 7, 1929; "Society of Cinemaland," *LAT,* May 26, 1929; and "On the Air at the Local Airports," *LAT,* May 26, 1929.

93   *about her age:* According to US Census records for the Crosson family, Marvel was her given name.

Fifth and C Streets in San Diego: In the 1926 San Diego city directory, Marvel listed her occupation as "saleslady" at the department store Stahel Dohrman.

"sure winner": Santa Monica Evening Outlook, August 18, 1929.

"best pilots in the world": "Tragic Air Death Forecast in Article by Miss Crosson," *San Diego Union,* August 30, 1929.

two weeks after Crosson: According to the *Wichita Eagle,* Marvel left Wichita bound for Los Angeles on July 27; according to the *LA Times,* Thaden left Wichita on August 13.

was blue: "Mrs. Thaden Is Derby Victor," CPD, August 27, 1929.

flawed from the start: HWF, 45.

was to begin: "More Women in Air Race," *LAT,* August 14, 1929.

forced landings: Nichols recounts the forced landings in WFL, 80; newspapers in Wichita, El Paso, and New York also covered the events.

march for miles: "Motor Sent Ruth Nichols, Forced Down in Arizona," NYHT, August 17, 1929.

94   *obvious misgivings:* WFL, 90.

"I'm very sorry": Fox Movietone newsreel, August 1929, Moving Image Research Collection, University of South Carolina Libraries.

"Come on out here, Louise": Ibid.

"Long Flight to Cleveland": Advertisement, *Santa Monica Evening Outlook,* August 16, 1929.

"Find it": "STF," 2.

95   *"never mind that":* Correspondence from Mary Avery to Henderson, April 12, 1929, Avery letters, CHC, HSPD.

"history of the country": "Praise Work on Air Show," *Cleveland News,* August 19, 1929.

Henderson figured: "Scores of Famous Flyers Arrive for National Events," *Cleveland News,* August 24, 1929.

"inside of it": "Ask Hoover Here to See Air Races," *CPD,* June 20, 1929.

"greatest show on Earth": "Scores of Famous Flyers Arrive for National Events."

96   *on the earthen runway:* Descriptions of the scene at Clover Field come from the *LAT,* the *NYHT,* and the *Santa Monica Evening Outlook,* August 19, 1929.

"Win $10": *Santa Monica Evening Outlook,* August 18, 1929.

turn to take off: "STF," 4.

"have been foolish": "Miss Earhart Says Derby Must Be Safe," *Santa Monica Evening Outlook,* August 15, 1929.

"unduly careful": Letter from Thaden, April 8, 1929, WIAA, USC.

"Good luck, old girl": "STF," 3.

97   *"you take off":* Ibid.

2,890-foot: "Clover Field, Santa Monica," *Aero Digest,* December 1929.

98   *"at all fastidious":* Viola Davis, "The Art of Taking Care of a Powder Puff," nationally syndicated column, August 4, 1929.

"Cosmetic Caravan": "Women in Aviation," *Flying,* December 1929.

"she derby": Will Rogers, syndicated columns, August 19 and August 20, 1929.

as previously planned: "Derby Fliers Ban Calexico as Stop Point," *San Bernardino County Sun,* August 19, 1929.

"Beware of sabotage": Pilot Thea Rasche received this telegram and shared it with the press, who ran stories of it across the country.

"primer, everything": "Women Derby Fliers Reach City," *Arizona Republican,* August 20, 1929.

99   *"all make it"*: "STF," 9.

   nearest large city: "Women Derby Fliers Reach City."

   "yes, there is": This and other quotes about the flight to Phoenix come from "STF," 9.

100   *seven thousand people*: "Women Derby Fliers Reach City."

   "too far ahead of us": "Famous Women Fliers Are Honored Guests at Exchange Club Banquet," *Arizona Republican*, August 20, 1929.

101   *"down in the mountains"*: HWF, 50.

   eyewitness accounts: "Famous Women Fliers Are Honored Guests."

   "moment she struck": "Miss Crosson Dies in Crash Near Wellton," *Arizona Republican*, August 21, 1929.

102   *for their daughter*: "Girl Flyer's Body Is Brought to S.D.," *San Diego Union*, August 21, 1929.

   and down the street: "Throng Attends Simple Funeral for Girl Flier," *San Diego Union*, August 24, 1929.

   "at the crossroads": "Women Fliers Have Little to Say About Sabotage Question," *WE*, August 24, 1929.

   "cut by pliers": *San Bernardino County Sun*, August 21, 1929.

   "flying in circles": "Women Derby Fliers Reach City."

103   *"before takeoff"*: *San Bernardino County Sun*, August 21, 1929.

   on their side: "No Traces of Interference Found at Quiz," *San Bernardino County Sun*, August 22, 1929.

   "not mastered successfully": "Women Indignant at Effort of Oklahoma Man to Halt Derby," *WE*, August 24, 1929.

   "confined to men": Arthur Brisbane, nationally syndicated column, August 21, 1929.

   "no time to stop": "Women Indignant at Effort of Oklahoma Man to Halt Derby."

104   *"Hey, Thaden"*: "STF," 21.

   "in advance": "Strain Is Telling."

   "Nothing to it": "Sabotage Is the Bunk," *WE*, August 23, 1929.

   "on our abilities": "Girls Peeved," *PP*, August 25, 1929.

   "Stop now": "Women Indignant at Effort of Oklahoma Man to Halt Derby."

105   *on day six*: Details of the city's preparations come from the *WE* in the following stories: "Night Turned into Day as Huge Beacon Light Floods Port," August 20, 1929; "Dinner Dance for Women Fliers Will Be Big

Affair Here," August 21, 1929; "Plans Completed for City's Welcome of Derbyists," August 23, 1929; and "Program at a Glance," August 23, 1929.
"precious minutes": "STF," 26.
"didn't you": Ibid., 28.
"a Wichita ship": "Louise Sets a Hot Pace to Wichita," *WE*, August 24, 1929.

106 *"Louise, darling"*: *HWF*, 55.
"Knight of the Air": "For Five Years Beech Has Been Smashing Records as a Wichita Aviator," box 3, WOABC, Wichita State University Libraries.
"nice race, Louise": "STF," 30.
"Hell's bells": Ibid., 36.
"Blanche beat me": "Fifteen Women Flyers Land at East Side Airport on Seventh Day of Race," *St. Louis Post-Dispatch*, August 25, 1929.
"momentarily lost": "STF," 42.

107 *"tomorrow night"*: "Nerves Growing Taut," *WE*, August 25, 1929.
fidgety: "STF," 39.
into Terre Haute, Indiana: "Ladybirds in Indiana," *Indianapolis Star*, August 26, 1929.
"Good luck, everybody": "STF," 43.
"direction is Columbus": Ibid., 46.
"around here someplace": Ibid., 48.
still no Columbus: Ibid., 46.

108 *"getting fat"*: "Mrs. Thaden Is Derby Victor," *CPD*, August 27, 1929.
from Lake Erie: "Mrs. Noyes to Fly Mail Lane," March 8, 1929, *Cleveland Press*.
Halle Brothers: Advertisement, *CPD*, August 28, 1929.

109 *"squashed beetle"*: *WFL*, 92.
given her the plane: Letter to Rearwin, October 23, 1929, folder FL-01, National Women's Air Derby, RNC, IWASM.
"could have won": The details of Thaden's arrival in Cleveland come from multiple papers on August 27, 1929, including the *Cleveland News*, the *Cleveland Press*, Thaden's first-person account published in the *WE*, "Dedicate Cup to Memory of Sister Flier," and the *CPD*'s detailed coverage in two different stories, "Mrs. Thaden Tells Own Story of How She Won Derby Race" and "Mrs. Thaden Is Derby Victor."

110 *"leading now"*: "Nerves Growing Taut."

111   *other issues:* "Flying Colonel Gets His Privacy," *CPD*, August 27, 1929.
       "mustn't ask me those": UPI, "Modest Flier Gets Ovation at Cleveland,"
       San Bernardino County Sun, August 27, 1929.
       "Understand": Gene Coughlin, undated article, Lindbergh clip file,
       Charles A. Weyerhaeuser Memorial Museum, Little Falls, Minnesota.
       "I'm sorry": "Flying Colonel Gets His Privacy."
       "bursting with pride": "Honor Fliers at Banquet," *Pittsburgh Post-Gazette,*
       September 3, 1929.
       "her revenge": "Gladys O'Donnell Winner in Race of Women Fliers,"
       Pittsburgh Post-Gazette, September 3, 1929.

112   *$4,600:* Tabulated from news accounts in the *CPD* and *Pittsburgh Post-*
       Gazette.
       in 1929: Statistical Abstract of the United States, 1930, table no. 368,
       "Average Weekly and Hourly Earnings: All Wage Earners and Classi-
       fied Groups of Labor, 25 Manufacturing Industries." The chart shows
       that women in these fields made, on average, $17.62 per week, a little
       more than $916 per year. Even when accounting for the fact that an
       office manager might make $20 a week, Thaden's winnings dwarfed a
       woman's average earnings in 1929.
       talk it over: There are varying accounts about who came up with
       the idea to form an organization and when. The idea dates back to
       at least 1927, when Earhart first suggested the plan to Ruth Nichols,
       and other women had similar plans. What's clear is that the idea was
       discussed under the trees at the air races in Cleveland. Recollections
       from Gladys O'Donnell, August 24, 1965, Gladys O'Donnell Collec-
       tion, IWASM.

Chapter 11: Good Eggs

113   *600,000 people:* "Air Races Succeed Financially; 600,000 See Events at
       Port," *Cleveland News*, September 3, 1929.
       and they did: "National Air Races Show First Profit," *Washington Post*,
       November 24, 1929.

114   *"can't describe it":* "Races Here Set New Air Marks," *CPD*, September 3,
       1929.
       almost 9,500: Aeronautical Chamber of Commerce of America, *Aircraft*
       Year Book, 1929.

Elementary Aeronautics: "Instruction in Aviation for Special Students," *BG,* September 17, 1929.

in American history: Aeronautical Chamber of Commerce of America, *Aircraft Year Book,* 1929.

"future for aviation": "Sky Pilots—Feminine Gender," *Independent Woman,* April 1929.

"just doesn't fly": "Amelia Says Few Women Air-Minded," *PP,* January 13, 1930.

"decoration": "Lady Mary Heath Tells Women's Aid to Flying," *Detroit Free Press,* April 5, 1929.

paid less: Statistical Abstract of the United States, 1931, tables 351 and 353.

"wasn't making enough": Ibid.

Swanee Taylor: Details about Taylor come from US Census records and his obituary on May 31, 1955.

115   *six basic categories:* "Women and Aviation," *Flying,* December 1929.

around a bigger issue: Women in Aviation 10 (November 19, 1929).

"on our planes": Letter from female pilot and original Ninety-Niner Opal Kunz, December 31, 1929, Ninety-Nines Museum.

116   *"influential and powerful":* Earhart letter, November 16, 1929, Ninety-Nines Museum.

"to oppose us": Opal Kunz, letter to Gladys O'Donnell, January 24, 1930, Ninety-Nines Museum.

"absolutely amazing": LT, *Air Facts,* July 1970, LTC, NASM.

"rolled up into one": Verses from poem "My Darling Thadie," sent to Thaden on March 13, 1930, LTC, box 2, NASM.

117   *"the keynote": Pittsburgh Post-Gazette,* February 21, 1930.

modeling the new: Ibid., February 8, 1930.

By January: The Aviation column in the *Pittsburgh Post-Gazette,* on January 31, 1930, written by Thaden, mentioned that ten women were currently enrolled, and according to other local stories, at least three others had enrolled in the fall of 1929.

"this sort of thing": Women in Aviation 34 (May 11, 1930).

seen it herself: "Training Women Pilots," *Western Flying,* February 1931.

"otherwise, by train": Letter from Nichols to Thaden, January 27, 1930, folder CN-11, RNC, IWASM.

118   *"Where are you going":* LT, Aviation column, *Pittsburgh Post-Gazette,* May 16, 1930.

"ever welcomed me": "Many Roads Lead Women into Politics," *NYT Magazine,* October 28, 1928.

$750: "Pitt Co-Ed Award Scholarship by Air Club," *PP,* March 22, 1930; "Homewood Avenue Girl Wins Air Scholarship," *Pittsburgh Post-Gazette,* March 22, 1930.

119 *"downhearted as he can be"*: Letter from Thaden to her mother, May 1930, LTC, NASM.

mishap in Harrisburg: "Noted Aviatrix Nearly Crashes After Inspecting City Airport," *Harrisburg Evening News,* April 24, 1930.

"can't be helped": Letter from Thaden to her mother, May 1930, LTC, NASM.

cost of baby clothes: Letter from Thaden to her parents, July 3, 1930, LTC, NASM.

120 *"fastest thing on wheels"*: Letter from Thaden to her mother, May 1930, LTC, NASM.

"something awful": Letter from Thaden to her parents, July 3, 1930, LTC, NASM.

"That's all": "Plane to Be Cradle of Son Born to Flying Thadens," *PP,* July 31, 1930.

Chapter 12: Mr. Putnam and Me

121 *"flying a great deal"*: Earhart, letter to her mother, November 22, 1929, AOE Papers, SLRC.

return to New York: Ibid.

"without Sam": Earhart, letter to her mother, August 12, 1928, AOE Papers, SLRC.

122 *"refer them to Mr. Putnam"*: Earhart, letter to her mother, August 26, 1928, AOE Papers, SLRC.

"a public menace": SW, 78.

"with my lips closed": Fellow aviator Elinor Smith didn't like George Putnam, who she felt tried to damage her career, so I have disregarded her comments about Putnam. However, she claimed to like Earhart, whom she described as a "very real and warm individual." She recalled the comment about the gap between Earhart's teeth in an early meeting; see Elinor Smith, *Aviatrix* (New York: Harcourt Brace Jovanovich, 1981), 70.

"than you think you will take": SW, 79–80.

wasn't fond of him: Louise Thaden interview, 1971, PTW Family Files.

123 *thirty-five dollars a week:* CITP, 166.

$500 a week: Smith, *Aviatrix*, 70.

home in California: CITP, 175.

a regular arrangement: Ibid.

"Fifth Avenue Bank": Earhart, letter to her mother, February 17, 1930, AOE Papers, SLRC.

endorsement fee: Receipt for $1,500 contributed by Earhart to Byrd Aviation Associates, AE Papers, Purdue University.

"gray with fatigue": LT, interview with Page Shamburger, IWASM.

two hundred in a single day: CITP, 168.

124 *failure to provide:* "Decree for Mrs. Putnam," *NYT*, December 20, 1929.

"need me anymore": Corey Ford, *The Time of Laughter* (Boston: Little, Brown, 1967), 205.

"no mystery of it": Associated Press, June 5, 1930.

"throws away life": Handwritten notes, personal musings on marriage, undated, AE Papers, Purdue University.

"cave-man expedients": Carl B. Allen, unpublished manuscript, "Ladybird in Revolt," 8, NASM.

for Stonington, Connecticut: "Amelia Earhart to Wed Publisher," *BG*, November 9, 1930.

into the open: In the early 1930s, there were few aviation reporters more respected than C. B. Allen. His suggestion that the marriage rumor was "allegedly planted by Putnam with one or more reporters" carries significant weight; Carl B. Allen, unpublished manuscript, "The True Amelia Earhart," 2, NASM.

"that much time": Associated Press, November 10, 1930.

125 *"the first edition":* "Putnam and Amelia Keep Plans Secret," *BG*, November 11, 1930.

"extreme pressure": Louise Thaden interview, 1971, PTW Family Files.

"if possible": Earhart's request for marriage advice and the dialogue in this scene come from C. B. Allen's written memories of that day; Allen, "The True Amelia Earhart," 3–5.

sold his stake: "Geo. P. Putnam Sells Publishing Firm to Cousin," *NYHT*, August 14, 1930.

member of her family: "Amelia Earhart Weds G. P. Putnam," *NYT*, February 8, 1931.

"gently to Mother": CITP, 176.

126   *"seem to want"*: Letter from Amelia Earhart to George Putnam, February 7, 1931, GPP Papers, Purdue University.

Chapter 13: Law of Fate

127   *"get a good ship"*: In May 1931, Richard Massock, an Associated Press staff writer and well-known author based in New York, penned a five-part series on Nichols, carried in newspapers across the country; this is from part 5.

128   *"commercially safe"*: Planning for Around the World memo, 1928–30, folder FL-10, RNC, IWASM.
over the ocean: Ibid.
"across the Atlantic": Letter from Paul Block to Nichols, January 26, 1928, folder FL-10, RNC, IWASM.
for modifications: Letter from Hilton Railey, April 28, 1931, folder BI-03, RNC, IWASM.

129   *forty-three minutes:* "Radio Station Installed in Airplane," *Cincinnati Enquirer,* August 4, 1930.
"on my way east": Undated telegram from Nichols, Trips Planned/Proposed, folder FL-11, RNC, IWASM.
in the Allegheny mountains: Accounts of Nichols's forced landing in Manns Choice, Pennsylvania, come from multiple sources, including *WFL,* 109; *HWF,* 136; "Noted Aviatrix Leaves Manns Choice Field," *Bedford Gazette,* November 27, 1930; "Aviatrix Forced Down," *Cincinnati Enquirer,* November 20, 1930; and part 5 of "Wings East," the five-part story of Nichols's life written by C. B. Allen and John Forbes that appeared in the *New York World-Telegram* in June 1931.

130   *"well-padded Eskimo"*: "Ruth Nichols Up Nearly Six Miles in Record Flight," *NYHT,* March 7, 1931.

131   *"Congratulations"*: Crosley telegram, Crosley Radio Sponsorship, folder BU-09, RNC, IWASM.
"Keep it up": Letter from Dorothy Binney Upton to Nichols, December 13, 1930, Transcontinental Record, folder FL-13, RNC, IWASM.
sent Nichols roses: Roses acknowledged by Nichols in letter to Earhart, March 13, 1931, Altitude Record, folder FL-14, RNC, IWASM.
high in the heavens: Letter to Nichols from fan in San Francisco, 1931, in ibid.

young girls: These letters from the young girls and Nichols's replies can be found in Fan Mail, 1928–32, folder CN-05, RNC, IWASM.

132 *"destroy this letter":* Letter from Ruth Nichols, April 17, 1931, RNC, IWASM.

"were to be opened": Letter from Ruth Nichols, March 21, 1931, RNC, IWASM.

133 *began rolling in:* Transatlantic Financing, folder FL-19, RNC, IWASM.

"Early in May": Letter to Railey, folder BI-03, RNC, IWASM.

"Don't help me": The office dialogue between Nichols and Railey was reported by Allen and Forbes, "Wings East," part 5.

134 *acknowledged receipt:* Letter from Nichols, April 10, 1931, and Railey contract, folder BI-03, RNC, IWASM.

worsening Depression: "Nichols Hopes for $200,000 on Hop," *Brooklyn Daily Eagle,* July 7, 1931.

"not to be considered": Telegram from Railey to Nichols, April 21, 1931, folder BI-03, RNC, IWASM.

"a closed issue": Memo from Railey to Nichols, April 25, 1931, in ibid.

135 *"go at that":* Letter from Railey, April 27, 1931, in ibid.

"PLEASE take me": Letter from Alice Campbell, April 24, 1931, Transatlantic Passenger Offers, folder FL-26, RNC, IWASM.

"bring you good luck": Letter from W. O. Barnes to Nichols, April 1931, Transatlantic Gifts/Charms, folder FL-28, RNC, IWASM.

to bring with her: Transatlantic Things to Take, folder FL-25, RNC, IWASM.

"the other side": Letter from Nichols to Railey, April 10, 1931, folder BI-03, RNC, IWASM.

136 *"London and Paris":* Letter from Railey's secretary to Nichols, May 22, 1931, in ibid.

"discover or explore": "Ruth Nichols Ready to Start on Sea Flight," *NYHT,* June 14, 1931.

"weeks into months": Letter from Railey to Nichols, June 19, 1931, folder BI-03, RNC, IWASM.

"sex competition": "Women Pilots Race for Ocean Flight," *NYT,* May 7, 1931.

"a slight delay": Telegram from brother Snowden Nichols to Ruth Nichols, May 25, 1931, Transatlantic Before Flight, folder FL-20, RNC, IWASM.

137   *"no in between"*: Letter from Mildred Morgan to Nichols, May 3, 1931, in ibid.

      Rockaway, Queens: Details about Nichols's flight come from multiple news sources on June 23, 1931, including the *NYT*, the *NYHT*, the *Brooklyn Daily Eagle*, and the *New York World-Telegram*.

      miles to the east: "Heat Subsides After 4 Deaths, 14 Drownings," *NYHT*, June 22, 1931.

      in a personal notebook: Handwritten prayers, Transatlantic Flight Notebook, folder AL-43, RNC, IWASM.

138   *"veritable trap"*: Letter from Nichols, July 27, 1931, Transatlantic Crash Letters, folder FL-29, RNC, IWASM.

      in the middle: Detailed accounts of Nichols's landing in New Brunswick can be found in the *NYT*, the *NYHT*, and the *St. John Telegraph Journal*, June 23 and June 24, 1931.

139   Get out: *WFL*, 157.

      "for another plane": "Injured Aviatrix Is Looking Forward to Ocean Hop in Fall," *St. John Telegraph Journal*, June 24, 1931.

      vertebrae in her back: In personal letters, Nichols wrote that she'd broken four vertebrae. Doctors told newspapers it was two.

      "out of it alive": "Ruth Nichols' Spine Splintered in Crash," *Brooklyn Daily Eagle*, June 23, 1931.

Chapter 14: Give a Girl Credit

140   *quarter of a million dollars*: 1929 Henderson tax return, Money and Taxes folder, CHC, HSPD.

      "this year's event": 1930 Air Races folder, CHC, HSPD.

141   *in the world*: "35,000 Gaze at Sky as Curtiss Airport Opens," *Chicago Tribune*, October 21, 1929; "Curtiss-Wright Airport to Add Second of Units," *Chicago Tribune*, December 29, 1929.

      "exploiting us": Letter from Thaden, July 25, 1930, Ninety-Nines correspondence, folder GR-22, RNC, IWASM.

      "to kindergarten": "Women Flyers Kick at Rules for Air Races," *Chicago Tribune*, July 20, 1930.

142   *thirty thousand cars*: *Chicago Daily News*, August 25, 1930.

      for an airplane race: "$10,000 Posted for Air Races," *CPD*, June 1, 1930.

flaming disasters: Coverage of the plane crashes and deaths at the 1930 races can be found in the *Chicago Tribune* and other Chicago daily newspapers on August 28, August 30, and September 2.

barely broke even: Proposal for the 1934 air races listing the financial figures for each previous year, CHC, NASM.

143 *Elm Court:* Chateau Bendix has been reborn today as the Trinity School at Greenlawn, a private school for students in grades seven through twelve. Tom Noe, director of the school's development office, gave me a tour of the estate in January 2017 and opened up the school's files on the old building, making this description possible.

5,500 in all: "Have You the Courage to Make Money?," *American Magazine* (June 1932).

144 *"humorous looking Swede":* "The Champion Gadget Maker Who Has Defied the Depression," *St. Louis Post-Dispatch Sunday Magazine,* August 7, 1932.

Bendix stock prices: "The Story of the Bendix Corporation," *Bendix Technical Journal* (Spring 1968), 4.

hulking Norwegian: Details about Bendix's habits come from two places, "The Champion Gadget Maker" and Bendix's daily office journals, located in the Bendix Archives, History Museum, South Bend.

145 *"and where":* "FWTF," 8.

got lucky: Ibid., 9.

haze of the club car: Don Dwiggins, *They Flew the Bendix Race* (Philadelphia: J. B. Lippincott, 1965), 13.

"for some months": Dwiggins and Henderson each recount the same story of the meeting with slightly different dialogue. In this, I am relying on Henderson's version, "FWTF," 9.

146 *"the radio and press":* Dwiggins, *They Flew the Bendix Race,* 103.

"Doolittle's coming": "Sets New Trans-U.S. Flight Record," *CPD,* September 5, 1931.

147 *"indulge in anymore":* "Jimmie Doolittle Back at Job as Commercial Pilot After 3362 Miles Within 21 Hours," *St. Louis Post-Dispatch,* September 6, 1931.

"scientific aeronautical knowledge": Nichols, letter to Swanee Taylor, May 6, 1931, Transatlantic Press Coverage, folder FL-18, RNC, IWASM.

"and take notice": Women in Aviation 47 (September 21, 1930).

"and what have you": Letter from someone who appears to be C. B. Allen, aviation editor at the *New York World-Telegram,* June 26, 1931, Transatlantic Press Coverage, folder FL-18, RNC, IWASM.

148 *"might have happened":* Correspondence between Nichols and Thaden, July 3 and July 6, 1931, Correspondence: Thaden, Louise, folder CN-11, RNC, IWASM.

"get the money": "Ruth Nichols Bravely Faces Future Although Hurt; Visions City as Coming Air Terminus," *St. John Telegraph Journal,* and "Ruth Nichols Is Overjoyed with Assurance That 'Akita' Can be Reconditioned for Help," *St. John Telegraph Journal,* June 26, 1931.

"all ready": Telegram from Nichols, August 17, 1931, Transatlantic Correspondence, folder FL-21, RNC, IWASM.

"winter weather approaching": "Ruth Nichols Seeks Record," *OT,* October 22, 1931.

loaned her money: Letter from Nichols, October 3, 1931, Transatlantic After Crash, folder FL-21, RNC, IWASM.

149 *"through other efforts":* Ibid.

"distance record": "Ruth Nichols Seeks Record."

"attending a prom": This quote and all other details about Ruth's takeoff in Oakland come from "Ruth Nichols Quits Oakland on N.Y. Hop," *OT,* October 25, 1931.

By one a.m.: "Ruth Nichols Lands Here, Claims Record," *Louisville Courier-Journal,* October 26, 1931.

by dawn: WFL, 192.

150 *"all the way":* The details of Nichols's doomed takeoff in Louisville all come from "Girl Flier Undaunted After Plane Burns," *Louisville Courier-Journal,* October 27, 1931.

Chapter 15: Grudge Flight

151 *"the public eye":* Carl B. Allen, unpublished manuscript, "Ladybird in Revolt," 3, NASM.

152 *inexperienced pilot:* "Autogiro's Advantages Give It Leading Place in Commercial Aviation, Declares Developer," *Philadelphia Inquirer,* November 16, 1930.

"my own medicine": "Noted Aviatrix, Touring Country in Autogiro, Talks on Aviation," *Chapel Hill Daily Tar Heel,* November 10, 1931.

"*Only my pride*": "Around the Town," *Detroit Free Press*, September 15, 1931.

"*death warrant*": "Flying at Its Best Revealed in 'Giro' Ride with Amelia," *Zanesville Times Recorder*, August 23, 1931.

"*nice old maid*": Allen, "Ladybird in Revolt," 7.

153   "*grudge flight*": Ibid., 1.

"*earliest convenience*": All details related to Nichols's requests for money and the corporate rejections come from Potential Sponsor Rejections, folder BU-15, RNC, IWASM.

"*with What*": "Ruth Nichols' Wings Clipped," *Inside Stuff*, February 20, 1932.

154   *lunch in Rye:* Accounts differ as to exactly which day Earhart and Nichols had lunch. What's clear is that it was right before Earhart left, which is confirmed by *WFL*, 209, and Allen, "Ladybird in Revolt."

155   "*conduct of its affairs*": Earhart, letter to Thaden, May 18, 1932, AE Papers, Marion Stabler Collection, IWASM.

route north: Unless otherwise noted, all details concerning Earhart's 1932 transatlantic takeoff, flight, and landing come from the primary news accounts of the day in the *NYT*, the *NYHT*, and the *BG*, May 21 and May 22, 1932.

"*get there, eh*": Movietone footage, 1932, AE Papers, Purdue University.

156   *useless: FOI*, 214.

158   "*splendid job*": Nichols's comments and others' congratulating Earhart come from 1932 Solo Transatlantic Flight, Post-Flight Correspondence, AE Papers, Purdue University.

"*suffrage in aviation*": *Ninety-Niner* (February 1932), Ninety-Nines Museum Archives.

Chapter 16: Spetakkel

161   "*look at Florence Klingensmith*": "Death Stalks the Air Racers," *Popular Aviation* (March 1934).

"*dangerous curves*": Handwritten photo caption, Klingensmith Family Archives, courtesy of Wayne Chapman.

"*I want to go*": "City Aviatrix May Fly Ocean," *Minneapolis Star*, July 25, 1932.

162   *spetakkel:* Ingvald Stensland, interview with Mark Piehl, May 2, 1991, FKC, HCSCC.

in their diaries: Details about farm life during Florence's childhood come from Levi Tjortvedt's handwritten diary, 1914–1916, HCSCC.

his car: Mark Piehl, oral history interviews, 1991, FKC, HCSCC.

busied herself elsewhere: Ibid. and Moorhead High School yearbooks, 1921 and 1923.

163 *July 1927:* Klingensmith divorce records, HCSCC.

for "Lindbergh Day": Details of Lindbergh's visit to Fargo, including his arrival and the parade route, come from coverage in the *Fargo Forum,* August 25 and August 26, 1927.

just five foot four: Star Tribune, May 18, 1931.

"these things, too": Ibid.

164 *crowds down below: Minneapolis Journal* article and photo, undated, FKC, HCSCC.

"ladder to climb": Ninety-Niner (September 15, 1933), Ninety-Nines Museum Archives.

"risk my money": St. Louis Post-Dispatch, April 30, 1930.

aviatrix: Fargo City Directory, 1930.

everyone to see: Wayne Chapman, Florence's great-nephew, interview with the author.

"famous woman flier": "Florence Klingensmith, 'Loop the Loop' Artist," *Star Tribune,* May 10, 1930.

"Extraordinary: Florence Klingensmith": "Airmeet," *Eau Claire Leader,* July 2, 1930.

"flying my own plane": Ninety-Niner (September 15, 1933).

165 *"It just isn't done":* "Women Pilots Compete with Men on Equal Terms for First Time in Races," *CPD,* August 28, 1932.

the wrong direction: "Women's Air Race Turns to Comedy," *CPD,* September 3, 1932.

"on guard against Florence Klingensmith": "Women Pilots Compete with Men on Equal Terms."

how he wanted it: "The Gee Bee Story," *Sport Aviation,* March 1971; *BG,* May 4, 1929.

edge of the White Mountains: "The Gee Bee Story."

"fails and why": "Yankee, Here with Novel Plane, Seeks Funds for Manufacture," *Sport Aviation,* 1929.

166 *could have hoped:* "Tests New Plane Whose Makers Seek Plant Here," *Sport Aviation,* 1929.

"takeoff and climb": Granville Brothers Aircraft company literature, Gee Bee Airplanes, vol. 1, SHLA.

and intense: Lowell Bayles pilot's license application at US Department of Commerce, Lowell R. Bayles Collection, SHLA.

167 *no one had seen before:* "Gee Bee Super-Sportster," *Aero Digest,* October 1931.

buying shares for a hundred dollars each: Springfield newspaper clips, summer 1931, Gee Bee Airplanes, vol. 1, SHLA.

erupted in celebration: "Bayles' Victory Thrills Airport Holiday Crowd," *Springfield Union,* September 8, 1931.

"stuck on a cloud": "Acrobatics—Sane and Asinine," *Sportsman Pilot,* April 1931.

168 *"fighting the controls":* Undated news clips related to Johnny Kytle's crash and death, February 1931, Gee Bee Airplanes, vol. 1, SHLA.

in Indianapolis: "Boardman, Ocean Air Hero, Lies in Hospital Wing as Life Ebbs," *Indianapolis Star,* July 2, 1933.

shooting star on a string: Witness report of Joseph Brandenburg, December 7, 1931, Record Group 342, Airplane Accidents 1931–1932, Department of Defense central files, National Archives, College Park, Maryland.

169 *"A ripping noise":* Ibid.

"came the crash": Witness report of Ray Cooper, December 22, 1931, in ibid.

"obtain any more": Granville letter to investigator, 1931, in ibid.

"of one's finger": "Russell Boardman Victim of Fate," *Indianapolis Star,* July 6, 1933.

"let me know": Letter from Henderson to Florence Klinginsmith [*sic*], August 14, 1933, CHC, HSPD.

170 *"friendly enemies":* *Santa Cruz Evening News,* July 13, 1933.

"out of the race": "Turner Shatters Own Mark to Win Trans-U.S. Derby," *Philadelphia Inquirer,* July 2, 1933.

Klingensmith groused: Postcard from Florence in Chicago to her mother, April 12, 1933, Klingensmith Family Files, courtesy of Wayne Chapman.

"interest to everyone": Henderson letter, August 1, 1933, CHC, WRHS.

thirteen million people had visited: "Labor Day Advance Crowds Break Saturday Records," *Chicago Daily Times,* September 3, 1933.

"and character": The details about events at the World's Fair come from the following sources in 1933: *Chicago Tribune,* August 20; *Chicago Daily News,* August 22; *Chicago Tribune,* January 16.

four hundred thousand visitors: "Nearly 400,000 Expected for Weekend,"
Chicago American, July 2, 1933.

171   *"seen in the United States":* Henderson letter, 1933 air races, CHC, WRHS.
"hello to the crowd": "Death Stalks the Air Racers."

172   *"after it's over":* Ibid.
"lucky today": "Aviatrix, Ill, Met Death in Proving Women Can Equal
Men, Inquest Told," *Chicago Daily News,* September 5, 1933.
and the money: 1933 Chicago air-race prize-money list, CHC, WRHS.
"can fly it": "Aviatrix, Ill, Met Death."
"as any man": Ibid.
panel before her: Tom Nallen, Gee Bee historian, interviewed by the
author in March 2017, described how Klingensmith would have worked
the controls to get the Gee Bee in the air.
670 horsepower: There is some discrepancy in news reports and eyewitness interviews about the horsepower of the engine in Klingensmith's
borrowed Gee Bee. In news accounts, it is reported as 420. In interviews
conducted by the coroner, it was reported to be 670. Either way, what's
clear is that it was at least twice the horsepower of the engine intended
for the plane, and perhaps bigger still.
"structural safety": "Aviatrix Thought of Crowd's Safety Rather Than of
Own," *Fargo Forum,* September 7, 1933.

173   *"beautiful race":* Ibid.
"stole the show": "Death Stalks the Air Racers."
"Jump NOW!": Ibid.

174   *pulled back:* Witnesses on the ground reported seeing the plane's elevators go up and the plane rise in the sky. To do this, Klingensmith would
have had to pull back on the stick.
250 feet: There is some discrepancy about how high the plane rose. Some
witnesses suggested it was as high as 600 or 800 feet. Aviators on the
ground, by and large, claim it was closer to 200 or 250, which is why the
author chose this number.
maybe twenty: Eyewitness testimony varies; some say Klingensmith may
have flown for as long as thirty seconds after the fabric fell off the wing,
but most agree it was closer to fifteen seconds.
"absolutely": This quote and others about the investigation into Klingensmith's crash come directly from the transcript of the coroner's inquest
in Chicago; see Cook County Coroner Inquest transcript and report no.
456969, Cook County Criminal Court, September 5, 1933, FKC, HCSCC.

175 *to be licensed:* "Physical Standards for Airplane Pilots," 1928–1933, RG 149, Records of the Government Printing Office, Commerce Department, National Archives, College Park, Maryland.

176 *"the menstrual period":* Starting in 1930, the aeronautics branch of the Department of Commerce specifically began listing its concerns over women flying while menstruating. The passages quoted here were laid out again on June 1, 1933, just three months before Klingensmith's crash, in "Physical Standards for Airplane Pilots: A Confidential Guide for the Use of Medical Examiners," RG 149, National Archives.
"off the right wing": Cook County Coroner's Verdict, September 5, 1933, FKC, HCSCC.

177 *"can 'take it'":* "Aviatrix, Ill, Met Death."
"shipped thousands": Paul and Jack Albinson, oral history interview conducted by Noel Allard, December 21, 1987, FKC, HCSCC.
well attended: Details about Florence's funeral come from the *Minneapolis Journal,* September 11, 1933, and "Dozen Pilots Here Today in Last Tribute to Girl Flier," *Fargo Forum,* September 7, 1933.
cut red roses: Funeral home flower-order list, FKC, HCSCC.

178 *"property and life":* Memo to air bureau director Gene Vidal, November 29, 1933, Record Group 40, box 570, US Department of Commerce central files, National Archives.
"what I already knew": "Should Women Race Planes?," *CSM,* January 16, 1935.

Chapter 17: All Things Being Equal

179 *nightmares lately:* Thaden wrote about her flying nightmares both in her memoir *HWF* and in a first-person article for the *WB.*
"Put it out!": *HWF,* 90.

180 *"Frightfully inadequate":* This detail and others about the flight come from "Famous Woman Flier Tells Experiences of Record Flight," *WB,* December 19, 1932.

181 *"be a knockout":* Handwritten note from flight coordinator Casey Jones to Thaden and Frances, PTW Family Files.
"see how it feels": *HWF,* 87.
"going to land": "Famous Woman Flier Tells Experiences."
"Doctor's orders": *HWF,* 89.

"between two loves": Ibid., 92.

182   *"scientific engineering skill"*: Birth announcement, September 1933, PTW Family Files.

    Herb could feel it: HWF, 92.

    "equal basis with men": Ninety-Niner (September 15, 1933), Ninety-Nines Museum.

    "nearly penniless": "A Real Problem for America — 250,000 Wandering Women," *Chicago Daily Times,* September 2, 1933.

    "simple supper": "Report on Educational Camps for Unemployed Women, 1934 and 1935," 5, Federal Emergency Relief Administration, Wirtz Labor Library, US Department of Labor.

    "demand less": Bulletin of the Women's Bureau, no. 139, "Women Unemployed Seeking Relief in 1933," 18, Wirtz Labor Library, US Department of Labor.

183   *mailed surveys:* All quotes and details regarding the employment surveys sent out in 1933 come directly from the surveys themselves saved for decades by Ruth Nichols and kept in 99s Labor Questionnaire, folder GR-25, IWASM.

    "almost impossible": Nichols mentioned her concerns on this front in many letters over the years. This quote comes from a letter to fellow pilot Thea Rasche, General Letters, folder CB-10, RNC, IWASM.

184   *"freelancing"*: Letter to Powel Crosley, October 17, 1933, Potential Sponsor Rejection, folder BU-15, RNC, IWASM.

    "at this time": Letter from Powel Crosley, October 27, 1933, in ibid.

    five hundred dollars to appear: Letter from Ruth Nichols, October 24, 1929, Lectures Correspondence, folder AU-05, RNC, IWASM.

    to get fifty dollars: Schedule of fees, Lectures Material 1933–37, folder AU-08, RNC, IWASM.

    "news flight left": Letter to Powel Crosley, October 17, 1933, Potential Sponsor Rejection, folder BU-15, RNC, IWASM.

185   *from loudspeakers:* "1,450 Crowd Church for Lecture by Amelia Earhart," *Mason City Globe-Gazette,* October 11, 1933.

    three hundred dollars to appear: "A $300 Talk," *Des Moines Register,* October 19, 1933.

    "building this evening": "Large Crowd for Amelia Earhart," *Emporia Gazette,* October 14, 1933.

186 *"when a girl does"*: Helen Welshimer, "Fly, Girls, Fly," nationally syndicated column, July 1932.

"differently from men": Associated Press, November 10, 1933.

"this decision": "Banning of Women Pilots in New Orleans Races Re-
vives Equal Rights Controversy," *NYHT,* February 4, 1934.

"Do your part": Advertisement, *New Orleans Times-Picayune,* February 13,
1934.

188 *"my purpose"*: "Turner Tells of Flight," *LAT,* July 2, 1933.

"big-shot": Roy Rutherford, *Colonel Roscoe Turner, Knight-Errant of the Air*
(Cleveland: n.p., 1947), 14, WRHS.

"better than crowds": "Flight Record Set by Turner," *LAT,* May 28, 1930.

a teenager: Benny Howard personal data, filled out by Howard on April
30, 1941, Library of Congress.

"in your care": Carnation Milk Company, letter to Howard, April 13,
1929, Benny Howard files, NASM.

189 *an everyman's hero:* "The Howard Flyabout," *Aviation,* August 9,
1926.

"of the crowds": "B. F. Howard's Tiny Homemade Airplane Earns Cost
at Races," *Chicago Tribune,* September 3, 1930.

"into these planes": "Flying 'Pete' Balks at Entry Fee for Races," *Cleveland
Press,* August 23, 1932.

"Go-Grease": "Go-Grease Benny Howard," *Saturday Evening Post,* September 2, 1939.

blond wife: "One Arm, One Leg Left, Parachutist Still Takes Jumps,"
CPD, August 31, 1935.

"Kiss him again": "Brave Wives Who Wait for Ships from Clouds Get
Loving Kiss at Journey's End as Their Reward," *Cleveland Press,* August
31, 1935.

"on this occasion": "New $4,000,000 Airport Dedicated Despite Heavy
Rain Shortening Program," *New Orleans Times-Picayune,* February 10,
1934.

190 *blue-and-yellow Gee Bee:* News clippings, Gee Bee Airplanes, vol. 4, SHLA.

didn't last long: The details about the mishaps in New Orleans come
from "Stunt Flier Meets Fiery Death in Fall Before Grandstand," *New
Orleans Times-Picayune,* February 15, 1934, and "Aviator and Jumper
Killed as Airplane Plunges into Lake," *New Orleans Times-Picayune,* February 18, 1934.

Chapter 18: *That's What I Think of Wives Flying*

193   *more than $43,000:* Income and Expenses spreadsheet, Aviation Air Races 1934, CHC, HSPD.

       "where are they": "Grand National Air Racing Circuit," *Aero Digest,* February 1933.

194   *"up to scorn":* "Women Flyers Threaten Boycott Over 'Men Only' Rule for Cleveland Race Entries," *NYHT,* July 29, 1934.

       "as contestants": Cooper letter to NAA secretary W. R. Enyart, July 27, 1934, Jacqueline Cochran Papers, box 2, A76-4, 1934 Correspondence, Dwight D. Eisenhower Library, Abilene, Kansas.

       625 women: Ninety-Niner (January 1934), Ninety-Nines Museum.

       "of all types": Cliff Henderson, letter to Cooper, August 3, 1934, Jacqueline Cochran Papers, box 2, A76-4, 1934 Correspondence, Dwight D. Eisenhower Library, Abilene, Kansas.

195   *just $175:* "Michigan Flyer Wins Race Program Feature," *Dayton Daily News,* August 5, 1934.

       $8.63 herself: Handwritten letter from Frances Marsalis to Earhart, September 30, 1933, Jacqueline Cochran Papers, box 2, A76-4, 1933 Correspondence, Dwight D. Eisenhower Library, Abilene, Kansas.

196   *"that $1,000":* "Flyer Had Laugh About Fatal Last Lap on Race," *Dayton Daily News,* August 6, 1934.

       six thousand locals: In 1934, there were three daily newspapers in Dayton: the *Daily News,* the *Journal,* and the *Herald.* There is some discrepancy in these accounts as to how many people attended the races that Sunday; the *Journal* estimated it at six thousand.

       "the last lap": "Flyer Had Laugh About Fatal Last Lap on Race."

       to the front: Accounts of the crash come from the next day's detailed news coverage in two local newspapers, the *Dayton Daily News* and the *Dayton Journal,* August 6, 1934.

197   *and was stunned:* HWF, 96.

       their historic flights: "Plane to Carry Woman Pilot's Body East for Funeral Rites," *Dayton Herald,* August 6, 1934; "Wright Pilots in Tribute as Flyer's Body Goes East," *Dayton Daily News,* August 7, 1934; "Aviation Field Rites Held for Mrs. Marsalis," *NYDN,* August 8, 1934.

198   *"one grand splurge":* HWF, 97.

       "the best pilots": "Women Aviators Honor Memory of Mrs. Marsalis," *NYDN,* August 7, 1934.

"theory is right": "Fair Fliers Wrathy Over Racing Ban," *Akron Beacon Journal*, August 24, 1934.

"this enterprise": Henderson letter to Paul Bellamy, editor of *CPD*, March 10, 1934, Aviation Air Races 1934, CHC, HSPD.

"aviation display": "Court of Flags to Thrill Crowds," *CPD*, August 31, 1934; "Today Is the Day," *CPD*, August 31, 1934; "Cleveland, Host," *Cleveland News*, August 31, 1934.

"a man's business": "Women Flyers on Sidelines, 'Don't Like It,'" *Cleveland News*, September 1, 1934.

199 *"quite agree"*: "Speed Pilot's Wife Sees Woman's Place on Ground," *Cleveland Press*, September 3, 1934.

"wives flying": "Women Flyers on Sidelines, 'Don't Like It.'"

for the job: "Amelia Earhart Boycotts Races Starting Today," *NYHT*, August 31, 1934.

"awful beating": "Rough All the Way; Took Awful Beating, Says Derby Victor," *CPD*, September 1, 1934.

200 *"to get killed"*: "Doug Davis, Air Winner, Killed in Trophy Race Crash, 100,000 Watch," *CPD*, September 4, 1934.

"the public thinks": "Best Meet Ever, Says National Aeronautic Head," *CPD*, September 3, 1934.

"take any chances": "Ask Longer Race Course Due to Davis Death," *Cleveland News*, September 4, 1934.

two-man race: The details about Davis's fatal race come from the daily news coverage in three newspapers, the *CPD*, the *Cleveland News*, and the *Cleveland Press*, on September 4, 1934.

202 *"Doug Davis"*: WHK radio script, September 4, 1934, CHC, WRHS.

"fly with Doug": "'Pals' Carry Doug Davis to His Last Resting Place," *Atlanta Constitution*, September 6, 1934.

"racing pilots killed": "Ask Longer Race Course Due to Davis Death."

"further to investigate": "Plane Structure Failure Blamed for Fatal Crash," *Cleveland Press*, September 5, 1934.

Chapter 19: They'll Be in Our Hair

203 *"other, Tradition"*: Changing Standards, Fourth Annual *New York Herald Tribune* Conference on Current Problems, 1934, speech transcript, William Brown Meloney Papers, Columbia University Rare Book and Manuscript Library.

"aptitude places her": "Aviatrix Arrives After 'Longest Ride on Train,'" *Minneapolis Star,* November 30, 1934.

204 *"Turns Back the Clock"*: *Ninety-Niner* (August 1934), Ninety-Nines Museum.

"races as men have": "Women Aviators Honor Memory of Mrs. Marsalis," *NYDN,* August 7, 1934.

"Air Races": Ninety-Nines resolution, signed by president Margaret Cooper, September 1934, Ninety-Nines Museum.

205 *"still be alive"*: "Women Fliers Organize to Boycott Air Races That Refuse Them Place on Program," *NYHT,* September 9, 1934.

voted to support: "Aviation Editors Want Women on Race Program," *CPD,* September 4, 1934.

"a brave man": "The Aero-Sportswoman," *Popular Aviation* (November 1934).

"they keep trying": Letter from Turner to Ruth Osgood, October 9, 1935, box 30, folder 1, Roscoe Turner Collection, University of Wyoming American Heritage Center.

"wouldn't let her": Oral History interview with Ben Howard (1960), Aviation Project, 44, Columbia Center for Oral History Archives, Rare Book & Manuscript Library, Columbia University in the City of New York.

"goggles on": "Pilots Suggest Ban on Women Flyers at Races," *CPD,* September 4, 1935.

206 *"inefficient and dangerous"*: "Youthful M.P. Objects to Female Aviators," *Ninety-Nine Club of New England* (April 1932), Ninety-Nines Museum.

"foreground of the picture": "Women Fliers 'Muscle In' at Races; Win Major Roles in National Show," *Cincinnati Enquirer,* August 25, 1935.

"hard to say no": "Pilots Suggest Ban on Women Flyers at Races."

weekend in Cleveland: "Women Fliers 'Muscle In' at Races."

"of Hollywood": Letter from Henderson, 1935 Air Races folder, CHC, HSPD.

207 *but close:* In *HWF,* page 99, Thaden writes that by 1935, the Depression and other missteps had hit the Thadens with "a stiff wallop."

"entrance on duty": Letter to Thaden, US Department of Commerce, August 31, 1935, LTC, NASM.

"job for nothing": *WFL,* 235.

"$1 per passenger": Advertisement, *Fitchburg Sentinel,* September 27, 1935.

"was living": *WFL,* 235.

Eight months before: Details of Earhart's solo Pacific flight in this section come from the following sources: Purdue University Special Collections, scrapbook #12, *Honolulu Advertiser* and other clippings, and the *OT* news coverage of her arrival on January 12 and January 13, 1935.

208   *twenty-four hundred miles:* "Throngs Cheer Perfect Hop Across Pacific," *OT*, January 13, 1935.

"publicity stunt": The original story appeared in the *San Francisco News* but was picked up by wire services and published in papers across the country.

"land plane": "Earhart Plan for Solo Hop Opposed Here," *Honolulu Star-Bulletin,* December 29, 1934.

209   *"what you like":* Ibid.

"unexplained mishap": Letter from Earhart to Putnam, January 8, 1935, AE Papers, Purdue University.

210   *staggered start:* "9 Flyers Get Set for Start of Air Derby," *Los Angeles Illustrated Daily News,* August 29, 1935.

211   *"conquests of the air":* "Roaring 'Round the Pylons at the National Air Races," *Young America,* August 30, 1935.

$17,000: "Go-Grease Benny Howard," *Saturday Evening Post,* September 2, 1939.

off the ground: "L.A. Crash Kills Bendix Racer; Howard 1st at Cleveland," *Los Angeles Herald Express,* August 30, 1935.

"family bus": "Earhart, in Family Bus, Sweeps to Bendix Place," *CPD,* August 31, 1935.

and she knew it: "Air Race Score," *Los Angeles Examiner,* August 31, 1935.

212   *"Let's go":* This quote and other details about Allen's final moments and his crash come from the daily coverage, including the following: "L.A. Crash Kills Bendix Racer"; "Death Plane Bore Banner of Religion," *Cleveland News,* August 30, 1935; "Allen Sixth Victim of Notorious Killer Plane; Tragedy Bares Romance," *Los Angeles Illustrated Daily News,* August 31, 1935; and "Race Crash Kills Flyer," *LAT,* August 31, 1935.

"Hell": "Howard Wins Race for Bendix Trophy," *NYT,* August 31, 1935.

"speed for safety": "Roaring 'Round the Pylons at the National Air Races."

storms into Ohio: Details of the close finish to the 1935 Bendix Trophy race come from the following: "Earhart, in Family Bus, Sweeps to Bendix Place"; "Air Race Score"; "Race Crash Kills Flyer"; and "Mister Mulligan," *Aviation* (October 1935).

Chapter 20: *Playing Hunches*

215   *bothered him:* Walter Beech's quotes about the things that upset him come from memos in the Beech Office Files in Wichita, courtesy of his daughter Mary Lynn Oliver.

216   *"guess you'll do":* The information about their meeting and early relationship comes from one of the only detailed profiles ever written about Olive Ann Beech: "Danger: Boss Lady at Work," *Saturday Evening Post,* August 8, 1959.

     as a carpenter: US Census records and the Beech Family Tree records, kept by the Beeches' daughter Mary Lynn Oliver.

     Interstate 135: US Census records for Olive Ann's father, Frank Mellor.

     "bother you, either": "Danger: Boss Lady at Work."

217   *grammar school:* In the Library of Congress biographical files, Walter Beech reports he did not finish grammar school.

     he might need: "Annie Can Handle This," March 17, 1947, Beech Office Files.

     "lies in speed": "Beech Organizes Company to Build Speedy Airplanes," WB, March 22, 1932.

     warmer, at least: The celebration was covered by both the WE and the WB on May 4, 1932.

218   *"world that failed":* "Airplane Industry to Lead U.S. on Road Back to Prosperity," WB, May 4, 1932.

     in the nose: The image of the new Beechcraft first appeared in the WE on June 29, 1932.

     in the autumn sky: WE, November 14, 1932.

     more profitable: Annual sales figures for the 1930s, box FF, WOABC, Wichita State University Libraries.

     "starving": Edward H. Phillips, *The Staggerwing Story* (Toronto, ON: Flying Books International, 1996), 24.

219   *in recent weeks:* Nichols estimated in WFL that they flew one thousand passengers that Sunday; the NYT put the number at eighteen hundred.

     "going to make it": "Ruth Nichols Gains; Will Go On Flying," NYT, October 28, 1935.

220   *"jumped clear":* "Ruth Nichols Hurt, Her Pilot Killed," NYT, October 22, 1935.

     amid the trees: News accounts of the crash and Nichols's personal account in her memoir differ on one detail: Nichols says Hublitz climbed through the hole in the cockpit, but at least one news story says he also was thrown from the plane.

"thing of beauty": "Ruth Nichols Gains; Will Go On Flying."

want photographers there: "Ruth Nichols' Photo Ban Blocks Hospital Inquest," *NYT,* November 1, 1935.

and swollen: "Ruth Nichols to Fly Soon," *Rochester Democrat and Chronicle,* December 5, 1935.

221   Oh, please, God, not yet: *WFL,* 240.

"it was darkness": "Ruth Nichols Gains; Will Go On Flying."

Thanksgiving dinner: "Ruth Nichols Eats Turkey in Bed off Hospital Tray," *NYHT,* November 29, 1935.

mansion yet again: "Ruth Nichols Flies Homes from Troy Crash Scene," *NYHT,* December 7, 1935.

"sidelines for long": Telegram from Earhart to Nichols, October 22, 1935, AE Papers, Marion Stabler Collection, IWASM.

feeling well either: Letter from Putnam to Helen Schleman, director of the Women's Residence Hall at Purdue, December 9, 1935, President Elliott's Correspondence with GPP and AE, AE Papers, Purdue University.

for her that winter: "A Woman's New York," *Louisville Courier-Journal,* December 15, 1935.

222   *"to be a person":* "Amelia Earhart Resting; Trying to 'Be Herself,'" *Dayton Daily News,* August 25, 1935.

offered her $2,000: Elliott proposal to Earhart, May 18, 1935, President Elliott's Correspondence with GP and AE, AE Papers, Purdue University.

"to your coming": Letter from Helen Schleman, director of the Women's Residence Hall, to Earhart, September 7, 1935, in ibid.

lucky to enroll: Helen Schleman, oral history, 1970, 5, Purdue University.

But the university: Advertisement, *Purdue Exponent,* October 3, 1935; "Student Pilot Code Framed," *Purdue Exponent,* October 3, 1935.

pulled up on campus: Alice Price, "The Sound of Wings," memories of Alice Price, resident nurse in the Women's Residence Hall, 1935–1937, 7, Purdue University.

"call me Miss Earhart": "Amelia Leaves Air to Guide Purdue Girls in Careers," *Lafayette Journal and Courier,* November 8, 1935.

questions of her own: AE, "Purdue University Questionnaire for Women Students, 1934–35," AOE Papers, SLRC.

"it's baloney": "Sees Education Failing to Prepare Young for Careers," *Lafayette Journal and Courier,* November 27, 1935.

223 *"in this project"*: Letter from Putnam to Elliott, November 12, 1935,
President Elliott's Correspondence with GPP and AE, 1935, AE Papers,
Purdue University.
"on its toes": Letter from Elliott to Putnam, November 14, 1935, in ibid.
At a dinner party: Ruth Freehafer, *R. B. Stewart and Purdue University*
(West Lafayette, IN: Purdue University Press, 1983), 59.
put up $40,000: Letter from Elliott to Earhart, March 20, 1936, President
Elliott's Correspondence with GPP and AE, AE Papers, Purdue University.
"outstanding flights": Letter from Putnam to Elliott, November 12, 1935,
in ibid.
224 *"getting old"*: Letter from Thaden to Earhart, January 12, 1935, folder 4,
AE Papers, Purdue University.
225 *"reduce accidents"*: "Marker Plan Advanced to Help Lost Aviators," *Salt
Lake Telegram*, December 12, 1935.
two men on board: Details of Dewey Noyes's crash come from "2 Flyers Killed at Nunda; Plane Rams Hill in Fog," *Rochester Democrat and
Chronicle*, December 12, 1935; "18 Questioned in Air Deaths," *Rochester
Democrat and Chronicle*, December 21, 1935; "Noyes, Pilot, Is Killed in
Plane Crash," *CPD*, December 13, 1935; US Department of Commerce
press release, April 19, 1936, IWASM.
"his idea, always": Oral History interview with Blanche Noyes (1960),
Aviation Project, 9, Columbia Center for Oral History Archives, Rare
Book & Manuscript Library, Columbia University in the City of New
York.
"near me": Blanche Noyes, "Dear Dewey Letter," date unknown,
Blanche Noyes files, IWASM.
"to interview her": Letter from Earhart to Gene Vidal at the Department
of Commerce, May 8, 1936, in ibid.
226 *"close to me"*: LT, "Father's Day, 1937" (poem penned, apparently, on the
one-year anniversary of her father's death), PTW Family Files.
"don't you": HWF, 109.

Chapter 21: A Woman Couldn't Win

227 *almost said no*: HWF, 109.
228 *beat Earhart*: Pat Thaden Webb interview, Bendix Collection, NASM.
215 miles an hour: "Amelia Hops in New Ship," *LAT*, July 22, 1936.

$64,000: Order form for AE's new Electra from the Lockheed Aircraft Corporation, March 20, 1936, Paul Mantz Papers, Purdue University.

"in North Hollywood": "Amelia Earhart Denies Plans for World Flight," *NYHT,* May 23, 1936.

229 *"a poker face":* "From Sagehens to Eagles," *LAT Sunday Magazine,* August 30, 1936.

"sensationally fast": "Bendix Race List Grows," *LAT,* August 20, 1936.

"famous plane": Popular Aviation (November 1935).

"dealer at once": Popular Aviation (May 1936).

"with Mister Mulligan": "Preparations for 1936 Air Races Go On Behind Closed Doors," *Aviation,* September 1936.

"all race pilots": "What's New in World of Airplanes and Air Transportation," *Chicago Tribune,* August 23, 1936.

found Walter stewing: In her memoir, Thaden writes that Walter thought Olive Ann "mentally unbalanced" for entering the Beechcraft in the race and that the factory pilot "was mad" that women were at the controls; see *HWF,* 110–11.

"trim blue princess": Ibid., 110.

230 *"we will win it":* "Race Is Business Affair, Not Stunt, to Louise Thaden," *WE,* September 5, 1936.

technical adviser Paul Mantz: "Amelia Earhart Lands at Kansas City Airport," *NYHT,* August 30, 1936, and "Ms. Earhart Is Found Safe Here," *CPD,* August 31, 1936.

"write poetry about": "Amelia Earhart Here; Will Fly in Bendix Race," *NYHT,* September 1, 1936.

231 *and forty-five minutes:* "Howard and Wife Set Chicago-N.Y. Air Mark of 2 Hrs. 45 Minutes," *Chicago Tribune,* September 2, 1936.

"and reliability": "Claim Records in Performance for New Plane," *Chicago Tribune,* April 26, 1936.

$35,000 contract: 1936 contract, 1936 Air Races folder, CHC, HSPD.

"bits of femininity": "Chatterbox," *LAT,* August 25, 1936.

no Roscoe Turner: Details about Roscoe Turner's ill-fated trip across the country for the Bendix race come from multiple sources, including the *LAT* and the *Gallup Independent,* August 31, 1936.

232 *Bad country:* "A Sinister Land Claimed the Wrecked Airliner," *NYT,* September 15, 1929.

"around by itself": "Turner Hurt, Returns Here," *LAT*, September 1, 1936.

233   *"this year"*: "Turner Hurt in Plane, Out of Air Races," *Santa Rosa Press Democrat*, September 1, 1936.

a different man: "Col. Turner Crashes in New Mexico," *LAT*, August 31, 1936.

"pretty shaky": "Turner Hurt in Plane, Out of Air Races."

"I'm not, too": "Turner Hurt, Returns Here."

"Bless Mother": "Breaking Air Records No Novelty for This Woman Flyer," *St. Louis Post-Dispatch*, September 8, 1936.

telephone switchboard: "Four Planes Soar for Los Angeles in Bendix Race," *NYHT*, September 4, 1936.

"of winning": "Boro Pilot Seeks Bendix Air Prize," *Brooklyn Daily Eagle*, September 3, 1936.

234   *the Half Moon Hotel:* WFL, 227.

meeting at ten thirty: HWF, 112.

private weather services: LT interview, 1971, PTW Family Files.

"generally good": "3 Air Teams Off on Race to Coast," *NYT*, September 4, 1936.

got off first: The *New York Post,* on September 4, 1936, published the exact time that each flier in the Bendix race took off.

hadn't checked: "Luck with Flier," *WE*, September 5, 1936.

"can't stand this": HWF, 112.

235   *"Goodbye, dear"*: Ibid., 114.

"Good luck": Jean Adams and Margaret Kimball, *Heroines of the Sky* (New York: Doubleday, Doran, 1942), 132.

"Well, so long": WFL, 256.

5:56 a.m.: Accounts over the years have stated different takeoff times, but the local press in the next day's papers recorded it as 5:56 a.m.

236   *"serious predicament"*: "Ex-Pittsburgh Flier Is Winner," *PP*, September 5, 1936.

on the horizon: Details about Jacobson's crash come from his first-person accounts given to three different newspapers: "Pilot Unaware Plane Exploded, Tells of Miraculous Leap," *Albuquerque Journal*, September 5, 1936; "Nerve Unshaken by Narrow Escape from Death, Flier Heads to Races," *WE*, September 5, 1934; and "Pilot Tells Close Call When Plane Blows Up," *LAT*, September 6, 1936.

237   *"valuable ship"*: "Misses Death by Narrow Margin," *WE*, September 5, 1936.

sixteen-minute stop: Brooklyn Daily Eagle, September 4, 1936.

city hall downtown: "Aviation History on Parade," *Los Angeles Examiner,* September 5, 1936.

238 *spinning propeller:* Details about *Mister Mulligan*'s crash come from several sources, including Columbia University's oral history of Ben and Maxine Howard, April 1960; on-the-ground reporting and first-day news coverage of the crash in "Crownpoint Crash Victims Gain in Struggle to Survive," *Gallup Independent,* September 5, 1936; "Go-Grease Benny Howard," *Saturday Evening Post,* September 2, 1939; and Don Pratt, "Damned Good Airplanes: The Ben Howard Story," *Sport Flying* (August and October 1967), a two-part story about Benny Howard's career that included interviews with both Benny and Maxine.

"to land": Ben Howard, oral history, 47, Columbia University.

"Too hard": Ibid.

239 *Sky ghosts:* "Crownpoint Crash Victims Gain in Struggle to Survive."

"hell is one": Ben Howard, oral history, 51.

240 *"be all right":* "Benny, 'Mike' Howard Recovering from Plane Crash Injuries, Will Fly Again," *Cleveland Press,* November 16, 1936.

"start a fire": "Crownpoint Crash Victims Gain in Struggle to Survive."

"How is my plane": "Women Capture Bendix Laurels," *Akron Beacon Journal,* September 5, 1936.

"IRRATIONAL": "Damned Good Airplanes: The Ben Howard Story."

"are you awake": This and other quotes from inside the plane come from HWF, 112 and 115.

241 *"A potato race":* Ibid., 116.

eleven-minute stop: "Misses Death by Narrow Margin."

242 *had made it:* "Best Routes to Air Races Outlined," *Los Angeles Illustrated Daily News,* September 4, 1936.

"done wrong now": HWF, 118.

243 *"won the Bendix":* Thaden's and Noyes's recollections of this quote are slightly different, but Blanche never wavered in hers, repeating the same version of this quote over and over again for decades — in speeches, news stories, and oral histories — even while Henderson was still alive. Noyes, oral history, 22, Columbia University.

"If we win": "$15,000 Bendix Air Race Won by Louise Thaden," *Arkansas Gazette,* September 5, 1936.

"couldn't win, eh": HWF, 119.

"from your home town": Bendix victory telegrams, September 1936, LTC, NASM.

"Splendid": "Misses Death by Narrow Margin."

"We won": Telegram from Thaden to her mother, Bendix victory telegrams, September 1936, LTC, NASM.

Chapter 22: The Top of the Hill

244 *"in open competition"*: "Air Successes Open New Fields to Women," *LAT*, September 8, 1936.

earful about it: These comments come from Henderson's 1936 air-race scrapbook signed by friends and fliers at the air races; Cliff Henderson scrapbook, miscellaneous pages, Purdue University.

"news value": LT interview, partial transcript, 1977, CHC, HSPD.

245 *"skirts or trousers"*: "Air Successes Open New Fields to Women."

246 *"you girls"*: "Detroit Airport Possibilities Praised by Builder of Huge Zeppelins, Bendix Boosts Race Prize," n.d., Detroit article about trophy ceremony, LTC, box 8, NASM.

"more will enter": "Women's Timidity Undesirable Habit, Amelia Earhart Asserts," *Binghamton Press and Sun-Bulletin*, December 16, 1935.

"place in the Bendix": Cliff Henderson, 1936 air-race scrapbook, page signed by Earhart, with personal note to Henderson, Purdue University.

"wanted to do it": "Amelia Prepares to Fly Round the World," *CSM*, February 12, 1937.

"to prove anything": "Amelia Earhart Will Fly Around the World in March," *NYHT*, February 12, 1937.

247 *"a nightmare"*: "Airplane Island," *Digest*, September 18, 1937.

have to be perfect: "Amelia Set for Flight to Howland Isle," *Oakland Post-Enquirer*, March 19, 1937.

"at the beginning": "Amelia Prepares to Fly Round the World."

"everything to lose": Thaden recounted this scene in two different places, her memoir, *HWF*, 150, and an article she wrote for the journal *Air Facts* in July 1970 titled "Amelia." In each, the dialogue differs slightly, but the sentiment is the same. These quotes come from the *Air Facts* account.

"challenge to others": Statement from Earhart, 1937 World Flight Attempt One, AE Papers, Purdue University.

248 *"crashed in Honolulu"*: "Companions Laud Amelia," *Honolulu Star-Advertiser*, March 21, 1937.

thirty thousand people: "Gale Halts Earhart," *San Francisco Examiner,* March 16, 1937.

"I'll be back": "Amelia Dodges Death in Crash," *LAT,* March 21, 1937.

"not sunsets": "Earhart May Hop Off Today," *OT,* May 30, 1937.

wanted to stop her: "Washington Bans Paris Air Race as Risking a Needless Loss of Life," *NYT,* May 18, 1937.

primitive runway: "Amelia Earhart Ready to Fly to Howland Island," *NYHT,* June 30, 1937.

249   *voice in his ears:* The Earhart radio log was released at the time and published in the *NYHT.* It also appears, in full, in Record Group 237, National Archives.

preflight miscommunication: "Radio Slip-Up Seems Costly to Amelia Earhart," *NYHT,* July 8, 1937.

"keep us busy": Ibid.

250   *"close to breaking":* Bellarts Papers, National Archives.

"very weary": "Is Amelia Earhart Still Alive?," *Popular Aviation* (December 1939).

as the fuel supply: "Radio Slip-Up Seems Costly to Amelia Earhart."

251   *"ragged transmission":* Records Regarding the Loss of Amelia Earhart, Record Group 38, Records of the Office of the Chief of Naval Operations, National Archives.

"Phoenix Island region": Ibid.

until five a.m.: "Amelia on Land, Claim," *OT,* July 6, 1937.

"Nothing discovered": "Hope Wanes for Amelia; Storm Retards Hunt," *OT,* July 9, 1937.

"hope otherwise": "Radio Slip-Up Seems Costly to Amelia Earhart."

Three thousand people: "Navy Ends Search for Miss Earhart," *NYT,* July 19, 1939.

252   *finally accepted:* "Lexington Is Final Hope for Earhart," *OT,* July 10, 1937.

"the weirdies": C. B. Allen letter, May 14, 1971, C. B. Allen Papers, NASM.

knowledge of Earhart's death: "Japan Denies Amelia Earhart Still Alive," *LAT,* September 22, 1945.

reported flying low: John Terry, an Associated Press reporter, was on board the USS *Colorado,* which was searching the Phoenix Islands with the use of three planes. After their daily search ended on July 10, 1937, he reported the pilots had searched Gardner Island.

253   *"that final transmission":* Bellarts Papers, National Archives.

254   *"right to the bottom":* Record Group 237, National Archives.

"to help sufferers": "Ruth Nichols, of Relief Wings, Is Good Samaritan of the Air Ways," *NYHT*, August 31, 1942.

"meet a challenge": "Women Best for Space, Pioneering Aviatrix Says," *Washington Post*, August 16, 1959.

"be flying them": WFL, 314.

255   *alma mater, Wellesley College:* Correspondence dated July 26, August 5, and August 18, 1938, Search for Employment, folder BU-20, RNC, IWASM.

"in that capacity": Letter written by Nichols to Northeast Airlines, April 10, 1945, Employment Applications, 1942–43, folder BU-25, RNC, IWASM.

"of aeronautics": Letter written to Nichols by United's R. F. Ahrens, March 30, 1943, in ibid.

255   *"hospital is interesting"*: Letter from Nichols, March 7, 1947, Personal Letters, folder CP-16, RNC, IWASM.

"MOVED AGAIN": Letter from Thaden, July 24, 1941, Correspondence, Thaden, Louise, 1929–1951, folder CN-11, RNC, IWASM.

"that you will": Letter from Nichols to Thaden, July 31, 1941, in ibid.

passed her by: Letter to Thaden, March 7, 1947, in ibid.

"those who have": Letter, March 7, 1947, Personal Letters, folder CP-16, RNC, IWASM.

"aren't, you know": All of Thaden's comments to Nichols about her depression come from personal letters written to her in the 1950s, kept by Nichols and cataloged in folder CN-11, Correspondence, Thaden, Louise, 1929–1951, folder CN-11, RNC, IWASM.

257   *private journals:* Ruth kept careful note of her dreams, her meetings with psychologists, and her feelings in hundreds of pages of typed and handwritten notes in Dreams, 1948–50, folder FA-13, RNC, IWASM.

258   *"there was nothing"*: "Ruth Elder Dies; Winged to Fame in 1927," *LAT*, October 10, 1977.

hide from the world: The details of Ruth's hard times and suicide attempt come from the *San Diego Union-Tribune*'s coverage in July 1950, including the following stories: "Ruth Elder in Hospital Here," July 14, 1950; "Ruth Elder Reported Victim of Sleeping Pills," July 17, 1950; "Elder Case Pills Traced to Tijuana," July 18, 1950; and Sleeping Pills Curb Lacking in Tijuana," July 30, 1950.

"married again": "Ruth Elder Dies; Winged to Fame in 1927."

259   *"a lovely life"*: "Ruth Elder: From Beauty Contestant to Heroine," *AS*, July 4, 1976.

      "defeat, after defeat": LT interview, 1971, PTW Family Files.

260   *"parcel of air racing"*: "FWTF," 267.

      "peach of a guy": LT interview, 1971, PTW Family Files.

      4,000 percent: "Kansas Air Plants Show Alert Spirit," *NYT*, May 19, 1942.

      $7 million: "Danger: Boss Lady at Work," *Saturday Evening Post*, August 8, 1959.

      $615 million: "Beech's Co-Founder and Chairman Retiring," *NYT*, May 31, 1982.

      "see you so tired": Letter from Thaden to Olive Ann, December 21, 1966, box 23, FF 4, WOABC, Wichita State University Libraries.

      "I keep busy": Letter from Olive Ann to Thaden, July 21, 1966, in ibid.

      "I love you, Ann Mellor Beech": Letter from Thaden to Olive Ann, August 11, 1973, in ibid.

261   *"for her own good"*: WFL, 109.

      "the way it is": Letter from Thaden to Blanche Noyes, January 26, 1949, PTW Family Files.

      "saved my life": "Old Barn Holds Special Memory," *USA Today*, December 6, 2002.

262   *the airwaves*: Thaden's speech and interview were recorded and kept by her daughter, Patricia Thaden Webb; the recording was given to me by Pat in October 2016.

263   *stops in a single day*: "Skids at 90 Miles Per Hour Cause Her to Prefer the Air," *Harrisburg Telegraph*, July 1, 1937.

      "American should know": "Flying with Al Williams," *PP*, May 18, 1937.

      growing in the yard: Pat Thaden Webb, interview with the author.

264   *an incident inside their home*: Ibid.

      "top of the hill": Letter from Thaden, August 8, 1951, Correspondence, Thaden, Louise, 1929–1951, folder CN-11, RNC, IWASM.

      "Welcome aboard, Mom": HWF, 163.

265   *"one of the best"*: Olive Ann Beech speech, rough drafts, August 2, 1976, box 23, FF 4, WOABC, Wichita State University Libraries.

      "nor will I ever": Letter from Thaden to her daughter, June 6, 1956, PTW Family Files.

Index